OPERA AND DRAMA

Richard Wagner

TRANSLATED BY
William Ashton Ellis

University of Nebraska Press
Lincoln and London

Manufactured in the United States of America

⊖ The paper in this book meets the minimum requirements of American National Standard for Information Sciences—Permanence of Paper for Printed Library Materials, ANSI Z39.48-1984.

First Bison Book printing: 1995

Library of Congress Cataloging-in-Publication Data
Wagner, Richard, 1813–1883.
[Literary works. English. Selections]
Opera and drama / Richard Wagner; translated by William Ashton Ellis.
p. cm.
Originally published: London: K. Paul, Trench, Trübner, 1900.
2nd ed. (Richard Wagner's prose works; v. 2)
Includes index.
ISBN 0-8032-9765-3 (pbk.)
1. Music—Philosophy and aesthetics. 2. Opera. 3. Drama.
I. Title.
ML410.W1A1268   1995
782.1—dc20
95-5263   CIP
MN

Reprinted from the 1893 translation of volume 2 (*Opera and Drama*) of *Richard Wagner's Prose Works,* published by Kegan Paul, Trench, Trübner & Co., Ltd., London.

CONTENTS

CORRIGENDUM.

Page 193, line 23, *after* "for the Future." *read* "But to organise Society in this sense, means to base it on the free self-determining of the Individual, as its eternally exhaustless source." This sentence was accidentally omitted from the first edition.—W. A. E.

TRANSLATOR'S PREFACE.

BEFORE plunging into the thick of the accompanying treatise, I believe it will interest the reader to gather a few details about its history. Fortunately these are obtainable at first hand; therefore I can take no credit for supplying them, further than that they have not hitherto been set forth in any connected form. The very first we hear of *Oper und Drama* is in a letter from Wagner to Theodor Uhlig dated December 27, 1849: "I have still very much to say to those before whom I am placing my *Art-work of the Future* [then in the printer's hands]; I therefore made inquiries respecting a newspaper in which—if only in outline—I might be able to utter my thoughts about certain matters." A fortnight later (Jan. 12, '50) we find our author again referring to his *Art-work of the Future*, and adding: "I quite understand that you take chief interest in music; perhaps I shall return to it at greater length on some future occasion." Again, on February 8, 1850, and even before receiving a printed copy of the work just named, he writes: "I am resolved to publish *Papers on Art and Life* entirely on my own acccount; perhaps fortnightly." Nothing definite comes of this proposal, except the article on *Art and Climate*—already translated in Vol. i of the present series—and in August the article on *Judaism in Music*, published in the *Neue Zeitschrift* September '50. We next read in Letter 14 that Liszt is pressing for the composition of *Siegfried*—i.e. the *Siegfried's Tod*—and significantly enough Wagner says: "the *choice* as to what I should take next in hand has tortured me: was it to be a poem, a book, or an essay?" and later on in the same letter (undated, but apparently written in August '50) he adds, "I had intended to set to work at another book—*The Redemption of Genius*—which should cover the whole ground. Feeling the uselessness of this book, I determined to content myself with two little essays: first, *The Monumental;* then, *The Unbeauty of Civilisation*, deducing the conditions of the beautiful from the life of the future. But what should I effect by that? Fresh confusion —and nothing else!" Leaving aside the easy handle that the

b

last remark affords to those who are pleased to call Wagner "an imperfectly equipped thinker"—as was done in a recent English criticism—this extract is interesting, as affording a clue to his method of literary composition at that period ; for the essays, or sketches for essays, on *Genius* and *The Monumental* have been incorporated in the *Communication to my Friends*, written about a year later, whilst that on *Civilisation* and the life of the future has evidently found its way into Chapter IV of Part II. of *Oper und Drama*.

By this time the literary longing was approaching a tangible shape, for on Sept. 20, 1850, Wagner writes again to Uhlig, and again after a reference to *Siegfried :* " I am thinking of doing some literary work this autumn and winter.   All generalities in art are, for the moment, repugnant to me ; no one understands them until his nose is driven into particulars.   Now my particular work would be music, and, above all, opera. . . . In any case, I will shortly send you rather a long article on modern opera,—about Rossini and Meyerbeer."   This we may take to be the first unmistakable shadowing forth of *Oper und Drama*, although the title and magnitude of the eventual book are not yet within clear range of vision.   Another point in this letter is the allusion in the very next sentence, already quoted in my preface to Volume i, to the receipt of a letter from Feuerbach, apparently accompanied by *all* that author's philosophical treatises.

At last on October 9, 1850, we find that the book is really begun, though with no definite idea of the size to which it will later swell, and under a title which points merely to the first Part of the work as we now have it.   This reference, in Letter 17 to Uhlig, runs as follows : " My would-be article on opera is becoming rather a voluminous piece of writing, and will perhaps be not much less in size than the *Art-work of the Future*.   I have decided to offer it to J. J. Weber [publisher] under the title, ' *Das Wesen der Oper.*' . . . I have only finished the first half ; unfortunately I am at present quite hindered from continuing the work.   Every day I must hold rehearsals " &c.   On the 22nd of the same month Uhlig is informed : " I say nothing here about all æsthetic scruples roused in you and others by my artistic tenets and writings, since I propose to treat the whole matter thoroughly and exhaustively in my *Wesen der Oper*—which I hope to be able to send you in a month.   I shall even be compelled to speak my mind about my former operas. The essay is becoming somewhat bulky."—In passing, I may note that this discussion of his own operas came to be reserved, and very properly, for the *Communication.*—

In Letter 19 to Uhlig, written early in December, 1850, we get the final title of the book, and a brief synopsis of its contents. This letter is peculiarly interesting, as it shews how the work grew under Wagner's hands and became a real assistance to him, through clearing up his theretofore half-conscious artistic procedure. He says : " You can have no idea of the trouble I am giving myself, to call forth a whole understanding in those who now understand but half ; yes, even my foes, who either do not or will not understand at all as yet, even them I fain would bring to understanding :—and lastly I rejoice for the mere reason that I am always coming to a better understanding myself. My book, which is now to be called ' *Oper und Drama,*' is not yet ready : it will be at least twice as big as the *Art-work of the Future.* I still shall require at least the whole of December before I come to the end, and then the whole of January, for certain, for the copying and revising. I can tell you nothing about it in advance, except the general outline : I. Exposition of the essence of Opera, down to our own day ; with the conclusion, ' Music is a bearing organism (Beethoven, as it were, practised it in the bearing of Melody)— therefore a womanly.'—II. Exposition of the essence of Drama, from Shakespeare down to our own day ; conclusion, ' the poetic Understanding is a begetting organism, the poetic Aim the fertilis- ing seed which takes its rise in nothing but the emotion of Love, and is the impulse to the fecundation of a female organism, which must bear the seed—received in Love.' III. (Here, first, do I really begin) ' Exposition of the act of bearing the poetic Aim, achieved through perfected Tone-speech.'—Alas ! I would I had told you nothing—for I see that I have told you nothing really.—Only this, as well : I have spared no pains, to be exact and circumstantial ; therefore I resolved, from the start, not to let myself be pressed for time, so as not to scamp any part." He then adds the diagram which I have reproduced on page 2, and about which I ought to remark that the arrow-heads are somewhat misleading, as it is evident, from page 224, that the evolutionary line is meant to proceed from the left base-angle to the apex of the triangle, and thence to the right base-angle.

By January 20, 1851—i.e. exactly four months from the first

definite thought of it!—the whole book appears to have been finished, and a portion of it fair-copied, for on that day Wagner writes his next letter to Uhlig, informing him: "At last I was seized with a fury to finish my book, and not to write you until I could send you one part of it fair-copied: this resolution I took in hand and have carried out. To-day I send you the first of the three Parts, and propose to send you the second so soon as ever it is tidy, and afterwards the third in the same manner. . . . The first Part is the shortest and easiest, perhaps also the most entertaining; the second goes deeper, and the third is a piece of work which goes right to the bottom. The whole will be a book of 400 to 500 pages." In the next letter, "beginning of February," he says, in addition to the words I have quoted on page 118: "I confess that I cherish the daring thought of not selling my book for less than 60 louis d'or. It has cost me four months of intense exertion."—Poor man, he only got 20 louis d'or for it, with the promise of a like amount when the first edition, of 500 copies, should be exhausted!—Finally we read in Letter 22, dated middle of February '51, "Here you have my testament: I may as well die now—anything further that I could do, seems to me a useless piece of luxury!—The last pages of this copy I have written in a state of mind which I cannot intelligibly describe to anyone." Then follows that touching anecdote of the death of his little parrot, which seems destined for an immortality like that of Newton's dog. This little household event acquires an additional importance from another pair of sentences in the letter: "Three days have passed, and nothing can comfort me. . . . I only wish sincerely to get the hateful manuscript out of the house. . . . There will still be many faults in the manuscript—I have only been able to just glance very inattentively through it once." These lines should be remembered, in reading Part III of *Opera and Drama*, as they account for many a knotty passage.

The manuscript being now finished and despatched to Uhlig, let us briefly trace its history as a completed work. Letter 23, of March 10, '51, says: "Strike out a whole passage on the first page of the Introduction [*not* the "Preface," as appears in the English version of these Letters]—I wrote this Introduction when I still thought that the whole thing would become a series of musical newspaper articles: now, as the opening of a larger book, such a tone would give the reader an impression of snappiness, if not of pettiness. It would be too terrible, if the book came to be looked on as a mere attack on Meyerbeer. I wish I still could withdraw much of this kind. When I read it myself, the taunts do not sound venomous—when others read it, I perhaps shall often seem to them a passionate and embittered person; which is about the last thing I should care to appear, even to my enemies." Later on in the letter one finds proof of the astounding energy of the man. Most people would have thought that a book of these dimensions would have exhausted, at least for a time, its author's fund of literary matter; but no, he writes " How do *I* feel now? —Well, if only I could describe it! The one thing that I now could set to work at, with any appearance of use, would be art-literature: and that is just what no one asks for. . . . Would it perhaps be better to compose another opera, for myself alone?— It's enough to make one die of laughing ! " He *did* write again and at once, to wit the pamphlet on *A Theatre for Zurich*, re-printed in Vol. v of the *Ges. Schr.*

I may pass over the difficulties in finding a publisher, and merely glancing at the facts recorded on page 118, to which I shall presently return, I come to Letter 27, of June 3, '51 : " You already know that Weber, after all, will print my book. Recently I received four sheets of proof; to my astonishment I see that he is going to publish it in three volumes, small octavo and very wide-spaced—in fact quite noble—type. Thus he will put up the selling price. O, you book-dealers ! " Again, Letter 28, of June 18, '51, where Wagner writes : " My book at Weber's progresses at a very slow pace. My " readings " here consisted of a selection from ' *Oper und Drama*,' given quite privately before a group of acquaintances and friends." Letter 31, September 8, '51, is more important; Wagner is ill, and writes: " I have a fresh prayer to make to you. There are still about twelve sheets of ' *Oper und Drama* ' to be corrected. To-day I am writing to Weber, asking him to send them to *you*, together with the manuscript. You really must see to them for me. . . . Don't be angry with me for thus disposing of your time." This ' proof,' handed over to Uhlig for ' correction,' would wellnigh cover the whole Third Part, since in the original edition that Part occupied 247 pages, and to the 192 for the " twelve sheets " we must add a certain number for the " about." We thus see that it was almost a decree of Fate, that Part III should not be properly revised, firstly in the manu-

script stage, and secondly in that of ‘proof.’ Uhlig's labours would
necessarily be confined to the correction of printer's errors, nor—
even had there been time for any extensive alterations—was he
quite the best adviser that could be found, on the point of clearness of meaning; his own articles in the *Neue Zeitschrift* are often
admirable in matter, but whenever he attempts to follow his
master into the depths of æsthetic speculation he loses his way in
intricate sentences, unrelieved by any of those flashes of intuition
which light up even the hardest page of Wagner's prose and make
his darkest sayings all the more worth unravelling. To this consideration, also, I shall have to return; but I wished to emphasise
in situ the lack of revision of Part III.

To resume the historical course—on Oct. 20 a couple of lines
give Uhlig instructions, for Weber, as to the precise title for the
book; merely "OPER UND DRAMA, von Richard Wagner." On
Nov. 20th a significant message to the faithful friend: "Why three
articles on Part I. of ‘ *Oper und Drama*,’ which contains little else
but criticisms, and only two on Part III? Yet this Third Part is
really the most important—to bring to people's thorough understanding—since it goes to the very bottom of the thing. Don't
forget to lay stress on ‘Stuff’—Part II.—as centre and axis of
the whole; for *here* is the crucial point, that I set forth Form
solely in the light of Substance, whilst it has hitherto been treated
quite regardless of all substance." Finally on Nov. 28th comes
the announcement: "Well, I have received ‘ *Oper und Drama*.’
. . . I shall have one copy interleaved, so as to use it for the
preparation of a—possible—second edition."

To complete the history of the manuscript, however, there is
still one document to cite; and this, unlike the previous references, has the merit of novelty for the English public. When
Oper und Drama had passed through its last stage, namely its
issue to the press and public, Wagner made Uhlig a present of
the manuscript, with a little private Dedication. Uhlig died in
1853, and the manuscript was returned by his family to the author,
at Wagner's own request, apparently in 1879. A copy of the
private Dedication found its way into an Austrian newspaper of the
latter year, and thence into the treasure-house of Herr Nicolaus
Oesterlein—the founder, and up to the present the owner, of the
invaluable Richard-Wagner-Museum in Vienna—by whose kind-
ness I am enabled to give it in an English dress. It runs thus:

'Dear Uhlig! You once let slip that you still were guilty of a conservative weakness for collecting autographs. As Christmas is just upon us, it gives me pleasure to supply that weakness with a friendly sop. In the name of God, then, conserve this manuscript as pertaining to your household goods. But above all take cheer from the binding, in which I have endeavoured to reverse Goethe's saying : 'Grey, my friend, is every theory,' so that I may call to you with a good conscience: 'Red, o friend, is this my theory!' Zurich, December 21, 1851. Yours, Richard Wagner."—It is perhaps scarcely necessary to point out the semi-political allusion to the revolutionary tendency of the art-theories embodied in this book.

Having watched *Oper und Drama* proceed through all the stages of its first edition, I may add that its second edition did not appear until 1868-9, practically unaltered. If that "interleaving" was ever effected, there appears to have been no use made of the blank pages—unlike Schopenhauer and his continued additions to *Die Welt als Wille und Vorstellung*—so that a revision would be quite out of the question; a man's views will generally alter, or develop, so much in seventeen years, that it is quite impossible to tinker at the original work without destroying its spontaneity. Moreover, when a book has already become the subject of considerable controversy, it is almost an act of literary disingenuousness, to subject it to an entire recasting ; Wagner felt this, and thus has left us a record of the most important stage in his intellectual career, for the loss of which no smoothing down of spurs and angles could possibly have compensated.—The third edition of *Oper und Drama* forms one-third of Volume iii and two-thirds of Volume iv of the *Gesammelte Schriften* issued in 1872. The fourth, and as yet the last, edition is that contained in the "Volksausgabe," issued in 1888.

I must now turn back to an incident in the early career of the book, the discussion of which in its proper order would have broken the historical thread, as it calls for rather more detailed treatment. If the reader will refer to my note on page 118 he will find an extract from a letter to Uhlig, in which Wagner alludes to certain "articles," taken from Part II., for the *Deutsche Monatsschrift*. Beside that extract I must now place another, this time from a letter to Liszt dated July 11, 1851, and the only important allusion to this book in any of Wagner's published correspondence apart from those I have cited above. In this letter we read: "'*Oper und Drama*' is passing through the press very slowly, and will scarcely be ready before two months. Out of this book I have, by special desire, contributed to the *Deutsche Monatsschrift* one or two articles upon modern dramatic poetry; but I now regret it,—for, torn from their context, they do not sound particularly clear. I send them to you all the same, although I am half inclined to ask you to ignore them now. . . . How delighted I am about my *Junge Siegfried* [i.e. about the Weimar proposals, through Liszt, for a performance of the work so soon as completed]; he will deliver me once for all from all article- and essay-writing. I shall spend all this month in gaining back my health, so as next month to throw myself into the music." Now, if we compare those articles in the *Monatsschrift* with the parallel passages of *Oper und Drama*, we find a large number of minor alterations and one very important addition. Wherever these minor alterations constitute a substantial divergence between the two texts, I have noted them in the accompanying translation; but there is scarcely a sentence, of these "articles," which has not been retouched in some trifling detail, such as the punctuation or the order of the words. In this particular section of Part II., therefore, Wagner indisputably took advantage of the opportunity for reflection, as afforded by its having already made an appearance in print; and in almost every instance these retouches add clearness to the original matter. This point I wish to emphasise, in connection with the letter of September '51 in which he declares himself too unwell to go on correcting his proofs of Part III; nor was it at all against his custom, to make amendments to a work while passing through the press, for we find him saying in a letter to Uhlig, of September '50 : "It is *most essential* that I should be able to look once more through the whole [a pamphlet on Theatre Reform] before it comes out, so as to be able to make, perhaps some small alterations, perhaps some mere omissions."

But the most interesting fact about these *Monatsschrift* articles is this—that they do not contain a word about the Œdipus-Antigone myth. I notice that Mons. Noufflard, on page 20 of Volume ii of his excellent *Wagner d'après lui-même*, considers this passage an "intercalation," i.e. an addition to the original text of *Oper und Drama*, and assigns it to the period mentioned on page 358 of the *Communication* (Vol. i of this series) when Wagner was balancing in his mind the respective merits of History and Myth as subjects for Drama, namely the years 1848 to 1849 when *Barbarossa* and *Siegfried* were dividing his attention. This really involves two questions : the one as to *whether* the passage existed in the original M.S., the other as to *when* it was written. The first question, I think, may be easily decided, although there is no documentary evidence to assist one—at least, none accessible at present. If the reader will take page 180 of the accompanying book, and pass straight from the asterisk to the passage quoted in the footnote, and then skip the intervening pages until he arrives at the asterisk on page 192, he will have before him a translation of the text exactly as it stood in the *Monatsschrift;* he will find that there is absolutely *no* break of continuity in the chain of thought, and that certain words such as "Fate," "sinfulness," and "erroneous views of Society" are brought quite close together, in a manner evidently intended by Wagner at the first writing of the chapter. True, that this would reduce Chapter III to little more than three pages; but it is quite intelligible that those three pages should originally have formed the opening of what is now Chapter IV, for there was no break in the magazine "article," beyond the commencing of a fresh paragraph. When I further find that there is no other allusion to Œdipus throughout the book, except a foot-note evidently *added* to the close of Part II, to me it seems quite clear that Wagner—dissatisfied with portions of what he had already written, now that he had seen it in print—decided on relieving a somewhat stiff chapter by the introduction of these superb pages. Had there been any letter to Uhlig of about the same date as that to Liszt above-cited, we should doubtless have heard all about the change; but there was none, for the very good reason that in this letter Wagner tells Liszt that Uhlig is now *with him* at Zurich.

The second question as to *when* this Œdipus-episode was written, is not quite so easy to settle, and it really lies quite apart from the question of its being an afterthought; for in either case it might well date from an earlier period, and have been an instance of working up old material that was lying by, just as we are told that a theme from the *Liebesverbot* found its way into *Tannhäuser*, that the 'Charfreitagszauber' of *Parsifal* dates from these Zurich years, &c. &c. This, in fact, is what I believe to have actually occurred, judging by internal evidence. The style of much of this episode is quite different from the style of the rest of the book—however composite that may be—and closely resembles the *manner* of the " Vaterlandsverein speech " and the *matter* of "*Jesus of Nazareth.*" Those strings of rhetorical questions on pages 184 and 189 are so much like the " speech," that I cannot but think that the major part of the episode was originally intended for a contribution to August Roeckel's " *Volksblätter* " of 1848-9. One or two other considerations confirm me in this belief:—namely the occurrence (a) of the expression " public opinion" three times in this episode (pages 180, 186, and 191), an expression which I do not remember to have come across in Wagner's writings, until those of many years later, but which would be the word most likely to come to the pen of anyone writing for a political newspaper; (b) of the allusion to " oaths," which we find dwelt-on in both the speech and the dramatic sketch, and I fancy nowhere else; (c) of a line which ushers in the episode, with the words " significant in so many *other* respects." I am aware that there are many sentences here which are not at all likely to have been written in the Dresden period, and are in perfect harmony with the rest of the book; but no author, with the slightest feeling for literary workmanship, would dream of pitchforking an earlier sketch into a later work without retouching it in many a particular. It would be quite a simple matter to point out the lines where the old matter is embroidered with the new—upon the hypothesis shared by Mons. Noufflard and myself,—but it would serve no other present purpose than to strengthen our position. At any rate, if it *is* an addition, there is a sentence in the upper part of page 180 that not only would make possible its introduction, but would most probably have suggested it.

To criticise the book as a whole, is scarcely the province of its translator ; for the mere work of carefully inspecting each sentence, to ensure its correct rendering, gives one far too much of a microscopic habit to be able to take a general survey ; moreover the continual revision of parts, both in the manuscript and the ' proof ' stage, leaves one with a most confused impression as to how those parts are arranged—for example, one may be writing the manuscript of Chapter VII while correcting the ' proof ' of

Chapter I and going over the 'revise' of Chapter IV. Some
months hence, I hope to be able to take up the whole matter in a
series of articles for " *The Meister*," when I shall have had time
to get the sections back into their proper order in my brain.
Meanwhile, before saying a word about the separate Parts, I may
add that my own study has convinced me of the general truth of
what Mr H. S. Chamberlain once said in the "*Revue Wagnérienne*"
(1888): " These two works [i.e. the present and *The Art-work*]
may, and in fact ought to be considered as intimately connected
with the *Ring des Nibelungen*. . . . If it was his dramatic projects,
that inspired him in the first place with the idea of writing these
studies, it was those also that he had before his eyes when—in
Opera and Drama—he entered into details upon alliteration, &c.
I even think that this preoccupation with the particular poem that
he had in view, is a fault in this fine work, and that the *Art-work
of the Future*, written at a moment when the *Ring* was less in the
forefront of his thought, is in many respects its superior." But, to
admit that there are faults in any great work, is only to say that it
is human, especially when one remembers the enormous range of
subjects treated in it; whilst, to claim superiority for its predecessor
" in many respects," is not to place the present work on a really
lower level. The superiority of *The Art-work* I consider to lie in
its more methodical arrangement and its greater balance of
diction ; it is far more readable in the German, and in fact there
are only about a couple of sentences in the whole of that work
which present any real ambiguity of meaning. *Opera and Drama*,
on the other hand, is a work which combines all the advantages
and disadvantages of having been written at a terrific pace—for it is
almost incredible that a book of this magnitude, in every sense of
the term, should have been dashed off *in four months;* the advantages might have been retained, and the disadvantages removed,
by laying aside the completed manuscript for a few months, and
then taking it up, for purposes of revision, with the impartial eye
of practically a stranger. This, however, was not to be : the
Communication was waiting to be written, and even that was con-
tending for pride of place, in Wagner's mind, with the rapidly
approaching project of the *Ring;* all these theories— beyond all
value, as they are, to a student of Wagner's dramas—were yet but
the antechamber to " Walhall." Thus the very work which was
to enlighten the uninitiate as to the great artistic reforms the

poet-composer had in his brain, was here and there obscured by the critic-philosopher taking for granted that everyone would be able to follow the many intercrossing lines of his association of ideas. It was as though a musician should set his full 'score' before persons who had only just learnt to read two 'staves.' Nor do I mean this merely as a metaphor, for even his music does not afford a stronger proof of the 'polyphonic' nature of Wagner's mind, than many pages of this *Opera and Drama*. It is not that a sentence is discursive, wandering off into mere byways like those of Jean Paul Richter : no, even the most complex sentence in this work loses a considerable amount of its force and import by the omission of a single subsidiary clause, or even of an adjective which at first sight seems unimportant. To reduce this 'score' to two 'staves' would be an infinitely more difficult task than that which Hans von Bülow accomplished with *Tristan und Isolde ;* some of the 'motives' would be bound to drop out, and, upon their recurrence later on, one would have lost their *raison d'être.* But I see that I am beginning to touch on the translator's fate ; and *that* I must reserve to the close of my Preface.

I proposed, just now, to glance at the separate Parts. Well, the First presents one with next to no difficulties at all ; merely an occasional sprinkling of Feuerbachian tricks of phrase, such as "will and can," "essence" and "is and should be"; the chief thing that strikes one in it, is the remarkable manner in which all its criticisms have become prophecies fulfilled, and the studious care with which Wagner has avoided any reference to his own operas, even where it must have been on the tip of his tongue to say "*Rienzi*" when attacking Meyerbeer's *Prophète.*—The Second presents us with considerable difficulties in Chapter IV—mainly political—and in the latter part of Chapter V ; but it is of far wider-reaching import than anything else its author wrote, either before or after, and this he himself appears to have recognised later : nay even at the time, for he writes to Uhlig, in February '51, " I feel inclined to dedicate my book ' To thinking musicians and—poets.' What's your opinion ? Would not the poets cry out that I am madly arrogant ? " Here it is obvious that Aristotle's "*Poetics* " was consulted by Wagner (naturally, in a German version), and possibly Lessing's "*Dramaturgy*," though reference is made solely to the "*Laocöon* " ; and I firmly believe that in times to come this Second Part will rank as the third—and most important—link in the chain commenced by the two earlier writers : at any rate any obscurities here will wellnigh vanish upon consulting Aristotle and Lessing, especially the latter as rendered into such fluent English by Mr Edward Bell.

The Third Part is undeniably a difficult piece of work, and I am not ashamed to confess misgivings as to my rendering of certain passages, for I know that even at "Wahnfried" a few of the pages are considered doubtful of interpretation. The causes I have already hinted at, namely over-haste in production coupled with want of careful revision ; but to these I must add two others, an almost entire oblivion, on the part of the author, that he was writing for anyone but himself, and a method which combines synthesis and analysis almost in one breath. I have already protested against the accusations that Wagner was an "ill-equipped thinker," and that his style was "involved and discursive" ; the truth is that he was too *well* equipped a thinker and forgot, at times, to make concessions to the weaker vessels, whilst there are very few of his sentences which are really long-winded, as distinct from being packed with positively *necessary* clauses : no, the difficulty of many passages in this Third Part consists in their intense condensation of thought, their saying in two or three words what it would take a page to set before any reader who requires to be told that "four" is virtually "two multiplied by two."

I think that my readers must be nearly tired of the name of Feuerbach, and I promise them that there will be no occasion to refer to him in future volumes. Personally I should like to strangle his ghost, if that were a possible feat ; but I suppose he had his uses in the development of Wagner's thought, for I cannot believe that it is mere Chance that brings one mind to influence another. Anyhow the Feuerbachian terminology is writ large upon much of this Part III, and that unlucky present of treatises must account for the recrudescence of a phase of thought which seemed to be passing away in *Judaism in Music* and the early chapters of *Opera and Drama*. Here again, however, I cannot insist too strongly upon the fact that it was mere *terminology*, and only portions of *that*, which Wagner borrowed from Feuerbach ; thus we shall find "necessary" occurring so often in the Feuerbachian sense, that I think needful to caution readers against taking it in the everyday meaning. Moreover Wagner was just then in the stage of philological study which makes one see in every "root" the stem, the branches, and the leaves that have, may, or may have sprung from it; in every sense this was the period, with him, of deification of the Word.

Thus I come at last to my own labours in this book; for the literal translator's task is almost confined to dealings with the *word*.

Unlike *Das Kunstwerk der Zukunft* (Art-work of the Future), *Oper und Drama* had been translated before, and that so long ago as 1855-6, in the columns of the departed "*Musical World*" (London). Before starting on my translation I glanced at the older version in that journal; but the reading of two or three pages, at random here and there throughout the work, soon convinced me that there was no assistance to be derived therefrom. At a meeting of the Musical Association, held December 13 of last year, I read a paper on "Richard Wagner's Prose," and as it has since been published in their "Proceedings of Session 1892-3" I need not here go into the matter, except to confess a feeling of greater lenience—*not* towards the editor of that old journal—but towards the earlier translator of this book; when that paper of mine was written I had only just commenced the present version,—its conclusion has convinced me that it is better to be humble. For a work of this kind is enough to knock the vanity out of any man, the conditions being so entirely unique. No other of Richard Wagner's literary writings presents one half the difficulties of Part III, and portions of Part II of *Oper und Drama;* one is presented with a theory absolutely *in the making;* and to step from the path of literal exactness—either to the right, by narrowing, or to the left by widening the meaning—would rob the work of all historic value. It is of no use to flatter oneself with the thought that *later* works of Wagner, either literary or musico-dramatic, justify such and such an interpretation; for the point here, the grand instructiveness, is *what* particular stage a certain line of thought, a certain characteristic proposal, had arrived-at in the author's mind. Then, again, there are certain words employed over and over again, and acting as a kind of *leitmotiven* through the work : to find satisfactory English equivalents has scarcely ever been an easy, often an impossible task. "Moments," for instance—for that word one might rest content with drawing attention to its specific use; but "bedingen" and "bestimmen,"—one had to take refuge in such cumbrous and disfiguring terms as "condition" (used as a verb) and "determine"; whilst "Zusammenhang" could only very rarely be allowed to appear as "hang-together" (its best and strictly etymological equivalent) or even "continuity," but had to ring the changes on "cohesion, conjunction, connection" &c., &c. Then there were combinations, such as "the poetic aim," which must be stereotyped at once, to avoid confusion; and lastly one had passages where the tantalising epithets seemed to group themselves into a coruscation baffling all description. Such passages I may expect to see selected as choice specimens of either the author's or the translator's style; but to the general reader—not reading for the mere sake of finding things to carp at—I may safely leave these passages in trust, knowing that if he reads the book from beginning to end, and not a mere sentence here and there, he will find the thoughts explain each other. To others I would offer the following quotation : "As for the third Unity which is that of Action, the ancients meant no other by it than what the Logicians do by their *Finis*, the end or scope of any action: that which is the first in Intention, and last in Execution: now the Poet is to aim at one great and compleat action, to the carrying on of which all things in his Play, even the very obstacles, are to be subservient; and the reason of this is as evident as any of the former. For two Actions equally labour'd and driven on by the Writer, would destroy the unity of the Poem; it would be no longer one Play, but two : not but that there may be many actions in a play . . . but they must be all subservient to the great one" &c. This is *not* from Richard Wagner's writings—though it well might be—but from "*An Essay of Dramatick Poesie*" by John Dryden (1684), whose claims as prose-writer are by many considered to rank higher than his claims as poet. I have quoted it for a double purpose: in the first place, to illustrate Wagner's use of "aim" and "great action"; in the second to justify my own frequent employment of 'capitals.' I am perfectly aware that the use of a capital A for "Art" is jeered at by those whose own art had better be printed upside down; yet I have felt that it was not only allow-able, but helpful, to *capitalise* such words as "Understanding and Feeling" and several others, rather than run a greater risk of misunderstanding. I ought to say, however, that all nouns are decorated with capitals, in the German; therefore, that my selection of any particular word for this mark of distinction is purely arbitrary, though guided by a definite purpose.

I may add a word about the Summary and Index. These I have tried to make supplementary to one another, so that the one shall shew the horizontal, the other the vertical, lines of cleavage. Moreover, an index is generally called a "subject-index": in this instance, I have endeavoured to make it also an index to the 'predicates.' Such an attempt is most difficult to carry out, and I am not thoroughly satisfied with the result; but at least something approaching a 'concordance' was necessary for a work of this unique character,—something that should afford a faint clue to the marvellous meshwork of thought that binds this treatise into one organic whole, whatever apparent defects there may be in its arrangement of minor parts.

In conclusion I must thank the general body of my critics for a reception, accorded to Volume i., by far more cordial than my most sanguine expectations could ever have prefigured. It has encouraged the Wagner Society (London Branch), for whom this work is undertaken in the first place, to enable me to double the speed of publication; so that the present volume makes its appearance a year earlier than I had promised, and the remaining four or five will, it is hoped, follow year by year. I may add that Volume iii will contain, *inter alia*, "A Theatre for Zurich," "Judaism in Music," "On the Performance of Tannhäuser" &c., &c.; also that, the style of the originals being simpler, my readers may reasonably anticipate an improvement in my own.

WM. ASHTON ELLIS.

LONDON, *Christmas* 1893.

OPERA AND DRAMA.

"OPER UND DRAMA."

In a letter to Theodor Uhlig, dated December 1850, *Wagner says : " My book on* Opera and Drama *will be at least twice as big as* The Art-work of the Future. . . . *I add a diagram, as to which I am not sure whether I shall put it into my book or not."*

The diagram in question did not find its way into Opera and Drama, *but has been published, since the author's death, in his* Letters to Uhlig, Fischer & Heine, *from which, with permission of Messrs. H. Grevel & Co., it is here reproduced :—*

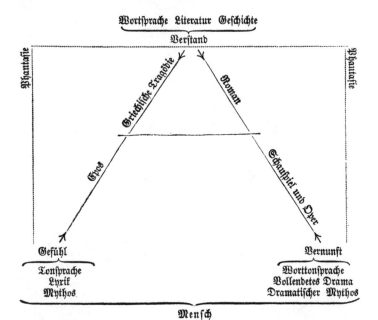

In English this would read : " Word-speech, Literature, History," bracketed by " Understanding"; on either side, " Fancy"; the left-hand slanting line, " Epic—Greek Tragedy," the right-hand, " Romance (or Fiction)—Play and Opera"; below these, on the left, " Tone-speech, Lyric, Myth," bracketed by " Feeling"—on the right, " Word-Tone-speech, Completed Drama, Dramatic Myth," bracketed by " Reason" (or "Intuition"?); and the whole figure governed by the last word, " Man."

TRANSLATOR'S NOTE.

DEDICATION OF THE SECOND EDITION

(of the Original).

To Constantin Frantz.

BOUT the same time last year as I received from you a letter, in which you so delighted me by the account of your impressions on reading this book of mine, I learnt that its first edition had been exhausted some little while back. As I had been advised not long before, that a tolerably ample stock of copies was still on hand, I asked myself, in wonder: What could be the reasons for an evidently greater interest, shewn of recent years, in a literary work whose very nature precluded it from being destined for any Public? My previous experiences had taught me that its First Part, containing a criticism of Opera as an art-genre, had been skimmed by music-reviewers for the newspapers, and its incidental jocular remarks had met with some notice; while a few real musicians had earnestly discussed the contents of this first portion, and even gone so far as to read the constructive Third Part. Of an actual consideration of the Second Part, devoted to the Drama and dramatic Stuff (*Stoff*), no sign had reached me: obviously my book had fallen only into the hands of professional Musicians; to our Literary-poets it had remained completely unknown. From the superscription of the Third Part: "The Arts of Poetry and Tone in the Drama of the Future," a title "*Zukunftsmusik*" ("Music of the Future") was derived, to characterise a latest musical "departure," as whose originator I unexpectedly was brought into full-blown world-celebrity.

Now, however, I have to thank that earlier, quite neglected second portion for an otherwise inexplicably increased demand for my book, occasioning its second edition. There seems to have arisen, among certain folk to whom I was utterly indifferent as poet or musician, an interest in the task of searching my writings, of which one had heard all kinds of curious things, for dangerous remarks on politics and religion. How far these gentry have succeeded in fastening on me any dangerous tendencies, to their own thorough satisfaction, I have as yet to learn: at any rate, they were able to induce me to attempt an explanation * of what I meant by demanding the "Sinking of the State" (" *Untergang des Staates* "). I must confess that this placed me in some perplexity; and, in order tolerably to extricate myself, I readily consented to the admission that I had not meant the thing so very badly, and that, upon mature reflection, I really had no serious objection to the continuance of the State.

The upshot of my various experiences with this extraordinary book was this: that its publication had been altogether useless, had only brought annoyances upon myself, and had provided no one else with any comforting instruction. I felt inclined to consign it to oblivion, and shirked the worry of a new edition for the simple reason that I should have to read it through once more ; a thing which, ever since its first appearance, I had had a great repugnance against doing. Your so expressive letter, however, has all at once reversed my purpose. It was no mere chance, that you were attracted by my musical dramas whilst I was filling my brain with the contents of your political writings. Who can measure the depth of my astonished joy, when you cried to me, in recognition, from that so misconstrued middle portion of my refractory book: "Your Foundering of the State is the Founding of my German Empire!" Seldom can there have been so

---

* Evidently the series of articles on " *German Art and German Politics* " that appeared in the *Süddeutsche Presse* in 1867, and were subsequently reprinted in Vol. VIII. Ges. Schr.—TR.

complete a mutual supplementing, as here had been
prepared upon the broadest basis betwixt the politician
and the artist. And in this *German spirit* which has
brought us two, while starting from the utmost opposites
of customary vision, to the deeply-felt perception of the
grand fore-calling of our Folk, we well may now believe
with strengthened courage.

But it needed our encounter, to strengthen our belief.
The eccentricity of my old opinions, as still apparent in
the accompanying book, was certainly occasioned by the
despair there lay in any opposite views. And even now,
the antidote for this despair would prove of little virtue,
had we to solely seek it in the aspect of our public life :
each contact with that public life can only bring men, filled
with our belief, into associations promptly to be rued ;
whereas a thorough isolation, with all its sacrifices, affords
the only rescue. The sacrifice you laid upon yourself, in
this sense, consisted in the renouncement of any general
recognition of your noble political writings, in which, with
most persuasive clearness, you point the Germans to the
weal that lies so near their door. Smaller seemed to be
the sacrifice the artist had to bring, the dramatic poet and
musician whose works spoke loud from all our public
theatres to you, and kindled so your hope that you saw
already a strengthening food supplied to that belief. It
came hard to you, not to misunderstand me, not to see
a morbid overstraining in my denial of your confident
assumptions, when I tried to teach you the little inward
worth of my successes with the theatre-public. Yet at
last you taught yourself that fundamental lesson by an
exact acquaintance with the contents of this book, now
dedicated to you, on Opera and Drama. For sure, it
opened up to you the wounds concealed from all the
world, the wounds of which, before my own unshaken
conscience, my successes as a German " opera-composer "
are bleeding still. In truth, and even to this day, can
nothing reassure me that these successes, in their weightiest
factor, are not still grounded on a misconception

which downright baffles all the real, the only aimed
success.

The explanations of this seeming paradox I laid before
the public, now wellnigh eighteen years ago, in the form
of a detailed handling of the problem—Opera and Drama.
What I must wonder at above all else, in those who grant
this work a searching scrutiny, is this : that they should
not allow themselves to be tired out by the difficulties of
the exposition, which were thrust upon me by the very
nature of that detailed handling. My desire to get to
the bottom of the matter and to shirk no detail that, in
my opinion, might make the difficult subject of æsthetic
analysis intelligible to the simple Feeling, betrayed me into
a stubbornness of style, which to the reader who looks
merely for entertainment, and is not directly interested in the
subject itself, is extremely likely to seem a bewildering
diffuseness. As regards the present revision of the text,
however, I have decided to change nothing therein of importance,* since just in that aforesaid difficulty of my book
have I, on the other hand, perceived its special recommen-
dation to the earnest thinker. For this I almost feel that
an apology would be both superfluous and misleading.
The problems, to whose handling I was impelled, have
never before been investigated in that connexion wherein
I recognised them, and not at all by artists, to whose
Feeling they most immediately address themselves, but
merely by theorising æstheticians, who, with the best will
in the world, could not avoid the evil of employing a
dialectic form of exposition for subjects whose fundamental essence has lain hitherto as far from the cognition
of Philosophy as has Music itself. Shallowness and
ignorance find it easy, by drawing on the garnered stores
of Dialectics, to prattle about things they do not under-

---

* Excepting where they involve mere alterations of grammar, punctuation,
or altogether synonymous terms, these few Variants will be noted below the text
in their proper places. For their discovery I have again to thank Vol. I.
of Dr Hugo's ' *Richard Wagner's geistige Entwickelung,*' mentioned in the first
volume of the present series.—TR.

stand, and in a manner to make a brave show in the eyes of the equally uninitiate : but he who does not merely wish to juggle with philosophic notions before a public which has none itself,—he who, the rather, in facing difficult problems desires to turn from erring notions to the right Feeling of the thing itself, may learn perchance from the following pages how much trouble it costs a man to fulfil his task to his own inward satisfaction.

In this sense, then, do I venture to commend afresh my book to earnest notice.   Where it meets with this, as was the case with you, my honoured Friend, it will serve towards the filling of that yawning gulf which lies between the mistaken spirit of the success of my musico-dramatic works, and the only effect that hovers in the air before me as their right one.

(The original of the above
was written at Lucerne, April
28, 1868.—TR.)

PREFACE TO THE FIRST EDITION

(of the Original).

 FRIEND has told me that, with my earlier utterances on Art, I angered many persons far less by the pains I took to unmask the grounds of the barrenness of our nowadays art-making, than by my endeavours to forecast the conditions of its future fruitfulness. Nothing could more aptly characterise our situation, than this verdict of experience. We all feel that we are not doing right, and do not even attempt to deny the fact when roundly told it; only, when shewn *how* we might do right, and that this right is nothing humanly impossible, but something very possible indeed, nay an absolute Necessity of the Future, then we feel hurt because, once forced to admit that possibility, we are robbed of our only excuse for abiding in unfruitfulness. For we have been indoctrinated with so much sense-of-honour, as to wish not to appear cowardly and slothful; but we lack true Honour's natural spur to courage and activity.—This selfsame wrath I shall be obliged to call down again upon my head, by the pages that now lie before me; and that the more, as I have been at some pains therein to show, not merely in general terms—as in my *Art-work of the Future*—but by a minute entry into particulars, the possibility and necessity of a more salutary tillage of the soil of Poetry and Music.

I must almost fear, however, that another grudge will this time gain the upper hand : a grudge occasioned by my exposition of the worthlessness of our modern opera-affairs. Many, even who mean well by me, will not be able to comprehend how I can presume to attack, in such unsparing fashion, a personage famous in the daily roll of opera-composers ; and this, too, in that capacity, of Opera-composer, in which I also am involved and thus exposed so lightly to the charge of most unbridled envy.

I will not deny that I battled long with myself, before I decided upon doing, and doing thus, what I have done. After writing, I quietly read over all that was contained in this attack, every turn of phrase and each expression, and carefully pondered whether I should hand it in this garment to publicity; until at last I have convinced myself that—with my sharply-outlined views on the weighty topic of discussion—I should only be a coward and unworthily concerned for self, did I not utter my opinions of that most dazzling phenomenon in the world of modern operatic composition exactly as I have done. What I say thereon, is only what has long ceased to be a matter of doubt among the generality of honest artists. Not a smothered growl, however, but alone an openly-proclaimed and categorical defiance, can bear good fruit; for it brings about the needful shock that cleans the air, divides the murky from the clear, and winnows what there is to winnow.   Yet it has not been my object to sound this challenge for its own dear sake, but I *needs must* sound it, since after delivering myself of more general opinions, as heretofore, I now felt the necessity of a definite excursion into the particular ; for it was my concern, not merely to arouse, but also to make my meaning unmistakable.   To make myself intelligible, I was forced to point my finger at our art's most salient features ; nor could I withdraw this finger and thrust it back, clenched in my fist, into my pocket, while faced with that phenomenon which shows the plainest an artistic error crying to us for solution.   For this error, the more brilliant its appearance, the more it blinds the captive eye : and that eye must see completely clearly, if it is not to be completely robbed of sight. Wherefore, if I had held my hand from sheer regard for this one personage, I either must have given up all thought of writing the accompanying work—to which, on the other hand, I felt engaged by my convictions—or else I must

have purposely lamed its effect; for I should wittingly
have had to put out of sight the most obvious facts, and
those the most necessary to a careful survey.

Whatever, then, may be the verdict on my book, one
thing at least must be admitted by even the most hostilely
disposed : and that is the *earnestness* of my intention. To
whomsoever I am able to convey this earnestness, by the
comprehensive nature of my argument, he will surely not
only forgive me that attack, but also understand that I
have not engaged in it from flippancy, still less from envy ;
and further, he will justify me in that, while exposing the
repugnant features of our modern art, I have from time to
time exchanged this earnestness for the quiet mirth of
irony,—the only mood that can help us tolerate a painful
sight, while, on the other hand, it always gives the least
offence.

But, even of that artistic personality, I had only to attack
that side which is turned towards our public art-affairs.
Only after I had set this side alone before my eyes, was I
able to conceal from my sight, as here was needful, that
other side on which it fronts considerations amid which I
myself was once brought into contact with it ; but which
lie so completely aloof from art's publicity, that they ought
not to be dragged before it,—even though I almost feel
compelled thereto, in order to admit how much I, also,
once went astray,—an admission I candidly and gladly
make, now that I have grown conscious of my former error.

If I thus was able to purge my conscience, I had the less
call to regard the dictates of prudence as I should be blind
if I did not clearly see that, from the moment when I struck
in my artistic works that path which in the following pages
I advocate as Writer, I fell into the exile from our public
artist-world in which I find myself to-day, alike politically
and as an artist, and from which it is quite certain that I
cannot be redeemed apart from others.—

But quite another reproach might be made me, by those
who hold that the worthlessness of That which I assail
is already so made out, that it will not repay the pains of so

circumstantial an attack.   Such persons are altogether in
the wrong.   What they know, is only known to few ; whilst
what is known to these few, the most of them do not *choose* to
know.   Of all things the most dangerous is the half-heartedness so much in vogue, which hampers each artistic effort
and every judgment.   I, however, have been forced to
speak out sharply, and enter definitely into details on this
side too, since I was not so much preoccupied with that
attack, as with the demonstration of artistic possibilities
which cannot plainly show themselves until we step upon a
soil from which half-heartedness is hunted clean away.
But he who holds *for accidental or overlookable* the artistic
feature that rules to-day the public taste, is involved, at
bottom, in the selfsame error from which that feature is
itself derived : and to show precisely this, was the foremost
object of my present work, whose *ulterior* object cannot be
so much as conceived by those who have not completely
cleared their minds as to the nature of that error.

The hope to be understood as I desire, I can put alone in
those who have the courage to break with every prejudice
May it be fulfilled me by many !

Zurich, January, 1851.

INTRODUCTION.

O phenomenon can be completely grasped, in all its essence, until it has itself come to fullest actuality ; an error is never done with, until all the possibilities of its maintenance have been exhausted, all the ways of satisfying a necessary need within its bounds been tried and measured out.

The essence of *Opera* could only become plain to us as an unnatural and flimsy one, when its un-nature and its flimsiness first came to openest and noisomest of show ; the error that lay behind the evolution of this musical art-form could only be brought home to us, after the noblest geniuses had spent their whole artistic life-force in exploring all the windings of its maze without finding any outlet, but on every hand the mere way back to the error's starting-point,—until at last this maze became the sheltering asylum for all the madness in the world.

The doings (*Wirksamkeit*) of Modern Opera, in their bearings on the public, have long become an object of deepest and heartiest aversion to all honour-loving *artists ;* but they have only complained of the corruption of taste and the frivolity of those artists who turned it to their purpose, without its ever occurring to them that that corruption was an altogether natural one, and therefore this frivolity a quite necessary result. If *Criticism* were really what it mostly pretends to be, it must have long-since solved the riddle of this error, and have radically justified the aversion of the honest artist. Instead thereof, even it has only felt the promptings of aversion, but the riddle's solution it has merely fumbled-at as confusedly as the artist, caught within the error, bestirred himself to find an exit.

In this matter, Criticism's greatest ill lies rooted in its very nature. The Critic does not feel within himself the imperious Necessity that drives the Artist to that fanatical stubbornness wherewith he cries at last: *So is it, and not otherwise!* The Critic, if he fain would herein imitate the Artist, can only fall into the repulsive fault of arrogance, i.e. of the confident assertion of some view, no matter what, upon a thing which he does not perceive with the instinct of an artist, but as to which he merely utters, with bald æsthetical caprice, opinions that he seeks to uphold from the standpoint of abstract learning. If, on the other hand, the Critic recognises his *proper* position toward the world of art-phenomena, then he feels himself constrained to that timidness and prudence which bid him merely range his objects side by side, and hand over the collection to some new inquirer, but never dare speak out with enthusiastic certainty the final word. Thus Criticism lives on "gradual" progress, i.e. upon the everlasting *maintenance* of Error ; it feels that, Error broken with for good, then steps upon the scene the naked actual Truth, the Truth whereat men only can rejoice, but nevermore may criticise,—just as the lover, in the exaltation of the love-emotion, can surely never fall a-pondering on the essence and the object of his love. Of this full saturation with the essence of Art, must Criticism, so long as it subsists and *can* subsist, fall ever short. It can never be *completely* with its object ; its one full half must it ever turn away ; and that the half which is its own sheer essence. This Criticism lives by "Though" and "But." Were it to plunge right down into the depth of a phenomenon, it then must manfully speak out this one and only thing, the depth that it had seen,—provided always that the critic had at all the needful faculty, i.e. a Love for the object of his criticism. But this One-thing is generally of such a kind that, once spoken squarely out, it must make all further criticism clean impossible. So Criticism prudently, for dear life's sake, holds ever by the merest surface of the matter ; weighs out its ounces of effect ; waxes wary ; and—look ye !—the unmanly, coward

"Ne'ertheless" uplifts its head, the possibility of endless
criticism and indecision is won afresh !

And yet we all have now to set our hands to criticism ;
for through it alone can the error of an art-tendency, as
unveiled by its products, come fully to the consciousness
of each of us ; and only through the knowledge of an error,
shall we be rid thereof. Have Artists unawares propped
up this error, and finally raised it to the height of its
further impossibility : so must they, to completely overcome it, make one last manly effort, themselves to practise
criticism. Thus will they alike crush Error and root-up
Criticism ; thenceforth to be again, and then first truly
Artists who may yield themselves uncaring to the
stream of inspiration, untroubled by æsthetic definitions of
their task. The hour that calls aloud for this upgirding
has struck already : we *must* do what we dare not leave
undone, if we would not prove a laughing-stock forever.

What, then, is the *Error* boded by us all, but not yet
fathomed ?

There lies before me, in Brockhaus' "*Gegenwart*," a
lengthy article entitled "Modern Opera," the work of an
able and experienced art-critic. The author ranges side
by side all the notable phenomena of modern Opera, in
most instructive fashion, and quite plainly teaches by them
the whole history of the error and its unveiling : he almost
lays his finger on this error, almost unveils it before our
eyes ; but then he feels himself so unable to speak boldly
out its ground, that, arrived at the point when such utterance becomes imperative, he prefers to lose his way among
the most mistaken expositions of the thing itself ; so that
he in a measure fouls again the mirror which, up to then,
had begun to reflect upon us a brighter and yet brighter
light. He *knows* that Opera has no historical—or more
correctly : natural—origin, that it has not arisen from the
Folk, but from an art-caprice ; he correctly *divines* the
noxious character of this caprice, when he calls it an arrant
blunder of most now-living French and German opera-
composers "that they strive on the path of *musical*

characteristique for effects that one can reach alone by
the *sharp-cut, intellectual Word of dramatic Poetry"*; he
gets as far as the well-grounded doubt, whether Opera
is not after all a quite self-contradictory, unnatural genre
of art; he shows in the works of *Meyerbeer*—here, to be
sure, almost unconsciously—this Un-nature driven to its
most vicious pitch; and—instead of speaking roundly out
the needful thing, already almost on the tongue of every
one—he suddenly veers round, to keep for Criticism an
everlasting life, and heaves a sigh that *Mendelssohn's* too
early death should have hindered, i.e. staved off, the
solution of the riddle!

What does this critic signify by his regret? Is it merely
the assumption that Mendelssohn, with his fine intelligence
and unusual musical gifts, either would have been in the
position to write an opera in which the evident contradictions of this art-form should be brilliantly set right and
reconciled, or else, supposing that despite those gifts and
that intelligence he were unable to effect this, he would
thereby have certified these contradictions for good and
all, and proved the genre unnatural and null?—Did the
critic, then, imagine he could make this proof dependent
on the pleasure of one peculiarly gifted—musical—personality? Was *Mozart* a lesser musician? Is it possible to
find anything more perfect than every piece of his *Don
Juan*? But what could Mendelssohn, in the happiest
event, have done beyond the delivering, number for
number, of pieces that should equal Mozart's in their
perfectness? Or does our critic wish for something other,
something more, than Mozart ever made?—There we
have it: *he demands the great one-centred fabric of the
Drama's whole; he demands—between his lines—the Drama
in its highest fill and potence.*

But to whom does he address this claim?—*To the
Musician!*—The harvest of his exhaustive survey of
Opera's accomplished facts, the solid knot into which he
had bound each thread of knowledge in his skilful hand,—
he lets it slip at last, and casts the whole thing back again

into its ancient chaos! He wants a house built for him, and turns to the carver or upholsterer; the *architect*, who includes within himself the carver, the upholsterer and all the other needful aids for decking-out the house, since he gives their joint endeavours aim and order,—he never thinks of *him!*—He had solved the riddle; yet its solution brought him, not the light of day, but only a lightning-flash in pitch-dark night, after whose vanishing the pathway suddenly becomes but still more indiscernible. So now at last he gropes around in utter darkness, and where the error rears itself in nakedest abomination and baldest prostitution, plain enough for any hand to grasp, as in the Meyerbeerian opera, there the wholly-blinded of a sudden deems he spies the lighted exit: he staggers and stumbles every moment over stock and stone; at every finger-touch he shudders; his breath forsakes him, stifled by the unnatural fumes he cannot but suck in;—and yet he believes himself upon the sound sure way to saving; wherefore he puts his best foot foremost, and dupes himself as to the very things that block that pathway with their evil bodings.—Nevertheless, did he only know it, he is travelling on the pathway of salvation. This is, in very truth, the road that leads from Error. Nay, it is more, it is the end of that road; for it is Error's crown of errors, blazoning forth its fall. That fall means here: *the open death of Opera,*—the death that Mendelssohn's good angel sealed, when it closed its charge's eyes in pitying season!—

That the solution of the riddle lies before our eyes, that it speaks aloud from the very surface of the show, but that Critics and Artists alike can still turn their heads from its acknowledgment—this is the veritable woe of our art-epoch. Let us be ever so honestly concerned to occupy ourselves alone with Art's true substance, let us be ever so righteously wroth in our campaign against the Lie: yet we deceive ourselves about that substance, and with all the powerlessness of such deception we fight against that lie the while, anent the essence of the most puissant art-form in which Music greets the public ear, we persistently abide in the selfsame error from which that art-form sprang all unawares, and to which alone is to be ascribed its open shattering, the exposure of its nulity.

It almost seems to me as though ye required a mighty courage, an uncommonly bold resolve, to acknowledge and proclaim aloud that error. It is to me as though ye felt the ground would slip away from all your present musical producings, if once ye made that necessary avowal, and that it therefore needs an unparalleled self-sacrifice to bring yourselves to do it. But yet, meseems, it calls for no excess of strength or trouble, and least of all, of pluck or daring : when it is nothing but a question of simply, and without any outlay upon wonder and amazement, acknowledging a patent fact, long felt but now grown past denial. I almost blush to speak with *lifted* voice the brief formula that bares the error, for I well might be ashamed to give the air of a weighty novelty to something so clear, so simple, and in itself so certain, that I should fancy all the world must long ago have got the thing by heart. If nevertheless I pronounce this formula with stronger accent, if I declare aloud that *the error in the art-genre of Opera consists herein :*

that a Means of expression (Music) has been made the end, while the End of expression (the Drama) has been made a means,

I do it nowise in the idle dream of having discovered something new, but with the object of posting the Error so plain that every one may see it, and of thus taking the field against that miserable half-heartedness which has spread its pall above our Art and Criticism. If we take the torch of truth provided by the enucleation of this error, and light therewith the features of our operatic art and criticism, we shall see amazed in what a labyrinth of fancies we have hitherto been wandering, with our makings and our judgings ; it will show us clearly why, not only in our Making must every high endeavour founder on the breakers

B

of impossibility, but also in our Judging have the evenest
of heads reeled to and fro in dotage and delirium.

Is it, by any chance, first necessary to prove the justice
of that proclamation of the Error innate in the art-genre
of Opera? Can it possibly be doubted, that in Opera
music has actually been taken as the end, the drama merely
as the means? Surely not. The briefest survey of the
historic evolution of Opera teaches us this, quite past dis-
puting ; every one who has busied himself with the account
of that development has—simply by his historical research
—unwillingly laid bare the truth. Not from the medieval
Folk-plays, in which we find the traces of a natural coöperation of the art of Tone with that of Drama, did Opera
arise ; but at the luxurious courts of Italy — notably
enough, the only great land of European culture in which
the Drama never developed to any significance—it occurred
to certain distinguished persons, who found Palestrina's
church-music no longer to their liking, to employ the
singers, engaged to entertain them at their festivals, on
singing *Arias,* i.e. Folk-tunes stripped of their naïvety and
truth, to which 'texts' thrown together into a semblance
of dramatic cohesion were added waywardly as underlay.*
This *Dramatic Cantata,* whose contents aimed at anything
but Drama, is the mother of our Opera ; nay more, it is
that Opera itself. The more it developed from this its
point of origin, the more consistently the purely musical
Aria, the only vestige of remaining Form, became the
platform for the dexterity of the Singer's throat : the more

---

* Our author makes no pretence of entering upon a historical discussion
of the first beginnings of Opera, the materials for which were certainly not
accessible to him in Zurich ; otherwise it would be necessary to qualify his
present statement, in certain details, by reference to the later-written Histories
of Music by Ritter and Naumann. That the pioneers of Opera (Bardi,
Galilei, Peri and Monteverde) started with the assumption that they were
reviving the *form* of the old Greek drama, however, makes little difference in
the *spirit* of their attempt, which was admittedly dictated by a feeling of dissatis-
faction with the contrapuntal music of their day. But, indeed, as is shewn by
the rapidity with which he reaches Metastasio and "150 years ago," Wagner
passes over the musico-dramatic efforts of the seventeenth century as of little
real moment.—Tr.

plainly did it become the office of the *Poet,* called-in to
give a helping hand to their musical diversions, to carpenter
a poetic form which should serve for nothing further than to
supply the needs both of the Singer and of the musical Aria-
form with their verse-requirements. *Metastasio's* great
fame consisted in this, that he never gave the musician
the slightest harass, never advanced an unwonted claim
from the purely dramatic standpoint, and was thus the
most obedient and obliging servant of this Musician.

Has this relation of the Poet to the Musician altered by
one hair's-breadth, to our present day? To be sure, in
respect of that which, according to purely musical canons,
is now held as dramatic, and which certainly differs widely
from the old-Italian opera; but by no means in respect of
what concerns the chief characteristic of the situation.
This holds as good to-day as 150 years ago : that the Poet
shall take his inspiration from the Musician, that he shall
listen for the whims of music, accommodate himself to
the musician's bent, choose his stuff by the latter's taste,
mould his characters by the timbres expedient for the
purely musical combinations, provide dramatic bases for
certain forms of vocal numbers in which the musician may
wander at his ease,—in short, that, in his subordination to
the musician, he shall construct his drama with a single eye
to the specifically musical intentions of the Composer,—or
else, if he will not or cannot do all this, that he shall be
content to be looked on as unserviceable for the post of
opera-librettist.—Is this true, or not? I doubt that any
can advance one jot of argument against it.

The aim of Opera has thus ever been, and still is to-day,
confined to Music. Merely so as to afford Music with a
colourable pretext for her own *excursions* (Ausbreitung), is
the purpose of Drama *dragged on,*—naturally, not to curtail the ends of Music, but rather to serve her simply as a
means. Unhesitatingly is this admitted on every hand ;
no one so much as attempts to deny this statement of the
position of Drama toward Music, of the Poet toward the

Tone-artist; only, in view of the uncommon spread and effectiveness (*Wirkungsfähigkeit*) of Opera, have folk believed that they must make friends with a monstrosity, nay, must even credit its unnatural agency with the possibility of doing something altogether new, unheard, and hitherto undreamt : namely, of *erecting the genuine Drama on the basis of Absolute Music.*

Since, then, I have made it the goal of this book to prove that by the collaboration of precisely *our* Music with dramatic Poetry a heretofore undreamt significance not only can, but *must* be given to Drama : so have I, for the reaching of that goal, to begin with a complete exposure of the incredible error in which those are involved who believe they may await that higher fashioning of Drama from the essence of our *modern Opera,* i.e. from the placing of Poetry in a contra-natural position toward Music.

Let us, therefore, first turn our attention exclusively to the nature of Opera !

FIRST PART.

OPERA AND THE NATURE OF MUSIC.

(DIE OPER UND DAS WESEN DER MUSIK.)

I.

VERYTHING lives and lasts by the inner Necessity of its being, by its own nature's Need. It lay in the nature of the art of Tone, to evolve herself to a capability of the most definite and manifold expression; which capability, albeit the need thereof lay hid within her soul, she would never have attained, had she not been thrust into a position toward the art of Poetry in which she saw herself compelled to will to answer claims upon her utmost powers, even though those claims should ask from her a thing impossible.

Only in its Form, can a being utter itself: the art of Tone owed all her forms to Dance and Song. To the Word-poet, who merely wished to make use of Music for the heightening of his own vehicle of expression, in Drama, she appeared solely in that narrowed form of song-and-dance ; in which she could not possibly betray to him the wealth of utterance whereof, in truth, she still was capable. Had the art of Tone remained once for all in a position toward the Word-poet such as the latter now occupies towards herself in Opera, then she could only have been employed by him in her meanest powers, nor would she ever have reached the capability of becoming that supremely mighty organ of expression that she is to-day. Music was therefore destined to credit herself with possibilities which, in very truth, were doomed to stay for her *im*possibilities; herself a sheer organ of expression, she must rush into the error of desiring to plainly outline the thing to be expressed ; she must venture on the boastful attempt to issue orders and speak out aims *there*, where in truth she can only have to subordinate herself to an aim *her* essence cannot ever formulate (*fassen*), but to whose realising she gives, by this her subordination, its only true enablement.—

Along two lines has Music developed in that art-genre which she dominates, the Opera : along an *earnest*—with all the Tone-poets who felt lying on their shoulders the burthen of responsibility that fell to Music when she took upon herself alone the aim of Drama ; along a *frivolous*— with all the Musicians who, as though driven by an instinctive feeling of the impossibility of achieving an unnatural task, have turned their backs upon it and, heedful only of the profit which Opera had won from an uncommonly widespread popularity, have given themselves over to an unmixed musical empiricism. It is necessary that we should commence by fixing our gaze upon the first, the *earnest* line.

The musical basis of Opera was—as we know—nothing other than the *Aria ;* this Aria, again, was merely the Folk-song as rendered by the art-singer before the world of rank and quality, but with its Word-poem left out and replaced by the product of the art-poet to that end commissioned. The conversion of the Folk-tune into the Operatic-aria was primarily the work of that art-Singer; whose concern was no longer for the right delivery of the tune, but for the exhibition of his throat-dexterity.   It was he, who parcelled out the resting-points he needed, the alternation of more lively with more placid phrasing, the passages where, free from any rhythmic or melodic curb, he might bring his skill to bearing as it pleased him best. The Composer merely furnished the singer, the Poet in his turn the composer, with the material for their virtuosity.

The natural relation of the artistic factors of Drama was thus, at bottom, as yet not quite upheaved : it was merely distorted, inasmuch' as the Performer, the most necessary condition for Drama's possibility, represented but one solitary talent—that of absolute song-dexterity—and nowise all the conjoint faculties of artist Man. This one distortion of the character of the Performer, however, sufficed to bring about the ultimate perversion of the natural relation of those factors: to wit, the absolute preferment of the Musician before the Poet. Had that Singer been a true, sound and whole Dramatic-performer, then had the Composer come necessarily into his proper position toward the Poet; since the latter would then have firmly spoken out the dramatic aim, the measure for all else, and ruled its realising. But the poet who stood nighest that Singer was the Composer,—the composer who merely helped the singer to attain his aim ; while this aim, cut loose from every vestige of dramatic, nay even poetic bearing, was nothing other, through and through, than to show-off his own specific song-dexterity.

This original relation of the artistic factors of Opera to one another we have to stamp sharply on our minds, in order to clearly recognise, in the sequel, how this distorted relation became only all the more entangled through every attempt to set it straight.—

Into the Dramatic Cantata, to satisfy the luxurious craving of these eminent sirs for change in their amusements, there was dovetailed next the Ballet. Dance and Dance-tune, borrowed just as waywardly from the Folkdance and its tune as was the operatic Aria from the Folksong, joined forces with the Singer, in all the sterile immiscibility of un-natural things ; while it naturally became the Poet's task, midst such a heaping-up of inwardly incongruous matter, to bind the samples of the diverse art-dexterities, now laid before him, into some kind of patchwork harmony. Thus, with the Poet's aid, an ever more obviously imperative dramatic cohesion was thrust on *That* which, in its actual self, was crying for no cohesion whatever ; so that the aim of Drama—forced on by outward Want—was merely lodged (*angegeben*), by no means housed (*aufgenommen*). Song-tune and Dance-tune stood side by side in fullest, chillest loneliness, for exhibition of the agility of singer or of dancer ; and only in that

which was to make shift to bind them, to wit the music-
ally-recited dialogue, did the Poet ply his lowly calling,
did the Drama peep out here and there.

Neither was Recitative itself, by any means, some new
invention proceeding from a genuine urgence of Opera
towards the Drama. Long before this mode of intoning
was introduced into Opera, the Christian Church had used
it in her services, for the recitation of biblical passages.
The banal singsong of these recitals, with its more listlessly
melodic than rhetorically expressive incidence of tone, had
been early fixed by ritualistic prescript into an arid
semblance, without the reality, of speech ; and this it was
that, merely moulded and varied by musical caprice, passed
over into the Opera. So that, what with Aria, Dance-tune
and Recitative, the whole apparatus of musical drama—
unchanged in essence down to our very latest opera—was
settled once for all. Further, the dramatic groundplans laid
beneath this apparatus soon won a kindred stereotyped
persistence. Mostly taken from an entirely misconstrued
Greek mythology, they formed a theatric scaffolding from
which all capability of rousing warmth of human interest
was altogether absent, but which, on the other hand,
possessed the merit of lending itself to the good pleasure
of every composer in his turn ; in effect, the majority of
these texts were composed over and over again by the most
diverse of musicians.—

The so famous revolution of *Gluck*, which has come to
the ears of many ignoramuses as a complete reversal of the
views previously current as to Opera's essence, in truth
consisted merely in this : that the musical composer
revolted against the wilfulness of the singer. The Composer, who, next to the Singer, had drawn the special
notice of the public to himself—since it was *he* who provided
the singer with fresh supplies of stuff for his dexterity—felt
his province encroached upon by the operations of the
latter, in exact measure as he himself was busied to shape
that stuff according to his own inventive fancy, and thus
secure that *his* work also, and perchance at last *only* his

work, might catch the ear of the audience. For the reaching of his ambitious goal there stood *two* ways open to the Composer: either, by use of all the musical aids already at his disposal, or yet to be discovered, to unfold the purely sensuous contents of the Aria to their highest, rankest pitch; or—and this is the more earnest path, with which we are concerned at present—to put shackles on Caprice's execution of that Aria, by himself endeavouring to give the tune, before its execution, an expression answering to the underlying Word-text. As, by the nature of these texts, they were to figure as the feeling discourse of the dramatis personæ, so had it already occurred, quite of itself, to feeling singers and composers to furnish forth their virtuosity with an impress of the needful warmth; and Gluck was surely not the first who indited feeling airs, nor his singers the first who delivered them with fit expression. But that he *spoke out with consciousness and firm conviction* the fitness and necessity of an expression answering to the text-substratum, in Aria and Recitative, this it is that makes him the departure-point of an at any rate thorough change in the quondam situation of the artistic factors of Opera toward one another. Henceforth the sceptre of Opera passes definitely over to the Composer: the Singer becomes the *organ of the Composer's aim*, and this aim is consciously declared to be the matching of the dramatic contents of the text-substratum with a true and suitable expression. Thus, at bottom, a halt was only cried to the unbecoming and heartless vanity of the singing Virtuoso; but with all the rest of Opera's unnatural organism things remained on their old footing. Aria, Recitative and Dance-piece, fenced-off each from each, stand side by side as unaccommodated in the operas of Gluck as they did before him, and as, with scarcely an exception, they still stand to-day.

In the situation of the *Poet* toward the Composer not one jot was altered; rather had the Composer grown more dictatorial, since, with his declared consciousness of a higher mission—made good against the virtuoso Singer—he set

to work with more deliberate zeal at the arrangement of
the opera's framework. To the Poet it never occurred to
meddle with these arrangements; he could not so much
as dream of Music, to which the Opera had owed its
origin, in any other form than those narrow, close-ruled
forms he found set down before him—as binding even
upon the Musician himself. To tamper with these forms
by advancing claims of dramatic necessity, to such an
extent that they should cease to be intrinsic shackles on
the free development of dramatic truth, would have seemed
to him unthinkable ; since it was precisely in these forms
alone—inviolable even by the musician—that he could
conceive of Music's essence. Wherefore, once engaged in
the penning of an opera-text, he must needs pay even
more painful heed than the musician himself to the observance of those forms ; at utmost leave it to that musician,
in his own familiar field, to carry out enlargements and
developments, in which he could lend a helping hand
but never take the initiative. Thus the Poet, who looked
up to the Composer with a certain holy awe, rather confirmed the latter's dictatorship in Opera, than set up rival
claims thereto ; for he was witness to the earnest zeal the
musician brought to his task.

It was Gluck's successors, who first bethought them to
draw profit from this their situation for the actual widening of the forms to hand. These followers, among whom
we must class the composers of Italian and French descent
who wrote for the Paris opera-stage at quite the close
of the past and beginning of the present century, gave
to their vocal pieces not only a more and more thorough
warmth and straightforwardness of expression, but a more
and more extended formal basis. The traditional divi-
sions of the Aria, though still substantially preserved, were
given a wider play of motive ; modulations and connecting
phrases (*Übergänge und Verbindungsglieder*) were themselves drawn into the sphere of expression ; the Recitative
joined on to the Aria more smoothly and less waywardly,
and, as a necessary mode of expression, it stepped into

that Aria itself. Another notable expansion was given
to the Aria, in that—obediently to the dramatic need—
more than *one* person now shared in its delivery, and
thus the essential Monody of earlier opera was beneficially
lost. Pieces such as Duets and Terzets were indeed known
long before; but the fact of two or three people singing
in one piece had not made the slightest essential difference
in the character of the Aria: this had remained exactly
the same in melodic plan and insistence on the tonality
once started (*Behauptung des einmal angeschlagenen thema-
tischen Tones*)—which bore no reference to any individual
expression, but solely to a general, specifically-musical
mood—and not a jot of it was really altered, no matter
whether delivered as a monologue or duet, excepting at
the utmost quite materialistic details, namely in that its
musical phrases were either sung alternately by different
voices, or in concert through the sheer harmonic device
of combining two, three, or more voices at once. To
apply that specifically-musical factor in such a way that
it should be susceptible of a lively change of individual
expression, was the object and the work of these composers, as shown in their handling of the so-called *dramatic-
musical Ensemble*. The essential musical substance of this
Ensemble was still, indeed, composed of Aria, Recitative
and Dance-tune: only, when once a vocal expression in
accord with the text-substratum had been recognised as
a becoming claim to make on Aria and Recitative, the
truthfulness of such expression must logically be extended
to everything else in the text that betrayed a particle
of dramatic coherence. From the honest endeavour to
observe this logical consistency arose that broadening of
the older musical forms, in Opera, which we meet in the
serious operas of *Cherubini, Méhul* and *Spontini*. We
may say that in these works there is fulfilled all that
Gluck desired, or could desire; nay, in them is once for
all attained the acme of all natural, i.e. in the *best*
sense consequential, evolution on the original lines of
Opera.

The most recent of these three masters, *Spontini*, was
moreover so fully convinced that he had actually reached
the highest point attainable in the genre of Opera; he
had so firm a faith in the impossibility of ever seeing
his exertions capped, that, in all the later art-productions
wherewith he followed up the works of his great Paris
period, he never made even the slightest attempt, as to
form and import, to overstep the standpoint taken in
those works. He obstinately refused to look upon the
later, so-called "romantic" development of Opera as anything but its manifest decadence; so that he gave to
people, with whom he afterwards discussed this matter,
the impression of a man who was positively eaten up with
himself and his works; whereas he was really only uttering a conviction based, in truth, upon a thoroughly sound
view of the essence of Opera. Surveying the demeanour
of our Modern Opera, Spontini could say, with perfect
iustice: "Have you in any way developed the essential
Form of the musical constituents of Opera, beyond what
you find with me ? Or have you, perchance, been able to
bring forth any intelligible or healthy thing by actually
quitting that form? Is not all the. unpalatable in your
works the mere result of your stepping outside that form,
and all the palatable a simple outcome of your adherence
to it? Where will you find this Form more majestic,
broader, or more capacious, than in my three grand Paris
operas? And who will tell me that he has filled this
Form with more glowing, more feeling, or more energic
Contents, than I ?"—
It would be hard to give Spontini's question any
answer that should bewilder him; still harder, to prove
to him that *he* is mad for taking *us* for madmen. Out
of Spontini speaks the honest, confident voice of the
absolute-musician, who there proclaims : "If the Musician
per se, as ordainer of the Opera, desires to bring to pass
the Drama, he cannot go a step farther than *I* have gone,
without betraying his total incapacity for the task." But
in this there unwittingly lies the corollary : "If you desire

more, you must address yourselves, not to the Musician, but—*to the Poet."*

Now how did this Poet bear himself towards Spontini and his colleagues? With all the maturing of Opera's musical Form, with all the development of its innate powers of Expression, the position of the Poet had not altered in the slightest. He still remained the platform-dresser* for the altogether independent experiments of the Composer. When the latter, by attained success, felt growing his power of freer motion within those forms of his, he simply bade the poet serve him his material with less fear and trembling; he, as it were, shouted to him: " See what I can do ! Don't incommode yourself; trust me to dissolve even your daringest dramatic combinations, gristle, bone and all, into my music ! "—So the Poet was merely hurried along with the Musician; he would have been ashamed to bring his master wooden hobby-horses, now that master was able to mount a real live horse, for he knew the rider had bravely learnt to ply the reins— those musical reins which were to school the horse's prancings in the well-strewn opera-circus, and without which neither Poet nor Musician would have dared to mount, for fear the steed should clear the ring and gallop home to its own wild wind-blown pastures.

Thus, in the wake of the Composer, the Poet certainly won an access of importance; but only in exact degree as the musician mounted upwards in advance, and bade him merely follow. The strictly musical possibilities, as pointed out by the composer, the poet had to keep in eye as the only measure for all his orderings and shapings, nay even for his choice of Stuff; and thus, for all the fame that *he* began to reap also, he remained ever but

------

* The word " *Bereiter* " (preparer, or dresser) seems, by its second meaning, " rough-rider, or horse-breaker " (cf. the French " *dresseur*") to have suggested to Wagner the metaphor in the latter half of this paragraph. —TR.

the skilful servant who was so handy at waiting on the
"dramatic" composer.   Seeing that the composer had
gained no other view of the relative position of the poet
than the one he found laid down already by the very
nature of Opera, he could only regard himself as the
de facto responsible agent, and thus in all good conscience
stay rooted to the standpoint of Spontini as the fittest;
for thereon he might flatter himself that he was doing
all that lay within the powers of a musician who fain
would see the Opera, as a Musical Drama, maintain its
claim to rank as an artistic form.

That in the Drama itself, however, there lay possibilities
which could not be so much as approached within that art-
form—if it were not to fall to pieces,—this, perhaps, is *now*
quite clear to us, but could by no chance occur to the poet
or composer of that epoch.   Of all dramatic possibilities,
they could only light on such as were realisable in that
altogether settled and, of its very essence, hampered
Opera-music form.   The broad expansion, the lingering
on a motive, which the Musician required in order to speak
intelligibly in his form,—the purely musical accessories
he needed as a preliminary to setting his bell a-swinging,
so that it might sound out roundly, and especially might
sound in a fashion to give fitting expression to a definite
character,—made it from the first the Poet's duty to con-
fine himself to dramatic sketches of one settled pattern,
devoid of colour and affording ample elbow-room to the
musician for his experiments.   Mere stereotyped rhetoric
phrases were the prime requirement from the poet, for on
this soil alone could the musician gain room for the
expansion that he needed, but which was yet in truth
entirely undramatic.   To have allowed his heroes to speak
in brief and definite terms, surcharged with meaning, would
have only drawn upon the poet the charge of turning out
wares impracticable for the composer.   Since, then, the
poet felt himself constrained to put trite and meaningless
phrases in the mouth of his heroes, even the best will in
the world could not have enabled him either to infuse a

real character into persons who talked like that, or to stamp the sum-total of their actions with the seal of full dramatic truth.   His drama was forever a mere *make-believe* of Drama; to pursue a *real dramatic aim* to its legitimate conclusions could not so much as occur to him. Wherefore, strictly speaking, he only translated Drama into the language of Opera, and, as a matter of fact, mostly adapted long-familiar dramas already played to death upon the acting stage, as was notably the case in Paris with the tragedies of the Théâtre Français.   The dramatic aim, thus bare within and hollow, passed manifestly over into the mere intentions of the Composer; from him was That awaited which the Poet gave up from the first.   To him alone—to the Composer—must it therefore fall, to clothe this inner void and nullity of the whole, so soon as ever he perceived it ; and thus he found himself saddled with the unnatural task of, from his standpoint—from the standpoint of the man whose only duty it should have been to help to realise by the *expression* at his command an already fully-fledged dramatic aim—imagining and calling into life that aim itself.   The Musician thus had virtually to pen the drama, to make his music not merely its expression but its *content;* and yet this content, by the very nature of affairs, was to be none other than the Drama's self!

It is here that the predicate " dramatic " most palpably begins to work a strange confusion in men's notions of the nature of Music.   Music, which, as an art of *expression*, can in its utmost wealth of such expression be nothing more than *true*, has conformably therewith to concern itself alone with *what* it should express : in Opera this is unmistakably the Feeling of the characters conversing on the stage, and a music which fulfils this task with the most convincing effect is all that it ever can be.   A music, however, which would fain be more than this, which should not connect itself with any object to be expressed, but desire to fill its place, i.e. to be alike that object : such a music is no longer any kind of music, but a fantastic, hybrid emanation from Poetry and Music, which in truth can only materialise itself as caricature. With all its perverse efforts, Music, the in any way effective music, has actually remained naught other than Expression. But from those efforts to make it in itself a Content—and that, forsooth, the Content of a Drama—has issued That which we have to recognise as the consequential downfall of Opera, and therewith as an open demonstration of the radical un-nature of that genre of art.

If the foundation and intrinsic Content of Spontinian opera were void and hollow, and its musical investiture of Form both threadbare and pedantic, yet with all its narrowness it was a plain, sincere avowal of the limits that must bound this genre, without one is to drive its un-nature into raving madness. *Modern opera*, on the contrary, is the open proclamation of the actual advent of that madness. In order to approach its essence closer, let us now turn to that other line of Opera's evolution which we have denoted above as the *frivolous*, and by whose intercrossing with the *serious* line just dealt-with there has been brought to light that indescribable medley which we hear spoken of, and not seldom even by seemingly reasonable beings, as " modern Dramatic Opera."

ONG before the time of Gluck—as we have already mentioned—it had occurred quite of itself to nobly-gifted, nobly-feeling singers and composers to equip the phrasing (*Vortrag*) of the operatic Aria with a more sincere (*innig*) expression ; amid all their song-dexterity, and despite their virtuose *bravura*, to work upon their hearers by conveying genuine feeling and true passion wherever the text permitted, and even where it brought nothing to meet such expression half-way. This step was due entirely to the individual disposition of the *musical* factors of Opera ; and therein the true essence of Music was so far victorious over formalism, as she proclaimed herself that art whose very nature it is to be the immediate language of the heart.

If, in the evolution of Opera, we may call the line (*Richtung*) on which this noblest attribute of Music was raised *on principle* by Gluck and his followers into the ordainer of the drama, that of *reflective* Opera : on the other hand, we must call that other line, on which this attribute— especially on the Italian opera-stage—was unconsciously evinced by naturally-gifted musicians, the *naïve* line. It is characteristic of the first, that, coming to Paris as a foreign product, it matured under the eyes of a public which, in itself entirely unmusical, gives a far more cordial welcome to well-balanced, dazzling turns of speech than to any feeling Content of that speech ; whereas the second, the naïve line, remained preeminently the property of the sons of Italy, the home of modern music.

Admitted that it was again a German, who displayed the utmost splendour of this line : yet was he called alone to this high office because his artist nature was as clear, as spotless, as unruffled as a shining sheet of water, to which the rare, the brightest flower of Italian music bent down its

head ; to see therein, to know, to love the mirrored likeness
of itself. This mirror, however, was but the surface of a
deep, unending sea of yearning, which from the measureless
fill of its being reached upwards to that surface, as for the
utterance of its meaning ; from the gentle greeting of that
fair vision, bending down to it as though in thirst for knowledge of itself, to win a form, a fashioning, a beauty.

Whosoever insists on seeing in Mozart an experimenting
musician who turns, forsooth, from one attempt to solve the
operatic problem to the next, can only counterpoise this
error by placing alongside of it another, and, for instance,
ascribing naïvety to Mendelssohn when, mistrustful of his
own powers, he took his cautious, hesitating steps along
that endless stretch of road which lay between himself and
Opera.* The naïve, truly inspired artist casts himself with
reckless enthusiasm into his artwork ; and only when this
is finished, when it shows itself in all its actuality, does he
win from practical experience that genuine force of Reflection which preserves him in general from illusions (*die ihn
allgemeinhin vor Täuschungen bewahrt*), yet in the specific
case of his feeling driven again to art-work by his inspiration, loses once more its power over him completely. There
is nothing more characteristic of Mozart, in his career of
opera-composer, than the unconcernedness wherewith he
went to work : it was so far from occurring to him to
weigh the pros and cons of the æsthetic problem involved
in Opera, that he the rather engaged with utmost unconstraint in setting any and every operatic textbook offered
him, almost heedless whether it were a thankful or
a thankless task for him as pure musician. If we piece
together all his æsthetic hints and sayings, culled from
here and there, we shall find that the sum of his Reflection
mounts no higher than his famous definition of his "nose."
He was so utterly and entirely a musician, and nothing
but musician, that through him we may also gain the
clearest and most convincing view of the true and proper

---

* Both things are done by the author of the article on " Modern Opera "
mentioned in the Introduction.—R. WAGNER.

position of the Musician toward the Poet. Indisputably his weightiest and most decisive stroke for Music he dealt precisely in Opera,—in Opera, over whose conformation it never for a moment struck him to usurp the poet's right, and where he attempted nothing but what he could achieve by purely musical means. In return, however, through the very faithfulness and singleness of his adoption of the poet's aim—wherever and howsoever present—he stretched these purely musical means of his to such a compass that in none of his absolute-musical compositions, and particularly his instrumental works, do we see the art of Music so broadly and so richly furthered as in his operas. The noble, straightforward simplicity of his purely musical instinct, i.e. his intuitive penetration (*unwillkürlichen Innehabens*) into the arcana of his art, made it wellnigh impossible to him *there* to bring forth magical effects, as Composer, where the Poem was flat and meaningless. How little did this richest-gifted of all musicians understand our modern music-makers' trick of building gaudy towers of music upon a hollow, valueless foundation, and playing the rapt and the inspired where all the poetaster's botch is void and flimsy, the better to show that the Musician is the jack in office and can go any length he pleases, even to making something out of nothing—the same as the good God! O how doubly dear and above all honour is Mozart to me, that it was *not* possible to him to invent music for *Tito* like that of *Don Giovanni*, for *Cosi fan tutte* like that of *Figaro!* How shamefully would it have desecrated Music!

Music Mozart always made, but *beautiful* music he could never write excepting when inspired. Though this Inspiration must ever come from within, from his own possessions, yet it could only leap forth bright and radiant when kindled from without, when to the spirit of divinest Love within him was shewn the object worthy love, the object that in ardent heedlessness of self it could embrace. And thus would it have been precisely the most absolute of all Musicians, Mozart himself, who would have long-since solved the

operatic problem past all doubt, who would have helped
to pen the truest, fairest and completest *Drama*, if only
he had met the *Poet* whom he only would have had to
help. But he never met that Poet: at times it was a
pedantically wearisome, at times a frivolously sprightly
maker of opera-texts, that reached him Arias, Duets, and
Ensemble-pieces to compose ; and these he took and so
turned them into music, according to the warmth they each
were able to awake in him, that in every instance they
received the most answering expression of which their last
particle of sense was capable.

Thus did Mozart only prove the exhaustless power
of Music to answer with undreamt fulness each demand
of the Poet upon her faculty of Expression ; for all
his un-reflective method, the glorious musician revealed
this power, even in the truthfulness of dramatic expression, the endless multiplicity of its motivation, in far richer
measure than Gluck and all his followers. But so
little was a fundamental principle laid down in his
creations, that the pinions of his genius left the *formal*
skeleton of Opera quite unstirred : he had merely poured
his music's lava-stream into the moulds of Opera. Themselves, however, they were too frail to hold this stream
within them ; and forth it flowed to where, in ever freer
and less cramping channels, it might spread itself according
to its natural bent, until in the Symphonies of Beethoven
we find it swollen to a mighty sea. Whereas in Instrumental music the innate capabilities of Music developed
into boundless power, those Operatic-forms, like burnt-out
bricks and mortar, stayed chill and naked in their pristine
shape, a carcase waiting for the coming guest to pitch his
fleeting tent within.

Only for the history of Music in general, is Mozart of so
strikingly weighty moment ; in no wise for the history of
Opera in particular, as a specific genre of art. Opera,
whose unnatural being was bound to life by no laws of
genuine Necessity, was free to fall a ready booty to the first
musical adventurer who came its way.

The unedifying spectacle presented by the art-doings of so-called followers of Mozart, we here may reasonably pass by. A tolerably long string of composers figured to themselves that Mozart's Opera was a something whose form might be imitated ; wherewith they naturally overlooked the fact that this form was Nothing in itself, and Mozart's musical spirit Everything. But to reconstruct the creations of Spirit by a pedantic setting of two and two together, has not as yet succeeded in the hands of any one.

One thing alone remained to utter in those forms. Albeit Mozart, in unclouded naïvety, had evolved their purely musical-artistic content to its highest pitch, yet the real secret of the whole opera-embroglio, in keeping with its source of origin, was still to be laid bare to nakedest publicity in those same forms. The world was yet to be plainly told, and without reserve, what longing and what claim on Art it was, that Opera owed its origin and existence to : that this longing was by no means for the genuine Drama, but had gone forth towards a pleasure merely seasoned with the sauces of the stage; in no sense moving or inwardly arousing, but merely intoxicating and outwardly diverting. In *Italy*, where this—as yet unconscious—longing had given birth to Opera, it was at last to be fulfilled with open eyes.

This brings us back to a closer dealing with the essence of the *Aria*.

So long as Arias shall be composed, the root-character of that art-form will always betray itself as an absolute-musical one. The Folk-song issued from an immediate double-growth, a consentaneous action of the arts of Poetry and Tone. This art—as opposed to that almost only one we can now conceive, the deliberate art of Culture—we ought perhaps to scarcely style as Art; but rather to call it an instinctive manifestment of the Spirit of the Folk through the organ of artistic faculty. Here the Word-poem and the Tone-poem are one. It never happens to the Folk, to sing its songs without a 'text'; without the Words (*Wortvers*) the Folk would brook no Tune (*Ton-*

weise). If the Tune varies in the course of time, and with
the divers offshoots of the Folk-stem, so vary too the
Words. No severing of these twain can the Folk imagine ;
for *it* they make as firmly knit a whole as man and wife.

The man of Luxury heard this Folk-song merely from
afar; in his lordly palace he listened to the reapers passing by ; what staves surged up into his sumptuous chambers
were but the staves of Tone, whereas the staves of Poetry
died out before they reached him. Now, if this Tone-
stave may be likened to the delicate *fragrance* of the
flower, and the Word-stave to its very *chalice*, with all its
tender stamens : the man of luxury, solely bent on tasting
with his nerves of smell, and not alike with those of sight,
squeezed out this fragrance from the flower and distilled
therefrom an extract, which he decanted into phials to
bear about him at his lief, to sprinkle on his splendid
chattels and himself whene'er he listed.   To gladden his
eyes with the flower itself, he must necessarily have sought
it closer, have stepped down from his palace to the wood-
land glades, have forced his way through branches, trunks
and bracken ; whereto the eminent and leisured sir had
not one spark of longing.   With this sweet-smelling residue
he drenched the weary desert of his life, the aching void of
his emotions; and the artificial growth that sprang from
this unnatural fertilising was nothing other, than the
Operatic Aria.   Into whatsoever wayward intermarriages it
might be forced, it stayed still ever-fruitless, forever but
itself, but what it was and could not else be : a sheer
musical Substratum.

The whole cloud-body of the Aria evaporated into
Melody; and this was sung, was fiddled, and at last was
whistled, without its ever recollecting that it ought by
rights to have a word-stave, or at the least a word-sense
under it.   Yet the more this extract, to give it some
manner of stuff for physically clinging to, must yield itself
to every kind of experiment—among which the most
pompous was the serious pretext of the Drama,—the more
folk felt that it was suffering by mixture with the thread-

bare foreign matter, nay, was actually losing its own pungency and pleasantness.

Now the man from whom this perfume, unnatural as it was, acquired again a corpus, which, concocted though it was, at least imitated as cleverly as possible that natural body which had once breathed forth its very soul in fragrance; the uncommonly handy modeller of *artificial* flowers, which he shaped from silk and satin and drenched their arid cups with that distilled substratum, till they began to smell like veritable blooms;—this great artist was *Joachimo Rossini*.

In the glorious, healthy, single-hearted artist-nature of Mozart that melodic scent had found so fostering a soil, that it eke put forth again the bloom of noble Art which holds our inmost souls as captives still. Yet even with Mozart it only found this food when the akin, the sound, the purely-human offered itself as Poetry, for wedding with his wholly musical nature; and it was wellnigh a stroke of Luck, that this repeatedly occurred for him. Where Mozart was left unheeded by this fecund god, there, too, the artificial essence of that scent could only toilsomely uphold its false, unnecessary life by artificial measures. Melody, however costly were its nurture, fell sick of chill and lifeless Formalism, the only heritage the early sped could leave his heirs; for in his death he took away with him—his Life.

What *Rossini* saw around him, in the first flower of his teeming youth, was but the harvesting of Death. When he looked upon the serious, so-called Dramatic Opera of France, he saw with the keèn insight of young Joy-in-life a garish corpse; which even Spontini, as he stalked along in gorgeous loneliness, could no longer stir to life, since—as though for some solemn sacrament of Self—he had already embalmed himself alive. Driven by his prickling sense of Life, Rossini tore the pompous cerecloths from this corpse, as one intent on spying out the secret of its former being. Beneath the jewelled and embroidered trappings he disclosed the true life-giver of even this majestic mummy:

and that was—*Melody.*—When he looked upon the native
Opera of Italy and the work of Mozart's heirs, he saw
nothing but Death again ; death in empty forms whose only
life shewed out to him as *Melody,*—Melody downright,
when stripped of that pretence of Character which must
seem to him a hollow sham if he turned to what of
scamped, of forced and incomplete had sprung therefrom.

To live, however, was what Rossini meant ; to do this,
he saw well enough that he must live with those who had
ears to hear him. The only living thing he had come
upon in Opera, was absolute Melody ; so he merely needed
to pay heed to the *kind* of melody he must strike in order
to be heard. He turned his back on the pedantic lumber
of heavy scores, and listened where the people sang without a written note. What he there heard was what, out of
all the operatic box of tricks, had stayed the most un-
bidden in the ear : the *naked, ear-delighting, absolute-
melodic Melody ;* i.e. melody that was just *Melody* and
nothing else ; that glides into the ear—one knows not
why ; that one picks up—one knows not why ; that one
exchanges to-day with that of yesterday, and forgets again
to-morrow—also, one knows not why ; that sounds sad
when we are merry, and merry when we are out of sorts ;
and that still we hum to ourselves—we haven't a ghost of
knowledge why.

This Melody Rossini struck ; and behold !—the mystery
of Opera was laid bare. What reflection and æsthetic
speculation had built up, Rossini's opera-melodies pulled
down and blew it into nothing, like a baseless dream. The
" dramatic " Opera met the fate of Learning with her problems : those problems whose foundation had really been
mistaken insight, and which the deepest pondering could
only make but more mistaken and insoluble ; until at last
the sword of Alexander sets to work, and hews the leathern
knot asunder, strewing its thousand thongs on every side.
This Alexander-sword is just the naked Deed ; and such a
deed Rossini did, when he made the opera-public of the
world a witness to the very definite truth, that people were

merely wanting to hear "delicious melodies" where mistaken artists had earlier fancied to make Musical Expression do duty for the aim and contents of a Drama.

The whole world hurrahed Rossini for his melodies:
Rossini, who so admirably knew how to make the employment of these melodies a special art. All organising of
Form he left upon one side; the simplest, barrenest and
most transparent that came to hand, he filled with all the
logical contents it had ever needed,—with narcotising
Melody. Entirely unconcerned for Form, just because he
left it altogether undisturbed, he turned his whole genius
to the invention of the most amusing hocus-pocus for
execution within those forms. To the singers, erstwhile
forced to study the dramatic expression of a wearisome
and nothing-saying 'text,' he said: "Do whatever you
please with the words; only, before all don't forget to get
yourselves liberally applauded for risky runs and melodic
entrechats." Who so glad to take him at his word, as the
singers? — To the instrumentists, erstwhile trained to
accompany pathetic snatches of song as intelligently as
possible in a smooth ensemble, he said: "Take it easy;
only, before all don't forget to get yourselves sufficiently
clapped for your individual skill, wherever I give you each
his opportunity." Who more lavish of their thanks, than
the instrumentists?—To the opera-librettist, who had erstwhile sweated blood beneath the self-willed orderings of
the dramatic composer, he said: "Friend, you may put
your nightcap on; I have really no more use for you."
Who so obliged for such release from sour, thankless toil,
as the opera-poet?

But who more idolised Rossini, for all these deeds of good,
than the whole civilised world—so far as the Opera-house
could hold it? And who had better reason, than it had?
Who, with so much talent, had shewn it such profound consideration as Rossini?—Did he learn that the public of one
city had a particular fancy for prima donna's runs, while
another preferred a sentimental song : straightway he gave

his prima donnas nothing but runs, for the first city ; for
the second, only sentimental songs.   Did he discover that
here folk liked to hear the drum in the band : at once he
made the overture to a rustic opera begin with a rolling of
the drum.   Was he told that people *there* were passionately
fond of a crescendo, in ensemble-pieces : he sat down and
wrote an opera in the form of a continuously recurring
crescendo.—Only *once* had he cause to rue his complaisance.   For Naples he was advised to be more careful with
his construction : his more solidly built-up opera did not
take ; and Rossini resolved never in his life again to think
of carefulness, even if advised to.—

Not the smallest charge of vanity or overweening self-
conceit can we bring against Rossini, if, looking at the vast
success of his treatment of Opera, he laughed people in the
face and told them he had found the true secret for which
his predecessors had groped in vain.   When he maintained
that it would be easy for him to consign to oblivion the
operas of his greatest forerunners, not excepting Mozart's
Don Juan, by the simple expedient of composing the same
subject over again in *his own* fashion, it was by no means
arrogance that spoke out here, but the certain instinct of
what the public really asked from Opera.   In very deed,
our musical pietists would have only had to see their own
complete confusion, in the appearance of a Rossinian
" Don Juan " ; for it may be taken for granted that, with
the genuine, verdict-giving theatrical public, Mozart's *Don
Juan* must have had to yield—if not for ever, still for long
enough—to that of Rossini.   For this is the real turn that
Rossini gave the opera-question : down to their last rag, his
operas appealed *to the Public ;* he made this Public, with all
its whims and wishes, the determinative factor in the Opera.

If the opera-Public had at all possessed the character
and significance of the *Folk*, in the proper sense of the
word, Rossini must have seemed to us the most thorough-
paced *revolutionary* in the whole domain of Art.   In face of
one section of our society, however, a section only to be
regarded as an unnatural outgrowth from the Folk, and

which in its social superfluity, nay harmfulness, can only
be looked on as the knot of caterpillars that erodes the
healthy, nourishing leaves of the natural Folk-tree, and
thence at most derives the vital force to flutter through a
day's luxurious existence as a giddy swarm of butterflies ;
in face of such a Folk's-scum, which, gathering above a
sediment of sordid filth, can rise to vicious elegance but
never into sterling human culture ; in short,—to give the
thing its fittest name,—in face of our *Opera-Public*, Rossini
was no more than a *reactionary :* whereas we have to view
Gluck and his followers as methodic *revolutionaries* on
principle, though powerless for radical results.   Under the
banner of the luxurious but only genuine Content of the
Opera and its logical development, *Joachimo Rossini* reacted
just as successfully against the doctrinaire maxims of the
revolutionary Gluck as P rince *Metternich*, his great protec-
tor, under the banner of the inhuman but only veritable
Content of European Statecraft and its logical enforcement,
reacted against the doctrinaire maxims of the Liberal revolutionaries who, *within* this system of the State and without a total upheaval of its unnatural Content, desired to
instal the Human and the Reasonable in the selfsame
forms which breathed that Content out of every pore.   As
Metternich,* with perfect logic on his side, could not conceive the *State* under any form but that of *Absolute Monarchy :* so Rossini, with no less force of argument, could
conceive the *Opera* under no other form than that of *Absolute Melody.*   Both men said : " Do you ask for Opera and
State ?   Here you have them ;—there are no others ! "

With Rossini the real *life-history of Opera* comes to end.
It was at end, when the unconscious seedling of its being
had evolved to nakedest and conscious bloom ; when the
Musician had been avowed the absolute factor of this art-
work, invested with despotic power ; when the taste of the
theatre-Public had been recognised as the only standard

* It should not be forgotten that Metternich, only two years before the
writing of this sentence, had played an important part in suppressing the
Austro-German revolutionary movement.—TR.

for his demeanour. It was at end, when all pretence of
Drama had been scrupulously swept away ; when the Performers had been allotted the showiest virtuosity of Song
as their only task, and their hence-sprung claims on the
Composer had been acknowledged as their most inalienable
of rights. It was at end, when the great musical public
had come to take quite characterless Melody for music's
only Content, a bandbox of operatic 'numbers' for the
only joinery of musical Form, the intoxication of an opera-
night's narcotic fumes for the sole effect of music's Essence.
It was at end—that day the deified of Europe, *Rossini*
lolling in the rankest lap of luxury, deemed it becoming to
pay the world-shy anchorite, the moody *Beethoven*, already
held for half-insane, a ceremonial visit——which the latter
did not return. What thing may it have been, the wanton,
roving eye of Italy's voluptuous son beheld, when it
plunged unwitting in the eerie glance, the sorrow-broken,
faint with yearning—and yet death-daring look of its unfathomable opposite ? Did there toss before it the locks of
that wild shock of hair, of the Medusa-head that none
might look upon and live ?—Thus much is certain : with
Rossini died the Opera.—

In Paris, however, that great city where the most
educated connoisseurs and critics can even yet not comprehend what distinction there can possibly be between
two famous composers, such as Beethoven and Rossini,
excepting mayhap that the one turned his heaven-sent
genius to the composition of Operas, the other to writing
Symphonies,—in this splendid seat of modern music-wisdom
was still to be drawn up a wonderful fresh lease of life for
Opera. There is always a masterful hold on being, in
everything that once exists. The Opera was an accomplished fact, just like the Byzantine Cæsardom ; and just
like that will it endure, so long as shall remain in force the
unnatural conditions that uphold it—dead at core—in
lingering life : until at last the untutored Turks arrive, who

once already put an end to the Byzantine Empire, and were even so unmannerly as to stable their wild horses in the gorgeous sanctuary of S. Sophia.

Spontini erred, when he deemed the Opera buried with himself, inasmuch as he took the Opera's "dramatic tendence" for its essence : he forgot the possibility of a Rossini, who very well could prove to him the contrary. When *Rossini*, with far more reason, held the Opera concluded with himself, he certainly erred less ; inasmuch as he had recognised its essence, had laid it bare and brought it into general acceptance, and thus was justified in assuming that he might indeed be imitated, but never overbid. However, it had escaped even *his* reckoning, that from all the quondam tendencies of Opera a caricature might be cobbled up, which should be greeted not only by the Public, but also by the wiseacres of Art, as a new and substantial shape of Opera ; for in the flower of his prime he never could have dreamt that it would some day occur to the Bankers, for whom he had always made their music, to make it for themselves.

Ah ! how wroth he waxed, the else so easy-going master ; how fierce he grew and evil-whimmed ; to see himself outdone, if not in talent, yet in skill at exploiting the good-for-nothingness of public art ! Ah ! how was he now the "*dissoluto punito*," the cast-off courtezan ; and with what rankling indignation at this shame, did he reply to the Paris Opera-director—who invited him, amid a momentary lull, to blow off a little tune again for the Parisians—that he would never come back until "the Jews had finished with their Sabbath there !" He was made to learn that, so long as God's wisdom rules the world, each fault will find its punishment : even the candour wherewith he had told the crowd the truth concerning Opera.—In righteous expiation of his sins, he became a fish-purveyor and church-composer.—

However, it is only by a wider circuit that we can reach an intelligible exposition of the essence of our modernest Opera.

III.

HE history of Opera, since Rossini, is at bottom nothing else but the history of *operatic melody;* of its application from an art-speculative, its execution from an effect-hunting standpoint.

Rossini's hugely successful method of procedure had unconsciously turned composers from all seeking for the dramatic Content of the Aria, all attempt to read into it any dramatically-consistent meaning. *The Essence of Melody itself,* into which the whole scaffolding of Aria had evaporated, was the thing that now led captive both the instinct and the speculation of the Composer. One could not but perceive that, even in the Aria of Gluck and his followers, the Public had only been edified in exact measure as the general sentiment indicated in the text-substratum had received in the purely melodic portion of that Aria an expression which, in its kindred generality, merely shewed itself as absolute, ear-pleasing Tune. If this is already visible enough in the case of Gluck, it becomes quite palpable in that of his latest follower, Spontini. They all, these serious Musical-dramatists, had more or less deceived themselves, when they ascribed the effect of their music less to the purely melodic essence of its airs, than to the realisation of the dramatic aim with which they had written them. The opera-house in their time, and especially in Paris, was the rendezvous of æsthetic *beaux esprits,* and of a world of notables which plumed itself on likewise being witty and æsthetic. The serious æsthetic intention of these masters was greeted by this public with all respect ; the nimbus of an artistic lawgiver streamed from the Musician who undertook to write the Drama *in notes;* his public, nothing loath, imagined it was being moved by the dramatic " declamation," whereas, in truth, it was only carried away by the

charm of the Aria's melody.   When the Public then, at last
emancipated by Rossini, dared to confess this openly and
unabashed, it simply avowed an undeniable truth, and
proved how logical and natural it was that, where Music was
the main affair, the end and aim,—not merely by an outward
assumption, but in keeping with the whole artistic basis of
this form of art,—there Poetry the handmaid, with all her
hints of dramatic purpose, must stay helpless and effectless,
leaving Music herself to call forth the whole effect by her
individual powers.   Every attempt to pass for dramatic and
characteristic could only disfigure Music's genuine essence ;
and—once that Music wills not merely to help and co-
operate in the reaching of a higher aim, but to *operate*
entirely by and for herself—this essence speaks out alone
in Melody, as the expression of a *general* emotion.

Every Opera-composer was plainly shewn this by
Rossini's indisputable success.   If a rejoinder still stood
open to deeper-feeling musicians, it could only be the following : that they looked on the *character* of Rossinian
melody not only as shallow and distasteful, but as by no
means *exhausting* the essence of Melody.   To such musicians the artistic project could not but present itself, to give
this unquestioned power of Melody the whole full utterance
of beauteous human Feeling (*Empfindung*) that is its own
by birthright.   In the effort to fulfil this task, they carried
the reaction of Rossini—right back behind the nature and
the origin of Opera—to the very fount from which the Aria
once had drawn its artificial life, *to the restoration of the
primal strains* (Tonweise) *of the Folk-song.*

It was a *German* musician who first, and with remarkable success, called this transformation of Melody into
being.   *Karl Maria von Weber* reached his artistic manhood in an epoch of historic evolution wherein the
waking pulse of Freedom as yet stirred less in *men* as units,
than in the Folks as *national masses.*   The feeling of Independence—not yet applied in politics to the Purely-human,
and therefore not yet reading itself as absolutely and unconditionally an aspiration for purely-human independence

—sought still for grounds of vindication, as though inexplicable to itself and rather roused by chance than of necessity, and thought to find them in the National roots of Race. The resultant movement was more akin, in truth, to Restoration than to Revolution. In its farthest strayings it took the form of a passion for re-setting up the old and lapsed ; and alone in quite recent days have we been taught the lesson, how this error could only lead to fresh-forged fetters on our evolution into truly human freedom. But in that we have been compelled to learn this, have we now been driven, with knowledge too, into the right road ; and that by painful, aye, but healing force.

I have no idea of attempting to show the development of Opera as marching hand in hand with our political evolution ; such a thesis allows too much room to wilful phantasy, for it not to run riot in the most absurd vagaries, —as indeed has already happened, in this reference, to a most unedifying pitch. I am far more concerned to demonstrate the unnatural and contradictory element in this art-genre, together with its manifest incapacity to really reach its professed aim, solely by a survey of its essence. However, the *national line*, as taken in the treatment of Melody, has in its import and its strayings, and finally in its ever plainer cleavages and barrenness,—the tokens of its error,—far too much parallelism with the errors of our political evolution of the last forty years, for the relationship to be quite passed by.

In Art, just as in Politics, this line has for its distinctive mark, that the error, lying at its base, appeared under a garment of bewitching beauty in its first instinctive innocence; but in its final selfish, cramped stiffneckedness, under one of loathsome hideosity. It was beautiful, so long as the first lispings of the soul of Freedom spoke out in it ; it is repulsive now, when the soul of Freedom has already broken through it, and only vulgar Egoism can hold it artfully together.

In the case of Music the national line shewed all the more genuine beauty in its beginnings, as the specific character of Music fits it more for the utterance of general, than of particular emotion. What with our romanticising *poets* betrayed itself as an ogling with the one eye at Roman-catholic mysticism and with the other at feudal-chivalric amours,* expressed itself in Music as homelike, deep and broad-breathed Tune, instinct with noble grace,—Tune as listened from the last vanishing sigh of the naïve spirit of the Folk.

The tone-poet of *Der Freischütz*, above all worth our love, was cut to the very heartstrings of his artistic purity by the voluptuous melodies of Rossini, in which the whole world had gone a-revelling. He could not allow that in *them* was bared the fount of genuine Melody ; he needs must show the world that they were but an impure outflow of that fountain, and that the source itself, had man the wit to find it, still flowed in undisturbed limpidity. If those so eminent founders of the Opera had only bent a careless ear to the Folk's sweet song, now *Weber* hearkened to it with all the strain of fixed attention. If the scent of the lovely Folk's-bloom had risen from the fields and pierced the mansions of the luxurious music-world, to be there imprisoned in its portable distillates : a yearning for the vision of the flower itself † drove Weber down from the sumptuous halls into the meadow ; and there he saw the bloom on the brink of the rippling brook, amid odorous wood-grasses, upon a bed of wondrous crinkled moss, beneath the dreamy whispering branches of trees grown gnarled with age. How the happy artist felt his heart-beat quicken at the sight, his breath grow light with all this fill of fragrance ! He could not withstand the loving impulse, to bring to nerveless fellow-men this healing vision, this livening perfume, for a ransom from their madness ; to tear the bloom itself from the godlike nurture of its woodlands, and hold it, the hallowedest of all created things, before a world of Luxury

* Compare Vol. I. of this series, pages 42 and 311-2.—TR.

† The "blue floweret" of Novalis : that ideal bloom which, ever since his time, has been the synonyme for all the hidden mysteries of Art and Nature.—TR.

bereft of blessing:—*he plucked it!*—Unhappy man!—Aloft
in the banquet-hall he set the sweet shy flower, in a costly
vase ; daily he sprinkled it with freshest water from the
forest stream.   But lo !—the petals, chastely clasped before,
unfold themselves as though to lax delights ; unshamed the
bloom lays bare its dainty stamens, and offers them, with
horrible indifference, to the prying nose of every ribald rake.
"What ails thee, flower ? " the master cries, in agony of
soul : "forget'st so soon the verdant meadow, that fostered
thy virginity ? "   But one by one the petals fall ; weary and
wan, they shower upon the carpet ; with one last breath of
its own sweet scent, the flower sighs to the master : " I die
but—since thou pluck'dst me ! "—And with the bloom the
master died.   For it had been the soul of all his art, and
this Art the upholding secret of his life.—In the meadow
no more grew a flower !—From their uplands came the
Tyrolean singers : they sang before Prince Metternich ; he
gave them letters of safe conduct to every court ; and all
the Lords and Bankers amused themselves, in their reeking
salons, with the merry *Jodel* of the children of the Alps,
with their songs in honour of their "*Dierndel*" (lassie).
Now the ploughboys march to Bellinian Arias to the murder of their brothers, and dance with their Dierndel to
Donizettian Opera-melodies ; for — *the flower bloomed no
more !*—

   It is a characteristic feature of the *German* Folk-melody,
that it less affects a brisk, compact and lively rhythm, than
a long-breathed, lusty (*froh*) and yet plaintive swell.   A
German song without its harmony is to us unthinkable :
everywhere we hear it sung in two ' voices' at the least ;
art instinctively feels challenged to supply the bass and so
easily filled-in second ' inner voice,' and thus to have the
whole body of Harmonic-melody before it.   This melody is
the basis of the Weberian Folk-opera : leaving aside all
local-national idiosyncrasies, it is of broad and general
emotional expression ; has no other adornment than the
smile of sweetest and most natural sincerity (*Innigkeit*) ;
and thus, by the indwelling force of its undisfigured grace,

it speaks directly to the hearts of men, no matter what their national peculiarity, simply because in it the Purely-human comes so unbesmeared to show. In the world-spread potency of Weber's Melody may we better recognise the essence of the *German* spirit, and its supposed predestination, than in those sham specific qualities with which the German people now is credited !—*

According to this Melody, does Weber shape the whole. Filled to the brim with *it*, whatever he had seen and would give forth, whatever in the farthest nook of Opera he had recognised as capable, or found means of making capable, of expression in this Melody,—be it only by breathing over it the perfume, or shaking on to it a dewdrop from the chalice, of the flower,—*that* he was bound to succeed in bringing to an exquisitely true and pertinent effect. And *this* Melody it was, that Weber made the actual factor of his Opera : through this melody the figment of Drama found in so far its realisement, as his whole drama was *ab initio* poured out in yearning to be taken up into this Melody, by it to be consumed, in it redeemed, and through it justified. If we look at the " *Freischütz* " drama in this light, we must give its poem exactly the same relation to Weber's music, as we give the poem of " *Tancredi* " towards its music by Rossini. Rossini's Melody laid down the lines of the poem of " *Tancredi*," precisely as much as Weber's Melody ordained Kind's poem of " *Der Freischütz* " ; and Weber *here* was nothing other than Rossini *there*, excepting that *this* man was noble and senseful (*sinnig*) whereas *that* was frivolous and sensual (*sinnlich*).† Weber only opened

---

* "Möchten wir in der weltverbreiteten Wirkung der Weber'schen Melodie das Wesen *deutschen* Geistes und seine vermeintliche Bestimmung besser erkennen, als wir in der Lüge von seinen spezifischen Qualitäten es thun !—" I have thought it best to give the original of this sentence, as in the English rendering I have been obliged to add a few words, in order to make the meaning (as I take it) clear. It appears to refer back to the "national " question, as touched on by the author above, page 50, and also in Vol. I. (*Art-work of the Future*) pages 89-90.—TR.

† As to what I here intend by "*sinnlich*," in distinction from the *Sinnlichkeit* (physicality) which I have claimed as the *realising* moment of the art-work, I may give an illustration from the shouts of an Italian audience, enraptured by the singing of a castrato : " God bless the knife ! "—R. WAGNER.

his arms so much the wider to take up the Drama, as his
Melody was the veritable language of the heart, all true
and undefiled : whatever ascended thereinto, was sheltered
safe and sure from all disfigurement. Yet, for all its truthfulness, whatsoever was *not* utterable in this language, by
reason of its limitation, even Weber toiled in vain to bring
from out it. His stammering here may stand, for us, as
the honest avowal of Music's inaptitude to herself become
the genuine Drama : in other words, to allow the genuine
Drama—and not one merely cut out to her order—to be
taken up (*aufgehen*) into her ; whereas, in right and reason,
it is Music that must *herself* be taken up into this genuine
Drama.

We have now to continue the history of Melody.

When Weber in his search for Melody had harked back
to the *Folk*, and when in the *German* Folk he found the
happy attribute of naïve heartiness (*Innigkeit*) without the
cramp of national insularity (*Sonderlichkeit*), he had led the
operatic composers of all the world to a stream which now,
wherever they could spy it out, was pounced on as a not
unlikely source of profit.

The first to follow, were the *French* composers ; who bethought them of serving up the herb they found a native of
their soil. For years the witty or sentimental "Couplet"
had flourished on their Folk-stage, in the spoken play. By
its nature more adapted for a gay—or if for a tender,
certainly never for a tragic expression, it has quite of itself
laid down the character of the dramatic genre into which it
was taken with set purpose. The Frenchman is not made
so as to allow of his emotions rising altogether into music ;
if his agitation mounts to a longing for Musical Expression,
he must still retain the right of speech withal, or at the
very least, of dancing. With him, where the Couplet ends
there begins the Contredanse ; without that, there is no
room for music in his economy. In his Couplet *speech* is

so much the main affair, that he insists on singing it *alone*, and never with another ; for otherwise one would not clearly understand the matter spoken.   In the Contredanse, too, the dancers for the most part stand singly facing one another; each does by himself what he has to do, and mutual claspings of the pair only occur when the general character of the dance makes them absolutely inevitable. Thus, in the French *Vaudeville*, all the items of the musical apparatus stand singly side by side, merely strung together by the prattling Prose ; and where the Couplet is sung by several people at once, this is accomplished in the most painful musical *unison* imaginable.   The *French Opera* is an enlarged Vaudeville ; its broader musical apparatus is borrowed, *as to Form*, from the so-called Dramatic-opera, but *as to Content*, from that virtuosic element which reached its rankest outgrowth in the hands of Rossini.

The distinctive blossom of this opera is now, and ever has been, the more *spoken* than chanted Couplet; its *musical* essence, the Rhythmic-melody of the Contredanse. To this national product, which had remained a mere subsidiary of the dramatic aim, and had never been strictly taken up into it, the French opera-composers turned back with set intention so soon as they observed on the one side the death of Spontinian-opera, on the other, the world-inebriating effect of Rossini's and, above all, the heart-searching influence of Weber's Melody.   But the living Content of that native French production had already vanished ; Vaudeville and Comic Opera had sucked so long at it, that its source could no longer flow within its parched-up bed.   Where the nature-craving art-musicians listened longingly for the babbling of the brook, they could no more hear it for the prosy clip-clap of the mill, whose wheel their selves were working with the water turned from out its natural channel and brought in wooden conduits.   Where they wanted to hear the People sing, there hummed nothing for them but the Vaudeville-factories that they were sick to death of.

So the great hunt for Folk-melodies in foreign lands

was given tongue. Already Weber himself, who found his
home-bred flower a-dying, had diligently thumbed the
pages of Forkel's illustrations of Arabian music, and taken
thence a march for harem-guarders. Our Frenchmen were
nimbler on their legs ; they merely thumbed the pages of
tourists' handbooks, and at once set off themselves to hear
and see, at closer quarters, if anywhere a morsel of Folk's
naïvety were left, and how it looked and sounded. Our
greybeard civilisation became a child again ; and childish
greybeards have short shrift !—

Far off in fair, but much soiled Italy, whose musical
fat Rossini had skimmed so elegantly for the starving art-
world, there sat the careless master at his ease, looking out
with an astonished smile at the picking and grabbing of
the brave Parisian hunters for Folk-melodies. One of
these was a capital horseman, and, whenever he dismounted
after a smart canter, people knew that he had unearthed
a right good melody which would bring him in a heap of
money. This time he galloped, as one possessed, through
all the piles of fish and fruit in the Naples market, sending
everything flying right and left ; cackles and curses sped
behind him, threatening fists were reared in front,—and so
with lightning-speed he scented out the notion of a splendid
revolution of fruiterers and fishmongers. But there was
still more yet to be made of the idea ! Out to Portici
stormed the Paris horseman, to the nets and wherries of
the simple fisher-folk, who sing as they ply their trade ;
who pass their lives between sleeping and wrangling, playing with their wives or children and hurling knives at one
another ; who stab to death, but keep on singing. Master
Auber, say now ! that was a mighty fine ride, and better
worth than one upon the Hippogryph that only soars
into the clouds,—where, when all's said and done, there's
nothing to be caught but colds and sneezing !—The rider
rode home ; got off his horse ; made Rossini an uncommonly handsome bow (he knew well enough the reason
why) ; took extra-post for Paris ; and what he polished off

with a turn of his wrist, was his famous "*Stumme von Portici.*" *

This *Stumme* was the dumb-struck Muse of Drama, who wandered broken-hearted between the singing, raging throngs, and, tired of life, made away at last with herself and her hopeless sorrow in the artificial fury of a stage-volcano!—

Rossini gazed on the glittering spectacle from afar. Travelling to Paris, he thought it well to rest a while amid the snowy Alps of Switzerland, and there to hearken how the sturdy, healthy peasants divide their musical pastimes between their mountains and their cows. Arrived in Paris, he made Auber his civilest of bows (for he, too, knew what he was about), and, with all a happy father's pride, he shewed the world his youngest child, in a lucky moment christened " *William Tell.*"

The " *Dumb Girl of Portici*" and "William Tell" henceforth became the poles round which the world of speculative opera-music revolved. A new recipe for galvanising the half-paralysed body of Opera had been found ; so it now might live for just as long as one could discover anywhere a remnant of national peculiarity. All the countries of the Continent were ransacked, each province plundered, every Folk-stem drained of its last drop of musical blood ; and the ardent extract was let off in blinding fireworks, to the supreme satisfaction of the princes and peddlers of the grand world of Opera. The German art-critics, on their side, discovered here a notable approximation of the Opera to its goal; for, behold! it had struck the "national," aye —if you will—the "historic" path. When all the world goes crazy, the Germans are in their seventh heaven ; for they have so much the more to ponder, to unravel, to expound, and finally—so as to make themselves *quite* comfortable—to classify!—

Let us consider the operation of the *National* on Melody, and through it upon Opera.

The Folk-element has ever been the fruitful fount of

---

* *Masaniello,* or the Dumb Girl (*Stumme*) of Portici.—TR.

Art, so long as—free of all Reflection—it was able to lift
itself by natural channels into Art-work. In Society, as
in Art, we have merely fed upon the Folk, without our
even knowing it. In our complete aloofness from the Folk,
we have taken the fruit on which we lived for manna, for a
gift dropped out of the clouds by heavenly Caprice into
the mouths of us privileged persons, us elect of God, us
plutocrats and geniuses. But when the manna was de-
voured, we looked ravenously round upon the orchards of
the earth ; and, robbers by the grace of God, we robbed
their fruits with barefaced impudence, uncaring whether
we had planted them or nursed them. Yea, the trees
themselves we tore up by the roots,—to see if these might
not be made quite tasty, or at any rate swallowable, by
scientific cooking. And so have we dug up the whole fair
native forest of the Folk, that *with it* we now stand naked,
starving beggars.

Thus, so soon as ever it discovered its own sterility and
drought, has Operatic Music thrown itself upon the Folk-
song, and sucked it empty to its roots ; in odious opera-
melodies it flings the plundered Folk the stringy fruit-sheath,
for pitiful and health-destructive food. But it too, this
Operatic Melody, is now without a shadow of a prospect
of fresh food. It has swallowed all there was to swallow ;
without one chance of fresh manuring, it falls unfruitful to
the ground. In the death-throes of an expiring glutton,
it gnaws at its own flesh ; and this horrible assault upon
itself is called by German critics a " Striving for higher
Charakteristik," just as they christened the uprooting of
those plundered orchards of the Folk " *Emanzipation* of the
Masses " !—

The true Folk-element the opera-composer had not the
wit to grasp; to have done this, he must himself have
worked in the spirit and with the notions of the Folk, i.e.
have been himself a part and parcel of it. Only the *Insular*
(das *Sonderliche*), in which the particularity of Folkhood
shows itself to him, could he lay hold of ; and this is
the *National.* The national colouring, already washed

entirely from out the upper classes, now lived on only in those sections of the Folk which, fastened to the furrow of the field, the shore, the upland valley, had been held back from any fertilising interchange of idiosyncrasies. It was therefore but a fossilised memento of the past, that fell into the hands of those freebooters; and in these hands,—which must pluck out the last fibre of its reproductive organs, or ever they could use it for their own luxurious caprice,— it could become nothing but a *modish curiosity.* Just as the modistes take at lief some hitherto-neglected foreign item of Folk-costume, and force it into their new-fangled finery: so Opera stripped the life of secluded nationalities of its scraps of melody and rhythm, and decked therewith the motley carcase of its outlived empty forms.

Upon the general demeanour of Opera, however, this procedure could not but exert a by no means unimportant influence: to wit, it brought about that change in the relation of Opera's executant factors to one another which, as already said, has been termed the " Emancipation of the Masses." Into this we must now look closer.

IV.

N exact measure as any art-tendency draws near its prime, does it gain the power of closer, plainer, surer shaping. In the beginning, the Folk expresses by cries of Lyric rapture its marvel at the constant wonders of Nature's workings ; in its efforts to master the object of that marvel, it condenses (*verdichtet*) the many-membered show of Nature into a God, and finally its God into a Hero. In this Hero, as in the convex mirror of its being, it learns to know itself; his deeds it celebrates in Epos, but itself in Drama re-enacts them. The tragic Hero of the Greeks stepped out from amid the Chorus, and, turning back to face it, cried : "Lo !—so does, so bears himself, a human being ! What ye were hymning in wise saws and maxims, I set it up before you in all the cogence of Necessity."

Greek Tragedy, in its Chorus and its Heroes, combined the Public with the Art-work : the latter held before the Folk, not only itself, but also its own judgment on itself— as it were, a concrete meditation. Now the Drama ripened into Art-work in exact measure as the interpretative judgment of the Chorus so irrefutably expressed itself in the actions of the Heroes, that the Chorus was able to step down from the stage and back into the Folk itself ; thus leaving behind it only actual partakers in the living Action.* *Shakespeare's* Tragedy unconditionally stands above that of Greece, in so far as it has enabled artistic technique to dispense with the necessity of a Chorus. With Shakespeare, the Chorus is resolved into divers individuals directly in-

---

* "Und genau in dem Grade reifte das Drama als Kunstwerk, als das verdeutlichende Urtheil des Chores in der Handlungen der Helden selbst sich so unwiderleglich ausdrückte, dass der Chor von der Scene ab ganz in das Volk zurücktreten, und dafür als belebender und verwirklichender Theilnehmer der Handlung—als solcher—selbst behülflich werden konnte."—TR.

terested in the Action, and whose doings are governed by
precisely the same promptings of individual Necessity as
are those of the chief Hero himself. Even their apparent
subordination in the artistic framework is merely a result
of the scantier points of contact they have in common with
the chief Hero, and nowise of any technical undervaluing
of these lesser personages ; for wherever the veriest subordinate has to take a share in the main plot, he delivers
himself entirely according to his personal characteristics,
his own free fancy.

If, in the further course of modern dramatic art, the
sharply outlined personalities of Shakespeare have lost
more and more of their plastic individuality, and sunk at
last to fixed and rigid character-masks, this must solely be
ascribed to the influence of a State which has put everything into a regulation livery, and has crushed out with
ever direr violence the right of free personality.   The
shadow-pantomime of hollow masks like these, all bare of
inner individuality, is what became the dramatic basis of
the Opera.   The more void of contents were the personalities beneath these masks, the more fitted were they deemed
for singing Operatic Arias.   " Prince and Princess,"—that
is the dramatic pivot round which the Opera has revolved,
and round which, if one would only look a little closer, it
still revolves to-day.   No Individualism could possibly
come to these operatic masks, excepting by a coat of paint ;
and so at last a local peculiarity of scene must make good
what they forever lacked inside.   Composers having exhausted all the melodic productivity of their art, and being
obliged to borrow from the Folk its local tunes, at last the
whole *locale* itself was seized upon : scenery, costume, and
the moveable stock to fill them out—the *Opera-Chorus*,
became at last the main affair, the Opera itself, and must
cast from every side their rainbow light upon the " Prince
and Princess," so as to keep the poor wretches in their
paint-daubed singer-life.

So was the Drama's circle rounded back upon itself, to
its eternal shame : the individual personages into which the

chorus of the Folk had crystallised, were melted down into
a motley, conglomerate Surrounding, without a centre to
surround. In the Opera this Surrounding, and nothing
but it, cries out to us from the whole gigantic scenic
apparatus, from the machinery, the painted canvas and the
piebald dresses; and its voice is the voice of the Chorus,
singing: "I am I, and there is none other Opera beside
me!"

Undoubtedly, noble artists had earlier employed the
trappings of the National; but it had only been able to
exert a veritable charm where it was added as an occasional
embellishment to a dramatic Stuff already livened by a
characteristic plot, and where it was introduced without
the slightest ostentation. How admirably did *Mozart* infuse a national colouring into his Osmin and his Figaro,
without having to seek in Turkey or in Spain, or any handbooks, for the tint he wanted. That Osmin and that Figaro,
however, were genuine individual characters, the happy in-
spirations of a poet, furnished with a true expression by the
musician, and utterly impossible to be misrendered by any
common-sense performer. The national trimmings of our
modern opera-composers, on the other hand, are not applied
to individualities like these, but are intended to give to
a quite characterless subject some vestige of a spurious
character, in justification and enlivement of its intrinsically
meaningless and colourless existence. The summit toward
which all healthy Folkhood tends, the characterisation of
the *purely human,* has been from the first degraded in our
Opera to a colourless and nothing-saying mask for Aria-
singers. This mask, forsooth, is now to be artfully enlivened
by reflexion of the surrounding colours; wherefore the surrounding is painted thick with the glaringest and cryingest
of splotches.

The Folk having been robbed of its Melody, at last the
Folk itself has been dragged upon the stage, in order to
brighten up the scene around the Aria-singer; yet this
naturally could not be *that* Folk which had invented the

tune, but the well-schooled *Mass*, which now is marched
hither and thither in beat with the operatic Aria.   It was
not the *Folk*, that was wanted, but the *Mass :* i.e. the
material leavings of the Folk, from which the living spirit
had been sucked dry.   The massive Chorus of our modern
opera is nothing else but the stage machinery set into motion
and song, the dumb pageant of the coulisses translated
into nimble noise.   " Prince and Princess," with the best
will in the world, had nothing more to say than their thousand-times repeated florid Aria : so one sought at last to
vary the theme by making the whole theatre, from the
wings right down to the last-hundredth chorister, join in the
singing of that Aria, and indeed—the higher was the effect
to mount — no longer in polyphonic harmony but in a
downright thundrous *unison*.   In the " Unisono," which
has to-day become so fashionable, there is quite palpably
revealed the inner purpose of this employment of the
Masses ; and, in an *operatic sense*, we hear the Masses quite
fittingly " emancipated " when we hear them, as in the most
famous passages of the most famous modern operas,
delivering the same old worn-out Aria in hundred-throated
unison.   Thus, too, has our State of nowadays emancipated
the Masses, when it makes them march battalion-wise in
military uniform, wheel left and right, present and shoulder
arms : when the Meyerbeerian " Huguenots " attain their
highest pitch, we *hear* the selfsame thing as we *see* in a
Prussian regiment of Guards.   German critics—as remarked
above—call it Emancipation of the Masses.

But, taken at bottom, the thus " emancipated " Surrounding was itself but a mask the more.   If a truly
characteristic life was absent from the chief personages of
the opera, it could certainly be still less instilled into the
mass-like apparatus.   The reflected rays, that were to fall
from this enlivening apparatus upon the hero and the
heroine, could therefore only be of any effective service if
the mask of this Surrounding also got itself, from here or

there outside, a coat of varnish that should cloak its inner
emptiness.   This varnish it gained from the *historic costume*,
which must lend the national colouring a still more striking
brilliance.

One might imagine that, with the introduction of the
Historic element, it must have necessarily fallen to the lot
of the Poet to take a determinative share in the shaping of
Opera.   Yet we shall soon be convinced of our mistake, if
we remember the previous evolutionary course of Opera :
how it owed each phase of its development solely to the
desperate struggle of the Musician to keep his work in
artificial life ; and how he had only been guided to the
choice of the *historic* element, by no means through an
imperious longing to yield himself to the Poet, but through
the force of purely musical circumstances,—through a force
which issued, in its turn, from the wholly unnatural proposal
of the Musician to provide the Drama with both object and
expression.   We shall have to return later to the situation
of the Poet toward our modernest Opera ; for the moment
let us follow undisturbed the actual factor of Opera, the
Musician, and see into what a quandary his mistaken
efforts were now to lead him.

Let him take on ne'er such airs and graces — the
Musician could only give Expression, and nothing but Expression ; he was therefore bound to lose even this faculty
of true and sound Expression, in exact measure as, in his
misguided eagerness to himself indite and shape the Object
of expression, he purposely degraded that object to a vague
and empty *schema*.   As he had not asked the Poet for *men*,
but the Mechanician for *puppets*, which he might drape
according to his fancy, and daze the eye by the mere
shimmer and arrangement of these draperies of his :
so now, since he could not possibly exhibit by these
puppets the warm pulsings of the human frame, he was
forced, amid the increasing poverty of his vehicle of expression, to hunt about at last for any new variety in the
disposition of his folds and colours.   But the Historic garb
of Opera—so rich in opportunities because it allows the

most checkered play of clime and period—is really the property of the Scene-painter and Stage-tailor, and these two auxiliaries have in effect become the most important allies of the modern opera-composer.   Still the Musician did not rest till he had adapted his tone-pallet to the requirements of Historic costume ; for how should he, the creator of Opera, he who had turned the Poet into his lacquey, not find a means of distancing the painter and the tailor ?   Had he not dissolved the whole drama, plot and characters and all, into his music : and how should it stay beyond his power, to turn into musical water the drawings and colours of the painter and the tailor ?   He managed to tear down every dam, to open every sluice, that hedged the ocean from the land ; and thus to drown the Drama, man and beast, paint-brush and scissors, in the deluge of his music !

The Musician was bound to fulfil his destiny of presenting German Criticism—for whom it is well-known that God's all-caring providence created Art — with the joy of an " *Historic music.*"   His high vocation full soon inspired him to find the way.

How must an " historic " music sound, to produce an effect in keeping with its name ?   To be sure, quite other-wise than a *not*-historic music.   But wherein lay the difference ?   Clearly in this : that the " historic music " should differ as much from that we are now accustomed to, as the costume of a former epoch from that of the present day.   Would it not be wisest then, just as one had copied faithfully the costumes of the date in question, to take one's music also from that epoch ?   Alas ! this was not quite so easy, for in those epochs, so piquant in their costume, there was, barbarically enough, no Opera : a general type of operatic speech was therefore not to be borrowed from them.   On the other hand, the people of those epochs sang in *churches*, and these church-hymns have about them, if one springs their chanting suddenly upon us, something strikingly foreign to our modern music. Excellent ! Fetch out the Hymns ! Religion shall take a turn upon the

E

stage ! * So Music's want of an historic costume became a Christian operatic virtue. For the crime of stealing the Folk's-melody one procured oneself Roman-catholic and Evangelical-protestant absolution, in return for the service rendered to the Church in that, just as earlier the Masses, now Religion too—to follow logically the expression of German Criticism—was "emancipated " by Opera.

Thus the opera-composer became the redeemer of all the world ; and in the deeply-inspired and self-lacerating rapture of the fervent *Meyerbeer* we have in any case to recognise the modern saviour, the bearer of the sins of the modern world.

However, this atoning "emancipation of the Church " could be only conditionally fulfilled by the musician. If Religion wished for the blessing of Opera, it must be reasonably content to take its fitting place among the other emancipates. Opera, as enfranchiser of the world, must rule Religion, and not Religion Opera ; if the opera was to be turned into a church, then Religion would certainly not be emancipated by it, but it by Religion. For sake of the purity of historic musical-costume, Opera would by all means have been only too delighted to have solely to do with Religion, since the only serviceable historic music was to be found in the Church alone. But to have to do with nothing but monks and clergy, would have seriously interfered with the gaiety of Opera : for the real thing that was to be glorified by the emancipation of Religion was the Operatic Aria, that luxuriantly unfolded germ of all the opera's being ; and its roots were nowise bathed in longing for devout self-concentration, but for an entertaining dissipation.† Strictly speaking, Religion was only to be used as a side-dish, just the same as in our well-regulated civic life : the 'piece of resistance' must still be " Prince and

---

* The reference to Meyerbeer's ' Huguenots ' and ' Prophète ' is obvious.— TR.

† It is not possible to convey in a word or two the antithesis between " *Sammlung,*" a " collecting " of one's thoughts, and " Zerstreuung," their distracting or "dissipation."—TR.

Princess," with a due seasoning of villain, court-choir and folk-choir, scenery and dresses.

How on earth, though, was this highly respectable Opera-symposium to be translated into Historic music ?—

Here stretched a blank expanse of clouds in face of the musician, a grey mist of unadulterated, absolute Invention : the challenge to *creation out of nothing.* But see, how quickly he took its measure ! He had only to look to it that his music should always sound a *shade different* from what one might have ordinarily expected, and his music would at once sound quite *outlandish* (fremdartig), while a skilful snip by the stage-tailor would suffice to make it out-and-out " historic."

Music, as the highest power of Expression, was now assigned a quite new, an uncommonly piquant task: to take this Expression, which she had already gone so far as to turn into the Object of expression, and contradict it out of its own mouth.   Expression—which, without an object worth expressing, was already in itself completely *null*— now *denied itself* in its endeavour to pose as that object ; so that the resultant of our theories of the world's-creation, according to which a Something has been brought about by two negations, was to be set up for entire attainment by our opera-composers.   We commend the outcome to German criticism, as " *Emancipated Metaphysics.*"

Let us follow this course a little farther.—

If the composer wished to furnish a straightforward and appropriate Expression, he could not, with the best will in the world, do it otherwise than in that musical dialect which we recognise to-day as an intelligible musical utterance ; but as he meant to henceforth lend it an Historic colouring, and as he could only deem this attainable, at bottom, by giving it a generally outlandish and unaccustomed twang, there stood chiefly at his service the expressional manner of an earlier musical epoch, which he might copy at his pleasure or borrow from according to his whim.   In this way has the composer patched together from all the tasty peculiarities of style of various periods a

piebald jargon, which, taken on its merits, was in a fair
way to meet his quest for outlandishness and unaccustomed-
ness.   But musical-speech, once it is cut adrift from any
Object worth expressing, once that it means to speak without a Content and according to the bare caprice of Operatic
Aria,—i.e. to merely chirp and chatter,—is so completely
given over to the tender mercies of the *Mode*, that it either
has to submit itself to this Mode or, if luck is favouring, to
rule it : that is, to bring it the *very latest thing* in modes.
So that, in the event of his success, the jargon which the
composer had invented in order to speak *outlandishly*—for
sake of his Historic ends—becomes at once another Mode,
which suddenly *ceases to sound outlandish* and turns into
the dress we all are wearing, the speech we all are speaking.
The composer cannot help despairing, to find himself thus
everlastingly balked by his own inventions, in his effort to
appear outlandish ; he is therefore forced to hit upon some
method of appearing outlandish for good and all, if he
means to keep faith with his calling to "historic" music.
Once for all, then, he must take pains to dislocate the very
backbone of his most distorted utterance—since it has
positively become a thing of Fashion by his own example :
to cut the story short, he must make up his mind to say
"No" where he really means "Yes," to give himself a
joyous bearing where he has to express sorrow, to whine
and whimper where his business is supreme delight.   Yes
indeed, only thus is it possible for him in every case to
seem outlandish, odd, and as though sprung from God
knows where ; he must feign to be rightdown crazy, so as
to appear "historico-characteristic."   Thus have we won
a truly brand-new element: the passion for the "historic"
has turned into *hysteric* mania, and when the lights are
turned up, this mania is found, to our intense delight, to be
nothing else than—how shall we call it ?—Eh!—*Neoromantic.*

V.

O the distortion of all truth and nature, that we see practised on musical expression by the French so-called *Neoromantists*, there was furnished from a sphere of Tone-art lying entirely aside from Opera a seeming vindication, and above all a food-stuff, which we may easiest sum together under the title of a *misunderstanding of** *Beethoven.*

It is very important to notice that, down to the present day, everything which has had a real and determinant influence upon the shaping of Opera has issued *simply from the domain of Absolute Music ;* never from that of Poetry, nor from a healthy coöperation of both arts. As we found that from Rossini onwards the history of Opera had definitely narrowed itself to the history of operatic *melody,* so do we also see the whole bias given in recent times to the more and more historico-dramatic pose of Opera proceeding from *that* opera-composer who, in his forced endeavour to vary operatic-melody, has been driven step by step to take up into this melody of his even the figment of an historical Characteristique, and who has accordingly instructed the Poet what to supply to the Musician in keeping with his plan. But as this melody had hitherto been propagated artificially as *vocal* melody,—i.e. melody which, parted from the poetic conditions of its base, yet obtained in the Singer's mouth or throat fresh conditions for its further cultivation,—and as it had chiefly gained these fresh conditions by a renewed eavesdropping of the primal nature-melody from the mouth of the Folk : so did it turn its greedy ears at last to where Melody, parted this time from the Singer's mouth, had won its further life-conditions from the mechanism of the Instrument. Thus

* The " of " is here to be understood in a transitive, not in a possessive sense. —TR.

Instrumental-melody, translated into the melody of operatic Song,* became the main factor in this fictive *drama :*—and this, in fact, was what was bound to happen in the long run to the unnatural genre of Opera !—

Whereas Operatic-melody, deprived of any actual fecundation by Poetry, could only pass from violence to violence, in its endeavour to uphold a toilsome, barren life : Instrumental-music, taking the harmonic strains of Dance and Song, separating them into smaller and ever smaller portions, augmenting and diminishing these portions, and building them up again into constantly varying forms, had won itself an idiomatic speech ; a speech which, in any higher artistic sense, however, was arbitrary and incapable of expressing the Purely-human, so long as the longing for a clear and intelligible portrayal of definite, individual human feelings did not become its only necessary measure for the shaping of those melodic particles. That the expression of an altogether definite, a clearly-understandable individual Content, was in truth impossible in this language that had only fitted itself for conveying the general character of an emotion,—*this* could not be laid bare, before the arrival of that instrumental composer with whom the longing to speak out such a content first became the consuming impulse of all his artistic fashioning.

The history of Instrumental-music, from the moment when that longing first evinced itself, is the history of an artistic error ; yet of one that ended, not in the demonstration of an impotence of Music's, like that of the Operatic genre, but with the revelation of a boundless inner power. The error of *Beethoven* was that of Columbus,† who merely

---

* We must already notice that vocal-melody, when *not* taking its vital conditions from the word-verse, but merely laid thereon, was in itself nothing but an instrumental melody ; in a more appropriate place, however, we shall have to return to a closer consideration of the position of this melody towards the orchestra.—R. WAGNER.

† I have already compared Beethoven with Columbus, in my "*Art-work of the Future*"; nevertheless I must here return to the comparison, because it further contains an important resemblance which I did not then touch on.— R. WAGNER.

meant to seek out a new way to the old known land of
India, and discovered a new world instead. Columbus
took his error with him to the grave : he made his comrades swear a solemn oath, that this new world of his was
still the ancient India ; but, never so involved in error, his
deed tore off the bandage from the old world's eyes, and
taught it to see, past all denial, the actual figure of the
earth in its undreamt fulness.—For us, too, has there been
unveiled the exhaustless power of Music, through Beethoven's all-puissant error. Through his undaunted toil,
to reach the artistically Necessary within an artistically
Impossible, is shown us Music's unhemmed faculty of
accomplishing every thinkable task, if only she consent
to stay what she really is—an *art of Expression.*

Beethoven's error, however, alike with the boon of his
artistic deed, we could not fully estimate until we were
in a position to survey his works in their totality, until
he and his works had become for us a rounded whole, and
until the artistic labours of his followers—who adopted
into their own creations the error of the master, without
either the right of ownership or the giant force of that
longing of his—had shewn us the error in its clearest
light. The contemporaries and immediate successors of
Beethoven, on the other hand, saw in his separate works,
whether in the magical impression of the whole or the
peculiar shaping of its details, precisely That alone which,
always according to the strength of their receptivity and
comprehension, was obvious to them at a glance.   So long
as Beethoven was at unison with the spirit of his musical
era, and simply embedded the flower of that spirit in his
works : so long could the reflex of his art-production prove
nothing but beneficial to his surroundings.   But from the
time when, in concord with the moving sorrows of his life,
there awoke in the artist a longing for distinct expression of specific, characteristically individual emotions,—as
though to unbosom himself to the intelligent sympathy of
fellow men,—and this longing grew into an ever more
compulsive force ; from the time when he began to care

less and less about merely making music, about expressing himself agreeably, enthrallingly or inspiritingly in general, within that music ; and instead thereof, was driven by the Necessity of his inner being to employ his art in bringing to sure and seizable expression a definite Content that absorbed his thoughts and feelings :—thenceforth begins the agony of this deep-stirred man and imperatively straying (*nothwendig irrenden*) artist. Upon the curious hearer who did not understand him, simply because the inspired man could not possibly make himself intelligible to such an one, these mighty transports and the half-sorrowful, half-blissful stammerings of a Pythian inspiration, could not but make the impression of a genius stricken with madness.

In the works of the second half of his artistic life, Beethoven is un-understandable—or rather mis-understandable—mostly just *where* he desires to express a specific, individual Content in the most intelligible way. He passes over the received, involuntary conventions of the Absolute-musical, i.e. its anyway recognisable resemblance—in respect of expression and form—to the dance- or song-tune ; he chooses instead a form of speech which often seems the mere capricious venting of a whim, and which, loosed from any purely musical cohesion, is only bound together by the bond of a Poetic purpose impossible to render into Music with full poetic plainness. The greater portion of Beethoven's works of this period must be regarded as instinctive efforts (*unwillkürliche Versuche*) to frame a speech to voice his longing ; so that they often seem like sketches for a picture, as to whose *subject* indeed the master was at one with himself, but not as to its intelligible grouping. The picture itself he could not carry out, until he had tuned its subject to the pitch of his expressional powers, had seized it in its more general meaning and translated its individual features into the native tints of Tone, and thus in a measure had 'musicalised' his very subject. If there had come before the world only these finished pictures, in which Beethoven spoke out his thoughts with delightful clearness and comprehensibility, then the misunderstanding about

himself, that the master gave rise to, would at any rate
have had a less bewildering and misguiding effect on others.
But Musical Expression, in its divorce from the conditionments of expression, had already fallen a prey to the re-
lentless necessity of mere modish likes and dislikes, and
therefore to all the conditionings of Mode itself. Certain
melodic, harmonic, or rhythmic features would flatter the ear
to-day so temptingly, that people used them to satiety;
but after a brief to-morrow they would be worn out to such
a pitch, that they would suddenly sound intolerable or
ridiculous to ears of taste. Now, he who made it his
business to catch the public's fancy, could think nothing
more important than to appear as new as possible in those
features of absolute-musical expression which we have just
characterised; and seeing that the food for such a newness
could only come from the art-domain of Music itself,—was
nowhere to be borrowed from the changing shows of Life,
—that musician was bound to see a most productive quarry
in those very works of Beethoven which we have denoted
as the sketches for his greater paintings, and in which the
struggle for discovery of a new basis of musical language,
with its excursions in all directions, often shewed itself in
certain spasmodic traits (*kramphaften Zügen*) that perforce
must strike the unintelligent listener as odd, original, bizarre,
and in any case quite new. The abrupt contrastment, the
hasty intersection, and above all the often wellnigh simultaneous utterance, of accents of joy and sorrow, ecstasy and
horror, closely woven each with each,—such as the master's
seeking instinct mingled in the strangest harmonic melismi
and rhythms, to form fresh terms for definitely expressing
individual moments of emotion,—all this, seized merely by
its formal surface, fell into the technical forcing-pit of those
composers who in the adoption of Beethoven's peculiarities espied a rich manuring for their Music-for-all-the-
world. Whereas the majority of *older* musicians could only
comprehend and sanction that element in the works of
Beethoven which lay the farthest from the master's individual being and appeared but as the crowning flower of

an earlier, less anxious period of musical art: the *younger*
note-setters have chiefly copied the externals and singu-
larities of the later Beethovenian manner.

However, as there were only externals to be copied,
since the Content of those idioms was doomed to stay the
unspoken secret of the master, so necessity commanded that
some sort of inner subject should be sought for them, some
subject that, despite its inevitable generality, might afford
a pretext for employing those features which pointed so
strongly to the particular and individual. This subject
was naturally to be found alone beyond the bounds of
Music ; and this again, for unmixed Instrumental-music,
could only be within the realm of Phantasy. A programme, reciting the heads of some subject taken from
Nature or human Life, was put into the hearer's hands ;
and it was left to his imaginative talent to interpret, in
keeping with the hint once given, all the musical freaks that
one's unchecked license (*Willkür*) might now let loose in
motley chaos.

German musicians stood close enough to the spirit of
Beethoven, to keep aloof from the wildest antics that sprang
from this misunderstanding of the master. They sought
to save themselves from the consequences of that expressional manner, by polishing down its most jutting angles ;
by taking up again the older fashions of expression, and
weaving them into these newest, they formed themselves an
artificial mixture that we can only call a general Abstract
style of music, in which one might go on music-ing with
great propriety and respectability for quite a length of time
without much fear of its being seriously disturbed by drastic
individualities. If Beethoven mostly gives us the impression of a man who has something to tell us, which yet he
cannot plainly impart : on the other hand these modern
followers of his appear like men who, often in a charmingly
circumstantial fashion, impart to us the news that they have
nothing at all to say.—

It was in Paris, however, that great devourer of all artistic tendencies, that a Frenchman gifted with uncommon musical intelligence pursued the above-named tendence to its uttermost extreme. *Hector Berlioz* is the immediate and most energetic offshoot of Beethoven on *that* side from which the latter turned away so soon—as I have above described—as he pressed forward from the sketch to the actual picture. The often crabbed and hasty penstrokes in which Beethoven, without a closer scrutiny, jotted down his attempts at finding new methods of expression, were almost the only heirloom of the great artist that fell into the eager pupil's hands. Was it a suspicion that Beethoven's most finished picture, his Last Symphony, would also be the very last work of its kind, that restrained Berlioz in his own interest—for he, too, wished to create great works—from searching those pictures for the master's actual trend (*Drang*)?—a trend which surely headed somewhere else, than toward the appeasement of a mere fantastic whim. Certain it is, that Berlioz' artistic inspiration was fed upon an enamoured staring at those strangely crumpled penstrokes: horror and ecstasy seized him at the sight of the enigmatic symbols in which the master had bound both ecstasy and horror in one common spell, to show by them the secret which he never could speak out in Music and yet believed he could speak therein alone. At this sight the starer was seized at last with giddiness; in wild confusion there danced a garish, witch-like chaos before eyes whose natural vision yielded to a purblind polyopia (*Vielsichtigkeit*), in which the dazed one fancied he was looking on human forms with all the hues of flesh, when there were really nothing but ghostly skeletons playing their tricks upon his fancy. But this spectre-roused vertigo was Berlioz' only inspiration: when he woke from it he saw, with all the exhaustion of an opium-eater, a chilling void around him, which he now endeavoured to animate by artificially re-summoning the fever of his dream; and this he could only manage by a toilsome re-arrangement of his musical household-stuff.

In his struggle to note down the apparitions of his grue-somely excited fancy, so as to present them accurately and palpably to the incredulous, hidebound world of his Parisian surroundings, Berlioz forced his enormous musical intelli-gence to a hitherto undreamt-of technical power. What he had to say to people was so wonderful, so unwonted, so entirely unnatural, that he could never have said it out in homely, simple words : he needed a huge array of the most complicated machines, in order to proclaim by help of many-wheeled and delicately adjusted Mechanism what a simple human Organism could not possibly have uttered—just because it was so quite un-human. We know, now, the supernatural wonders wherewith a priesthood once deluded childlike men into believing that some good god was manifesting himself to them : it was nothing but Mechanism, that ever worked these cheating wonders. Thus to-day again the *super*-natural, just because it is the *un*-natural, can only be brought before a gaping public by the wonders of mechanics; and such a wonder is the secret of the *Berliozian Orchestra.* Each height and depth of this Mechanism's capacity has Berlioz explored, with the result of developing a positively astounding knowledge, and if we mean to recognise the inventors of our present industrial machinery as the benefactors of modern State-humanity, then we must worship Berlioz as the veritable saviour of our world of Absolute-music ; for he has made it possible to musicians to produce the most wonderful effect, from the emptiest and most un-artistic Content of their music-making, by an unheard marshalling of mere mechanical means.

Berlioz himself, in the beginning of his artistic career, was certainly not attracted by the glory of a mere mechanical inventor : in him there dwelt a genuine artistic stress (*Drang*), and this stress was of a burning, a consum-ing kind. That, in order to content this stress, he was driven by the unsound and the un-human along the line above-discussed, to such a point that he needs must sink as artist into mechanism, as supernatural, fantastic dreamer into an all-devouring materialism : this makes of him not

only a warning example,—but so much the more a deeply
to be deplored phenomenon as he to-day is still consumed with a genuinely artistic yearning, notwithstanding
that he lies already buried hopelessly beneath the desert
waste of his machines.

He is the tragic sacrifice to a tendency whose results
have been exploited from *another* side with the most
grievous unabashedness, the most heedless self - com-
placency in all the world.   The Opera, to which we shall
now return, has swallowed down the Neoromanticism of
Berlioz, too, as a plump, fine-flavoured oyster, whose
digestion has conferred on it anew a brisk and well-to-do
appearance.

From the sphere of Absolute-music an enormous increase in means of manifold Expression had been brought
to Opera by the *modern orchestra,* by the orchestra that—
in the opera-composer's sense—was now prepared to bear
itself "dramatically."   Formerly the Orchestra had never
been anything beyond the rhythmic and harmonic bearer
of the opera-melody : however richly equipped in this its
station, yet it was always subordinated to that melody ;
and where it even reached so far as to take a direct share or
interest in its delivery, still it really only served to render
mistress Melody more dazzling and more proud, by
sumptuously adorning, as it were, her court.   Everything
that belonged to the necessary accompaniment of the
dramatic-action was taken from the sphere of Pantomime
or Ballet, whose melodic expression had evolved from the
Folkdance-tune by precisely the same laws as Operatic
Aria had evolved from the tune of the Folksong.   Just as
the one tune had owed its development and tricking-out
o the wayward fancy of the Singer, and finally of the
novelty-hunting Composer, so had the other owed *its* to
that of the Dancer and Pantomimist.   In neither had it
been possible to tamper with its essential roots, since these
lay beyond the soil of operatic art, were incognisable and

inaccessible to the factors of Opera; and this essence
was enunciated in that hard-and-fast (*scharf gezeichneten*)
rhythmic and melismic Form, whose surface the composer
might haply vary, but never wash away its outlines without completely drowning himself in a chaos of the most
hopelessly indefinite expression. Thus Pantomime itself
had been domineered over by Dance-melody. The pantomimist could deem nothing expressible by gestures but
what this Dance-melody, sternly chained to certain
rhythmic and melismic conventions, was able to accompany with any degree of fitness. He was strictly bound
to measure his movements and gestures, and consequently
what they were intended to express, by the standard of
the music's powers; by these to mould and stereotype
himself and his individual powers,—exactly as in Opera
the singing-actor must temper his dramatic powers to
those of the stereotyped Aria-expression, and leave his
own quite undeveloped, albeit entitled by the nature of
the case to the real determinative voice.*

In this anti-natural relation of the artistic factors to one
another, in both Pantomime and Opera, musical-expression
had been starved into the barest formalism. Above all
the Orchestra, as accompanist of dance or pantomime, had
not been able to gain that faculty of expression which it
must needs have reached if this subject of accompaniment,
to wit the Dramatic pantomime, had ventured to evolve
according to its own exhaustless inner powers, and thus
in itself to offer the Orchestra the material for genuine
invention. Even in Opera nothing else had been possible
to the Orchestra, when accompanying pantomimic movements, but that tied-down, banal rhythmic-melodic expression : by luxuriance and glitter of surface colour alone, had
one sought to indue it with variety.

Now, in independent Instrumental-music this fixed
expression had been broken down, and that by actually
smiting its rhythmic and melodic Form to pieces, from

* " Und sein eigenes, nach der Natur der Sache in Wahrheit eigentlich zum
Gesetzgeben berechtigtes Vermögen unentwickelt lassen musste."

which new and endlessly diverse forms were moulded according to purely musical design. *Mozart* still commenced his Symphonies with an entire melody, which he then, as though in sport, divided contrapuntally into smaller and smaller portions. *Beethoven's* most distinctive creation began with these divided pieces, from which he built before our very eyes an ever loftier and richer edifice. *Berlioz*, however, was delighted with the intricate and gay confusion into which he shook those fractions ; and the hugely complicated machine, the kaleidoscope in which he rattled parti-coloured stones together, he took and reached it to the modern opera-composer in his *Orchestra*.

These splintered and atomic melodies, whose fragments he might join together at his lief—the more without rhyme or reason, the more quaintly and surprisingly—the Opera-composer now lifted from the orchestra *into the voice itself*. However fantastically whimsical this sort of melodic practice might appear in purely orchestral pieces, yet *here* everything could be excused ; for the difficulty, nay impossibility of expressing oneself in Music alone, with full distinctness, had already betrayed even the most earnest masters into a like fantastic whimsicality. But in Opera, where the sharp-cut word of Poetry afforded the musician a quite natural basis for a sure, infallible expression, this scandalous confounding of all expression, this supercilious maiming of each still healthy organ of expression, such as is exhibited in the modernest Opera's preposterous stringing-together of utterly alien and radically diverse melodic elements—this we can only ascribe to the complete development of madness in the composer ; who, in his arrogant pretension to bring about the Drama by his sole absolute-musical powers, with *merely labourer's assistance* from the Poet, was necessarily bound to arrive where we see him arrived to-day amid the ridicule of every man of common sense.

In virtue of his hugely swollen musical apparatus, the Composer, who since Rossini's time had only developed his frivolous side and lived on absolute Opera-melody, now felt

called to boldly advance from the standpoint of melodic
frivolity to the further stage of dramatic " Characteristique."
As such a " Characteristicist " is the most famous opera-
composer of modern times acclaimed ; and that not only
by the public, who had long-since been made his deeply
compromised accomplice in the assault upon Music's truth,
but also by the art-critics. In view of the greater melodic
purity of former epochs, and compared therewith, 'tis true
the Meyerbeerian melody is upbraided by our criticists as
frivolous and *flimsy* (gehaltlos) ; but in regard of the quite
new marvels in the way of " Characteristique " that have
blossomed from his music this composer is meted out a
plenary indulgence,—which involves the corollary that, after
all, one considers a *musical-dramatic Characteristique* only
possible when couched in a *frivolous and flimsy Melodique :*
a consideration which in its turn can only fill the æsthetician
with an utter distrust of the whole genre of Opera.—

Let us briefly survey the nature of this modern " Characteristique," as exhibited in Opera.

VI.

ODERN "CHARACTERISTIQUE," in Opera, is something essentially different from its counterpart in the *pre*-Rossinian era, in the tendency of Gluck or of Mozart.

In declaimed Recitative, as in be-sung Aria, *Gluck*—with full retention of these forms, and amid his instinctive carefulness to comply with the wonted claims upon their purely musical content—was consciously concerned to reproduce as faithfully as possible by his Musical Expression the emotion indicated in the 'text,' and above all to never sacrifice the purely declamatory accent of the verse in favour of this musical expression. He took pains to speak correctly and intelligibly in his music.

Mozart, by reason of a nature wholly sound at core, could never speak otherwise than correctly. He pronounced with the selfsame clearness the rhetorical 'pigtail' and the genuine dramatic accent : with him grey was always grey, and red red ; only that this grey and this red were equally bathed with the freshening dew of his music, were resolved into all the nuances of the primordial colour, and thus appeared as many-tinted grey, as many-tinted red. Instinctively his music ennobled all the conventional stage-characters presented him, by polishing, as it were, the rough-hewn stone, by turning all its facets to the light, and finally by fixing it in that position where the light could smite it into brightest play of colour. In this way was he able to lift the characters of "Don Juan," for instance, into such a fulness of expression that a writer like Hoffmann could fall on the discovery of the deepest, most mysterious relations between them, relations of which neither poet nor musician had been ever really conscious. Certain it is, however, that Mozart could not possibly have made his music characteristic in such sort,

F

had the characters themselves not been already present in the poet's work. The more we are able to look through the glowing tints of Mozart's music to the ground behind, with the greater sureness do we recognise the sharp and definite penstrokes of the Poet, whose lines and touches first pre-scribed the colours of the Musician, and without whose skill that wondrous music would have straightway been impossible.

But the amazingly lucky relationship between Poet and Composer, that we have found in Mozart's masterwork, we see completely vanishing again in the further evolution of Opera; until, as we have already noticed, *Rossini* quite abolished it, making absolute Melody the only authentic factor of Opera, to which all other interests, and above all the coöperation of the Poet, had wholly to subordinate themselves. We further saw that *Weber's* objection to Rossini was only directed against this Melody's shallow-ness and want of character; by no means against the unnatural position of the Musician toward the Drama. On the contrary, Weber only added to this unnaturalness, in that he assigned himself a still more heightened position, as against the Poet, by a characteristic ennobling of his Melody; a position loftier in exact degree as his melody outtopped Rossini's in just that point of nobility of char-acter. To Rossini the Poet hung on like a jolly trencher-man, whom the Composer—distinguished, but affable person that he was—treated to his heart's content with oysters and champagne; so that, in the whole wide world, the Poet found himself nowhere better off than with the famous maëstro. Weber, on the other hand, from unbending faith in the characteristic pureness of his one and indivisible Melody, tyrannised over the Poet with dogmatic cruelty, and forced him to erect the very stake on which the wretch was to let himself be burnt to ashes for the kindling of the fire of Weber's melody. The poet of "Der Freis-chütz," entirely without his own knowledge, had committed this act of suicide: from out his very ashes he protested, while the flames of Weber's fire were already filling all the air; he called to the world that these flames were really leaping forth from *him*. But he made a radical mistake; his wooden logs gave forth no flame until they were consumed—destroyed: their ashes alone, the prosaic dialogue, could he claim as his property after the fire.

After the "Freischütz" Weber sought him out a more accommodating poet; for a new opera he took into his pay a lady, from whose more unconditional subservience he even demanded that, after the burning of the funeral pile, she should not leave behind so much as the last ashes of her prose: she should allow herself to be consumed flesh and bone in the furnace of his melody. From Weber's correspondence with Frau von Chezy, during the preparation of the text of "Euryanthe," we learn with what painstaking care he felt again compelled to rack the last drop of blood from a poetic helper; how he rejects and prescribes, and once more prescribes and rejects; here cuts, there asks for more; insists on lengthenings here and shortenings there,—nay extends his orders even to the characters themselves, their motives and their actions. Was he in this, mayhap, a peevish malcontent, or a boastful parvenu who, inflated by the success of his "Freischütz," desired to play the despot where by rights he should have obeyed? No, no! Out of his mouth there spake alone the honourable artist-care of the Musician, who, tempted by stress of circumstance, had undertaken to construct the Drama itself from Absolute-melody. Weber here was led into a serious error, but into an error which was necessarily bound to take him. He had lifted Melody to its fairest, most feeling height of nobleness; he wanted now to crown it as the *Muse of Drama* herself, and by her strenuous hand to chase away the whole ribald pack of profaners of the stage. As in the "Freischütz" he had led each lyric fibre of the opera-poem into this Melody, so now he wished to shower down the Drama from the beams of his melodic planet. One might almost say that the melody for his "Euryanthe" was ready before a line of its poem; to provide the latter, he only

wanted someone who should take his melody completely
into ear and heart, and merely poetise upon it. Since this
was not practicable, however, he and his poetess fell into
a fretful theoretic quarrel, in which a clear agreement was
possible from neither the one side nor the other,—so that
in this case of all others, when calmly tested, we may
plainly see into what painful insecurity men of Weber's
gifts and artistic love of truth may be misled, by holding
fast to a fundamental artistic error.

After all was done, the Impossible was bound to stay
impossible for Weber too. Spite all his suggestions and
instructions to the Poet, he could not procure a dramatic
groundwork which he might entirely dissolve into his
Melody ; because he wished to call into being a genuine
drama, and not merely a play filled out with lyric
moments, where—as in " Der Freischütz "—he would need
to employ his music for nothing but those lyric moments.
In the text of " Euryanthe," besides the dramatic-lyric
elements,—for which, as I have expressed myself, the
melody was ready in advance,—there was still so much of
additional matter quite foreign to Absolute Music, that
Weber was unable to get command of it by his Melody
proper. If this text had been the work of a veritable
poet, who should only have called upon the musician for
aid, in the same manner as the musician had now called
upon the poet : then this musician, in his affection for the
proffered drama, would never have had a moment's hesi-
tancy. Where he recognised no fitting Stuff to feed or
vindicate his broader musical expression, he would only
have deployed his lesser powers, to wit of furnishing an
accompaniment subordinate but ever helpful to the whole ;
and only where the fullest musical expression was necessarily conditioned by the Stuff itself, would he have
entered with his fullest powers. The text of " Euryanthe,"
however, had sprung from the converse relationship between poet and musician, and wherever the Composer—
the virtual author of that opera—should by rights have
stood aside or withdrawn into the background, there he

now could only see a doubled task, namely that of im-
printing on a musically quite sterile stuff a stamp which
should be musical throughout.   In this Weber could have
succeeded only if he had turned to music's frivolous line ;
if, looking quite aside from truth, he had given rein to the
epicurean element, and set death and the devil to amusing
melodies *à la* Rossini. But this was the very thing against
which Weber lodged his strongest artistic protest : *his*
melody should be everywhere *characteristic*, i.e. true and
answering to each emotion of his subject. Thus he was
forced to betake himself to some other expedient.

Wherever his broad-breathed melody—mostly ready in
advance, and spread above the text like a glittering
garment—would have done that text too manifest a
violence, there Weber broke this melody itself in pieces.
He then took up the separate portions of his melodic
building, and, always according to the declamatory requirements of the words, re-joined them together into
a skilful mosaic ; which latter he coated with a film of
fine melodic varnish, in order thus to preserve for the
whole construction an outward show of Absolute Melody,
detachable as much as possible from the text-words.
The desired illusion, however, he did not succeed in
effecting.

Not only Rossini, but Weber himself had made Absolute
Melody so decidedly the main content of Opera, that,
wrested from its dramatic framework and even stripped of
its text-words, it had passed over to the Public *in its barest
nakedness.* A melody must be able to be fiddled and
blown, or hammered-out upon the pianoforte, *without*
thereby losing the smallest particle of its individual
essence, if it was ever to become a real melody for the
public. To Weber's operas, too, the public merely went
to hear as many of such melodies as possible, and the
musician was terribly mistaken when he flattered himself
that he would see that lacquered declamatory mosaic
accepted as Melody by this public : for, to tell the truth,
that was what the composer 'really made for. Though in

the eyes of Weber himself that mosaic could only be justified by the words of the text, yet on the one side the public was entirely indifferent—and that with perfect justice—to those words ; while on the other side it transpired that this text itself had not been quite suitably reproduced in the music. For it was just this immature half-melody that turned the attention of the hearer away from the words, and made him look out anxiously for the formation of a whole melody that never came to light,—so that any longing for the presentment of a poetic thought was throttled in advance, while the enjoyment of a melody was all the more painfully curtailed as the longing for it was roused indeed, but never satisfied. Beyond the passages in "Euryanthe" where the composer's artistic judgment could hold his own broad natural melody completely justified, we see in that work his higher artistic efforts only crowned with true and beautiful success where, for love of truth, he quite renounces Absolute-melody, and —as in the opening scene of the first act—gives the noblest, most faithful musical expression to the emotional dramatic declamation (*Rede*) as such; where he therefore sets the aim of his own artistic labours no longer in the music but in the poem, and merely employs his music for the furthering of that aim : which, again, could be attained by nothing but Music with such fulness and so convincing truth.

Criticism has never dealt with "Euryanthe" in the measure that its uncommonly instructive Content deserves. The Public gave an undecided voice, half stirred, half chagrined. Criticism, which at bottom always waits upon the public voice, in order—according to its own intention of the moment—either from that and the outward success to take its cue, or else to doggedly oppose it : this Criticism has never been able to take proper stock of the utterly contradictory elements that cross each other in this work, to sift them carefully, and from the composer's endeavour to unite them into one harmonious whole to find a warrant for its ill-success. Yet never, so long as Opera has existed,

has there been composed a work in which the inner contradictions of the whole genre have been more consistently
worked out, more openly exhibited, by a gifted, deeply-
feeling and truth-loving composer, for all his high endeavour to attain the best. These contradictions are : *absolute, self-sufficing melody, and—unflinchingly true dramatic
expression.* Here one or the other must necessarily be
sacrificed,—either Melody or Drama. Rossini sacrificed
the Drama ; the noble Weber wished to reinstate it by
force of his more judicious (*sinnigeren*) melody. He had
to learn that this was an impossibility. Weary and exhausted by the troubles of his " Euryanthe," he sank back
upon the yielding pillow of an oriental fairy-dream ;
through the wonder-horn of Oberon he breathed away
his last life's-breath.

What this noble, lovable Weber, aglow with a pious
faith in the omnipotence of his pure Melody, vouchsafed
him by the fairest spirit of the Folk,—what *he* had striven
for in vain, was undertaken by a friend of Weber's youth,
by *Jacob Meyerbeer ;* but from the standpoint of Rossinian
melody.

Meyerbeer passed through all the phases of this Melody's
development ; not from an abstract distance, but in a very
concrete nearness, always on the spot. As a Jew, he owned
no mother-tongue, no speech inextricably entwined among
the sinews of his inmost being : he spoke with precisely
the same interest in any modern tongue you chose, and set
it to music with no further sympathy for its idiosyncrasies
than just the question as to how far it shewed a readiness
to become a pliant servitor to Absolute Music. This attribute of Meyerbeer's has given occasion to a comparison of
him with *Gluck ;* for the latter, too, although a German,
wrote operas to French and Italian texts. As a fact,
Gluck did not create his music from the instinct of Speech
(which in such a case must always be the *mother*-speech) :
what he, as Musician, was concerned with in his attitude

toward Speech (*die Sprache*), was its Rhetoric (*die Rede*), that utterance of the speech-organism which merely floats upon the surface of this myriad of organs. Not from the generative force of these organs, did his productive powers mount through the Rhetoric into the Musical-expression ; but from the sloughed-off Musical-expression he harked back to the Rhetoric, merely so as to give that baseless Expression some ground of vindication. Thus every tongue might well come equally to Gluck, since he was only busied with his rhetoric: if Music, in this transcendental line, had been able to pierce through the Rhetoric into the very organism of Speech, it must then have surely had to entirely transform itself.—In order not to interrupt the course of my argument, I must reserve this extremely weighty topic for thorough investigation in a more appropriate place ; for the present I content myself with commending to notice, that *Gluck's* concern was with an animated Rhetoric in general—no matter in what tongue, —since in that alone did he find a vindication for his melody ; whereas since Rossini this Rhetoric has been completely swallowed up in Absolute-melody, leaving only its materialest of frameworks, its vowels and its consonants, as a scaffolding for musical tone.

Meyerbeer, through his indifference to the spirit of any tongue, and his hence-gained power to make with little pains its outer side his own (a faculty our modern education has brought within the reach of all the well-to-do), was quite cut out for dealing with Absolute Music divorced from any lingual ties. Moreover, he thus was able to witness on the spot the salient features in the aforesaid march of Opera-music's evolution : everywhere and everywhen he followed on its footsteps. Above all is it noteworthy that he merely *followed* on this march, and never kept *abreast* of, to say nothing of outstripping it. He was like the starling who follows the ploughshare down the field, and merrily picks up the earthworm just uncovered in the furrow. Not *one* departure is his own, but each he has eavesdropped from his forerunner, exploiting it with mon-

strous ostentation ; and so swiftly that the man in front
has scarcely spoken a word, than *he* has bawled out the
entire phrase, quite unconcerned as to whether he has
caught the meaning of that word ; whence it has generally
arisen, that he has actually said something slightly different
from what the man in front intended. But the noise of
the Meyerbeerian phrase was so deafening, that the man
in front could no longer arrive at bringing out his own real
meaning : willy-nilly, if only to get a word in edgeways, he
was forced at last to chime into that phrase.

In Germany alone was Meyerbeer unsuccessful, in his
search for a new-fledged phrase to anyhow fit the word of
Weber : what Weber uttered from the fill of his melodic
life, could not be echoed in the lessoned, arid formalism of Meyerbeer. At last, disgusted with the fruitless
toil, he betrayed his friend by listening to Rossini's siren
strains, and departed for the land where grew those raisins
(*Rosinen*). Thus he became the weathercock of European
opera-music, the vane that always veers at first uncertain
with the shift of wind, and only comes to a standstill when
the wind itself has settled on its quarter. Thus Meyerbeer
in Italy composed operas *à la* Rossini, precisely till the
larger wind of Paris commenced to chop, and Auber and
Rossini with their "*Stumme*" and their "*Tell*" blew the
new gale into a storm ! With one bound, was Meyerbeer
in Paris ! There he found, however, in the *Frenchified*
Weber (need I recall "*Robin des bois*"?) and the *be-Berliozed* Beethoven, certain moments to which neither Auber
nor Rossini had paid attention, as lying too far out of their
way, but which Meyerbeer in virtue of his cosmopolitan
capacity knew very well to valuate. He summed up all
his overhearings in one monstrous hybrid phrase, whose
strident outcry put Rossini and Auber to sudden silence :
" Robert," the grim " Devil," set his clutches on them all.

In the survey of our operatic history, there is something
most painful about being *only able to speak good of the dead*,
and being forced to pursue the living with remorseless
bitterness !—But if we want to be candid, since we *must*,

we have to recognise that the departed masters of this art
deserve alone the martyr's crown; if *they* were victims to
an illusion, yet that illusion shewed in them so high and
beautiful, and they themselves believed so earnestly its
sacred truth, that they offered up their whole artistic lives
in sorrowful, yet joyful sacrifice thereto. No living and
still active Tone-setter any longer strives from inner stress
for such a martyrdom; the illusion now is laid so bare,
that no more can anyone repose implicit trust in it. Bereft
of faith, nay, robbed of joy, operatic art has fallen, at the
hand of its modern masters, to a mere commercial article.
Even the Rossinian wanton smile is now no more to be perceived; all round us nothing but the yawn of ennui, or the
grin of madness! Almost we feel most drawn towards the
aspect of the *madness* (Wahnsinn); in it we find the last
remaining breath of that *illusion* (Wahn) from which there
blossomed once such noble sacrifice. The juggling side of
the odious exploitation of our modern opera-affairs we will
therefore here forget, now that we must call before us the
work of the last surviving and still active hero of operatic
composition : that aspect could only fill us with indignation,
whereby we might perhaps be betrayed into inhuman
harshness towards a personage, did we lay on it alone the
burden of the foul corruption of those affairs which surely
hold this personage the more a captive as to us it seems
set upon their dizziest peak, adorned with crown and sceptre.
Do we not know that Kings and Princes, precisely in their
most arbitrary dealings, are now the greatest slaves of all?
—No, in this king of operatic music let us only look upon
the traits of Madness, by which he appears to us an object
of regret and warning, not of scorn! For the sake of everlasting Art, we must learn to read the symptoms of this
madness; because by its contortions shall we plainest
recognise *the illusion* that gave birth to an artistic genre, as
to whose erroneous basis we must thoroughly clear up our
minds before ever we can gain the healthy, youthful
courage to set rejuvenating hands to Art itself.

To this inquiry we may now press on with rapid step, as

we have already shewn the essence of that Madness, and
have only to observe a few of its most salient features in
order to be quite sure about it.

———————————

We have seen the frivolous Opera-melody—i.e. that
robbed of any real connexion with the poem's text—grow
big with taking up the tune of National-song, and seen it
swell into the pretence of Historic Characteristique. We
have further noticed how, with an ever-dwindling in-
dividualisation of the chief rôles in the musical drama, the
character of the Action was more and more allotted to the
—" emancipated "—masses, from whom this Character was
then to fall as a mere reflex on the main transactors. We
have remarked that only by an Historic costume could the
surrounding Mass be stamped with any distinctive, at all
cognisable character; and have seen the Composer, so as
to maintain his supremacy against the Scene-painter and
Stage-tailor,—to whom had virtually fallen the merit of
establishing the historic Characteristique,—compelled to
outdo them by the most unwonted application of his
purely-musical nostrums. Finally, we have seen how the
most desperate departure in Instrumental-music brought
the composer an extraordinary sort of mosaique-melody,
whose waywardest of combinations offered the means of
appearing strange and outlandish, whenever he had a fancy
that way,—and how, by a miraculous employment of the
Orchestra, calculated solely for material surprise, he believed
he could imprint on such a method the stamp of a quite
special Characteristique.

Now we must not leave out of sight that, after all, this
whole conjuncture could never have arisen without the
Poet's confederacy; wherefore we will turn, for a moment,
to an examination of the modernest relationship of the
Musician to the Poet.

Through Rossini the new operatic tendency started
decidedly from Italy: *there* the Poet had degenerated into

an utter nonentity. But with the transshipment of Rossini's
tendency to Paris, the position of the Poet also altered. We
have already denoted the peculiarities of French Opera, and
found that its kernel was the entertaining conversation (*der
unterhaltende Wortsinn*) of the Couplet. In French Comic-
opera the Poet had erstwhile relinquished to the Composer
but a limited field, which he was to cultivate for himself
while the poet abode in undisputed possession of the ground-
estate. Now although, in the nature of the thing, that
musical terrain had gradually so encroached upon the rest
that it took up in time the whole estate, yet the Poet still
held the title-deeds, and the Musician remained a mere
feoffee, who certainly regarded the entire fief as his
hereditary property, but notwithstanding—as in the whilom
Romo-German Empire—owed allegiance to the Emperor
as his feudal lord. The Poet enfeoffed, and the Musician
enjoyed. In this situation alone, have there ever come to
light the healthiest of Opera's progeny, when viewed as a
Dramatic genre. The Poet honestly bestirred himself to
invent characters and situations, to provide an entertaining
and enthralling piece, which only in its final elaboration did
he trim for the Musician and the latter's Forms ; so that the
actual weakness of these French opera-poems lay more in
the fact that, by their very Content, they mostly called for
no music at all, than in that they were swamped by Music
in advance. On the stage of the *Opéra Comique* this entertaining, often delightfully witty genre was in its native
element ; and in it the best work was always done when the
music could enter with unforced naturalness into the poetry.

This genre was now translated by Scribe and Auber into
the pompous phraseology of so-called " Grand Opera." In
the " *Muette de Portici* " we still can plainly recognise a
well-planned theatric piece, in which the dramatic interest
is nowhere as yet subordinated with manifest intention to
a purely musical one : only, in this poem the dramatic-
action is already essentially transferred to the operations of
the surrounding Mass, so that the main transactors behave
more as talking representatives of the mass, than as real

Persons who act from individual necessity. So slack already, arrived before the imposing chaos of Grand Opera, did the Poet hold the reins of the opera carriage ; those reins he was soon to drop upon the horses' backs ! But whereas in the "Muette," and in "Tell," the Poet still kept the reins within his hand, since it occurred to neither Auber nor Rossini to do anything else but just take their musical ease and melodious comfort in the stately opera-coach—unworried as to how and whither the well-drilled coachman steered its wheels,—now Meyerbeer, to whom that rank melodic ease did not come so in the grain, felt impelled to seize the coachman's reins, and by the zig-zag of his *route* arouse the needful notice, which he could not succeed in attracting to himself so long as he quietly sat in the coach, with no other company than his own musical personality.—

Merely in scattered anecdotes has it come to our ears, what painful torments Meyerbeer inflicted on his poet, Scribe, during the sketching of his opera-subjects. But if we paid no heed to any of these anecdotes, and knew absolutely nothing of the mysteries of those opera-confabulations between Scribe and Meyerbeer, we should still see clearly by the resultant poems themselves what a pothersome, bewildering incubus must have weighed on the else so rapid, so easy-working and quick-witted Scribe, when he had to cobble up those bombastical, rococo texts for Meyerbeer. While Scribe continued to write fluent, often interestingly planned dramatic poems for other composers ; texts in any case worked out with considerable natural skill, and at least based always on a definite plot, with easily intelligible situations to suit that plot,—yet this uncommonly expert poet turned out for Meyerbeer the veriest fustian, the lamest galimathias ; actions without a plot, situations of the most insane confusion, characters of the most ridiculous buffoonery. This could never have come about by natural means : so easily does no sober judgment, like that of Scribe, submit to the experiments of craziness. Scribe must first have had his brain unhinged for him,

before he conjured up a " Robert the Devil " ; he must have
first been robbed of all sound sense for dramatic-action,
before he lent himself in the "Huguenots" to the mere
compilation of scene-shifters' nuances and contrasts; he
must have been violently initiated into the mysteries of
Historical hanky-panky, before he consented to paint a
"Prophet" of the sharpers.—

We here perceive a determinant influence of the Composer on the Poet, akin to that which Weber exerted on
the poetess of "Euryanthe ": but from what diametrically
opposite motives! Weber wanted a Drama that could
pass with all its members, with every scenic nuance, into
his noble, soulful Melody:—Meyerbeer, on the contrary,
wanted a monstrous piebald, historico-romantic, diabolico-
religious, fanatico-libidinous, sacro-frivolous, mysterio-
criminal, autolyco-sentimental dramatic hotch-potch, therein to find material for a curious chimeric music,—a want
which, owing to the indomitable buckram of his musical
temperament, could never be quite suitably supplied. He
felt that, with all his garnered store of musical effects,
there was still a something wanting, a something hitherto
non-existent, but which he could bring to bearing were
he only to collect the whole thing from every farthest
cranny, heap it together in one mass of crude confusion,
dose it well with stage gunpowder and lycopodium, and
spring it crashing through the air. What he wanted therefore from his librettist, was, so to speak, an inscenation
of the Berliozian Orchestra ; only—mark this well!—with
the most humiliating degradation of it to the sickly basis
of Rossini's vocal trills and *fermate*—for sake of "dramatic"
Opera. To bring the whole stock of elements of musical
effect into some sort of harmonious concord through the
Drama, would have necessarily appeared to him a sorry
way of setting about his business; for Meyerbeer was no
idealistic dreamer, but, with a keen practical eye to the
modern opera-public, he saw that by a harmonious concord he would have gained no one to his side, whereas by
a rambling hotch-potch he must certainly catch the moods

of all, i.e. of each man in his line. So that nothing was more important for him, than a maze of mad cross-purposes, and the merry Scribe must sweat blood to concoct a dramatic medley to his taste. In cold-blooded care the musician stood before it, calmly meditating as to which piece of the monstrosity he could fit out with some particular tatter from his musical store-room, so strikingly and cryingly that it should appear quite out-of-the-ordinary, and therefore—" characteristic."

Thus, in the eyes of our art-Criticism, he developed the powers of Music into *historical Characteristique*, and brought matters so far that he was told, as the most delicate compliment, that the texts of his operas were terribly poor stuff *but what wonders his music knew how to make out of this wretched rubbish !*—So the utmost triumph of Music was reached : the Composer had razed the Poet to the ground, and upon the ruins of operatic-poetry the *Musician* was crowned the only *authentic poet !*—

The secret of Meyerbeer's operatic music is—*Effect.* If we wish to gain a notion of what we are to understand by this " Effect " (" *Effekt* "), it is important to observe that in this connection we do not as a rule employ the more homely word " *Wirkung* " [lit. " a working "]. Our natural feeling can only conceive of " *Wirkung* " as bound up with an antecedent *cause :* but here, where we are instinctively in doubt as to whether such a correlation subsists, or are even as good as told that it does not subsist at all, we look perplexedly around us for a word to anyhow denote the impression which we think we have received from, e.g., the music-pieces of Meyerbeer ; and so we fall upon a foreign word, not directly appealing to our natural feeling, such as just this word " Effect." If, then, we wish to define what we understand by this word, we may translate " Effect " by " a Working, without a cause " (" *Wirkung ohne Ursache* ").

As a fact, the Meyerbeerian music produces, on those who are able to edify themselves thereby, a Working-without-a-cause. This miracle was only possible to the extremest music, i.e. to an expressional power which—in Opera—had from the first sought to make itself more and more independent of anything worth expressing, and had finally proclaimed its attainment of complete independence by reducing to a moral and artistic nullity the Object of expression, which alone should have given to this Expression its being, warranty and measure ; by reducing it to such a degree that this *object* now could only gain its being, warranty and measure from a mere act of grace on the part of Music,—an act which had thus itself become devoid of any real expression. This act of grace, however, could only be made possible in conjunction with other coefficients of absolute-Working. In the extremest Instrumental-music appeal had been made to the vindicating force of Phantasy, to which a programme, or mayhap a mere title, had given an extramusical leverage : in Opera this leverage was to be materialised, i.e. the imagination was to be absolved from any painful toil. What had there been programmatically adduced from moments of the phenomenal life of Man or Nature, was here to be presented in the most material reality, so as to produce a fantastic Working without the smallest fellow-working of the Phantasy. This material leverage the Composer borrowed from the scenic apparatus, inasmuch as he took also purely for their own sake the workings it was able to produce, i.e. absolved them from the only object that, lying beyond the realm of Mechanism and on the soil of life-portraying Poetry, could have given them conditionment and vindication.—Let us explain our meaning clearly by one example, which will at the same time characterise the most exhaustively the whole of Meyerbeerian art.

Let us suppose that a poet has been inspired with the idea of a hero, a champion of light and freedom, in whose breast there flames an all-consuming love for his downtrod brother-men, afflicted in their holiest rights. The poet

wishes to depict this hero at the zenith of his career, in the
full radiance of his deeds of glory, and chooses for his
picture the following supreme moment. With thousands
of the Folk—who have left house and home, left wife and
children, to follow his inspiring call, to conquer or to die in
fight against their powerful oppressors—the hero has
arrived before a fortressed city, which must be stormed
by his unpractised mob, if the work of freedom is to come
to a victorious issue. Through earlier hardships and
mishaps, disheartenment has spread apace ; evil passions,
discord and confusion are raging in his hosts : all is lost, if
all shall not be won to-day. This is a plight in which
heroes wax to their fullest grandeur. In the solitude of
the night just past the hero has taken counsel of the god
within him, of the spirit of the purest love for fellow-
men, and with its breath has sanctified himself ; and now
the poet takes him in the grey of dawn, and leads him
forth among those hosts, who are already wavering as to
whether they should prove coward beasts or godlike
heroes. At his mighty voice, the Folk assemble. That
voice drives home into the inmost marrow of these men,
who now alike grow conscious of the god within them :
they feel their hearts uplifted and ennobled, and their
inspiration in its turn uplifts the hero to still loftier
heights ; from inspiration he presses on to deed. He
seizes the standard and waves it high towards those
fearful walls, the embattled city of the foe, who, so
long as they lie secure behind their trenches, make impossible a better future for mankind. " On, then, comrades !
To die or conquer ! This city *must* be ours ! "—The poet
now has reached his utmost confines : upon the boards he
wills to show the one instant when this high-strung mood
steps suddenly before us with all the plainness of a great
reality ; the scene must now become for us the stage of all
the world ; Nature must now declare herself a sharer in
this exaltation ; no longer can she stay a chilling, chance
bystander. Lo ! sacred Want compels the poet :—he parts
the cloudy curtains of the morn, and at his word the

G

streaming sun mounts high above the city, that city henceforth hallowed to the victory of the inspired.

Here is the flower of all-puissant Art, and this wonder
blossoms only from the art of Drama.

Only, the opera-composer has no longing for wonders
such as blossom merely from the dramatic-poet's inspiration and may be effectuated by a picture taken lovingly
from Life itself : he wishes for the *effect* but not the
cause, since the latter lies outside his sway.   In a leading
scene of Meyerbeer's " Prophète," where the *externals*
resemble those just described, we obtain for the ear the
purely physical effect of a hymn-like melody, listened from
the Folk-song and swelled into a sound like thunder : for
the eye, that of a sunrise in which there is positively
nothing for us to see but a master-stroke of Mechanism.
The Object that should be fired by that melody, should be
shone on by this sun, *the inspired hero* who from very
ecstasy must pour his soul into that melody, who at the
stressful climax of Necessity called forth the dawning of
this sun,—the warranty, the kernel of the whole luxuriant
dramatic fruit,—*is absolutely not to hand.** In his place
there functions a characteristically-costumed tenor, whom
Meyerbeer has commissioned through his private-secretary
poet, Scribe, to sing as charmingly as possible and at the
same time behave a wee bit communistically, in order that
the gentry might have an extra dash of piquancy to think

---

* I may get for reply : " Your glorious Hero of the Folk we did not want :
the whole conception of him is only a pernicious outcome of your private
revolutionary fancy.   On the contrary, we wanted to exhibit an unfortunate
young man, who, embittered by unpleasant experiences and led astray by tricky
agitators, lets himself be driven into crime, which he later expiates by a most
sincere contrition."   I go on to ask for the meaning of the sun-effect, and
still I may be answered : " It is copied accurately from Nature.   Why should
the sun not rise in the early morning ? "   To be sure, that would be a very
practical apology for an involuntary sunrise ; yet I must still be obstinate,
and maintain that You would never have allowed that sun to steal a march
upon you, if you had not really been haunted by some such situation as that
which I have sketched above : the situation, indeed, did not suit your taste,
but all the same you intended its Effect.—R. WAGNER.—Our author might
have gone farther, and said : " and you stole it from *Rienzi*."—TR.

into the thing. The hero of whom we spoke before, is some
poor devil who out of sheer weakness has taken on the rôle
of trickster, and finally bewails in the most pitiful fashion
—by no means any error, any fanatical hallucination,
which might at a pinch have called for a sun to shine on it,
—but solely his weakness and mendacity.

What considerations may have joined forces to call into
the world such an unworthy object under the title of a
" Prophet," we will here leave unexplored ; let it suffice us
to observe the resultant, which is instructive enough in all
conscience. First, we see in this example the complete
moral and artistic dishonourment of the Poet, in whose
work even those who are most favourably disposed to the
Composer can find no single hair's-breadth of merit : so !—
the poetic aim is no longer to attract us in the slightest ;
on the contrary, it is to revolt us. The Performer is now
to interest us as nothing but a costumed Singer ; in the
above-named scene, he can only do this by his singing of
that aforesaid melody, which makes its effect entirely for
itself—as Melody. Wherefore the sun is likewise to work
entirely for itself, namely as a successful theatrical copy of
the authentic sun : so that the ground of its 'working'
comes not at all into the province of Drama, but into that
of sheer Mechanics,—the only thing left for us to think
about when it puts in its appearance ; for how alarmed the
composer would be, if one chose to take this appearance
as an intentional transfiguration of the hero, in his capacity
of champion of mankind ! No, no : for him and his public,
everything must be done to turn such thoughts away, and
guide attention solely to that master-stroke of mechanism.
And thus in this unique scene, so heaped with honours by
the public, the whole of Art is resolved into its mechanical
integers : the externals of Art are turned into its essence ;
and this essence we find to be—*Effect*, the absolute Effect,
i.e. the stimulus of an artificial love-titillation, without
the potence of an actual taste of Love.

I have not taken upon myself to offer a criticism of
Meyerbeer's operas, but merely to shew by them the
essence of our modernest Opera, in its hang with the whole
class in general. Though the nature of my subject has
often compelled me to give my exposition the character of
a historic survey, yet I have had to resist the being led
aside into historic detail-writing. If I had to characterise
in particular the calling and talent of Meyerbeer for
dramatic composition, I should have for very sake of truth,
which I here am labouring to bare completely, to lay the
strongest stress upon one remarkable phenomenon in his
works.—In Meyerbeer's music there is shewn so appalling
an emptiness, shallowness and artistic nothingness, that—
especially when compared with by far the larger number of
his musical contemporaries—we are tempted to set down his
specific musical capacity at zero. However, it is not that
despite all this he has reaped such great successes with the
European opera-public, which should fill us with wonder-
ment ; for this miracle is easily explained by a glance at
that Public itself :—no, it is a purely artistic observation,
which here should rivet and instruct us. We observe,
namely, that for all the renowned composer's manifest inability to give by his unaided musical powers the slightest
sign of artistic life, nevertheless in certain passages of his
operatic music he lifts himself to the height of the most
thoroughly indisputable, the very greatest artistic power.
These passages are products of a genuine inspiration, and
if we look a little closer we shall also see whence this inspiration derived its stimulus—namely, from the Poetic
situation. Where the poet forgot his hampering regard
for the musician, where amid his work of dramatic compilation he stumbled on a moment in which the free, the freshening breath of human Life might come and go,—there he
suddenly transmits this breath alike to the musician, as a
gust of Inspiration ; and now the composer, who had exhausted all the resources of his musical ancestry without
being able to strike one solitary spark of real Invention, is
at a blow empowered to find the richest, noblest, most

heart-searching musical Expression. I here would chiefly call to mind certain features in the well-known plaintive love-scene of the Fourth Act of the " Huguenots," and above all the invention of that wondrous moving melody in G-flat major, by side of which—sprung as it is, like a fragrant flower, from a situation which stirs each fibre of the human heart to blissful pain—there is very little else, and certainly none but the most perfect of Music's works, that can be set. This I signalise with the sincerest joy and frank enthusiasm, because precisely in this phenomenon is the real essence of Art presented in so clear and irrefutable a fashion, that we can but see with rapture how the faculty for genuine art-creation must come to even the most corrupted music-maker, so soon as he treads the soil of a Necessity stronger than his self-seeking Caprice ; of a necessity which suddenly guides his erring footsteps, to his own salvation, into the paths of sterling Art.

But, that here we can only mention separate features, and not one whole great track—not e.g. the entire love-scene to which I have referred, but only scattered moments in it, —this compels us to above all ponder well the gruesome nature of that Madness, which nips in the folded bud the musician's noblest faculties, and stamps upon his muse the sickly smile of odious complaisance, or else the ghastly grin of crazy tyranny. This madness is the musician's passion to supply for himself, and by his own powers, what he does not in himself and of his powers possess, and in whose joint establishment he can only *take a share* when it is brought him by the individual powers of another. Through this unnatural eagerness of the Musician to satisfy his vanity, namely to exhibit his possessions (*Vermögen*) in the dazzling light of a measureless capacity, he has reduced these possessions—ample enough, in all truth—to that beggarly array in which the Meyerbeerian opera-music now appears. In her self-seeking endeavour to force her narrow forms upon the Drama as of sole validity, this Opera-music has exposed their wretched stiffness and unyieldingness, till

they have grown past any bearing with. In her mania for
seeming rich and many-sided, she has sunk, as a musical
art, to the utmost spiritual penury, been driven to borrow-
ing from the most material Mechanism. In her egoistic
feint of affording an exhaustive dramatic Characteristique
by sheerly musical means, she has ended by losing all
power of natural Expression, and won instead the doubtful
honours of a contortionist and mountebank.—

As I said at the beginning, that the *error* in the Operatic
art-genre consisted in " that a Means of expression (Music)
had been made the end, while the End of expression (the
Drama) had been made a means,"—so the heart of the
illusion, and finally of that *madness* which has exposed the
Operatic art-genre in its rankest un-naturalness to the
ridicule of all, we must thus denote:

**that this means of Expression wanted of itself
to prescribe the aim of Drama.**

VII.

E have reached the end;—for we have followed Music's powers in Opera to the proclamation of her utter impotence.

When to-day we talk of Opera-music, in any stricter sense, we speak no longer of an Art, but of a mere article of Fashion. Only the Critic, who feels no stir of artistic necessity within him, can still expound his hopes or fears about the future of Opera. The Artist—provided he does not degrade himself into a speculator on the Public—shews by the very fact of his seeking for outlets aside from Opera, and particularly his soliciting the energetic participation of the Poet, that he takes the Opera itself for dead already.

But here, in this to-be-solicited *participation of the Poet*, do we touch the point as to which we must reach a conscious clearness, bright as day, if we want to grasp and set fast in its genuine, its healthy naturalness the relation between Musician and Poet. This relation must be one completely opposite to that wonted heretofore, so entirely changed that, for his own welfare, the Musician will only settle down to it when he dismisses every memory of the old unnatural union, whose last-remaining bond could but draw him back into the old unfruitful madness.

In order to get the clearest notion of this sane and only salutary relation that is to come, we must once more denote *the nature of our present music,* in brief but definite terms.—

We shall quickest reach a lucid survey, if we tersely sum up Music's nature in the concept, *Melody.*

As the inner is both ground and conditionment of the outer, but in the outer comes the inner first to plain and

definite show, so are *Harmony* and *Rhythm* indeed the
shaping organs, but *Melody* the first real Shape of music.
Harmony and Rhythm are the blood, flesh, nerves and
bones, with all the entrails, and like these, when we look
upon the finished, living man, stay closed against the
gazing eye; Melody, on the other hand, is this finished
Man himself, just how he shews his body to our eye. In
gazing on this man we view alone the supple shape, as
expressed in the form-giving demarcations of the outward
skin ; we linger on the most expressive aspect of this
shape, in the features of his face; and finally we pause
before the eye, the most life-full and communicative utterance of the whole man : who through this organ—which,
in its turn, obtains its power-of-imparting solely from its
quite universal faculty for taking up the utterances of the
surrounding world—at once reveals the most convincingly
his inner soul. So is Melody the most perfect expression
of the inner being of Music, and every true melody, conditioned by this inmost being, speaks also through that
eye to us ; that eye which most expressively imparts to us
this Inmost, but always so that we see alone the flashing
of the pupil, and not the inner, in itself still formless
organism in all its nakedness.

    When the *Folk* invented melodies, it proceeded like the
natural bodily-man, who, by the instinctive exercise of
sexual functions, begets and brings forth Man; this
finished Man, arrived at light of day, reveals himself at
once by his outer stature : not first, forsooth, by his hidden
inner organism. *Greek Art* still apprehended this Man
by his outer stature alone, and strove to mould his faithful, lifelike counterfeit—at last in bronze and marble.
Christianity, on the contrary, proceeded anatomically :
it wanted to find man's *soul ;* it opened and cut up
his body, and bared all that formless inner organism at
which our gaze rebelled, because it neither is nor should
be set there for the eye.* In searching for the soul, how-

* We here have a curious hint of Wagner's subsequent attitude toward
Vivisection.—TR.

ever, we had slain the body; in hunting for the source of
Life we had destroyed its utterance, and thus arrived at
nothing but dead entrails, which only in completely unbroken faculty of utterance could be at all conditionments
of Life. But the searched-for *soul*, in truth, is nothing
other than *the life:* wherefore what remained over, for
Christian anatomy to look upon, was only—*Death.*

Christianity had choked the organic impulse of the
Folk's artistic life, its natural force of procreation: it had
hacked into its flesh, and with dualistic scissors had
played havoc with even its artistic organism. Community,
in which alone the Folk's artistic force of procreation can
mount to the full power of perfect art-creation, belonged
to Catholicism: only in solitude, where fractions of the
Folk—far distant from the highways of associate life—
found themselves alone with Nature and each other, was
there preserved in its childlike simpleness and straitened
indigence the *Folkslied*, so indivorcibly ingrown with
Poetry.

If for the moment we turn aside from this, we see Music
taking in the realm of cultured-art an amazing new development: from its anatomically disjoined, its inwardly
slaughtered organism, we see it making for a new life-
evolution by piecing together its severed organs and allowing them to freshly coalesce.—In the Christian Church-song
Harmony had independently matured itself. Its natural
life-need now drove it of necessity to utterance as Melody;
for that utterance, however, it could not dispense with the
hold on form and movement given by the organ of Rhythm;
and this it took, as an arbitrary, more fancied than actual
standard, from Dance. The new union could only be an
artificial one. Just as Poetry had been constructed by the
rules which Aristotle had abstracted from the tragic poets,
so must Music be dressed by scientific canons and assumptions. This was at the time when *men*, in sooth, were to
be made by scholarly recipes, and from chemical decoctions.
Such a Man did bookish music endeavour to construct:
Mechanism was to set up *Organism*, or else replace it.

But, in truth, the restless mainspring of this mechanical inventiveness drove ever toward the genuine Man, the man who was to be re-erected from out the *Concept*, and thus was finally to wake to real organic life.—We here impinge upon the whole vast course of modern manhood's evolution !—

But the man whom Music wished to erect, was really none other than *Melody*, i.e., the moment of most definite, most convincing utterance of her actual living, inner organism. The farther Music evolved, in this necessary longing to become a human being, the more decisively do we see the struggle for a plain melodic message wax into a positively painful yearning ; and in the works of no musician do we see this yearning grow to such a stress and power, as in the great Instrumental works of *Beethoven*. In these we marvel at the gigantic efforts of Mechanism longing to become a Man ; efforts to resolve its every component part into the flesh and blood of an actual living organism, and through that to reach an unerring utterance as Melody.

In this respect, the characteristic, decisive course of our whole art-evolution shows out with Beethoven by far more genuinely than with our Opera-composers. These apprehended Melody as something lying outside the realm of their art-production, as something ready-made ; Melody, in whose organic generation they had taken absolutely no part, they snatched from the mouth of the Folk, thus tearing it loose from its Organism, and *applied* it just according to their wayward whim, without ever being able to justify it by anything but their own luxurious pleasure. If that Folk's-melody was the outward Shape of man, then in a sense the Opera-composers stripped this man of his skin and covered therewith a puppet, as though to give it a human look : but with it they could only dupe at most the civilised savages of our purblind opera-public.

With Beethoven, on the contrary, we perceive the natural thrust of Life, to breed Melody from out music's inner Organism. In his weightiest works, he by no means posits Melody as something ready in advance, but in a measure lets it *be born* from Music's organs before our very eyes ; he

inducts us into this act of bearing, inasmuch as he sets it
before us in all its organic Necessity. But his most decisive
message, at last given us by the master in his *magnum opus*,
is the necessity he felt *as Musician* to throw himself into
the arms of the Poet, in order to compass the act of *begetting* the true, the unfailingly real and redeeming Melody.
To become a *human being*, Beethoven perforce must become
an entire, i.e. a social (*gemeinsamer*) being, subjected to the
generic conditionments of *the manly and the womanly*.—
What an earnest, deep and yearning brooding unveiled at
last to the endless-gifted master the limpid melody wherewith he broke into the Poet's words : " Joy, thou fairest
spark of Godhead ! " (" *Freude, schöner Götterfunken !* ").—
With this Melody is solved withal the mystery of Music :
we *know* now, we have won the faculty, to be *with consciousness* organically-working artists.—

Let us linger now beside the weightiest point of our
investigation, and let us take the " *Freude* "-melody of
Beethoven for guide.—

The *Folk'smelody*, at its rediscovery on the part of Culture-
musicians, afforded us a twofold interest : that of joy in its
native beauty, where we met it undisfigured in the Folk,
and that of inquiry into its inner organism. The joy in it,
speaking accurately, was bound to stay unfruitful for our
art-production ; to imitate the form and content of this
melody too, with any success, we should have had to restrict
our movements within an art-variety similar to the *Folkslied*
itself ; nay, we should ourselves have had to be Folk-artists
in the strictest sense, in order to win the faculty for such
an imitation. We should thus have had—intrinsically—not
to imitate it at all, but as Folk ourselves, to invent it.

In bondage to another sort of art-procedure—differing by
all the breadth of heaven from that of the Folk—we could
at best apply this melody in the crudest sense, and that
amid surroundings and conditions which must necessarily
disfigure it. At bottom, the history of Operatic Music goes
always back to the history of this melody alone ; a history in
which according to certain laws like those of ebb and flow,

the periods of taking up and re-taking up the Folksmelody alternate with periods of advancing and finally overwhelming corruption and disfigurement thereof.—Those musicians who became the most painfully conscious of this evil attribute of the Folksmelody, when converted into Operatic Aria, saw themselves therefore driven with more or less plainly felt necessity to take thought for the organic Begettal of Melody itself. The Opera-composer stood the nearest to the discovery of the needful process ; yet with *him*, of all others, it must inevitably fail, because he stood in an utterly false relation to the only fructifying element, that of Poetry; because, in his unnatural and usurpatorial attitude, he had in a measure robbed that element of its begetting organs. In his distorted attitude towards the Poet the Composer might try his hardest, but wherever the Feeling soared to the height of a melodic outpour he must bring with him his ready-made melody, because the Poet had *à priori* to adapt himself to the entire *form* in which that melody was to declare itself : this Form, moreover, had so imperious an influence over the shaping of the opera-melody, that in truth it prescribed its substantial Content as well.

This Form was taken from the *Folkslied*-tune ; its outermost shape, the change and reiteration of movement in rhythmic time-measures, was even borrowed from the Dance-tune,—which latter, however, was originally one and the same thing as the Song-tune. This Form was merely varied in, but has itself remained the irremovable scaffold of the Opera-aria right down to the present day. Within it alone, was a melodic structure thinkable ; and naturally, this stayed always such a structure as was strictly governed by that scaffold in advance. The musician, seeing that once he stepped within this Form he could no longer invent but merely vary, was robbed in advance of all power for the organic generation of Melody ; for true Melody is, as we have seen, itself the utterance of an inner organism ; to arise organically, therefore, it must have *shaped for itself its very Form*, and a form entirely adequate to explicitly convey its inner essence. On the other hand, the melody that was constructed from the Form, could never be anything but an imitation of the pristine melody which had first spoken in that selfsame form.* With many opera-composers we therefore see an endeavour to break this Form : yet such an attempt could only have proved artistically successful, provided suitable new forms were found. Yet again, the new Form could only have been a genuine art-form, provided it shewed itself as the explicit utterance of a specific musical Organism : *but every musical organism is by its nature—a womanly ;* it is merely a *bearing,* and not a *begetting* factor ; the begetting-force lies clean *outside it,* and without fecundation by this force it positively cannot bear.—Here lies the whole secret of the barrenness of modern music !

We have denoted Beethoven's artistic procedure in his weightiest Instrumental works as "our induction into the act of bearing Melody." Let us keep well in view this characteristic fact, however, that though *only in the progress* of his tone-piece, does the master set his full melody before us as a finished whole, yet this melody is to be subsumed as already finished in the artist's mind *from the beginning.* He merely broke at the outset the narrow Form,—that very Form against which the opera-composer had striven in vain,—he shattered it into its component parts, in order to unite them by organic creation into a new whole ; and this he did, by setting the component parts of different melodies in changeful contact with each other, as though to show the organic affinity of the seemingly most diverse of such parts, and therewith the prime affinity of those different

* The Opera-composer, who saw himself condemned in the Aria-form to an eternal barrenness, sought a field for freer movement of his musical-expression, and sought it in *Recitative.* Only, this also was a settled form ; and if the musician quitted that sheer rhetorical expression which is proper to Recitative, in order to let bloom the flower of keener feeling, he found the admission of Melody driving him back into the Aria-form. If, therefore, he avoided the Aria-form on principle, he could only stay glued to the sheer rhetoric of Recitative, without ever soaring up to Melody; except—mark well !—where with noble self-oblivion he took into himself the Poet's fertilising seed.—R. WAGNER.

melodies themselves. Beethoven but discloses to us here
the inner organism of Absolute Music : his concern was, in
a sense, to restore this organism from its mechanical state
(*diesen Organismus aus der Mechanik herzustellen*), to vindicate its inner life, and to show it at its livingest in the very
act of Bearing. But what he employed to fertilise this
organism, was still the Absolute Melody ; he thus put life
into this organism only so far as he *practised it in Bearing*
—so to say—and indeed, let it *re*-bear an already finished
melody. Precisely through that process, however, he found
himself driven on to supply this musical organism, now
freshly quickened into bearing-power, with the fecundating
seed as well ; and this he took from the Poet's power of
begetting. Far as he was from any æsthetic experimenting,
yet Beethoven, here taking up unconsciously the spirit of
our whole artistic evolution, could not go to work otherwise
than speculatively, in a certain sense. He himself had by
no means been spurred to instinctive creation by the begetting Thought of a Poet, but in his desire for Music-
bearing he had looked around him for the Poet. Thus
even his "*Freude*"-melody does not as yet appear invented
for, or through, the Poet's verse, but merely conceived with
an eye to Schiller's poem after an incitation by its general
contents. First where, in the progress of this poem, Beethoven is worked-up by its contents into a dramatic directness,* do we see his melodic combinations springing ever
more definitely from the diction also ; so that at last the
unprecedented many-sidedness of his music's Expression
answers to the highest sense, at any rate, both of the poem
and its wording ; and with such directness, that the music,
once divorced from the poem, would appear to us no longer
thinkable or comprehensible.

This is the point where we see the results of our æsthetic
inquiry into the organism of the *Volkslied* confirmed with
startling plainness by an artistic Deed. Just as the living

---

* I may direct especial notice to the "Seid umschlungen Millionen !" and
the union of that theme with the "Freude, schöner Götterfunken !", in order
to make my meaning plain.—R. WAGNER.

Folk's-melody is inseparable from the living Folk's-poem, at pain of organic death, so can Music's organism never bear the true, the living Melody, except it first be fecundated by the Poet's Thought. Music is the bearing woman, the Poet the begetter; and Mùsic had therefore reached the pinnacle of madness, when she wanted, not only to bear, but also to *beget.*

Music is a woman.

The nature of Woman is *love:* but this love is a *receiving* (empfangende), and in receival (*Empfängniss*) an unreservedly *surrendering,* love.

Woman first gains her full individuality in the moment of surrender. She is the Undine who glides soulless through the waves of her native element, till she receives her soul through love of a man. The look of innocence in a woman's eye is the endlessly pellucid mirror in which the man can only see the general faculty for love, till he is able to see in it the likeness of himself. When he has recognised himself therein, then also is the woman's all-faculty condensed into one strenuous necessity, to love him with the all-dominant fervour of full surrender.

The true woman loves unconditionally, because she *must.* She has no choice, excepting where she does not love. But where she must love, there she experiences a vast *constraint* (Zwang), which withal develops for the first time her *Will.** This Will, which rebels against that constraint, is the first and mightiest stirring (*Regung*) of the individuality of the beloved object; and, taken up by sympathy into the woman, it is that individuality which has gifted her with Will and Individuality.† This is the honourable *pride* (Stolz) of woman, a pride that comes solely from the force of the

---

* Here again we have an interesting, and unconscious, coincidence with the philosophy of Schopenhauer.—Tr.

† "Dieser Wille, der sich gegen den Zwang auflehnt, ist die erste und mächtigste Regung der Individualität des geliebten Gegenstandes, die, durch das Empfängniss in das Weib gedrungen, es selbst mit Individualität und Willen begabt hat."

individuality that has won her and constrains her with all
the exigence (*Noth*) of Love. For sake of the cherished
boon she strives against the constraint of Love itself, until,
beneath the all-dominance of this constraint, she learns
that both it and her own pride are but the energising of
the individuality which she has taken up ; that Love and
the beloved object are one, that without them she has
neither force nor will, that from the instant when she first
felt pride she was already conquered (*vernichtet*). The
plain avowal of this conquest is then the effective offering
of woman's last surrender : her pride ascends with consciousness into that only thing which she can sense, can
feel, can think—nay, what she *is*,—into love for *this one*
man.—

A woman who loves not with this pride of surrender,
truly does not love at all. But a woman who does not love
at all, is the most odious, most unworthy spectacle in the
world. Let us adduce the characteristic types of such
ladies !

Some one has very appropriately called the modern
Italian opera-music a *wanton*. A courtezan may pride
herself on always remaining her self ; she never steps outside herself, never sacrifices herself but when she wishes for
either pleasure or profit in return, and in this case she only
offers to the joys of others that portion of her being which
she can lightly enough dispose of, since it has become an
object of her own caprice. In the embraces of the courtezan
the Woman is never present, but only a portion of her
physical organism : from love she reaps no individuality,
but gives herself in general to the general world. Thus
the wanton is an undeveloped, wasted woman : yet she at
least fulfils the physical functions of the female sex, by
which we can still—albeit with regret—detect the Woman
in her.

French opera-music passes rightly for a *coquette*. The
coquette adores to be admired, nay even loved : but her
peculiar joy at being admired and loved she can only taste,
providing she herself be snared by neither love nor admira-

tion for the object she inspires with each.   The profit she seeks is delight in herself, satisfaction of her vanity : the whole enjoyment of her life lies in being admired and loved ; and this would be instantly disturbed, were she herself to feel either love or admiration for another.   Were she in love, she would be robbed of her self-enjoyment ; for in Love she must necessarily forget herself, and make surrender to the distressful, often suicidal enjoyment of another.   From nothing, therefore, does the coquette so guard herself, as from Love, in order to preserve untouched the only thing she loves—to wit her Self; that being which yet gains its force of tempting, its practised individuality, from the love-approach of Man alone ; from whom the coquette thus withholds his own possession.   Wherefore the coquette loves from thievish Egoism, and her vital force is icy coldness.   In *her* the nature of Woman is perverted to its odious opposite ; from her chilling smile, which only mirrors back our broken likeness, we turn mayhap, in desperation, to the Italian wanton.

But there is still another type of unsexed dames, a type that fills us with the utmost horror : this is the *prude*, as which the so-called " German "* opera-music must pass for us.—It *may* happen to the courtezan, that the caresses of some ardent youth shall suddenly awake in her the sacrificial glow of Love,—as witness the God and the Bayadere!—; it may fall out that the coquette, who is always playing at love, shall one day find herself the victim of this game, and caught, for all the battlings of her vanity, in a net where she now bewails with tears the losing of her will.   But never will this beauteous human lot befall the

---

* By " German " Opera I naturally do not mean the Opera of Weber, but that modern phantasm of which people speak the more, the less is it really forthcoming,—just like the " German Realm " (*das " deutsche Reich "*).   The speciality of this Opera consists in its being a laboured fabrication of the modern German composers who do not arrive at setting French or Italian texts—the only thing that hinders them from writing French or Italian operas, but which affords them, in return, the proud consolation of bringing something quite specific and select to light, since they *understand Music so much better* than the Italians or the French.—R. WAGNER.

woman who guards her spotlessness with the fanaticism of
orthodox belief,—the woman whose virtue consists in
lovelessness on principle. The prude has been brought up
in all the regulations of decorum, and from earliest youth
has heard the word "love" pronounced with a flutter of
uneasiness. Her heart filled with Dogma, she steps into
the world, looks coyly round her, perceives the courtezan
and the coquette, smites her pious breast, and cries : "I
thank thee, Lord, that I am not as these!"—Her life-
force is Decorum, her only will the denial of love, which
she knows no else than in the likeness of the courtezan
and the coquette. Her virtue is the avoiding of crime, her
works unfruitfulness, her soul the pride of insolence.—And
yet how near is this woman, of all others, to the most disgusting fall! In her bigoted heart there stirs no love, but
in her ambushed flesh a vulgar lust. We know the
conventicles of the self-righteous, the respectable towns
where bloomed the flower of the "saints"!* We have
seen the prude fall headlong into all the vices of her
French and Italian sisters,—only, still further tainted by
the arch-vice of hypocrisy, and alas without one glimmer
of originality !—

Let us turn from this revolting sight, and ask: What
kind of woman must *true music* be ?

A woman *who really loves*, who sets her virtue in her
pride, her pride, however, in her *sacrifice ;* that sacrifice
whereby she surrenders, not *one portion* of her being, but
her whole being in the amplest fulness of its faculty—when

---

* "Muckerei."—It will be remembered that Wagner was Music-director at
the theatre of Königsberg (Prussia) in the year 1836. Now, it so happened that
in 1835 there had been commenced a legal prosecution of the "Muckers," the
trial continuing till 1842. This sect had been founded by J. W. Ebel, a follower
of the theosophist, J. H. Schönherr, and included many dames of high degree.
The "Muckers" (I believe the title was a nickname) were accused of immoral
practices carried on under the cloak of religion, and the trial ended by Ebel's
removal from his post. After his death in 1861, however—i.e. ten years after
the writing of *Oper und Drama*—an independent examination of the evidence
went to show that these accusations were unfounded, and that the trial had
been conducted with gross injustice.—See *Meyer's Konversations-Lexikon.*—
TR.

she *conceives*. But in joy and gladness to *bear* the thing conceived, this is *the deed* of Woman,—and to work deeds the woman only needs *to be entirely what she is*, but in no way *to will* something : for she can will but one thing—*to be a woman !* To man, therefore, woman is the ever clear and cognisable measure of natural infallibility, (*Untrüglichkeit*), for she is at her perfectest when she never quits the sphere of beautiful Instinctiveness (*Un-willkürlichkeit*), to which she is banned by that which alone can bless her being,—by the Necessity of Love.

And here, again, I point you to the glorious musician in whom Music was all that in a human being she ever can be, if in all the fulness of her essence she is to stay precisely *music* and nothing else but music. Look on *Mozart !*—Was he haply a lesser musician because he was Musician out-and-out, because he could not, would not, be anything other than *Musician ?* Take his "Don Juan"! Where else has music won so infinitely rich an Individuality, been able to characterise so surely, so definitely, and in such plenteous fill as here,—where the Musician, by the very nature of his art, was in no whit other than an unconditionally-loving Woman ?

—Yet, let us halt, and precisely here, to put ourselves the searching question : *Who* then must be *the Man*, whom this Woman is to love so unreservedly ? Before we give away this woman's love, let us well ponder whether the counter-love of the Man is something haply to be got by begging, or something that he also *needs* for his redemption.

Let us closely view *the Poet !*

SECOND PART.

THE PLAY AND THE NATURE OF DRAMATIC POETRY.

(DAS SCHAUSPIEL UND DAS WESEN
DER
DRAMATISCHEN DICHTKUNST.)

In Letters to Uhlig *No.* 21, *dated " Beginning of February '51," Wagner writes : " Herewith you receive the second part. The third will, I think, follow in a fortnight. . . . Kolatschek offered of his own accord to open negotiations with the publisher of the* Deutsche Monatsschrift *(now Kühtmann at Bremen) respecting my book. I accepted, so as in any case to have a choice. If I came to an understanding with Kühtmann, some sections of the book would first have to appear as special articles in the* Monatsschrift. *. . . In the accompanying manuscript you will find three articles already marked with pencil."—Kolatschek was the editor of the* Monatsschrift, *a literary and scientific monthly, which flourished for little more than a twelvemonth.*

Though Kühtmann did not become the publisher of Oper und Drama, *arrangements being finally concluded with J. J. Weber of Leipzig, early in May* 1851, *yet the three articles duly appeared in the* Monatsschrift; *the first in the March number, and the second and third in that for May '51. My footnotes to the text of this Second Part will indicate the passages selected, &c.*

Translator's Note.

HEN LESSING laboured in his "Laocöon" to discover and map out the bounds of Poetry and Painting, he had in his eye that poetry which was already mere description (*Schilderei*). He starts from lines of comparison and demarcation which he draws between the plastic group portraying the scene of Laocöon's death-struggle, and that description of the same scene as sketched by Virgil in his "Æneid," an epos written for dumb reading. Though in the course of his inquiry Lessing touches on Sophocles, again he has only in mind the literary Sophocles, such as alone exists *for us ;* or, if he takes into his purview the poet's Tragic Artwork in all its life of actual performance, he instinctively places it outside any comparison with the works of Sculpture or Painting : since not the living Tragic Artwork is bounded as against these plastic arts, but *these,* compared with *that,* find in their straitened natures their necessary bounds. Wherever Lessing sets up limits and boundaries for Poetry, he does not mean the *dramatic Artwork* directly brought before the senses by physical performance, that Artwork which sums in itself each factor of the plastic arts, in highest potence such as it alone can reach, and by its power has first brought to these their higher potentiality of artistic life ; but he means the exiguous phantom of this Artwork, the narrating, depicting, literary poem, appealing to the imagination and not the senses—the form in which that force of imagination has been turned into the virtual performer, toward which the poem merely acts as stimulus.

Such an *artificial* art, 'tis true, can only produce an effect at all by the exactest observance of boundaries and limits, since she must be ever on her watch to guard the unlimited force of imagination—which has here to play the performer's

rôle *in place of her*—from any bewildering digression, and
thus to guide it to the one fixed point at which she can
display her purposed object as definitely and distinctly as
possible. But it is to the force of imagination alone, that
all the egoistically severed arts address themselves; and
especially the Plastic art, which can only bring into play
the weightiest moment of Art, namely *motion*, by appealing
to the Phantasy. All these arts *merely suggest* : an *actual
representation* would to them be possible only could they
parley with the universality of man's artistic receptivity,
could they address his entire sentient (*sinnlichen*) organism,
and not his force of imagination ; for the true Artwork can
only be engendered by an advance from imagination into
actuality, i.e. physicality (*Sinnlichkeit*).

Lessing's honest endeavour to map out the boundaries
of those severed art-varieties, which can no longer directly
represent but merely figure (*schildern*), is foolishly misunderstood to-day by those to whom the huge difference
between those *arts* and the *one veritable Art* remains a thing
incomprehensible. Inasmuch as they keep before their eye
these separate art-varieties alone, all powerless in themselves for a direct impersonation, they naturally can only
assign to each of these arts—and thus (as they must deem)
to Art in general—the task of overcoming *with as little
disturbance as possible* the difficulty of giving the force of
imagination a firm leverage in their *figuring*. To *heap
the means* of this their figuring, can only confuse the Figuring itself—with which I quite agree,—and by distressing or
distracting the Phantasy through the presentation of dis-
parate means, can only turn it from a full grasp of the
object.

Purity of the art-variety is therefore the first requisite
for its comprehensibility, whereas an *alloy* (Mischung) from
other art-varieties can only foul this comprehensibility.
In fact we can imagine nothing more bewildering, than if
the Painter, for instance, should want to show his subject
in motion such as can be depicted by the Poet alone; the

acme of repulsiveness, however, we find in a painting where
the poet's verses are written as issuing from some person's
mouth.   When the Musician—i.e. the absolute musician—
attempts to paint, he brings-about neither music nor a
painting; but if he wanted to accompany with his music
the inspection of an actual painting, then he might be quite
sure that no one would understand either the painting or
his music.   He who can only conceive the combination of
all the arts into the Artwork as though one meant, for example, that in a picture-gallery and amidst a row of statues
a romance of Goethe's should be read aloud while a
symphony of Beethoven's was being played,* such a man
does rightly enough to insist upon the *severance* of the arts,
and to wish each unit left to help itself to the plainest
possible depicting of its subject in its own way.   But, that
our modern æstheticians [orig. ed. " State-æstheticians "]
should rank *the Drama* also as an art-*variety*, and as such
assign it to the Poet for his special property, in the sense
that the blending with it of another art, like that of Music,
would need *apology* but could by no means gain acquittal
—this is to draw from Lessing's definition a conclusion for
which there is not one trace of support in the original.
These people, however, see in Drama nothing but a *branch of
literature*, a species of poesy such as the romance or didactic
poem; only with this difference, that, instead of being merely
read, it is to be learnt by rote by several persons, declaimed,
accompanied with gestures, and lit up by the footlights.
To be sure, to the stage-performance of a literary-drama its
musical embellishment would bear almost the same relation as though it were executed in presence of an easel-ed
painting, and therefore the so-called Melodrama has been
branded as a genre of most pernicious medley.   But this

* This is really how certain childish-clever litterateurs [orig. ed. "Court-
litterateurs "] conceive what I have denoted "the united artwork," when
they think necessary to regard it as a "chaotic jumbling" of all the arts.
Moreover a Saxon critic sees good to treat my appeal to *Sinnlichkeit* as gross
"sensualism," whereby he naturally wishes to convey the 'lusts of the belly.'
—One can only explain the imbecility of these æsthetes, by their deliberate
mendacity.—R. WAGNER.

drama, the only one our literarians have in mind, is just as little a true Drama as a *clavichord* * is an orchestra, to say nothing of a troupe of singers. The literary drama owes its origin to the same egoistic spirit of our general art-development as does the clavichord, and by the latter will I endeavour to make plain this course in brief.

The oldest, truest, most beautiful organ of music, the organ to which alone our music owes its being, is the *human voice*. The most naturally was it counterfeited by the *wind-instrument*, and this again by the *stringed instrument :* the symphonic concord of an orchestra of wind and strings, again, was counterfeited by the *Organ ;* the unweildy Organ, in its turn, was replaced by the handy clavichord. The most noticeable thing in this march of events, from the primal organ of the human voice to the clavichord, is the sinking of music to an ever greater lack of Expression. The instruments of the orchestra, though they had already lost the articulations (*Sprachlaut*) of the human voice, were still able to sufficiently counterfeit the human tone, in its endless variety and lively alternation of expressional power ; the organ-pipes could only retain this tone in respect of its Time-duration, but no longer of its changeable Expression ; till at last the clavichord merely hinted at this tone itself, and left its actual body to be thoughtout by the ear's imagination. Thus in the clavichord we have an instrument which does nothing more than *delineate* music.

But how came it, that the musician finally contented himself with a toneless instrument ? From no other ground than a desire to make music for himself *alone*, without any mutual aid from others. The human voice, which intrinsically requires the use of Speech, to pronounce itself melodically, is *an individual ;* only the concurrence of several such

---

* A violin played to the pianoforte blends as little with the latter instrument, as would music played to a literary-drama.—R. WAGNER.—In this connection I have preferred, in the body of the text, the word "clavichord" (for "*Klavier*"), as the modern "pianoforte" would be an anachronism in the following paragraph ; whereas the older term is general enough to cover the whole ground, both ancient and modern.—TR.

individuals, can produce symphonic harmony. The wind and stringed instruments stood near the human voice in this degree, that they alike retained that individual character, whereby each of them possessed a definite, however richly modulable a colour, and for the production of harmonic effects they were likewise forced to work together. In the Christian Organ all these living individualities were already ranged into a register of dead pipes, which raised their mechanical voices to the glory of God at the masterful key-tread of the one and indivisible performer. On the clavichord at last the virtuoso, without so much as the help of another (the organ-player had still required a bellows-blower), could set a multitude of hammers a-clattering to his private glory; for the hearer, deprived of all delight from music's *tone*, was only left the entertainment * of bewondering the keyboard-hitter's skill. —Assuredly, our whole Modern Art is like the clavichord : in it each unit does the work of a community, but alas! in bare *abstracto* and with an utter dearth of tone. Hammers —but no Men!—

From the standpoint of the clavichord † let us follow back the Literary-drama, whose doors our æsthetes bar with such puritanic pride against the noble breath of Music; let us follow it back to the origin of this clavichord—and what do we find ? We find at last the living *tone of human speech*, which is one and the same with *the singing tone*, and without which we should have known neither clavichord nor Literary-drama.

* Our author has here made a tiny variation from the original edition, by substituting "*Beachtung*" for "*Amüsement*," evidently in his scrupulous care to avoid non-German words wherever possible.—TR.

† To me it is truly not without significance, that the very pianoforte-player who in modern days has shewn us the highest summit of virtuosodom, in every aspect, that the wonder-worker of the pianoforte, *Liszt*, is at present turning with such momentous energy to the sounding (*tönende*) orchestra, and, as it were *through* this orchestra, to the living human voice itself.—R. WAGNER.

HE MODERN DRAMA has a twofold origin : the one a natural, and peculiar to our historic evolution, namely *the Romance*,—the other an alien, and grafted on our evolution by reflection, namely the *Greek Drama* as looked at through the misunderstood rules of Aristotle.

The real kernel of all our poesy may be found in the Romance. In their endeavour to make this kernel as tasty as possible, our poets have repeatedly had recourse to a closer or more distant imitation of the Greek Drama.—

The topmost flower of that Drama which sprang directly from Romance, we have in the plays of *Shakespeare ;* in the farthest removal from this Drama, we find its diametrical opposite in the " Tragédie " of *Racine.* Between these two extremes our whole remaining dramatic literature sways undecided to and fro. In order to apprehend the exact character of this wavering, we must look a little closer into the natural origin of our Drama.

———

Searching the history of the world, since the decay of Grecian art, for an artistic period of which we may justly feel proud, we find that period in the so-called " Renaissance," a name we give to the termination of the Middle Ages and the commencement of a new era. Here the inner man is struggling, with a veritable giant's force, to utter himself. The whole ferment of that wondrous mixture, of Germanic individual Hero-dom with the spirit of Roman-

---

* This chapter, with the exception of its last paragraph but one, formed the first of the " three articles" mentioned in Wagner's letter of February '51 to Uhlig. It appeared in the March number of the *Deutsche Monatsschrift* for that year, under the title " Ueber moderne dramatische Dichtkunst," and with a footnote to the effect that it was "from a larger work by the author, presently to appear."

Catholicising Christendom, is thrusting from within outwards, as though in the externalising of its essence to rid itself of indissoluble inner scruples. Everywhere this thrust evinced itself as a passion for delineation of surface (*Schilderung*), and nothing more; for no man can give himself implicitly and wholly, unless he be at one within. But this the artist of the Renaissance was not; he only seized the outer surface, to flee from his inner discord. Though this bent proclaimed itself most palpably in the direction of the *plastic arts*, yet it is no less visible in *poetry*. Only, we must bear in mind that, whereas Painting had addressed itself to a faithful delineation of the living man, Poetry was already turning from this mere delineation to his *representment* (Darstellung), and that by stepping forward from Romance to Drama.

The poetry of the Middle Ages had already brought forth the Narrative poem and developed it to its highest pitch. This poem described men's doings and undergoings, and their sum of moving incident, in much the same way as the painter bestirred himself to present the characteristic moments of such actions. But the field of the poet who waived all living, direct portrayal of his Action by real men, was as unbounded as his reader's or hearer's force of imagination, to which alone he appealed. In this field he felt the more tempted into extravagant combinations of incidents and localities, as his vision embraced an ever wider horizon of outward actions going on around him, of actions born from the very spirit of that adventurous age. Man, at variance with himself, and seeking in art-production a refuge from his inward strife—just as he had earlier sought in vain to heal this strife itself by means of art *—felt no urgence to speak out a definite *something* of his inner being, but rather to go a-hunting for this Something in the world outside. In a sense he dissipated his inner thoughts, by an altogether wayward dealing with everything brought him from the outer world; and the more motley he could make his mixture of these diverse shows, the surer might he hope

* We need only recall the genuine Christian poetry.—R. WAGNER.

to reach his instinctive goal, of inward dissipation. The master of this charming art, but reft of any inwardness, of any hold on soul,—was *Ariosto.*

But the less these shimmering pictures of Phantasy were able, after many a monstrous divagation, to distract in turn the inner man ; and the more this man, beneath the weight of political and religious deeds of violence, found himself driven by his inner nature to an energetic counter-thrust: so much the plainer, in the class of poetry now under notice, do we see his struggle to become master of the multifarious stuff from within outwards, to give his fashionings a firm-set centre, and to take this centre, this axis of his art-work, from his own beholdings,* from his firm-set will-ing of Something in which his inner being may speak out. This Something is the matrix of the newer age, the condensing † of the individual essence to a definite artistic Will. From the vast mass of outward matters, which theretofore could never shew themselves diversified enough to please the poet, the component parts are sorted into groups akin ; the multiple points of action are condensed into a definite character-drawing of the transactors. Of what unspeakable weight it is, for any inquiry into the nature of Art, that this inner urgence of the Poet, such as we may see before our very eyes, could at last content itself with nothing but reaching the plainest utterance through direct portrayal to the senses : in one word, *that the romance became a drama !* This mastery of the outward stuff, so as to shew the inner view of the essence of that stuff, could only be brought to a successful issue by setting the subject itself before the senses in all

---

* "Aus der eigenen Anschauung." In this *Lebensanschauung,* which we shall meet often enough in the following pages, we have a good old German compound, current for God knows how long, and in "view of life" an equally ancient English term, both of which cover the whole ground—and more—of the much-vaunted "criticism of life" which Matthew Arnold and his disciples have run to death.—Tr.

† *Verdichtung* again, as the essence of *Dichtung* (poetry)—see footnote to Vol. I., p. 92, &c.—Tr.

the persuasiveness of actuality; and this was to be achieved in Drama and nothing else.

With fullest necessity did *Shakespeare's Drama* spring from Life and our historic evolution : his creation was just as much conditioned by the nature of our poetic art as the Drama of the Future, in strict keeping with its nature, will be born from the satisfaction of a need which Shakespearian Drama has aroused but not yet stilled.

Shakespeare—of whom we here must always think as in company with his forerunners, and only as their chief— condensed the narrative Romance into the Drama, inasmuch as he translated it, so to say, for performance on the stage.   Human actions, erewhile merely figured by the narrative talk of poesy, he now gave to actual talking men to bring before both eye and ear,—to men who, so long as the performance lasted, identified themselves in look and bearing with the to-be-represented persons of the romance. For this he found a stage and actors, who till then had hidden from the Poet's eye,—like a subterranean stream of genuine Folk's-artwork, flowing secretly, yet flowing ever, —but, now that Want compelled him to their finding, were discovered swiftly by his yearning gaze.   The characteristic of this Folk-stage, however, lay in that the *mummers* * addressed themselves *to the eye*, and intentionally, almost solely to the eye ; whence their distinctive name.   Their performances, being given in open places before a wide-stretched throng, could produce effect by almost nothing but gesture ; and by gesture only actions can be rendered *plainly*, but not—if speech is lacking—the inner motives of such actions : so that the Play of these performers, by its very nature, bristled with just as grotesque and wholesale

* "*Schau*spieler"—to lay stress on the "*Schau*" (Show), as Wagner has done by this mode of printing the word, I can find no better term than "mummers," which at least conveys the idea in a negative fashion ("mum"). We have kept the idea in "Showman," but whereas the Germans have retained the old expression with a new meaning, we have borrowed our "actors" from the Latin.   In this sentence our author also employs the compound "Folksschaubühne" ; but "Folk's-*show*-stage" would be a little too cumbrous.—Tr.

odds and ends of Action, as the romance whose scrappy plethora of Stuff (*zerstreute Vielstoffigkeit*) the poet was labouring to compress. The poet, who looked towards this Folk's-play, could not but see that for want of an intelligible speech it was driven into a monstrous plethora of action ; precisely as the narrative Romancist was driven thither, by his inability to actually display his talked-of persons and their haps. He needs must cry to these mummers : " Give me your stage ; I give you my speech ; and so we both are suited ! "

In favour of Drama, we see the poet narrowing-down the Folk-stage to the Theatre. Exactly as the Action itself, through a clear exposition of the motives that called it forth, must be compressed into its weightiest definite moments : so did the necessity become evident, to compress the show-place also ; and chiefly out of regard for the spectators, who now were not merely to see, but alike to plainly hear. Together with its effect upon the space, this curtailment had also to extend to the time-duration, of the dramatic play. The Mystery-stage of the Middle Ages, set up in spreading fields, in streets or open places of the towns, offered the assembled populace an entertainment lasting all day long, nay—as we even still may see—for several days on end : whole histories, the complete adventures of a lifetime, were represented ; from these the constant ebb and flow of lookers-on might choose, according to their fancy, what most they cared to see. Such a performance formed a fitting pendant to the monstrously discursive Histories (*Historien*) of the Middle Ages themselves : just as mask-like in their dearth of character, in their lack of any individual stir of life, just as wooden and rough-hewn were the much-doing persons of these Histories *be-read*, as were the players of those *beheld*. For the same reasons that moved the poet to narrow down the Action and the Show-place, he had therefore to curtail the Time-length of per-formance also, since he wanted to bring to his spectators, no longer fragments, but a self-included whole ; so that he took his spectator's power of giving continuous and

undivided attention to a fascinating subject, when set
before him, as the measure for the length of that performance. An artwork which merely appeals to Phantasy, like
the be-read romance, may lightly break the current of its
message; since Phantasy is of so wayward a nature, that
it hearkens to no other laws than those of whimsy chance.
But that which steps before the senses, and would address
them with persuasive, unmistakable distinctness, has not
only to trim itself according to the quality, faculty and
naturally bounded vigour of those senses, but to shew
itself complete from top to toe, from beginning to end: if
it would not, through sudden break or incompleteness of
its exposition, appeal once more for needful supplementing
to the Phantasy, to the very factor it had quitted for the
senses.

Upon this narrowed stage one thing alone remained
still left entirely to Phantasy,—*the demonstration of the
scene* itself, wherein to frame the performers conformably
with the local requirements of the action. Carpets hung
the stage around; an easily shifted writing on a notice-
board informed the spectator what place, whether palace
or street, forest or field, was to be *thought of* as the scene.
Through this one compulsory appeal to Phantasy, un-
avoidable by the stage-craft of those days, a door in the
drama remained open to the motley-stuffed Romance and
the much-doing History. As the poet, hitherto busied
only with a speaking, bodily representation of the Romance,
did not yet feel the necessity of a naturalistic representment of the surrounding Scene as well, neither could he
experience the necessity of compressing the Action, to be
represented, into a still more definite circumscription of its
leading moments. We here see plain as day how it is
Necessity alone that drives the artist toward a perfect
shaping of the artwork; the artistic necessity that determines him to turn from Phantasy to Sense, to assist the
indefinite force of fancy to a sure, intelligent operation
through the senses. This necessity which shapes all Art,
which alone can satisfy the artist's strivings, comes to us

I

solely from the definiteness of a universally sentient intuition (*universell sinnlichen Anschauung*): if we render
complete justice to all its claims, then it drives us withal
to the completest art-creation. Shakespeare, who did not
yet experience this one necessity, of a naturalistic representment of the scenic surroundings, and therefore only so
far sifted and compressed the redundance of his Dramatised
Romance as he was bidden-to by the necessity he did
experience,—to wit of narrowing the show-place, and
curtailing the time-length, of an Action represented by
men of flesh and blood,—Shakespeare, who within these
limits quickened History and Romance into so persuasive,
so characteristic a truth, that he shewed us human beings
with individualities so manifold and drastic as never a poet
before,—this Shakespeare nevertheless, through his dramas
being not yet shaped by that single aforesaid necessity,
has been the cause and starting-point of an unparalleled
confusion in dramatic art for over two centuries, and down
to the present day.

In the Shakespearian Drama the Romance and the
loose-joined History had been left a door, as I have expressed it, by which they might go in and out at pleasure:
this open door was the relinquishing to Phantasy the
representment of the Scene. We shall see that the consequent confusion increased in exact degree as that door
was relentlessly * shut from the other side, and as the felt
deficiency of Scene, in turn, drove people into arbitrary
deeds of violence against the living Drama.

Amongst the so-called Romanic nations of Europe, with
whom the adventure-hunting of the Romance—which
tumbled every Germanic and Romanic element into one
mass of wild confusion—had raged the maddest, this
Romance had also become the most ill-suited for drama-

* In the *Deutsche Monatsschrift*, " auf das brutalste."—TR.

tising.   The stress to seize the motley utterances of earlier
fantastic whim, and shape them by the strenuous inwardness of human nature into plain and definite show, was
only exhibited in any marked degree by the Germanic
nations, who made into their deed of Protestance the
inward war of conscience against tormenting outward
prescripts. The Romanic nations, who outwardly remained
beneath the Catholic yoke, clove steadfastly to the line
along which they had fled before the irreconcilable inward
strife, in order to distract from without—as I have above
expressed myself—their inward thoughts.   Plastic art, and
an art-of-poetry which—as descriptive—was kindred to the
plastic, if not in utterance, yet in essence : these are the
arts, externally distracting, diverting, and engaging, peculiar
to these nations.

The educated Frenchman and Italian turned his back
upon his native Folk's-play *; in its raw simplicity and
formlessness it recalled to him the whole chaos of the
Middle Ages, which he had just been labouring to shake
off him, like some heavy, troublous dream.   No, he harked
back to the historic feeders of his language, and chiefly
from Roman † poets, the literary copiers of the Greeks, he
chose his pattern for that drama which he set before the
well-bred world of Gentlemen, in lieu of the Folk's-play
that now could entertain alone the rabble.   Painting and
architecture, the principal arts of the Romanic Renaissance,

---

* As I am writing no History of the Modern Drama, but, agreeably to my
object, have only to point out in its twofold development the chief lines along
which the root-difference between those two evolutionary paths is plainest
visible, I have passed over the *Spanish Theatre*, since in it alone those diverse
paths are characteristically crossed with one another.   This makes it indeed
of the highest significance in itself, but to us it affords no antitheses so marked
as the two we find, with determinant influence upon all newer evolution of the
Drama, in Shakespeare and the French *Tragédie*.—R. WAGNER.

This note does not occur in the original edition (1852) ; nor does our author
appear to have made much acquaintance with the Spanish Drama till the end
of 1857, as we may see by letters 250 and 255 of the " *Briefwechsel*," in the
latter of which he gives Liszt a superb criticism, in the highest sense, of
Calderon.—TR.

† In the *D. M.* " Latin."—TR.

had made the eye of this well-bred world so full of taste,
so exacting in its demands, that the rough carpet-hung
platform of the British Shakespeare could not content it.
For a show-place, the players in the Princes' palaces were
given the sumptuous hall, in which, with a few minor
modifications, they had to erect their Scene. Stability of
Scene was set fast as the criterion for the whole drama ;
and in this the accepted line of taste of the well-bred world
concurred with the modern origin of the drama placed
before it, with the rules of Aristotle. The princely spectator, whose *eye* had been trained by Plastic-art into his
best-bred organ of positive sensuous pleasure, had no lief
that *this* sense of all others should be bandaged, to submit
itself to sightless Phantasy; and that the less, as he shrank
on principle from any excitation of the indefinite, medieval-
shaping Phantasy. At the drama's each demand for
Change of Scene, he must have been given the opportunity
of seeing that scene displayed with strict fidelity to form
and colour of its subject, to allow a change at all. But
what was made possible in the later mixing of the two
dramatic genres, it was by no means needful to ask for
here, since from the other side the rules of Aristotle, by
which alone this fictive drama was constructed, made
Unity of Scene its weightiest condition. So that the very
thing the Briton, with his organic creation of the drama
from within, had left disregarded as an outer moment,
became an outward-shaping 'norm' for the French drama ;
which thus sought to construct itself from without inwards,
from Mechanism into Life.

Now, it is important to observe closely, how this outward Unity of Scene determined the whole attitude of the
French drama, almost entirely excluding from this scene
any representment of the action, and replacing it by the
mere delivery of speeches (*Rede*). Thus the root poetic
element of medieval and more recent life, the action-packed
Romance, must also be shut out on principle from any
representment on this Scene, since the introduction of its

multifarious stuff would have been rightdown impossible without a constant shifting. So that not only the outward form, but the whole cut of the plot, and finally its subject too, must be taken from those models which had guided the French playwright in planning out his form. He was forced to choose plots which did not need to be first condensed into a compact measure of dramatic representability, but such as lay before him already thus condensed.

From their native Sagas the Greek tragedians had condensed such stuffs, as the highest artistic outcome of those Sagas : the modern dramatist, starting with outward rules abstracted from these poems, and faced with the poetic element of his own era's * life, which was only to be mastered in an exactly opposite fashion, namely that of Shakespeare, could never compress it to such a density as should answer to the standard outwardly imposed ; therefore nothing remained for him but a—naturally *disfiguring* —imitation and repetition of those already finished dramas. Thus in *Racine's* Tragédie we have Talk upon the scene, and behind the scene the Action ; grounds of movement, with the movement cut adrift and turned outside ; will-ing without can-ning. All art was therefore focused on *the mere outside of Talk,* and quite logically in Italy—whence the new art-genre had started—this soon lost itself in that musical delivery which we have already learnt to recognise as the specific content of opera-ware (*des Opernwesens*). The French Tragédie, also, of necessity passed over † into Opera: *Gluck* spoke aloud the actual content of this tragedy-ware. Opera was thus the premature bloom on an unripe fruit, grown from an unnatural, artificial soil. With what the Italian and French Drama *began,* to wit the outer form, to that must the newer Drama first attain by organic evolution from within, upon the path of Shakes-

---

* In the *D. M.* we find " and his nation's " (*seines Volkes und seiner Zeit*). —Tr.

† In the D. M. " under " (*unter*).—Tr.

peare's Drama; then first will ripen, also, the natural
fruit of Musical Drama.*

Between these two extremes, however, between the
Shakespearian and the *Racinian* Drama, did *Modern Drama*
grow into its unnatural, mongrel shape; ˈand *Germany* was
the soil on which this fruit was reared.
Here Roman Catholicism continued side by side, in
equal strength, with German Protestantism: only, each
was so hotly engaged in combat with the other, that,
undecided as the battle stayed, no natural art-flower came
to light. The inward stress, which with the Briton threw
itself into dramatic representment of History and Romance,
remained with the German Protestant an obstinate endeavour to inwardly appease that inward strife itself. We
have indeed a *Luther*, whose art soared up to the Religious
Lyric; but we have no Shakespeare. On the other hand,
the Roman-catholic South could never swing itself into
that genial, light-minded oblivion of the inward conflict,
wherewith the Romanic nations took up Plastic art: with
gloomy earnestness it guarded its religious dream (*Wahn*).
While the whole of Europe threw itself on Art, still
Germany abode a meditant barbarian. Only what had
already outlived itself outside, took flight to Germany,
upon its soil to blossom through an after-summer. English
comedians,† whom the performers of Shakespearian dramas
had robbed of their bread at home, came over to Germany
to play their grotesquely pantomimic antics before the
Folk: not till long after, when *it* had likewise faded out of
England, followed Shakespeare's Drama itself; German

* *Des musikalischen Drama's;*—this stood as "the musically-executed
Drama" (*des musikalisch vorgetragenen Drama's*) in the *D. M.*—The point is
interesting, as Wagner some twenty years later, in a little monograph "Ueber
die Benennung 'Musikdrama'" gave his reasons for objecting alike to the
terms "Music-drama" and "Musical drama."—Tʀ.
† "*Komödianten*"—perhaps "clowns" or "morris dancers" would be
better here, as Wagner does not usually employ this term for actors.—Tʀ.

players, fleeing from the ferule* of their wearisome dramatic tutors, laid hands on it and trimmed it for their use.

From the South, again, the Opera had forced its way in, —that outcome of Romanic drama. Its distinguished origin, in the palaces of Princes, commended it to German princes in their turn; so that these princes introduced the Opera into Germany, whereas—mark well!—the Shakespearian Play was brought in by the Folk.—In Opera the scenic penury of Shakespeare's stage was contrasted by its utmost opposite, the richest and most far-fetched mounting of the Scene. The Musical drama became in truth a *peep-show* (*Schau*spiel), whereas the *Play* (Schauspiel) remained a *hear*-play (*Hör*spiel). We need not here go far for reasons for the scenic and decorative extravagance of the opera-genre: this loose-limbed drama was constructed from without; and only from without, by luxury and pomp, could it be kept alive at all. One thing, however, it is important to observe: namely, that this scenic ostentation, with its unheard-of complexity and far-fetched change of exhibition to the Eye, proceeded from the same dramatic tendency which had originally set up unity-of-scene as its 'norm.' Not the Poet, who, when compressing the Romance into the Drama, had left its plethora of stuff thus far unhedged, as in that stuff's behoof he could change the scene as often and as swiftly as he chose, by mere appeal to phantasy,—not the Poet, from any wish to turn from that appeal-to-phantasy to a positive confirmation by the senses,—not *he* invented this elaborate mechanism for shifting actually presented scenes: but a longing for outward entertainment and constant change thereof, a sheer lust of the Eye, had called it forth. Had *the poet* devised this apparatus, we should have had to further suppose that he felt the necessity of a frequent change of Scene as a need inherent in the drama's plethora of Stuff itself; and since the poet, as we have seen, was constructing organically from within outwards, this supposition would have as good as proved that the historic and romantic plethora-of-

* *Zucht*,—in the *D. M. "pedantischen Zucht."*—TR.

stuff was a necessary postulate of the Drama : for only the
unbending *necessity* of such a postulate could have driven
him to invent a scenic apparatus whereby to enable that
plethora of Stuff (*Vielstoffigkeit*) to also utter itself as a
panoramic plethora of Scene (*Vielscenigkeit*). But the very
reverse was the case. Shakespeare felt a necessity im-
pelling him to represent History * and Romance dramatically ; in the freshness of his ardour to content this
impulse, there came to him no feeling of the necessity for
a naturalistic (*naturgetreuen*) representment of the Scene
as well ;—had he experienced this further necessity, toward
a completely convincing representment of the dramatic
action, he would have sought to answer it by a still more
careful sifting, a still more strenuous compression of the
Romance's plethora of Stuff : and that in exactly the same
way as he had contracted the show-place, abridged the
time-length of performance, and for their sakes had already
curtailed this plethora of Stuff itself. The impossibility of
still further condensing the Romance—an insight which he
certainly would have arrived at—must then have enlightened him as to the true nature of this Romance :
namely, that its nature does not really correspond with
that of Drama ; a discovery which *we* could never make,
till the undramatic plethora of History's Stuff was brought
to our feeling *by the actualisation* of the Scene, whereas the
circumstance that this Scene *need only be suggested* had
alone made possible to Shakespeare the dramatised
Romance.—

Now, the necessity of a representment of the Scene, in
keeping with the place of action, could not for long remain
unfelt ; the medieval stage was bound to vanish, and make
room for the modern. In Germany this was governed by
the character of the Folk's mimetic art, which likewise,
since the dying-out of Mystery and Passion plays, took its
dramatic basis from the History and the Romance. At
the time when German mimic art first took an upward
swing—about the middle of the past century—this basis

* In the *D. M.* " History and " did not occur here.—TR.

was formed by the Burgher-romance,* in its keeping with the then Folk-spirit. It was by far more manageable, and especially less cumbered with material, than the Historic or Legendary (*sagenhafte*) romance that lay to Shakespeare's hand : a suitable representment of its local scenes could therefore be effected with far less outlay than would have been required for Shakespeare's dramatisations. The Shakespearian pieces taken up by these players had to submit to the most hampering adaptation on every side, in order to become performable by them at all. I here pass over every other ground and measure of this adaptation, and lay my finger on that of the purely scenic requirements, since it is the weightiest for the object of my present inquiry.† These players, the first importers of Shakespeare to the German stage, were so honest to the spirit of their art, that it never occurred to them to make his pieces representable by either accompanying his constant change of scene with a kaleidoscopic shifting of their own theatric scenery, or even for his sake renouncing any actual exhibition whatsoever of the scene, and returning to the sceneless medieval stage. No, they maintained the standpoint of their art, once taken up, and to it subordinated Shakespeare's plethora-of-scene ; inasmuch as they downright left out those scenes which seemed to them of little weight, while the weightier ones they tacked together.

It was from the standpoint of Literature, that people first perceived what Shakespeare's art-work had lost hereby, and urged a restoration of the original form of these pieces for their performance too. For this, two opposite plans were broached. The first proposal, and the one not carried out, is Tieck's. Fully recognising the essence of Shakespearian Drama, *Tieck* demanded the restoration of

---

* "Der bürgerliche Roman"=the *bourgeois-*, or citizen-romance; "the Romance of domestic life," as opposed to the classical, the historical, the legendary, or the political.—TR.

† Footnote to the *D. M.* only : "This object is, to track (*aufsuchen*) the Artwork at every point where it emerges from Thought into realisement *to the Senses.*"—TR.

Shakespeare's stage, with its Scene referred to an appeal
to Phantasy. This demand was thoroughly logical, and
aimed at the very spirit of Shakespearian Drama. But,
though a half attempt at restoration has time out of mind
remained unfruitful, on the other hand a radical one has
always proved impossible. Tieck was a radical restorer,
to be honoured as such, but bare of influence.—The second
proposal was directed to employing the gigantic apparatus
of Operatic scenery for the representation of Shakespearian
Drama too, by a faithful exhibition of the constant change
of scene that had originally been only hinted at by him.
Upon the newer English stage, people translated Shakespeare's Scene into the most realistic actuality * ; wonders
of mechanism were invented, for the rapid change of the
most elaborate stage-mountings : marches of troops and
mimic battles were presented with astonishing exactitude.
In the larger German theatres this course was copied.

In face of this spectacle, the modern Poet stood brooding
and bewildered. As literature, Shakespearian Drama had
given him the exalting impression of the most perfect
poetic unity; so long as it had only addressed his
phantasy, that phantasy had been competent to form
therefrom a harmoniously rounded image : but now, with
the fulfilment of his necessarily wakened longing to see
this image embodied in a thorough representment to the
senses, he saw it vanish suddenly before his very eyes.
The embodiment of his fancy-picture had merely shewn
him an unsurveyable mass of realisms and actualisms, out
of which his puzzled eye absolutely could not reconstruct
it. This phenomenon produced two main effects upon
him, both of which resulted in a disillusionment as to
Shakespeare's Tragedy.† Henceforth the Poet either
renounced all wish to see his dramas acted on the stage,
so as to be at peace again to model according to his

---

* Not quite *every* scene, however, as our many ' acting editions ' will show.—
After "battles," in the last clause of this sentence, the *D. M.* had : " merely
suggested by conventional signs, on the older stage."—TR.

† In the *D. M.* "Drama," in place of "Tragödie."—TR.

intellectual aim the fancy-picture he had borrowed from Shakespearian Drama,—i.e. he wrote literary-dramas for dumb reading;—or else, so as to practically realise his fancy-picture on the stage, he instinctively turned more or less towards the reflective type of drama, whose modern origin we have traced to the pseudo-antique (*antikisiren-den*) drama, constructed according to Aristotle's rules of Unity.

Both these effects and tendencies are the guiding motives in the works of the two most important dramatic poets of modern times—*Goethe* and *Schiller*. With them I must therefore deal a little closer, so far at least as concerns the object of my present inquiry.

Goethe began his career, as dramatic poet, by dramatising a full-blooded Germanic Feudal-romance (*Ritterroman*), " *Götz von Berlichingen.*" The method of Shakespeare was quite faithfully followed here : the romance * with all its circumstantial details was in so far translated for the stage, as the narrowing of that stage and the abridgment of the time-length of performance would allow.   But Goethe was already faced with a stage on which the Action's *locale*, however scantily and roughly, was yet exhibited with a definite intention to meet that Action's claims.   This circumstance led the poet to revise for actual stage-performance a poem written rather from a literary, than a theatric standpoint.   In its second shape, given it

---

* In the *D. M.* " die romanhafte Historie," i.e. "the Romance-like History."   In this chapter Wagner has frequently used the term " Historie " as an equivalent of " Geschichte," the true German word for " History," albeit apparently with the purpose of conveying the idea of a certain amount of "traditional conventionality " in the former term ; this shade of meaning it is impossible to convey in English, as we have only one word, " History," for the thing *itself* and the thing *written about it*.   To any one who wishes to pursue this matter farther, I can only recommend a study of the original ; but I may add that six pages later, in referring to Schiller's abandonment of historic " Stuff," for his dramas, our author has substituted " Historie " for " Geschichte," seemingly to avoid the contrast originally offered, in the *D. M.*, by the juxtaposition of the two terms.—TR.

out of consideration for scenic requirements, the poem has lost the freshness of Romance, without gaining in its stead the perfect strength of Drama.

Goethe next chose the material for his dramas chiefly from the Burgher-romance. The characteristic of this *citizen romance* consists in this : that its plot is completely cut adrift from any wider group of historic actions and associations, that it holds only to the social precipitate of these historical events for its conditioning medium (*bedingende Umgebung*), and within this medium—which at bottom is but the reaction of those historic incidents, with all their colour blotted out—evolves itself more according to certain humours (*Stimmungen*) tyrannously imposed on it thereby, than according to any inner motives strong enough for a completely plastic utterance. This plot is just as cramped and poor, as the humours which gave it birth are bare of freedom and self-dependent inwardness. Its dramatisation, however, answered to both the intellectual view-point of the public and, more especially, the outward possibilities of scenic represberment ; and that inasmuch as these threadbare plots brought to the practical 'mounting' no necessities which it could not answer out of hand. What a mind like Goethe's composed (*dichtete*) amid such limitations we must take as coming almost solely from his felt necessity of submitting to certain cramping maxims, if he were to bring about a drama at all,* and certainly far less from any voluntary submission to the cramped spirit of the Burgher-romance, or to the humours of the public which favoured its style of plot. But Goethe rescued himself from this limitation, and won the most unfettered freedom, by completely giving up the 'acting-drama.' In planning out his "Faust" he merely retained for the literary poem the advantages of a dramatic mode of statement, but left purposely out of sight the possibility of a scenic represberment. In this poem, Goethe was the first to sound with full consciousness the keynote of the poetic element distinctive of the present age, *the thrust of Thought*

---

* In the *D. M.* "vor der Oeffentlichkeit," i.e. "before the public."—TR.

toward Actuality, though he could not yet give it artistic redemption in the actuality of Drama. Here stands the watershed (*Scheidepunkt*) between the medieval *romance,* sicklied to the shallowness of its burgher type, and the real *dramatic matter* of the Future. We must defer a closer entry upon the characteristics of this 'watershed': for the present let us hold it weighty, that Goethe, arrived at this watershed, could neither give us a genuine romance nor a genuine drama, but precisely a poem which enjoyed the advantages of both classes in an abstract artistic measure.

From this poem—which sent its plastic impulse threading through the poet's whole artistic life, like a welling vein of living water—let us here look aside, and follow Goethe's art-creation wherever we may find it turned, in fresh attempts, towards the Scenic Drama.

From the dramatised Burgher-romance — which in "Egmont" he had sought to raise to its highest pitch from within outwards, by extending its medium so as to embrace a widely-branching group of historical moments— Goethe had departed for good, with the sketch for his "Faust": if the Drama still had charms for him, as the most perfect branch of poetic art, it was chiefly through a regardal of it in its most perfect artistic form. This *Form* —which, in keeping with their degree of classical knowledge, had been only cognisable to the French and Italians as an outwardly constraining 'norm'—presented itself to the more enlightened gaze of German searchers as an integral moment-of-utterance of Greek *Life:* the warmth of that Form had power to enkindle them, when they had felt out for themselves the warmth of this life that lingered in its very monuments. The German poet grasped the fact, that the unitarian (*einheitliche*) Form of Grecian Tragedy could not be imposed upon the drama from outside, but must be vitalised afresh from within outwards, through a unitarian Content. The Content of modern life, which could utter itself intelligibly in nothing now but the Romance, it was impossible to compress into such plastic unity that with an at all intelligible dramatic treatment it could have spoken through the Form of Grecian Drama, could have justified this Form, could, in fact, have begotten it of necessity.   To the poet, here concerned with absolute-artistic Shaping, it was now only open to return—at least outwardly—to the method of the French ; in order to justify the use of the Form of Greek Drama, for his art-work, he must also employ the finished Stuff of Grecian Mythos.   But when Goethe laid hands on the finished stuff of "Iphigenia in Tauris," he proceeded exactly as did Beethoven in his weightiest symphonic pieces : just as Beethoven made himself master of the finished Absolute Melody, in a measure loosened it, broke it up, and fitted its limbs afresh together by a new organic vitalising, in order to make the organism of Music * itself capable of bearing melody,—so did Goethe lay hands on the finished Stuff of "Iphigenia in Tauris," resolved it into its component parts, and fitted these afresh together by an organi-cally-vitalising act of poetic Shaping, in order thus to make the organism of Drama itself capable of begetting the perfect dramatic art-form.

But only with this already finished Stuff, could Goethe succeed in such a procedure : with none borrowed from modern life, or from Romance, might the poet reach a like success.†   We shall come back to the reason of this pheno-menon : let it suffice for now, to establish from a survey of Goethe's art-creation that the poet turned away from *this* attempt in Drama too, so soon as ever he had a mind for the‡ exhibition of Life itself, and not for absolute Art-creation.   This Life, in its complex branchings, its will-less outward shaping by influences from far and near, even Goethe could subdue to an intelligible demonstration alone in Romance.   The choicest flower of his modern world-

---

* In the *D. M.* " Kunstmusik," i.e. "Art-music."—TR.

† In the *D. M.* and in the original edition of the book, this sentence was continued by "; already in ' Tasso' this Stuff was cooling markedly beneath his unitarian (*einheitlich gestaltenden*) hand,—in ' Eugenie ' it froze at last to ice."—TR.

‡ In the *D. M.* " verständliche," i.e. "intelligible," was here inserted.—TR.

view (*Weltanschauung*) the poet could only give us in a delineation, in an appeal to Phantasy, and not in a direct dramatic representment,—so that Goethe's most pregnant art-creation must lose itself again in the Romance; the Romance from which, at the beginning of his poetic career, he had turned with a true Shakespearian stress toward Drama.—

Schiller, like Goethe, began with the Dramatised Romance, beneath the influence of Shakespearian Drama. The domestic and political Romance engaged his dramatic shaping-force, till he reached the modern source of this Romance, reached naked *history* itself, and from that endeavoured to construct the Drama without an intervener. Here it was, that the stubbornness of Historic matter, and its incompetence for presentment in a dramatic form, became manifest.—Shakespeare translated the dry but honest historic Chronicle into the living speech of Drama. This Chronicle outlined with exact fidelity, and step by step, the march of historical events and the deeds of those engaged therein: it went about its task without any criticism or individual views, and thus gave a daguerreotype of historic facts. Shakespeare had only to vivify this daguerreotype into a luminous oil-painting; he necessarily had to unriddle from the group of facts their underlying motives, and to imprint these on the flesh and blood of their transactors. For the rest, the historic scaffolding stayed entirely undisturbed by him: his stage allowed him that, as we have seen.—But in presence of the modern Scene, the poet soon perceived the impossibility of dressing History, for the play, with the chronicler's fidelity of Shakespeare: he grasped the fact, that only to the Romance—all heedless as to brevity or length—had it been possible to deck the Chronicle with lifelike portraits of its characters; and that only Shakespeare's stage, again, had permitted the compression of the Romance into a drama. If Schiller, then, sought in History itself for the stuff for Drama, this was with the wish and effort to submit the historic subject from the first to so directly poetic an

adaptation that it might be presented in the dramatic
Form, which only in the utmost possible Unity can make
itself intelligible.   But in this very wish and effort, lies the
reason for the nullity of our* Historic Drama.   History is
only *history* in virtue of its shewing us, with unconditional
veracity, the naked doings of human beings : it does not
give us men's inner thinkings, but merely lets us infer these
thinkings from their doings.   If, then, we believe we have
rightly fathomed these thinkings, and if we wish to present
history as vindicated by them, we can only do it in pure
Historiography, or—with the utmost artistic warmth
attainable—in the Historical Romance, i.e. in an art-form
where we are not constrained by any outward consideration
to disfigure the naked facts of history through a wilful
sifting or compressing.   We can make thoroughly intelligible to ourselves the thoughts which we have unriddled
from the actions of historical persons, in no other way than
by a faithful portrayal of the identical actions from which
we have unriddled those thoughts.   If, however, in order to
make plain to ourselves the inner motives of action, we in
any item alter or disfigure the actions which have thence
arisen, for sake of their portrayal : then this necessarily
involves a disfigurement of the thoughts as well, and therefore a total falsification of history itself.   The poet who,
avoiding the chronicler's exactitude, attempted to adapt
historic subjects for the dramatic Scene,—and with this
object, treated the facts of history according to his own
artistic formula,—could bring neither History, nor yet a
Drama, into being.

If, in illustration of the above-said, we compare Shakespeare's Historic dramas with Schiller's " *Wallenstein*," we
shall see at a glance how *here* by the evasion of outward
historical fidelity, the history's very Content is set awry as
well ; whereas *there*, by maintenance of the chronicler's
exactitude,† the characteristic Content of the history is

* In the *D. M.* " sogenannten," i.e. "so-called."—TR.
† In the *D. M.* here occurred " in der Darstellung des historischen Thatbes-
tandes auch," i.e. "in the portrayal of historic matters-of-fact, the Content
also."—TR.

brought to light with most persuasive truth. Without a doubt, Schiller was a greater expert than Shakespeare in historical inquiry, and in his purely-historic works * he fully makes amend for his handling of History as dramatic poet. But our present business is the statistical proof, that for Shakespeare indeed, upon whose stage appeal was made to Phantasy, might the stuff for Drama be borrowed from history ; but not for *us*, who demand a sense-convincing exhibition of the Scene as well. For it was not possible even to Schiller, to compress the historic stuff, howsoever deliberately prepared by him, into the dramatic unity he had in mind. All which first gives to History its intrinsic life, the Surrounding that stretches far and wide,† and yet exerts its conditioning force upon the central point—all this, since he felt its delineation indispensable, he was forced to shift into an entirely independent, self-included adjunct, and to split his drama itself into two dramas: a very different matter to Shakespeare's handling of his serial historic dramas ; for there we have whole life-careers of persons, who serve for a historical focus, parcelled off into their weightiest periods, whereas in "Wallenstein" only *one* such period, proportionally not ‡ over-rich in matter, is divided into several sections merely for sake of circumstantially motivating a historical moment which is clouded into positive obscurity. In three plays, upon *his* stage, Shakespeare would have given the whole Thirty-years War.

This "dramatic poem"—as Schiller himself calls it— was nevertheless the most conscientious attempt to win from History, as such, material for the Drama.

In Drama's further evolution, we see Schiller henceforth dropping more and more his regard for History : on the

---

* "Studien" in the *D. M.* Moreover, "fully" has been substituted for "to a certain extent."—TR.

† The clause from "and yet" to "central-point" does not appear in the *D. M.*—TR.

‡ In the *D. M.* "by no means" (*keinesweges*) occurs in place of "verhält-nissmässig gar nicht."—TR.

one hand, to employ it * merely as itself a clothing for an
intellectual motive peculiar to the poet's own general phase
of culture—on the other, to present this motive more and
more definitely in a form of drama which, by the nature of
the thing and especially since Goethe's many-sided attempts,
had become the object of artistic speculation. With this
purposed subordination and arbitrary regulation of the
Stuff, Schiller fell ever deeper into the inevitable fault of a
sheer reflective and rhetorical presentment of his subject ;
until at last he ruled it merely by the Form, which he took
from Greek Tragedy as the most suitable for a purely
artistic purpose. In his " Bride of Messina " he even went
farther in his imitation of the Greek Form, than Goethe in
his " Iphigenia." Goethe only went so far back to this
Form, as thereby to fix the plastic *unity* of an Action :
Schiller sought to shape the drama's Stuff itself, from out
this Form. In this he approached the method of the
French tragic poets ; his only essential difference from
them being, that he restored this Form more completely
than had been possible to their limited knowledge of it,
that he sought to vivify its Spirit, of which they knew
absolutely nothing, and to stamp that spirit on the Stuff
itself. Further, he adopted from the Greek tragedy its
" Fate,"—at least so far as was possible to *his* understanding of it,—and constructed with this Fate a plot which, by
its medieval costume,† was meant to afford a halfway-
house between the Antique and our modern understanding.
Never was anything so purposely planned from a purely
art-historical standpoint, as this " Bride of Messina " : what
Goethe shadowed in his marriage of Faust with Helena,
was here to be embodied through artistic speculation. But

---

* " Historie "—this is the substitution of " Historie " for " Geschichte " (as
it stood in the *D. M.*) referred to on page 139.—TR.

† The portion of this sentence contained between the dashes, "at least so
far " &c. was not included in the *D. M.* article ; whereas, in place of " nach
ihrem mittelalterlichen Kostüm," we *there* find the pleonasm : " nach ihrem
mittelalterlichen, dem Verständnisse unserer Zeit wiederum näher als die Antike
liegenden, Tracht," i.e. " by its medieval garb, which, again, lay nearer to the
comprehension of our times, than did the Antique."—TR.

this embodiment would not succeed at all : stuff and form were made alike so turbid, that neither did the sophisticated medieval Romance come to any effect, nor the antique Form to lucid view.   Who may not learn a profound lesson, from this fruitless attempt of Schiller's ?—In despair, himself, he turned his back upon this form ; in his last dramatic poem, " William Tell," by taking up again the form of dramatised Romance he sought to save at least his poetic freshness, which had markedly flagged beneath his æsthetic experimentings.

Thus we see the dramatic creativeness of Schiller, also, swaying between History and Romance—the real life element of our era's poetry—on the one side, and the perfect Form of the Grecian drama on the other : with every fibre of his poetic life he clung to the former, while his higher artistic shaping-impulse was driving him towards the latter.

What specially characterises Schiller, is that in him the thrust (*Drang*) towards the pure, the antique art-form, took the line of a thrust towards the Ideal in general.   He was so bitterly distressed at not being able to fill this Form artistically with the contents of our own life-element, that at last he loathed any artistic employment of that element at all.   *Goethe's* practical sense reconciled itself with our life-element, by giving up the perfect art-form and developing farther the only one in which this life can enounce itself intelligibly.   Schiller never turned back again to the Romance proper ; the Ideal of his higher artistic vision, as revealed to him in the antique art-form he made into the essence of true Art itself.   But he only saw this Ideal from the standpoint of our present life's poetic incapacity ; and, confounding the things of *our* life with those of Human Life in general, he could at last but picture Art as a thing divorced from Life, the utmost plenitude of Art as a thing to be dreamt of, but never more than approximately reachable.—

Thus Schiller stayed hovering between heaven and earth ; and in this hovering hangs, after him, our whole dramatic poetry. That heaven, however, is really nothing but *the antique art-Form*, and that earth *the practical Romance of modern times*. The newest school of dramatic poetry—which, *as art*, lives only on the attempts of Goethe and Schiller, now turned to literary monuments—has developed the aforesaid hovering between opposite tendencies into a positive reeling. Wherever it has left the field of mere literary dramatics, and engaged in representing Life, it has fallen back upon the dead level of the dramatised Burgher-romance, in order to produce an at all intelligible scenic effect; or if it has wanted to give voice to any higher import of Life, it has seen itself compelled to gradually strip off again its spurious dramatic plumes, and present itself to the dumb reader as a naked six- or nine-volume novel.*

To take our whole art-literary doings at one hasty glance, let us range their notable phenomena in the following order.

Our modern life-element can only be displayed, at once intelligibly and artistically, in the *Romance*. In the endeavour for a more effectual, more direct display of its Stuff, the Romance becomes *dramatised*. As each new poet recognises afresh the impossibility of this attempt, the Stuff, which distracts by its too-much-doing, is pounded down into first an unveracious, and next a completely pur-

---

* The allusion is evidently to Gutzkow's "*Ritter vom Geiste*" (published 1850-51), a novel in the portentous form of *nine* volumes, averaging 450 pages apiece ! Gutzkow was Director of Plays at Dresden during the last two or three years of Wagner's residence there. In "*Letters to Uhlig*," No. 86 (Oct. 14, '52) Wagner writes, "In spite of Schlurk, I will never become acquainted with the '*Ritter vom Geiste*.' In that matter I stick to a terribly severe diet ! I have not even read Heine's '*Romanzero*.' I anticipate my complete ruin if I took to that sort of thing." Though the passage in the text, above, was written nearly two years before the letter from which I have quoted, most—if not, all—of the volumes of Gutzkow's extravagantly long work were then already published. Wagner would of course have known of their existence and been able to form a pretty good guess as to their contents, judging from earlier works of Gutzkow ; with which, as a Dresdener, he would naturally have become acquainted.—It is curious, too,—but characteristic—to find the same association of ideas cropping up again in the letter ; for the "literary-*Lyrics*," mentioned in the next paragraph of the book, are obviously those of Heine.—TR.

poseless foundation for the modern *stage-piece*, i.e. the Play; which, in its turn, becomes a mere platform for the modern theatre-Virtuoso. From this play, so soon as he grows aware of his wrecking on the routine of the coulisses, the poet returns to undisturbed presentment of his Stuff in the *romance;* the perfect dramatic Form, which he had striven for in vain, he gets set before him as something foreign out-and-out, in an actual performance of the genuine Greek drama.   Finally, in the literary-*Lyric* he attacks and ridicules,—laments and bewails the contrariness of our life-affairs ; which appears to him, in the matter of Art, a contradiction between stuff and form,—in that of Life, a contradiction between man and nature.

It is noteworthy that the most recent epoch has shewn this irreconcilable contradiction so conspicuously in the daily history of its art, that any continuance in error with regard thereto must seem clean impossible to any man with half an eye.   Whereas the Romance in every country (*überall*),—and especially among the French,*—after its last fantastic attempts at painting History, has thrown itself on the nakedest exhibition of the life of the present day; has taken this life by its most vicious social basis (*lasterhaftesten sozialen Grundlage*); and, with its own completed unloveliness as art-work, has employed its literary artifice † as a revolutionary weapon against this

---

* One has wellnigh to rub one's eyes, to convince oneself that this was written over forty years ago ; yet it stands verbatim both in the *Deutsche Monatsschrift* and all the editions of the book.   With that wonderful instinct which makes this whole volume almost a prophecy, our author here lays his finger on the beginnings of one of the most notable departures in the history of art, and one whose goal we apparently have not yet reached.—TR.

† "Das literarisches Kunstwerk des Romanes selbst." In the *D. M.* this stood simply as "den Roman selbst" : i.e., in view of the commencement of the sentence, "the Romance employed itself,"—a form of expression which naturally required amendment.—It is more important to notice, however, that to "den Roman" Wagner appended in the *D. M.* a foot-note : "German poets employ the same tactics (*üben dieselbe Wirksamkeit*) even in the Literary-drama,—as witness Hebbel." Friedrich Hebbel (1813-63) was then in what is now called in Germany his 'second period,' and his works appear to have been considered much too cold and bitter in their 'analysis'; he is best known by those of his 'third period,' such as "*Agnes Bernauer*" (Vienna, 1855) and

life-base ;—whereas the Romance, I say, has become an appeal to that revolutionary force of the Folk which shall destroy these life-foundations, — on the other hand a talented poet, who as creative artist had never found the ability to master any sort of Stuff for the actual Drama, induced an absolute monarch to command his Stage-intendant to produce before him with antiquarian fidelity a *real Greek tragedy*, for which a famous composer had to prepare the needful music.* In face of our present-day life, this *Sophocleian Drama* shewed itself as a clumsy artistic fib (*Nothlüge*): as a quibble patched up by artistic penury, to cloak the untruthfulness of our whole art-doings ; as a prevarication which tried to lie away the true Want of our times, under all manner of artistic pretexts. Yet *one* plain truth this tragedy could not help unbaring : namely, that *we have no Drama, and can have*

"*Gyges und sein Ring*" (ibid. 1856), the former work being still given, I believe, on the German stage. Singularly enough, Hebbel's masterpiece was a dramatic Trilogy, "*Die Nibelungen*" (Vienna, 1862) in which Kriemhild and Hagen form the central figures, the idea of the work being based on the conflict between Pagandom and Christendom.—See *Meyer's Konversations-lexikon.*—TR.

* The reference is, of course, to Friedrich Wilhelm IV. of Prussia (brother of the late German Emperor, Wilhelm I.) and the performances of old Greek dramas at Berlin and Potsdam (cf. the "*Communication*," Vol. I., p. 275, of this series). It will be remembered that Wagner had special reasons for keeping this monarch in his mind, as it was *he* who figured so largely in the opposition to the movement which led to the Dresden revolt, and also in its suppression. The "musician " was Mendelssohn, to whom the "*anfertigen musste*"—which I have rendered "had to prepare"—is peculiarly applicable, seeing how distasteful he found his duties at Berlin, chiefly owing to these orders for the Antique Drama. The "tragedy" was the *Antigone*, as will be seen by the close of Chapter III.; although Mendelssohn (Oct. 21, 1841) writes enthusiastically about this his *first* task of the kind, yet he adds : "at the beginning I thought, on the contrary, that I would not mix myself up with the affair." The "poet" was Ludwig Tieck, the romancist, whom Bunsen (Apr. 28, 1844,—in the "*Mendelssohn Letters*") calls "the great Chorodidas-kalos"; he was one of the group of talented men, including Friedrich Rückert, A. W. von Schlegel, Schelling and Mendelssohn, whom Friedrich Wilhelm IV. summoned to court soon after his accession in 1840. I may add that it was from Tieck's *almost solitary* dramatic poem, "Genoveva"—in combination with *Hebbel's* "Genoveva"—that Schumann took the chief materials for the text of his like-named opera, produced at Leipzig in June 1850.—TR.

no Drama; that our Literary-drama is every whit as far
removed from the genuine Drama, as the pianoforte from
the symphonic song of human voices; that in the Modern
Drama we can arrive at the production of poetry only by
the most elaborate devices of literary mechanism, just as
on the pianoforte we only arrive at the production of
music through the most complicated devices of technical
mechanism,—in either case, however, a soulless poetry, a
toneless music.—

With *this* Drama, at all events, true Music, the loving
wife, has nothing at all to do. The coquette can approach
this shrivelled man, to lure him into the net of her flirta-
tions; the prude can unite herself with the impotent one, to
journey with him into godliness; the wanton lets him pay
her, and laughs at him behind his back : but the true, love-
yearning woman turns away from him, unmoved !—*

If, now, we want to pry a little closer into *what* has made
this Drama impotent, we must get to the bottom of *the
Stuff* on which it has fed. This Stuff was, as we saw, the
Romance. To the essence of the Romance we must therefore turn our more particular attention.

* As mentioned earlier, this paragraph was omitted from the *Deutsche
Monatsschrift;* without the First Part of *Opera and Drama* it would have been
pointless. — With the succeeding paragraph the first "article" concluded.
—TR.

II.

AN is in a two-fold way a poet : in his *beholding*, and in his *imparting*.

His *natural* poetic-gift is the faculty of condensing into an inner image the phenomena presented to his senses from outside; his *artistic*, that of projecting this image outwards.

Just as the eye can only take up farther-lying objects in a proportionally diminished scale, so also the human brain—the inner starting-point of the eye, and that to whose activity, conditioned by the whole internal organism, the eye imparts the shows which it has gathered from without—can only grasp them in the diminished scale of the human individuality. Upon this scale, however, the functioning brain is able to take the phenomena, brought to it in a state of disruption from their native actuality, and shape them into new and comprehensive pictures by its double endeavour, to sift them or to group them ; and this function of the brain, we call it *Phantasy*.

The Phantasy's unconscious effort is directed to becoming familiar with the actual measure of these shows, and this drives it to impart its image to the outer world ; so to say—it tries to fit its image on to the reality, in order to compare it therewith. But this imparting to the outer world can only take an artistic, a mediated path ; the senses, which instinctively took up the outer shows themselves, demand, for any imparting to them of a fancy-picture, that the man who fain would address them intel-ligibly should first have exercised and regulated his organ of utterance. Completely intelligible in its externalisation will the fancy-picture never be, until it re-presents to the senses the phenomena in the selfsame measure as that in which the latter had originally presented themselves to them ; while by the final correspondence of the effect of

his message with his previous longing, ·does man first
become insofar acquainted with the correct measure of
the phenomena, as he recognises it for the measure in which
they address themselves to men in general. No one can
address himself intelligibly to any but those who see things
in a like measure with himself: but this measure for his
communication is the concentrated image of the things
themselves, the image in which they present themselves to
man's perception. This measure must therefore rest upon
a view in common; for only what is perceptible to this
common view allows, in turn, of being artistically imparted
thereto: a man whose mode of viewing is not that of his
fellow-men, neither can address himself to them artistically.
—Only in a finite measure of inner viewing of the essence of
things, has the artistic impulse-to-impart, since the memory
of man, been able to develop itself to the faculty of explicit
portrayal (*überzeugendster Darstellung*) to the senses : only
from the Greek world-view, has the genuine Artwork of
Drama been able as yet to blossom forth.   But this drama's
Stuff was the *Mythos ;* and from its essence alone, can we
learn to comprehend the highest Grecian art-work, and its
Form that so ensnares us.

In the *Mythos* the Folk's joint poetic-force seizes things
exactly as the bodily eye has power to see them, and no
farther ; not as they in themselves really are. The vast
multiplicity of surrounding phenomena, whose real association the human being cannot grasp as yet, gives him first
of all an impression of unrest: in order to overcome this
feeling of unrest he seeks for some connexion of the phenomena among themselves, some connexion which he may
conceive as their First Cause. The real connexion, however, is only discoverable by the Understanding, which seizes
the phenomena according to their reality ; whereas the
connexion invented by the man who is only able to seize
the phenomena according to their directest impression upon
himself, can merely be the work of Phantasy—and the
Cause, thus subsumed for them, a mere product of his
poetic imaginative-force.   God and gods, are the first

creations of man's poetic force : in them man represents to himself the essence of natural phenomena as derived from a Cause. Under the notion of this Cause, however, he instinctively apprehends nothing other than his own human essence ; on which alone, moreover, this imagined Cause is based. If the 'thrust' of the man who fain would overcome his inner disquietude at the multiplicity of phenomena, if this thrust makes toward representing as plainly as possible to himself their imagined cause,—since he can only regain his peace of mind through the selfsame senses wherethrough his inner being had been disquieted,—then he must also bring his God before him in a shape which not only shall the most definitely answer to his purely human manner of looking at things, but shall also be outwardly the most understandable by him. All understanding comes to us through love alone, and man is urged the most instinctively towards the essence of his own species. Just as the human form is to him the most comprehensible, so also will the essence of natural phenomena—which he does not know as yet in their reality—become comprehensible only through condensation to a human form. Thus in Mythos all the shaping impulse of the Folk makes toward realising to its senses a broadest grouping of the most manifold phenomena, and in the most succinct of shapes. At first a mere image formed by Phantasy, this shape behaves itself the more entirely according to human attributes, the plainer it is to become, notwithstanding that its Content is in truth a suprahuman and supranatural one : to wit, that joint operation of multi-human or omninatural force and faculty which, conceived as merely *the concordant action* of human and natural forces in general, is certainly both natural and human, but appears superhuman and supernatural by the very fact that it is ascribed to *one* imagined individual, represented in the shape of Man.* By its faculty of thus using its force of imagin-

* The *immediate* source of this idea, in the writings of Feuerbach, will be found in my footnote to " *Art and Climate*," pages 260-1, Vol. I. of this series.—TR.

ation to bring before itself every thinkable reality and
actuality, in widest reach but plain, succinct and plastic
shaping, the Folk therefore becomes in Mythos the creator
of Art; for these shapes must necessarily win artistic form
and content, if—which, again, is their individual mark—they
have sprung from nothing but man's longing for a *seizable*
portrait of things, and thus from his yearning to recognise
in the object portrayed, nay *first to know* therein, himself
and his own-est essence: that god-creative essence.   Art,
by the very meaning of the term, is nothing but the fulfilment of a longing to know oneself in the likeness of an
object of one's love or adoration, to find oneself again in
the things of the outer world, thus conquered by their representment.*   In the object he has represented, the Artist
says to himself: "So art thou; so feel'st and thinkest
thou. And so wouldst thou do; if, freed from all the strenuous caprice of outward haps of life, thou mightest do
according to thy choice."   Thus did the Folk portray in
Mythos to itself its *God;* thus its *Hero;* and thus, at last, its
Man.—

Greek Tragedy is the artistic embodiment of the spirit
and contents of Greek Mythos.   As in this Mythos the
widest-ranging phenomena were compressed into closer
and ever closer shape, so the Drama took this shape and
re-presented it in the closest, most compressed of forms.
The view-in-common of the essence of things, which in
Mythos had condensed itself from a view of Nature to a
view of Men and morals, here appeals in its distinctest,
most pregnant form to the most universal receptive-force of
man; and thus steps, as Art-work, from Phantasy into
reality.   As in Drama the shapes that had been in Mythos
merely shapes of Thought, were now presented in actual
bodily portrayal by living men : so the actually represented
Action now compressed itself, in thorough keeping with
the mythic essence, into a compact, plastic whole.   If a

---

* It would seem that our author here derives " Kunst " (art) from " kennen "
(to know), whereas in the " Art-work of the Future " (Vol I., p. 100, Eng.) he
derives it from " können " (to ' can ').—TR.

man's idea (*Gesinnung*) is only bared to us convincingly
by his action, and if a man's character consists in the complete harmony between his idea and his action : then this
action, and therefore also its underlying idea—entirely in
the sense of the Mythos—gains significance, and correspondence with a wide-reaching Content, by its manifesting
itself in utmost concentration. An action which consists of
many parts, is either over-weighted, redundant, and unintelligible—when all these parts are of equally suggestive,
decisive importance ; or it is petty, arbitrary and meaningless—when these parts are nothing but odds and ends of
actions. The Content of an action is the idea that lies at
the bottom of it : if this idea is a great one, wide of reach,
and drawing upon man's whole nature in any one particular line, then it also ordains an action which shall be
decisive, one and indivisible ; for only in such an action
does a great idea reveal itself to us.

Now, by its nature, the Content of Greek Mythos was
of this wide-reaching but compact quality ; and in their
Tragedy it likewise uttered itself, with fullest definition, as
this one, necessary, and decisive Action. To allow this
Action, in its weightiest significance, to proceed in a
manner fully vindicated by the idea of its transactors—
this was the task of the Tragic-poet ; to bring to
understanding the Necessity of the action, by and in the
demonstrated truth of the idea,—in this consisted the
solution of that task. The unitarian Form of his artwork,
however, lay already mapped out for him in the contours
of the Mythos ; which he had only to work up into a
living edifice, but in no wise to break to pieces and newly
fit together in favour of an arbitrarily-conceived artistic
building. The Tragic-poet merely imparted the content
and essence of the myth in the most conclusive and intelligible manner ; his Tragedy is nothing other than the
artistic completion of the Myth itself ; while the Myth is
the poem of a life-view in common.

Let us now try to make plain to ourselves, what is the life-view of the modern world which has found its artistic expression in *the Romance.*—

So soon as the reflective Understanding looked aside from the image, to inquire into the actuality of the things summed-up in it, the first thing it saw was an ever waxing multitude of units, where the poetic view had seen a whole. Anatomical Science began her work, and followed a diametrically opposite path to that of the Folk's-poem. Where the latter instinctively united, she separated purposely; where it fain would represent the grouping, she made for an exactest knowledge of the parts: and thus must every intuition of the Folk be exterminated step by step, be overcome as heresy, be laughed away as childish. The nature-view of the Folk has dissolved into physics and chemistry, its religion into theology and philosophy, its commonwealth into politics and diplomacy, its art into science and æsthetics,—and its Myth into the historic Chronicle.—

Even the new world won from the Myth its fashioning force. From the meeting and mingling of two chief mythic rounds, which could never entirely permeate each other, never lift themselves into a plastic unity, there issued the medieval Romance.

In the *Christian Mythos* we find that That to which the Greek referred all outer things, what he had therefore made the sure-shaped meeting-place of all his views of Nature and the World,—the *Human being,*—had become the *à priori* Incomprehensible, become a stranger to itself. The Greek, by a comparison of outward things with Man, had reached the human being from without: returning from his rovings through the breadth of Nature, he found in Man's stature, in his instinctive ethical notions, both quieting and measure. But this measure was a fancied one, and realised in Art alone. With his attempt to deliberately realise it in the State, the contradiction between that fancy standard, and the reality of actual

human self-will,* revealed itself: insofar as State and
Individual could only seek to uphold themselves by the
openest overstepping of that fancy standard. When the
natural custom had become an arbitrarily enacted Law, the
racial commonweal an arbitrarily constructed political State,
then the instinctive life-bent of the human being in turn
resisted law and state with all the appearance of egoistic
caprice. In the strife between that which man had recognised as good and right, such as Law and State, and that
toward which his bent-to-happiness was thrusting him—
the freedom of the Individual,—the human being must at
last become incomprehensible to himself; and this confusion as to himself, was the starting-point of the Christian
mythos. In this latter the *individual* man, athirst for
reconcilement with himself, strode on towards a longed-for,
but yet a Faith-vouchsafed redemption into an extramundane Being, in whom both Law and State were so far
done away with, as they were conceived included in his
unfathomable will. Nature, from whom the Greek had
reached a plain conception of the Human being, the
Christian had to altogether overlook: as he took for her
highest pinnacle redemption-needing Man, at discord with
himself, she could but seem to him the more discordant
and accurst. Science, which dissected Nature into fragments, without ever ·finding the real bond between those
fragments, could only fortify the Christian view of
Nature.

The Christian myth, however, won bodily shape in the
person of a man who suffered martyr's-death for the with-
standing of Law and State ; who, in his submission to
judgment, vindicated Law and State as outward necessities ; but through his voluntary death, withal, annulled

---

* " *Willkür*,"—in the edition of 1852 this stood as "*Unwillkür*" (Instinct).
The same alteration has been made by our author a few pages farther on :
Vol. IV., p. 54, line 6, of the *Gesammelte Schriften*. By reference to Volume
I. of the present series, page 26, it would appear that he had actually com-
menced the substitution there alluded to, but abandoned it after this pair of
fractional attempts.—TR.

them both in favour of an inner Necessity, the liberation of
the Individual through redemption into God. The enthralling power of the Christian myth consists in its portrayal
of a *transfiguration through Death.* The broken, death-rapt
look of an expiring dear one, who, already past all consciousness, for the last time sends to us the lightning of his
glance, exerts on us an impression of the most poignant
grief. But this glance is followed with a smile on the wan
cheeks and blanching lips ; a smile which, sprung in itself
from the joyful feeling of triumph over Death's last agony,
at onset of the final dissolution, yet makes on us the impression of a forebodal of over-earthly bliss, such as could
only be won by extinction of the bodily man. And just
as we have seen him in his passing, so does the departed
one stay pictured in our memory : it removes from his
image all sense of wilfulness or uncertainty in his physical
life-utterance ; our spiritual eye, the gaze of loving recollection, sees the henceforth but remembered one in the soft
glamour of unsuffering, reposeful bliss. Thus the moment
of death appears to us as the moment of actual redemption
into God ; for, through his dying, we think alone of the
beloved as parted from all feeling of a Life whose joys we
soon forget amid the yearning for imagined greater joys,
but whose griefs, above all in our longing after the trans-
figured one, our minds hold fast as the essence of the
sensation of Life itself.

This *dying*, with the yearning after it, is the sole true
content of the Art which issued from the Christian myth ;
it utters itself as dread and loathing of actual life, as flight
before it,—as longing for death. For the Greek, Death
counted not merely as a natural, but also as an ethical
necessity ; yet *only as the counterpart of Life*, which *in
itself* was the real object of all his viewings, including
those of Art. The very actuality* and instinctive necessity
of Life, determined of themselves the tragic death ; which

* " Wirklichkeit."—As the meaning of this term is somewhat less rigi than
that of our " reality," I have had to render it occasionally by " actuality,"
" genuineness," or " truth," according to circumstances.—TR.

in itself was nothing else but the rounding of a life fulfilled by evolution of the fullest individuality, of a life expended on making tell this individuality.   To the Christian, how- ever, Death was *in itself* the object.   For him, Life had its only sacredness and warranty as the preparation for Death, in the longing for its laying down.   The conscious strip- ping-off the physical body, achieved with the whole force of Will, the purposed demolition of actual being, was the object of all Christian art; which therefore could only be limned, described, but never *represented*, and least of all in Drama.*   The distinctive element of Drama is its artistic realising of the Movement of a sharply outlined content. A movement, however, can chain our interest only when it *increases ;* a diminishing movement weakens and dissipates our interest,—excepting where a necessary lull is given expression to in passing.   In a Greek drama the movement waxes from the beginning, with constantly accelerated speed, to the mighty storm of the catastrophe ; whereas the genuine, unmixed Christian drama must perforce begin with the storm of life, to weaken down its movement to the final swoon of dying-out.   The Passion-plays of the Middle Ages represented the sufferings of Jesus in the form of a series of living pictures : the chief and most affecting of these pictures shewed Jesus hanging on the cross : hymns and psalms were sung during the performance.—*The Legend*, that Christian form of the Romance, could alone give charm to a portrayal of the Christian Stuff, because it appealed only to the Phantasy,—as alone was possible with this Stuff,—and not to physical vision.   To Music alone, was it reserved to represent this Stuff to the senses also, namely by an outwardly perceptible motion ; albeit merely in this wise, that she resolved it altogether into moments of Feeling, into blends of colour without drawing, expiring

---

* Here it is not necessary to go back to Feuerbach, for our author's idea. His own abandonment of his dramatic sketch of " *Jesus of Nazareth* " must have arisen from a feeling that in *this* form it was impossible ; while, on the other hand, he had not yet developed for himself the broader basis which made possible his *Parsifal.*—TR.

in the tinted waves of Harmony in like fashion as the dying one dissolves from out the actuality of Life.*

Of the myths which have worked decisively upon the life-views and art-fashionings of the modern era we now come to the other circle, and that opposed to the Christian myths. It is the native Saga of the newer European, but above all the *German* peoples.

Like that of the Hellenes, the Mythos of these peoples waxed from beholdings of Nature into picturings of Gods and Heroes. In the case of one of these sagas—that of Siegfried—we now may look with tolerable clearness into its primordial germ, which teaches us no little about the essence of myths in general. We here see natural phenomena, such as those of day and night, the rising and the setting sun, condensed by human Phantasy into personal agents revered or feared in virtue of their deeds ; at last, from man-created Gods we see them transformed into actual human Heroes, supposed to have one-time really lived, and from whose loins existing stems and races have boasted themselves as sprung. The Mythos so reached into the heart of actual Life, giving shape and measure, revindicating claims and kindling men to deeds, where it not only was nurtured as a religious Faith but proclaimed itself as energised Religion. A boundless wealth of cherished haps and actions filled out the breadth of this religious Mythos, when fashioned into the Hero-saga : yet how manifold soever these sung and fabled actions might give themselves to be, they all arose as variations of one very definite type of events, which, on closer examination, we may trace back to one simple religious notion. In this

---

* " Die in der farbigen Zerflossenheit der Harmonie so erlosch, wie der Sterbende aus der Wirklichkeit des Lebens zerfliesst."—It is impossible to pass over the prefigurement of Kundry's release, in *Parsifal*, and Isolde's " Liebestod."—TR.

L

religious notion, taken from the beholding of Nature, the
most varied utterances of the endless-branching Sagas—
amid the undisturbed development of a specific Mythos—
had each their ever-fruitful source. Let the shapings of
the Saga enrich themselves as they might with fresh
stores of actual events, among the countless stems and
races : yet the poetic shaping of the new material was
instinctively brought about in the one and only way that
belonged to the poetic intuition for good and all, and this
was rooted deeply in the same religious beholding of
Nature which once had given birth to the primordial
Mythos.

Thus these peoples' poetic shaping-force was a religious
one withal, unconsciously common to them and rooted in
their oldest intuition of the essence of things.   On *this root*,
however, Christianity now laid its hands. The enormous
wealth of leaves and branches of the Germanic Folk-tree
the Christians' pious passion for conversion could not come
at ; * but it tried to drag up the root wherewith that tree
had anchored in the soil of being.   Christianity upheaved
the religious faith, the ground-view of Nature's essence,
and supplanted it by a new belief, a new way of beholding,
diametrically opposed to the older. Though it could not
completely root out the old belief, at least it robbed it of
its virile wealth of artist-force : and that which hitherto
had sprung from out this force, the teeming amplitude of
Saga, stayed now a bough cut off from stem and stringers,
un-nourished by its vital sap and offering but a sorry
sustenance to the Folk itself.   Whereas the religious
intuitions of the Folk had earlier formed a girth which bound
into one whole each never so varied shaping of the Saga :
since the rending of this girdle there now was nothing left
beyond a loose entanglement of motley shapes, flitting
holdless and disbanded to and fro, in a fancy henceforth
merely bent on recreation but no more in itself creative.

---

* Compare the brief preface to the original edition of the *Tannhäuser* text-
book, given in Mrs John P. Morgan's English version (Schott & Co.), and
also translated in *The Meister*, No. XV.—Tr.

The Mythos, grown incapable of procreation, dispersed itself into its individual hedged-off fractions ; its unity into a thousandfold plurality ; the kernel of its Action into a mass of many actions. These actions, in themselves but the individualisations of a great root-action—as it were the personal variations of the same *one action* that had been the necessary utterance of the spirit of the Folk— became splintered and disfigured to such a degree, that their separate parts could be pieced together again by arbitrary whim ; and this to feed the restless impulse of a Phantasy which, maimed within and reft of power to shape without, could now devour alone the outer matter, but no longer give the inner from itself. The splintering and extinction of the German Epos, as evinced to us by the whirring figures of the " Heldenbuch," shews itself in a monstrous mass of actions, swelling all the larger the more has every genuine Content vanished from them.—

Through the adoption of Christianity the Folk had lost all true understanding of the original, vital relations of this Mythos, and when the life of its single body had been resolved by death into the myriad lives of a swarm of fables, the *Christian religious-view* was fitted under it, as though for its fresh quickening. By its intrinsic property, this view could do absolutely nothing more, than light up *that corpse* of Mythos and deck it with a mystic apotheosis. In a sense it justified the death of Myth, inasmuch as it set before itself those clumsy actions, that tangle of cross-purposes—in themselves no longer explicable or vindicable by any intelligible idea still proper to the Folk—in all their whimsical caprice, and, finding it impossible to assign an adequate motive to them, conveyed them to the Christian Death as their redeeming issue.* The Christian

* This sentence will be better understood on reference to "*Art and Climate*" (Vol. I., page 256, of this series), where the idea of the *Eddas* being based on Christianity is rightly scouted. As Mons. Georges Noufflard has pointed out in his valuable work, "*Wagner d' après lui-meme*," this "*Opera and Drama*" seems to be written round the *Siegfried* drama (that is to say, its *incubating* germ), and the next sentence certainly confirms that view.—TR.

Ritter-Romance * gives a faithful expression to the life of
the Middle Ages, by beginning with the myriad leavings of
the corpse of the ancient Hero-Mythos, with a swarm of
actions whose true idea appears to us unfathomable and
capricious, because their motives, resting on a view of life
quite alien to the Christian's, had been lost to the poet : to
expose the utter lack of rhyme or reason in these actions,
and out of their own mouths to vindicate to the instinctive
Feeling the necessity of their transactors' downfall,—be it
by a sincere adoption of the Christian rules, which incul-
cated a life of contemplation and inaction, or be it by the
uttermost effectuation of the Christian view, the martyr's-
death itself,—this was the natural bent and purpose of the
spiritual-poem of Chivalry.

The original Stuff of the pagan Mythos, however, had
already swelled into the most extravagant complexity of
'actions,' by admixture of the Sagas of every nation—of
Sagas cut adrift, like the Germanic, from their vital root.
By Christianity every Folk, which adopted that confession,
was torn from the soil of its natural mode of viewing, and
the poems that had sprung therefrom were turned into
playthings for the unchained Phantasy.   In the multifarious intercourse of the Crusades, the orient and the
occident had interchanged these stuffs, and stretched
their manysidedness to a monstrosity.   Whereas in earlier
days the Folk included nothing but the *homelike* in its
myths : now that its understanding of the homelike had
been lost, it sought for recompense in a constant novelty of
the *outlandish*.   In its burning hunger, it gulped down
everything foreign and unwonted : its voracious phantasy
exhausted all the possibilities of human imagination,—to
digest them into the wildest medley of adventures.

This bent at last the Christian view could no more
guide, albeit itself, at bottom, had been its generator ; for
this bent was primarily nothing but the stress to flee from
an un-understood reality, to gain contentment in a world

---

* The Chivalresque Romance, such as the countless dragon-stories, among
which may be instanced our own " St George."—TR.

of fancy.   But this fancied world, however great the diva-
gations of Phantasy, still must take its archetype from the
actual world and nothing else : the imagination finally
could only do over again what it had done in Mythos ; it
pressed together all the realities of the actual world—all
that it could comprehend—into close-packed images, in
which it individualised the essence of totalities and thus
furbished them into marvels of monstrosity.   In truth this
newer thrust of Phantasy, just as with the Mythos, made
again toward finding the reality ; and that, the reality of a
vastly extended outer world.   Its effectuation, in this sense,
did not go long a-begging.   The passion for adventures, in
which men yearned to realise the pictures of their fancy,
condensed itself at last to a passion for undertakings whose
goal—after the   thousand-times   proved   fruitlessness   of
mere adventures—should be the knowledge of the outer
world, a tasting of the fruit of actual experiences reaped
on a definite path of earnest, keen endeavour.   Daring
voyages of discovery undertaken with a conscious aim, and
profound scientific researches grounded on their results, at
last uncloaked to us the world as it really is.—By this
knowledge was the Romance of the Middle Ages destroyed,
and the delineation of *fancied* shows was followed by the
delineation of their reality.

This reality, however, had stayed untroubled, undisfigured by our errors, in the phenomena of *Nature alone*,
unreachable by our activity.   On the reality of *Human
Life* our errors had lain the most distorting hand of
violence.   To vanquish these as well, to know the life of
Man in the Necessity of its individual and social nature ;
and finally, since that stands within our might, *to shape it*—
this is the trend of humankind since ever it wrested to itself
the outward faculty of knowing the phenomena of Nature
in their genuine essence; for from this knowledge have
we won the measure for the knowledge, also, of the essence
of Mankind.

The Christian life-view—which had unwittingly engendered this outward thrust of man, but of itself could
neither feed nor guide it—had withdrawn into itself before
this vision, had shrunk into a stolid Dogma, as though for
sanctuary against a thing it could not comprehend. It is
here that the intrinsic weakness and contradictoriness of
this view bewrayed itself. Actual Life, and the ground of
its phenomena, to it had ever been a thing incomprehensible.
The strife between the law-made State and the selfwill* of
the Individual it had been the less able to overcome, as the
roots of its own origin and essence lay in that strife alone :
were the individual man completely reconciled with the
commonwealth—nay, should he find therein the fullest
satisfaction of his bent toward happiness, then would all
necessity of the Christian view be done away with, and
Christianity itself be practically annulled. But as this view
had originally sprung from that discord in the human mind,
so Christianity, in its bearings toward the world, fed itself on
the continuance of that discord, nothing else ; and its *purposed maintenance* must therefore become the life-task of the
Church, so soon as ever she grew fully conscious of her lifespring.—

The *Christian Church* had also striven for unity: every
vital manifestment was to converge in her, as the centre of
all life. She was not, however, life's central, but its terminal point ; for the secret of the truest Christian essence was
Death. At the other terminus there stood the natural
fount of Life itself, of which Death can only become master
through its annihilation : but the power which ever led this
life towards the Christian-death, was none other than *the
State* itself. The State was the veritable lifespring of the
Christian Church ; this latter warred against herself, when
she strove against the State. What the Church of the
Middle Ages disputed, in her despotic *but honest* zeal for
the Faith, was the remnant of old pagan ideas which expressed itself in the individual self-sanction of the worldly
rulers. By imposing on these rulers the duty of seeking

* " Willkür " substituted for " Unwillkür," as pointed out on page 158.—TR.

their authority from divine sanction, through the Church as intermediary, she drove them to consolidate the absolute, four-square State,* as though she had felt that such a State was needful to her own existence. Thus the Church was obliged at last to help fortify her own antithesis, the State, so as to render possible her own existence by making it a dualistic one ; she became herself a political might, because she felt that she could exist in none but a political world. The Christian life-view,—whose inner consciousness, rightly speaking, did away with the State,—now that it had condensed into a Church, not only became the vindicatrix of the State, but she brought its standing menace to the freedom of the Individual to such a pitch that henceforth man's outward-thrust turned towards his liberation from Church and State alike, as though to find in human life itself a final realising of the nature of things, which he had now beheld in their true essence.

But first the actuality (*Wirklichkeit*) of Life and its shows themselves, was to be explored in like fashion as the actuality of natural phenomena had been explored by voyages of discovery and scientific research.   Men's thrust, directed heretofore to outward things, now turned back to the actuality of Social Life ; and that with all the greater zeal as, after flight to the uttermost ends of the earth, they had never been able to rid themselves of these social conditions, but everywhere had stayed subjected to them.   What man instinctively had fled from, and yet in truth could never flee away from, must at last be recognised as rooted so deeply in our own heart and our involuntary view of the essence of things human, that a flight from *it* to outer realms was clean impossible.   Returning from the endless breadths of Nature, where we had found the imaginings of our Phantasy refuted by the essence of things, we

* It will be remembered (Vide Vol. I. page 359) that Wagner, not long before writing these lines, had been engaged in collecting materials for a drama on the subject of *Barbarossa*,—simultaneously with his " Siegfried " researches,—and that at the end of 1849 he had published these materials under the title of "*Die Wibelungen.*" That essay (*Ges. Schr.* Vol. II.) contains a longer exposition of the present thesis.—TR.

were necessarily driven to seek in a plain and lucid contemplation of human affairs the selfsame refutation for a
visionary, a false opinion thereof ; for we felt that we must
have fed and formed those affairs themselves in the same
way as we had earlier formed our erroneous opinions of
the phenomena of Nature. The first and weightiest step
toward knowledge consisted, therefore, in grasping the
phenomena of Life according to their actuality : and that, at
first, without passing any judgment on them, but with the
single aim to bring before ourselves their actual facts and
grouping as perspicuously and truthfully as possible. As
long as seafarers had set before themselves the object of
discovery according to preconceived opinions, so long did
they always find themselves disillusioned by the reality at
last perceived ; wherefore the explorer of our life-affairs
held himself freer and freer from pre-judgment, the surer
to reach the bottom of their actual essence. The most
unruffled mode of looking at the naked, undisfigured truth
henceforth becomes the Poet's plumb-line: to seize and
exhibit human beings and their affairs as they *are*, and not
as one had earlier imagined them, is from now the task
alike of the Historian and of the Artist who fain would set
before himself in miniature the actuality of Life,—and
Shakespeare was the unmatched master in this art, which
let him find the shape for his Drama.

Yet not in the actual Drama, as we have seen, was this
actuality of Life to be portrayed artistically, but only in
the describing, delineating Romance ; and that for reasons
which this Actuality itself alone can teach us.

————————

Man * can only be comprehended in conjunction with

* With this paragraph, begins the second of the three extracts from *Oper
und Drama* which appeared in the *Deutsche Monatsschrift*. That second extract was contained in the number for May 1851, and included the succeeding
pages, down to the first third of Chapter IV. ; but with a considerable omission (?) from Chapter III., as will be pointed out *in loco*.—TR.

men in general, with his Surrounding: man divorced from this, above all *the modern man*, must appear *of all things the most incomprehensible.* The restless inner discord of this Man, who between 'will' and 'can' had created for himself a chaos of tormenting notions, driving him to war against himself, to self-laceration and bodiless abandonment to the Christian death,—this discord was not so much to be explained, as Christianity had sought to do, from the nature of the Individual-man himself, as from the confusion wrought on this nature by an unintelligent view of the essence of Society. Those torturing notions, which disturbed this view, must needs be referred back to the reality that lay at bottom of them; and, as this reality, the investigator had to recognise the true condition of Human Society. Yet neither could this condition, in which a thousandfold authority was fed upon a millionfold * injustice and man was hedged from man by infranchisable barriers, first imagined and then realised,—neither could *this* be comprehended out of its mere self; out of historical traditions converted into rights, out of the heart of facts and finally of the spirit of historical events, out of the ideas which had called them forth, must it be unriddled.

Before the gaze of the Investigator, in his search for the human being, these historic facts upheaped themselves to so huge a mass of recorded incidents and actions, that the medieval Romance's plethora-of-Stuff seemed naked penury compared therewith. And yet this mass, whose closer regardal shewed it stretching into ever more intricate ramifyings, was to be pierced to its core by the searcher after the reality of man's affairs, in order to unearth from amidst its crushing waste the one thing that might reward such toil, the genuine undisfigured Man in all his nature's verity. Faced with an expanse of matters-of-fact beyond what his two eyes could grasp, the historical investigator must perforce set bounds to his avidity of research. From a broader conjunction, which he could only have sug-

* In the *D. M.* "a thousandfold" (*tausendfache*) was here repeated, in place of the later "millionenfache."—TR.

gested, he must tear off fragments : by them to shew with
greater exactitude a closer coherence, without which no
historical representment can ever be intelligible. But even
within the narrowest bounds, this coherence, through which
alone an historic action is understandable, is only to be
made possible by the most circumstantial setting forth of
a Surrounding ; in which, again, we can never take any
sort of interest, until it is brought to view by the liveliest
description. Through the felt necessity of such description, the Investigator must needs become a Poet again :
but his method could only be one opposed outright to that
of the dramatic-poet. The dramatic-poet compresses the
Surrounding of his personages into proportions easy to
take in, in order to allow their Action—which again he
compresses, both in utterance and content, into a comprehensive main-action—to issue from the essential ' idea ' of
the Individual, to allow this individuality to come to a
head therein, and by it to display Man's common essence
along one of its definite lines.

The Romance-writer (*Romandichter*), on the other hand,
has to explain the action of an historic chief-personage by
the outer necessity of the Surrounding : in order to give
us the impression of historic truth, he has above all to
bring to our understanding the character of this Surrounding, since therein lie grounded all the calls which determine
the individual to act *thus* and not otherwise. In the
Historical Romance we try to make comprehensible to
ourselves the man whom we positively cannot understand
from a purely human standpoint. If we attempt to image
to ourselves the action of an historic man as downright
and purely human, it cannot but appear to us highly
capricious, without rhyme or reason, and in any case unnatural, just because we are unable to vindicate the ' idea '
of that action on grounds of purely-human nature. The
idea of an historic personage is the idea of an Individual
only in so far as he acquires it from a generally-accepted
view of the essence of things ; this generally-accepted view,
however,—*not* being a purely-human one, nor therefore

valid for every place and time,—finds its only explanation in a purely Historic relation, which changes with the lapse of time and is never the same at two epochs. This relation, again, and its mutation we can only clear up to ourselves by following the whole chain of historic events, whose many-membered series has so worked upon a simpler historic-relation that it has taken *this* particular shape, and that precisely *this* idea has enounced itself therein as a commonly current view. Wherefore the Individual, in whose action this idea is to express itself, must be degraded to an infinitesimal measure of individual freedom, to make his action and idea at all comprehensible to us :—his idea, to be in any way cleared up, is only to be vindicated through the idea of his Surrounding; while this latter, again, can only make itself plain in a number of actions, which have to encroach the more upon the space of the artistic portrait, as only in its most intricate branching and extension can the Surrounding, also, become understood of us.

Thus the Romance-writer has to occupy himself almost solely with a description of the Surrounding, and to become understandable he must be circumstantial. On what the dramatist *pre*supposes, for an understanding of the Surrounding, the romance-writer has to employ his whole powers of portrayal ; the current view, on which the dramatist takes his footing from the first, the romance-writer has to cunningly develop and fix in the course of his portrayal. The Drama, therefore, goes from within outwards,* the Romance from without inwards. From a simple, universally intelligible Surrounding, the dramatist rises to an ever richer development of the Individuality; from a complex, toilsomely explained Surrounding, the romance-writer sinks exhausted to a delineation of the

---

* In Vol. VII., pages 163-4, of the *Ges. Schr.* (given in English in No. XVII. of *The Meister*, page 39), Wagner has shewn this to be the root-idea, pre-eminently, of his *Tristan und Isolde*. With regard to the text above,—this sentence : "The Drama," etc., was in the *D.M.* placed after the two succeeding ones.—Tr.

Individual, which, poverty-stricken in itself, could be tricked-out with individuality by that Surrounding alone. In the Drama, a sinewy and fully self-developed individuality enriches its surrounding ; in the Romance, the surrounding feeds the ravenings of an empty individuality. Thus the Drama lays bare to us the Organism of mankind, inasmuch as it shews the Individuality as the essence of the Species ; whereas the Romance shews us the Mechanism of history, according to which the Species becomes the essence of the Individuality.* And thus also, the art-procedure in Drama is an *organic* one, in Romance a *mechanical :* for the Drama gives us the *man,* the Romance explains to us the *citizen;* the one shews us the fulness of Human nature, the other apologises for its penury on plea of the State. The Drama, then, shapes from innermost necessity, the Romance from outermost constraint.

Yet the Romance was no arbitrary, but a necessary product of our modern march of evolution : it gave honest artistic expression to life-affairs which were only to be portrayed by it, and not by Drama. The Romance made for representing Actuality (*Wirklichkeit*) ; and its endeavour was so sincere, that at last it demolished itself, as art-work, in favour of this Actuality.

Its highest pitch, as an art-form, was reached by the Romance when, from the standpoint of purely artistic necessity, it made its own the Mythos' plan of moulding

---

* Reference should here be made to the foot-note on pages 276-7, Vol. I., containing a passage from Feuerbach's *Essence of Christianity.* In the *D.M.* this sentence stood : " Das Drama deckt uns den Organismus der Menschheit auf, indem die Individualität in die Gattung aufgeht,—der Roman aber den Mechanismus der Geschichte, nach welchem die Gattung dem Individuum zur Verzehrung vorgeworfen wird ; und so ist " . . . ; Anglice, " The Drama lays bare to us the Organism of mankind, inasmuch as the Individuality ascends into the Species, — but the Romance the Mechanism of history, according to which the Species is flung before the Individual, for his consumption ; and thus also " . . . I cannot but think that the original, less Feuerbachian form was, in this case, the better of the two.—Moreover, the last sentence of this paragraph is an addition made since the *D.M.*, but appears in all the issues of the *book.*—TR.

types. Just as the medieval romance had welded into
wondrous shapes the motley shows of foreign peoples,
lands and climates : so the newer Historical-romance
sought to display the motleyest utterances of the spirit of
whole historic periods as issuing from the essence of one
particular historic individual.   In this procedure, the
customary method of looking at history could but countenance the Romance-writer.   In order to arrange the
excess of historical facts for easy survey by our eye, we
are accustomed to regard the most prominent personalities
alone, and in them to consider as embodied the spirit of
a period.   As such personalities, the wisdom of the
chronicler has mostly bequeathed us the Rulers ; those,
from whose will and ordering the historic undertakings
and State-economy were supposed to have issued.   The
unclear ' idea ' and contradictory manner of action of these
chiefs, but above all the circumstance that they never
really reached their aimed-for goal, allowed us in the first
place so far to misunderstand the spirit of history, that we
deemed it necessary to explain the caprice (*Willkür*) in
these rulers' actions by higher, inscrutable influences,
guiding and foreordering the course and scope of history.
Those factors (*Faktoren*) of history seemed to us will-less
tools—or if wilful, yet self-contradictory—in the hands
of an extrahuman, heavenly power.   The end-results of
history we posited as the cause of its movement, or as the
goal toward which a higher, conscious spirit had therein
striven from the beginning.   Led by this view, the ex-
pounders or setters-forth of History believed themselves
justified in deriving the seemingly arbitrary actions of its
ruling personages from ' ideas ' in which was mirrored back
the imputed consciousness of a governing World-spirit :
wherefore they destroyed the unconscious Necessity of
these rulers' motives of action, and, so soon as they
deemed they had sufficiently accounted for those actions,
they displayed them as arbitrary out-and-out.—
     Through this procedure alone, whereby historic actions
could be disfigured and combined at will, did the Romance

succeed in inventing types, and in lifting itself to a certain
height of art-work, whereon it might seem qualified anew
for dramatisation.   Our latter days have presented us with
many such an Historical-drama, and the zest of making
history in behoof of the dramatic form is nowadays so
great, that our skilled historical stage-conjurors fancy the
secret of history itself has been revealed for the sole benefit
of the play-maker.   They believe themselves all the more
justified in their procedure, as they have even made it
possible to invest History's dramatic installation * with the
completest Unity of place and time : they have thrust into
the inmost recesses of the whole historic mechanism, and
have discovered its heart to be the antechamber of the
Prince, where Man and the State make their mutual
arrangements between breakfast and supper.   That this
artistic Unity and this History, however, are equal forgeries,
and that a falsehood can only have a forged effect,—*this*
has established itself plainly enough in the course of our
present-day Historic Drama.   But, that true history itself
is no stuff for Drama,—this we now know also ; since this
Historical Drama has made it clear to us, that even the
Romance could only reach its appointed height, as art-
form, by sinning against the truth of history.

From this height the Romance stepped down again, in
order, while giving up its aimed-for purity † as art-work, to
engage in truthful portraiture of historic life.

The seeming Caprice in the actions of historical chief-
personages could only be explained, to the honour of mankind, through discovering the soil from which those actions
sprang of instinct and necessity.   As one had earlier
thought it incumbent to place this Necessity *above*, soaring
over the historic personages and using them as tools of its
transcendent wisdom ; and as one at last had grown convinced of both the artistic and the scientific barrenness of
this view : so thinkers and poets now sought for this

---

* "Herstellung"; in the *D.M.* this was "Darstellung," *i.e.*, "representment."—Tr.

† "Reinheit,"—in the *D.M.* this stood as "Einheit," *i.e*, "unity."—Tr.

explanatory Necessity *below*, among the foundations of all history.   The soil of history is *man's social nature :* from the individual's need to unite himself with the essence of his species, in order in Society (*Gesellschaft*) to bring his faculties into highest play, arises the whole movement of history.   The historic phenomena are the outward manifestments of an inner movement, whose core is the Social Nature of man.   But the prime motor of this nature is the *Individual*, who only in the satisfaction of his instinctive longing for Love (*Liebesverlangen*) can appease his bent-to-happiness.   Now, to argue from this nature's manifestments to its core,—from the dead body of the completed Fact to go back upon the inner life of man's social bent, from which that fact had issued as a ready, ripe, and dying fruit,—in *this* was evinced the evolutionary march of modern times.

What the Thinker grasps by its essence, the Poet seeks to shew in its phenomena : the phenomena of human society, which *he*, too, had recognised as the soil of history, the Poet strove to set before him in a conjunction through which he might be able to explain them.   As the most seizable conjunction of social phenomena he took the wonted surroundings of Burgher-life, in order by their description to explain to himself the man who, remote from any participation in the outward facts of history, yet seemed to him to condition them.   However, this *Burgher society*, as I have before expressed myself,* was nothing but a precipitate from that history which weighed upon it from above,—at least in its outward form.   Without a doubt, since the consolidation of the modern State, the world's new life-stir begins to centre in the burgher class : the living energy of *historic* phenomena weakens down in direct ratio as the burgher class endeavours to bring its claims to tell upon the State.   But precisely through its inner lack of interest in the events of history, through its dull, indifferent looking-on, it bares to us the burden wherewith they weigh it down, and under which it

* See page 140.—TR.

shrugs its shoulders in resigned ill-will. Our Burgher society is in so far no living organism, as its shaping is effected from Above, by the reaction of historic agencies. The physiognomy of Burgher society is the flattened, disfigured physiognomy of history, with all its expression washed out : what the latter expresses through living motion in the breath of Time, the former gives us in the dull expanse of Space. But this physiognomy is the mask of Burgher-society, under which it still hides from the human-seeking eye the Man himself : the artistic delineators of this society could only describe the features of that mask, not those of the veritable human being; the more faithful was their description, the more must the artwork lose in living force of expression.

If, then, this mask was lifted, to peer beneath it into the unvarnished features of human society, it was inevitable that *a chaos of unloveliness and formlessness* should be the first to greet the eye. Only in the garment of History had the human being—bred by this history, and by it crippled and degraded from his true sound nature,—preserved an aspect at all tolerable to the artist. This garment once removed, we were horrified to see nothing but a shrivelled, loathly shape, which bore no trace of resemblance to the true man, such as *our thoughts* had pictured in the fulness of his natural essence ; no trace beyond the sad and suffering glance of the stricken unto death,—that glance whence Christianity had derived the transports of its inspiration (*seine schwärmerische Begeisterung*). The yearner for Art turned away from this sight: like Schiller, to dream him dreams of beauty in the realm of Thought ; or like Goethe, to shroud the shape itself in a cloak of artistic beauty,—so well as it could be got to hang thereon. His romance of "Wilhelm Meister" was such a cloak, wherewith Goethe tried to make bearable to himself the sight of the reality : it answered to the naked reality of Modern Man for just so far as he was conceived and exhibited as struggling for an artistically beautiful Form.

Up to then the human shape had been veiled, no less for

the eye of the historical student than for that of the artist, in the costume of History or the uniform of the State: this costume left free play to fancy, this form * to disputations. Poet and Thinker had before them a vast assortment of discretionary shapes, among which they might choose at their artistic pleasure or arbitrary assumption a garment for the human being, whom they still conceived alone in that which was wrapped about him from without. Even Philosophy had allowed this garment to lead her astray, in respect of man's true nature; while the writer of Historical romances was—in a certain sense—a mere costume-drawer. With the baring of the actual shape of modern society, the Romance now took a more practical stand: the poet † could no longer extemporise artistic fancies, now that he had the naked truth unveiled before him, the actuality that filled the looker-on with horror, pity, and indignation. His business was only (*Er brauchte nur*) to display this actuality, without allowing himself to belie it,—he needed only to feel pity, and at once his passion became a vital force. He still could poetise (*dichten*), when he was bent alone on portraying the fearful immorality of our society: but the deep gloom, into which his own portrayings cast him, drove away all pleasure of poetic contemplation, in which he now could less and less delude himself; it drove him out into the actuality itself, there to strive for human society's now recognised real Need. On its path to practical reality the Romance-poem, too, stripped-off yet more and more its artistic garment: its possible Unity, as art-form, must part itself—to operate through the intelligence—into the practical plurality of everyday occurrences. An artistic bond was no longer possible, where everything was struggling to dissolve, where the strenuous bond of the Historic State was to be torn asunder. The Romance-poem turned to

* In the *D. M.* "Uniform."—TR.

† Just as we found the verb "dichten" used in a wider sense than "to make poetry," so we find our author here—and in fact, in many another passage—using the noun "Dichter" to cover a wider field than that of the "Poet" strictly so-called.—In the remainder of the paragraph we have the 'Ibsen question' put in a nutshell, a whole generation before it arose.—TR.

M

Journalism ; its content flew asunder, into *political articles ;* its art became the *rhetoric of the Tribune,* the breath of its discourse a *summons to the people.*

Thus the Poet's art has turned to *politics :* no one now can poetise, without politising.   Yet the politician will never become a poet, precisely until he ceases to be a politician : but in a purely political world * to be *not* a politician, is as good as to say one does not exist at all ; whosoever at this instant steals away from politics (*wer sich jetzt noch unter der Politik hinwegstielt*), he only belies his own being.   The Poet cannot come to light again, until we have no more Politics.

Politics, however, are the secret of our history, and of the state of things therefrom arising.   *Napoleon* put this clearly. He told Goethe that : the rôle of *Fate* in the ancient world is filled, since the empire of the Romans, by *Politics.*   Let us lay to heart this saying of him who smarted in St Helena !   In it is briefly summed the whole truth of what we have to comprehend before we can come to an understanding, also, about the Content and the Form of Drama.

* In the *Deutsche Monatsschrift* in place of "world" there appeared "Zeit,"—i.e. "time" or "era,"—while the "noch" (lit. "as yet") was absent from the clause which I have cited in brackets. These changes are only of importance as fixing the exact shade of meaning our author wished to convey ; but that meaning has acquired additional significance owing to the half blundering, half malicious assertions of those members of the English and German press who have accepted Ferd. Praeger's *mis*quotations as gospel. —Tr.

III.

HE Greek *Fate* is the *inner Nature-necessity*, from which the Greek—*because he did not understand it* *—sought refuge in the arbitrary political State. *Our Fate* is the arbitrary political State, which to us shews itself *as an outer necessity* for the maintenance of Society ; and from which we seek refuge in the Nature-necessity, because we have learnt to understand the latter, and have recognised it as the conditionment of our being and all its shapings.

The Nature-necessity utters itself the strongest and the most invincibly in the physical life-bent (*Lebenstrieb*) of the *Individual,*—less understandably, however, and more open to arbitrary interpretings, in the *ethical views of society* by which the instinctive impulse of the State-included Individual is finally influenced or judged. The life-bent of the Individual utters itself forever *newly* and *directly*, but the essence of Society is *use and wont* and its 'view' a *mediated* one. Wherefore the 'view' of Society, so long as it does not fully comprehend the essence of the Individual and its own genesis therefrom, is a hindering and a shackling one ; and it becomes ever more tyrannical, in exact degree as the quickening and innovating essence of the Individual brings its instinctive thrust to battle against habit. Recognising this thrust as a disturbance, from the standpoint of his ethical Wont, the Greek misinterpreted it in this wise : that he traced it to a conjuncture in which the individual agent was conceived as possessed by an influence robbing him of his freedom of action, of that freedom in which he would have done the ethically (*sittlich*) wonted thing. Since the Individual, through his deed committed against ethical Wont, had ruined himself in the eyes of

---

* In place of this parenthesis, the *D. M.* had " weil er sie der sittlichen Gewohnheit gegenüber endlich missverstand," i.e. " because at last, in face of ethical habit (or ' use and wont '), he *mis*understood it."—Tr.

Society (*vor der Gesellschaft*) ; but yet, with [later] conscience of his deed, in so far re-entered the pale of Society
as he condemned himself by its own conscience (*aus
ihrem Bewusstsein selbst*) : so the act of unconscious sinning appeared explicable through nothing but a curse which
rested on him without his personal guiltiness. This curse
—represented in the Mythos as the divine chastisement for
a primordial crime, and as cleaving to one special stock
until its downfall—is in truth nothing other than an embodiment of the might of Instinct (*Unwillkür*) working in
the unconscious, Nature-bidden actions of the Individual ;
whereas Society appears as the conscious, the capricious
(*Willkürliche*), the true thing to be explained and exculpated. Explained and exculpated will it only be, however,
when *its* manner of viewing is likewise recognised as an
instinctive one, and its conscience as grounded on an
erroneous view of the essence of the Individual.*

Through the *Myth of Œdipus*, significant in so many
other respects, let us make clear to ourselves this relation.

Œdipus had slain a man who affronted and finally drove
him into self-defence. In this, public opinion found nothing worthy of condemnation ; for such-like cases were of
common occurrence, and to be explained on the universally

* Here the corresponding passage in the *D. M.* continues thus : " This
knowledge, however, could never be won by the givers and guarders of the
Law, under whose hands Society, feeling itself entitled to absolute authority
(*absolut berechtigt*), at last hardened itself into the State, and from whom it was
demanded that according to an imagined ' norm ' they should make secure
against the perceived imperfections of its actual existence that Society itself,
which had been unsettled from its habit by the action of the Individual. Yet
that these politicians retained the very imperfections which had come to light
of day " &c.,—the sentence then dovetailing into one that occurs on page 82
of the *Ges. Schr.* Vol. IV. (the present being page 69 of that volume), and will
be noticed hereafter. The whole of the account of the Œdipus and Antigone
myth was thus omitted in that magazine,—or rather, appears to have been
added for the first edition of this book. As this subject, however, is too complex for treatment in a Note, I have relegated it to the 'Translator's Preface '
to the present volume.—TR.

intelligible principle of the necessity of warding off an attack. Still less did Œdipus commit a crime, in that, as payment for a benefit conferred upon the land, he took its widowed Queen to wife.

But it transpired that the slaughtered man was not only the husband of this Queen, but also the father—and thus his widowed wife the mother—of Œdipus himself.

To men the reverence of children for their father, their love toward him, and love's eagerness to cherish and protect him in old age, were such instinctive feelings, and upon these feelings was so founded of itself the most essential ground-view (*Grundanschauung*) of human beings united by that very view into a Society, that a deed which wounded these feelings in their tenderest spot must perforce appear to them both incomprehensible and execrable. These feelings, moreover, were so strong and insurmountable that even the consideration, how that father had first attempted the life of his son, could not overpower them : certainly there was recognised in the death of Laïus a punishment for that earlier crime of his, so that we are unmoved by his destruction ; nevertheless, this circumstance was incompetent to quiet us in any way concerning the deed of *Œdipus*, from which nothing could remove the stain of parricide.

Still more violently was roused the public horror, by the circumstance that Œdipus had wedded his own mother and begotten children of her.—In the life of the Family —the most natural, albeit the most straitened basis of Society—it had been established quite of itself, that betwixt parents and children, as betwixt the children of one pair, there is developed an inclination altogether different from that which proclaims itself in the sudden, violent commotion of sexual love. In the Family the natural ties between begetter and begotten become the ties of Wont ; and only from out of Wont, again, is evolved a natural inclination of brothers and sisters toward one another. But the first attraction of sexual love is brought the stripling by an unwonted object, freshly fronting him from Life itself ; this attraction is so overpowering, that it draws him from the wonted surroundings of the Family, in which this attraction had never presented itself, and drives him forth to journey with the un-wonted. Thus sexual love is the revolutionary, who breaks down the narrow confines of the Family, to widen it itself into the broader reach of human Society. The intuition of the essence of family-love and its distinction from the love between the sexes is therefore an instinctive one, inspired by the very nature of the thing: it rests upon Experience and Wont, and is therefore a view which takes us with all the strength of an insuperable feeling.

Œdipus, who had espoused his mother and begotten children of her, is an object that fills us with horror and loathing, because he unatonably assaults our *wonted* relations towards our mother and the views which we have based thereon.

But if these views, now thriven into ethical conceptions (*sittlichen Begriffen*), were of so great strength only because they had issued instinctively from human nature's feeling, then we ask: Did Œdipus offend against this Human Nature, when he wedded his own mother?—Most certainly not. Else would revolted Nature have proclaimed her wrath, by permitting no children to spring from this union: yet Nature, of all others, shewed herself quite willing; *Jocasta* and *Œdipus*, who had met as two un-wonted objects, loved each other; and it was only at the instant when it was made known to them from without that they were mother and son, that their love was first disturbed. Œdipus and Jocasta *knew* not, in what social relation they stood to one another: they had acted un-consciously, according to the natural instinct of the purely human Individual; from their union had sprung an enrich-ment of human Society, in the persons of two lusty sons and two noble daughters, on whom henceforth, as on their parents, there weighed the irremovable curse of that Society. The hapless pair, whose Conscience (*Bewusstsein*) stood within the pale of human Society, passed judgment on themselves when they became conscious of their unconscious crime:

by their self-annulling, for sake of expiation, they proved the strength of the social loathing of their action,—that loathing which had been their own through Wont, *even before* the action itself ; but in that they had done the deed, despite this social conscience, they testified to the far greater, more resistless might of unconscious individual Human Nature.

How full of meaning it is, then, that precisely this Œdipus had solved the riddle of the *Sphinx !* In advance he uttered both his vindication and his own condemnal, when he called the kernel of this riddle *Man.* From the half-bestial body of the Sphinx, there fronted him at first the human Individual in its subjection to Nature : when the half brute-beast had dashed itself from its dreary mountain-stronghold into the shattering abyss below, the shrewd unriddler of its riddle turned back to the haunts of men ; to let them fathom, from his own undoing, the whole, the Social Man. When he stabbed the light from eyes which had flamed wrath upon a taunting despot, had streamed with love towards a noble wife,—without power to see that the one was his father, the other his mother,— then he plunged down to the mangled carcass of the Sphinx, whose riddle he now must know was yet unsolved. —It is *we* who have to solve that riddle, to solve it by vindicating the instinct of the Individual from out Society itself; whose highest, still renewing and re-quickening wealth, that Instinct is.—

But let us next pursue the wider circuit of the Œdipus-saga, and see how *Society** behaved itself, and whither its moral conscience went astray !—

From the strifes of the sons of Œdipus there fell to *Creon,* brother of Jocasta, the rulership of Thebes. As

---

* " Gesellschaft,"—not to break our author's chain of argument by swerving from the one equivalent, I must beg readers to remember that the primary meaning both of " Society " and " *Gesellschaft* " is "a fellowship, or association."—TR.

lord, he decreed that the corpse of *Polynices*, one of these
two sons,—who together with *Eteocles*, the other, had fallen
in mutual combat,—should be given unburied to the winds
and vultures, whilst that of Eteocles was interred with all
befitting pomp: whoever should act in contravention of
the edict, should himself be buried alive. *Antigone*, the
sister of both brothers,—she who had followed her blind
father into banishment,—in full consciousness defied the
edict, interred the corpse of her outlawed brother, and
suffered the appointed punishment.—Here we see *the
State*, which had imperceptibly waxed from out the
Society, had fed itself on the latter's habit of view, and
had so far become the attorney (*Vertreter*) of this habit
that now it represented abstract Wont alone, whose core
is fear and abhorrence of the thing unwonted.   Armed
with the power of this Wont, the State now turns upon
Society itself, to crush it ; inasmuch as it wards from it the
natural sustenance of its being, in the holiest and most
instinctive social feelings.   The above-recited mythos
shews us plainly how this came about, if we will only
regard it a little closer.

What profit had Creon, from the decreeing of such a
ruthless edict ?   And what made him deem it possible,
that such an edict should *not* be abrogated by the general
indignation of his people ?   Eteocles and Polynices, after
the downfall of their father, had agreed to divide their
inheritance, the rulership of Thebes, in this wise : that they
should administer it by turns.   Eteocles, who was the first
to enjoy their common birthright, refused to make it over
to his brother, when Polynices at the appointed time
returned from voluntary exile to enjoy his spell of government.   Thus Eteocles forswore his oath.   Did oath-
revering Society mete him punishment therefor ?   No : it
supported him in his designs, designs which rested on a
broken oath.   Had men already lost all reverence for the
sacredness of oaths ?   No, on the contrary : they cried
aloud to the Gods, deploring the forswearal, for they feared

it would be avenged.   But, despite their evil conscience,
the citizens of Thebes acquiesced in the conduct of
Eteocles, because the oath's *object*, the compact sworn
between the brothers, at the moment seemed to them far
more flagitious than the consequences of an act of perjury,
which might haply be circumvented through gifts and
sacrifices to the Gods.   What pleased them not, was a
change of rulers, a constant innovation, because Wont had
already become their virtual lawgiver.   Moreover, in this
taking sides for Eteocles the citizens evinced their practical
sense* of the nature of Property,—which everyone was
only too glad to enjoy alone, without sharing it with
another.   Each citizen who recognised in Property the
guarantee of wonted quiet, was *ipso facto* an accomplice of
the unbrotherly deed of Eteocles, the supreme Proprietor.
The might of self-serving Wont thus lent support to
Eteocles; whilst against it fought the defrauded Polynices
with all the heat of Youth.   In him there only dwelt the
feeling of an injury meet to be avenged : he assembled a
host of like-feeling hero-hearted comrades, advanced upon
the citadel of broken oaths, and summoned it to drive
from out its walls the birthright-robbing brother.   This
mode of dealing, albeit prompted by a throughly justifiable
wrath, yet appeared to the good citizens of Thebes as but
another monstrous crime; for Polynices was unconditionally
a very *bad patriot*, when he besieged his father-city.   The
friends of Polynices had gathered from every race: a
purely human interest made them favour the cause of
Polynices; wherefore they represented the Purely-human,
Society in its widest and most natural sense, as against a
straitened, narrow-hearted, self-seeking society which was
imperceptibly shrinking, under their attacks, into the
ossified State.—In order to end the lengthy war, the
brothers called each other forth to single combat : *both* fell
upon the field.—

* "Instinkt," in the German; but Wagner so generally uses the word
" Unwillkür " for our notion of "instinct," that the latter term would only
prove confusing here.—TR.

The crafty Creon now surveyed these incidents in their conjunction, and recognised therein the essence of Public Opinion ; seeing its kernel to be nothing but Wont, Care, and dislike of Innovation.   The ethical view (*sittliche Anschauung*) of the nature of Society—which had still been so strong in the great-hearted Œdipus that, from loathing at his own unconscious outrage on it, he had annulled himself—lost its power in exact degree as the Purely-human, which inspired it, came into conflict with the strongest social interest, that of absolute Wont, i.e. of joint self-seeking.   Wherever this ethical conscience fell into conflict with the practice of society, it severed from the latter and established itself apart, as *Religion ;* whereas practical society shaped itself into *the State.*   *Morality* (Sittlichkeit), which in Society had heretofore been something warm and living, in Religion remained merely something *thought*, something wished, but no longer able to be carried out.   In the State, on the contrary, folk acted according to the practical judgments of Utility ; and, if the moral conscience came by an offence,—why ! it was appeased by religious observances quite innocuous to the State.   Herewith the great advantage was this, that one gained someone, both in Religion and State, upon whom to shift one's sins : the crimes of the State the Prince* must smart for, but the Gods had to answer for offences against religious ethics.—Eteocles was the practical scape-goat of the new-made State : the consequences of his oath-break, the accommodating Gods had had to bring home to him ; but the stability of the State—so they hoped, at least, though alas it did not so turn out !—the valiant

---

* The later *Democracy* was the open taking-over of the scapegoat's office by the united body of citizens ; herewith they admitted that they had so far come to a knowledge of themselves, as to know that they were themselves the basis of the royal Caprice.   Here, then, even Religion openly became an art, and the State a cockpit for the egoistic personality.   In flight before the individual Instinct, the State fell into the hands of the individual Caprice of forceful personalities ; after Athens had cheered an *Alcibiades* to the echo and deified a *Demetrius*, at last it licked, with ease and comfort, the spittle of a *Nero*.— RICHARD WAGNER.

citizens of Thebes were to enjoy all to themselves. Whoever felt inclined to offer himself anew as such a scapegoat,
was therefore to them most welcome : and that was the
crafty Creon, who well knew how to make his own
arrangements with the Gods; but not the over-heated
Polynices, who for the simple breaking of an oath, forsooth,
had knocked so rudely at the good city's gates.

But, from the intrinsic cause of the Laïds' tragic fate,
Creon further recognised how extremely indulgent the
Thebans were toward actual crimes, provided only they
did not disturb the peaceful burghers' Wont. The father
Laïus had been warned by the Pythia that a son, as yet
un-born, would one day murder him. Merely to forestall
any public annoyance, the honourable father gave secret
orders to slay the newborn child, in some secluded spot.
In this he shewed himself most considerate toward the
moral sentiment of the Theban burghers, who, had the
execution been carried out under their very eyes, would
simply have resented the scandal and been obliged to
pray an unwonted amount to their Gods, but would by no
means have felt the horror needful to impel them practically to hinder the deed and punish the conscious murderer
of his son ; for their horror would at once have been
choked down by the consideration, that through this deed
at least the public peace would be preserved, whereas it
must have been disturbed by the son—who, in any case,
could only turn out a ne'er-do-weel. Creon had remarked
that, on discovery of the inhuman deed of Laïus, that deed
itself had, strictly speaking, called forth no righteous indignation ; nay, that everyone would certainly have been
better pleased, had the murder been really consummated,
for *then* everything would have gone smoothly, and there
would have been no such atrocious scandal as that which
had so terribly upset the burghers for many a weary year.
Quiet and *Order*, even at the cost of the most despicable
outrage on human nature and the wonted morality itself,
—at the cost of a conscious, deliberate murder of a child

by its own father, prompted by the most unfatherly self-
regard,—this Quiet and Order were at any rate more worth
considering than the most natural of human sentiments,
which bids a father sacrifice himself to his children, not
them to *him*.—What, then, had this Society become, whose
natural moral-sense had been its very basis? The diametrical opposite of this its own foundation: the representative of *im*morality and hypocrisy. The poison which
had palsied it, however, was—*use-and-wont*. The passion
for use-and-wont, for unconditional quiet, betrayed it into
stamping down the fount from which it might have ever
kept itself in health and freshness ; and this fount was the
free, the self-determining Individual. Moreover, in its
utmost palsy, Society has only had morality brought back
to it, i.e. the truly *human* morality, by the Individual ; by
the Individual who, of the instinctive thrust of Nature's-
necessity, has lifted up his hand against and morally
annulled it. This glorious vindication of genuine Human
Nature, also, is further inscribed in plainest letters on the
world-historical myth we have before us.

Creon had become ruler: in him the people recognised
the legitimate successor to Laïus and Eteocles; and this
he confirmed in the eyes of every burgher, when he
doomed the corpse of unpatriotic Polynices to the terrible
shame of lack of burial, and thus his soul to eternal unrest.
This was an edict of the highest political wisdom: by it
Creon cemented his rule, inasmuch as he vindicated
Eteocles, who by his oath-break had preserved the Quiet
of the burghers ; and inasmuch as he thus gave plainly to
be understood that he, too, was willing to maintain the
State in quiet and order by taking on his shoulders
the burden of every offence against true human morals.
Through his edict he at like time gave the surest, strongest
proof of his friendly disposition toward the State: he
struck Humanity across the face, and cried—long live the
State !—

In this State there was but one sorrowing heart, in

which the feeling of Humanity had sought a shelter :—it was the heart of a sweet maiden, from whose soul there sprang into all-puissant beauty the flower *of Love.* Antigone knew nothing of politics ;—*she loved.*—Did she try to play the advocate for Polynices ? Sought she for special pleadings, points of circumstance or lawful right, to explain his mode of dealing, to exculpate or justify his deed ?—No ;—she loved him.—Was it *because* he was her brother, that she loved him ?—Was not Eteocles her brother, too,—were not Œdipus and Jocasta her parents ? After the horrors that had come to pass, could she think of her family ties without a shudder? From them, the hideously disrupted ties of nearest nature, was she to win the strength for Love ?—No, she loved Polynices because of his misfortune, and because the highest power of Love alone could free him from his curse.   What, then, was this love, which was not the love of sex, not love of child to parent, not love of sister for her brother ?—It was the topmost flower of all.   Amid the ruins of love of sex, of parents, and of brethren,—which Society had disowned and the State annulled,—there sprang, from the ineradicable seed of all these loves, the fullest flower of *pure Human-love.*

Antigone's love was *fully conscious.*   She knew, what she was doing,—but she also knew that do it she must, that she had no choice but to act according to love's Necessity ; she knew, that she had to listen to this unconscious, strenuous necessity of *self-annihilation in the cause of sympathy ;* and in this consciousness of the Unconscious she was alike the perfect Human Being, the embodiment of Love in its highest fill and potence.—Antigone told the godly citizens of Thebes : Ye condemned my father and my mother, because they loved unwittingly ; but ye condemned not Laïus, the witting murderer of his son, and ye sheltered Eteocles, his brother's foe: condemn then *me,* who deal from pure human-love alone,—so is the measure of your outrage brimmed !— —And lo !—*the love-curse of Antigone annulled the State !*—No hand was stirred to save

her, when she was led to death. The State-burghers wept,
and prayed the Gods to take away the pain of pity for the
wretched girl ; they followed her with words of comfort :
that so it was and so it must be ; that the quiet and order
of the State, alack! required Humanity to be made a
victim!—But there, where all Love was born, was also
born high Love's avenger. A stripling burned with sudden
love towards Antigone ; to his father he disclosed his
plight, and begged that father's love to spare the victim :
harshly was he thrust aside. Then the stripling stormed
his loved one's grave, that grave which had erst received
her living : he found her dead, and with his sword he
pierced his loving heart. But this was the son of *Creon*,
the son of the State personified : at sight of the dead body
of the son who through Love perforce had cursed his
father, the ruler became again a father. The sword of his
son's love drove a deadly gash into his heart : wounded
deep within, *the State* fell crashing to the ground, to
become in death a *Human Being.*—

*O holy Antigone ! on thee I cry ! Let wave thy banner,
that beneath it we destroy and yet redeem !*—

Wondrous! that, when the modern Romance had turned
to Politics, and Politics become a bloody field of battle ;
when the Poet, in anxious yearning for the sight of a
perfect art-form, induced a ruler to command the performance of an old Greek tragedy—this tragedy should have
been none other than our "Antigone." One sought for
the work in which *this art-form was shewn the purest;* and
lo !—it was precisely the work whose *content was the purest
essence of humanity*, the destructrix of the State!—How
rejoiced were the learned old children, at this "Antigone"
in the Court-theatre of Potsdam ! They got strewn upon
them from on high the roses which "Faust's" redeeming
host of angels scatter down upon the tail-decked "devils
thick and thin, with short and straight, and long and

crumpled horns":* but alas! the roses only roused in
them that repulsive itching which they kindled in Meph-
istopheles,—not Love!—The "Eternal Womanly drew"
them not "up," but the eternal old-womanly (*das ewig
Weibische*) brought them wholly down!—

The incomparable thing about the Mythos is, that it is
true for all time, and its content, how close soever its compression, is inexhaustible throughout the ages. The only
task of the Poet, was to expound it. Even the Greek
tragedian did not always stand in full unconstraint, before
the myth he had to expound : the myth itself was mostly
juster to the essence of the Individuality, than was the
expounding poet. The tragedian had completely taken
up the spirit of this Mythos into himself, however, in so
far as he made the essence of the Individuality the irremovable centre of his artwork, from which the latter fed
and refreshed itself on every hand. So undisfigured stood
before the poet's soul this all-begetting essence-of-the-
individuality, that therefrom a Sophocleian *Ajax* and
Philoctetes could spring forth,—heroes whom no side-
glance at the prudent world's opinion could lure from
their nature's self-annihilating Necessity and truth, to drift
into the shallow waters of Politics, on which the weather-
wise *Ulysses* understood so masterly to ship him to and
fro.

To-day we only need to faithfully expound the *myth of
Œdipus* according to its inmost essence, and we in it win
an intelligible picture of the whole history of mankind,
from the beginnings of Society to the inevitable downfall
of the State. The necessity of this downfall was foreboded
in the Mythos : it is the part of actual history (*der wirklichen Geschichte*) to accomplish it.

Since the establishment of the *political State*, no single

* From the 'stage-directions' of the penultimate scene of Goethe's "*Faust*."
—TR.

step has been taken in history but, let it be directed with
never so deliberate aim to that State's consolidation, has
led towards its downfall. The State, as *abstractum*, has
been ever on the point of going under, or more correctly,
it has never so much as come to actuality ; merely States
in concreto have found—in perpetual change, as constantly
incipient variations of an inexecutable theme—a violent,
but yet an ever interrupted and contested footing. The
State, as *abstractum*, is the fixed-idea of well-meaning but
mistaken thinkers,—as *concretum*, the booty for the caprice
of forceful or intriguing individuals, who fill the pages of
our history with the record of their deeds. With this
concrete State—whose substance Louis XIV. correctly
designated as *himself*—we need not further occupy ourselves ; *its* kernel, also, is bared us in the Œdipus-saga :
as the seed of all offences we recognise the *rulership* of
Laïus, since for sake of its undiminished possession he
became an unnatural father. From this possession grown
into an *ownership* (Eigenthum), which wondrously enough
is looked on as the base of all good order, there issue all
the crimes of myth and history.—Let us keep our eye upon
the abstract State alone. The Thinkers of this State
desired to plane down and equalise the imperfections of
actual Society, according to a thought-out 'norm' : yet
that they retained these very imperfections* as a given
thing, as the only thing to fit the "sinfulness" of human
nature, and never went back to the real Man himself,—who
from his at first instinctive, but at last erroneous views had
called those inequalities into being, exactly as through
Experience and the consequent correction of his errors he
must also bring about, quite of itself, the perfect Society,
i.e. one answering to the real Needs of men,—this was the
grand error through which the Political State evolved
itself to the unnatural height whence it fain would guide
our Human Nature far below ; that nature which it did

---

* Here we are brought back to the text as also contained in the *Deutsche
Monatsschrift ;* except that " individual " there occurred before " Man," and
the clause " i.e. one answering to the real Needs of men " was absent.—TR.

not understand at all, and understood the less, the more it
fain would guide it. The Political State lives solely on the *vices of society*,
whose *virtues* are derived solely from the *human individuality*. Faced with the vices of society, which alone it can
espy, the State cannot perceive the virtues which society
acquires from that individuality.* In this situation it [the
State] weighs on Society to such a degree, that the latter
further turns its vicious side towards the Individuality, and
thus must finally dry up its every source of sustenance, were
the Necessity of individual instinct not stronger of nature
than the arbitrary notions of the politician.—In their "Fate"
the Greeks mistook the nature of the Individuality, because it disturbed Society's moral-wont: to battle against
this Fate, they armed themselves with the political State.
Now, *our* Fate is the political State, in which the free
Individuality perceives its destroying Destiny (*Schicksal*).
But the essence of the political State is *caprice*, whereas
the essence of the free Individuality is *necessity*.† From
out this Individuality, which we have recognised as in the
right (*als das Berechtigte*) in its thousand-years' battle with
the political State,—from this *to organise*‡ Society, is the
conscious task imposed upon us for the Future. But, to
bring *the unconscious part* of human nature to *consciousness*

---

* In the *D. M.* "aus der Unwillkür der menschlichen Individualität,"—i.e.
"from the Instinct of that human individuality." Further, the immediately
preceding sentence contained "the Individual (*Individuum*)," in place of
"the human Individuality."—TR.

† Our modern State-politicians twist this round: they call the following of
State-edicts a *necessity*, whereas they derive their breaking from the *self-will*
of the Individual. Thus *freedom* seems to them Caprice, and *constraint*
Necessity. Whosoever employs these most weighty words according to their
natural sense, he expresses himself—as they write in the reviews—in "embarrassed language" ("*befangener Sprache*"). — RICHARD WAGNER.—This
note and its successor were contained in the original edition ('52) of the book
alone; not in the *D. M.*, nor in later editions.—TR.

‡ At any rate not in the sense of the Austrian Government, which at present
—as it puts it—is also "organising" its State. Let us here understand the word
in that same "embarrassed" sense of language: according to which it means,
not a mechanical arranging from on high, but a letting-arise from the root
itself.—RICHARD WAGNER.

within Society, and in this consciousness to know nothing other than *the necessity common to every member of Society*, namely of *the Individual's own free self-determining*,—this is as good as to say, *annul the State ;* for through Society has the State marched on to a denial of the free self-determining of the Individual,—upon the death of *that*, has it lived.

IV.

OR *Art*, with which alone our present inquiry is concerned,* there lies in the *annulling of the State* (Vernichtung des Staates) the following superlatively weighty 'moment.'

It all the more necessarily became the poet's task to display the battle in which the Individual sought to free himself from the political State or religious Dogma, as political life — remote from which the poet at last could merely lead a life of dreams—was more and more consciously filled by the changing hazards of that battle, as by its genuine Content. If we leave aside the religious State-poet, who even as artist offered up the human being with gruesome satisfaction to his idol, we then have solely before us the poet who, aching with undissembled fellow-feeling for the sufferings of the Individual, and as such an one himself, has turned to face the State, to face the world of Politics, with an exhibition of that Individual's struggle. By the nature of the thing, however, the individuality which the poet led into battle against the State was *no purely human one*, but an individuality *conditioned by the State itself.* It was of like genus with the State, included in it, and merely the opposite of that State's extremest apex.

A *conscious* individuality,—i.e. an individuality which determines us in this one particular case, to act *so* and not otherwise—we win *alone within society*, which brings us first the case in which we have to form decisions. The Individual without Society is completely unthinkable by us, *as*

---

* The article in the *Deutsche Monatsschrift* running on without a break, except for the starting of a fresh paragraph, this clause—between the commas —did not appear.—TR.

an individuality; for first in intercourse with other individuals, is shewn the thing wherein we differ from them,
wherein we are peculiar to ourselves. Now, when Society
had grown into the political State, it governed (*bedang*)
this Particularity of the individual by its own essence, just
as much as the free Society had done: only, as a State,
but far more strongly and categorically. No one can
depict an individuality, without the Surrounding which
conditions (*bedingt*) it as such : if this Surrounding was a
natural one, giving ample breathing-space to the development of the individuality, and freely, elastically, and
instinctively shaping *itself* anew by contact with that
individuality,—then this Surrounding could be truly and
strikingly denoted in the simplest of outlines ; for only
through an exhibition of the Individuality had the
Surrounding, itself, to gain its characteristic idiosyncrasy.
The State, however, is no such flexible, elastic Surrounding, but a stiff, dogmatic, fettering and domineering might ;
which lays down for the individual in advance, "So shalt
thou think and deal!" The State has assumed the
education of the individual's character : it takes possession
of him already in the mother's womb, through foreordaining
him an unequal share in the means toward social self-
dependence ; * by forcing its *morale* upon him, it takes
away the instinctiveness of his viewing; and it appoints to
him, as *its* own property, the standing he is to take toward
his surrounding. The State-citizen has to thank the State
for his individuality ; but it is strictly nothing more than
his predetermined standing toward the State, the standing
in which his purely-human individuality is annulled for all
his *dealings* and bounded, at the utmost, to the *thoughts* he
may keep entirely to himself.

The dangerous corner of the human brain, into which
the entire individuality had fled for refuge,—the State

* "Durch Vorausbestimmung eines ungleichen Antheiles an den Mitteln zu
sozialer Selbständigkeit." In the *D.M.* this read : " durch Vorausbestimmung
des Antheiles an dem Leben der Gesellschaft," i.e. " by foreordaining his share
in the life of Society."—TR.

endeavoured to sweep it out as well, by the aid of religious
Dogma ; but here the State was doomed to failure, since it
could merely bring up hypocrites, i.e. State-burghers who
deal otherwise than as they think. Yet it was *from thinking*,
that there first arose the force to withstand the State. The
first purely human stir of freedom manifested itself in
warding off the bondage of religious dogma ; and *freedom
of thought* the State at last was forced to yield. How,
then, does this sheer *thinking* individuality utter itself in its
dealings?—So long as the State is to hand, the helpless
thing will only be able to deal as a *State-burgher*, i.e. as an
individuality whose way of dealing is not the counterpart
of its way of thinking. The State-burgher is impotent to
take a single step which is not set down for him in advance,
as either a *duty* or a *crime*. The character of his duty and
his crime is not one proper to his individuality ; let him
try as he may, to act upon his never so free thinking, yet
he cannot step outside the State—to whom even his crime
belongs. Only through *death*, can he cease to be a citizen
of the State ; thus only where he also ceases to be a human
being.

The poet, then, who had to portray the battle of the
Individuality against the State, could *portray* the State
alone ; but the free Individuality he could merely *suggest
to Thought*. The State was the actual extant thing, in all
its pomp of form and colour : whereas the Individuality
was but the thing imagined, shapeless, colourless, and non-
extant. All the features, contours and colours, which lend
the Individuality its set, its definite and knowable artistic
shape, the poet had to borrow from a Society politically
divided up and compressed into a State ; not to take them
from the rightful individuality, which gains its own drawing
and colour from contact with other individualities. The
Individuality, thus merely *thought-out* but not *portrayed*,
could therefore be exhibited to nothing but the *thought*, and
not to the directly-seizing *feeling*. Our Drama has therefore been *an appeal to the Understanding*,—not to the
Feeling. It thus has taken the place of the Didactic-

poem, which exhibits a subject from the life only as far as
it suits the conscious aim, of imparting a thought to the
Understanding. But, to impart a thought to the Understanding the poet has to proceed just as *circumspectly* as,
on the contrary, he must go to work with the greatest
simplicity and straightforwardness when he addresses himself to the directly receptive Feeling. The Feeling seizes
nothing but the actual (*das Wirkliche*), the physically
enacted, the perceivable by the senses : to *it* one can only
impart the fulfilled, the rounded-off, the thing that is just
wholly what it is, just what at this instant * it *can* be. To
the Feeling the at-one-with-itself alone is understandable ;
whatsoever is at variance with itself, what has not reached
an actual and definite manifestment, confounds the Feeling
and drives it into thinking,—drives it into an act of
combination which does away with it as Feeling.

In order to convince it, the poet who turns towards the
Feeling must be already so at one with himself, that he
can dispense with any aid from the mechanism of Logic
and address himself with full consciousness to the infallible
receptive powers (*Empfängniss*) of the un-conscious, purely
human Feeling. With this message of his he has therefore
to proceed as straightforwardly and (in view of physical
perception) as unconditionally, as the Feeling is addressed
by the actual phenomenon itself—such as warmth, the
wind, the flower, the animal, the man. But, in order to
impart the highest thing impartable, and alike the most
convincingly intelligible—the purely human Individuality
—the *modern* dramatic poet, as I have pointed out, has to
move along a directly opposite path. From out the enormous mass of its actual surroundings—in the visible
measure-, form-, and colour-giving State, and in History
petrified into a State—he has first with infinite toil to
reconstruct this Individuality ; in order at last, as we have

---

* " Jetzt,"—this word was absent from the *D. M.*, as was also the short
bracketed clause of the next paragraph ; the brackets, in this instance, occurring in the *German* text.—TR.

seen, to do nothing more than exhibit it to the Thought.* The thing that our feeling involuntarily seizes in advance, is solely the form and colour of the State. From the earliest impressions of our youth, we see Man only in the shape and character given him by the State; the individuality drilled into him by the State our involuntary feeling takes for his real essence; we cannot seize him otherwise, than by those distinctive qualities which in truth are not his very own, but merely lent him by the State. To-day the Folk cannot conceive the human being otherwise than in the uniform of his 'class,' the uniform in which, from youth up, it sees his body clad; and the "Folk's-playwright," also, can address himself understandably to the Folk only when not for a single instant does he tear it from this State-burgherly illusion—which holds its unconscious Feeling captive to such a degree, that it would be placed in the greatest bewilderment if one attempted to reconstruct before it the actual human being beneath this visible semblance. †   Wherefore, to exhibit the purely-human

---

* In "Egmont" *Goethe* had employed the whole course of the piece in loosening this purely-human Individuality, with toilsome wealth of detail, from the conditions of its State-historical Surrounding; in the solitude of the dungeon, and immediately before its death, he now wished to shew it to the *Feeling* as coming into oneness with itself: for this, he must reach out hands to Marvel and to Music. How characteristic it is, that it was the idealising Schiller, of all others, who could not understand this uncommonly significant feature of Goethe's highest artistic truthfulness! But how mistaken, also, was it of Beethoven, not to reserve his music for this appearance of the Wondrous; instead of introducing it—at the wrong time—in the middle of the politico-prosaic exposition.—RICHARD WAGNER.—This Note did not appear in the *D. M.* It has a strong bearing upon the final scenes of the *Ring* and *Tristan und Isolde.*—TR.

† The Folk must be something like that pair of children who were standing before a picture of Adam and Eve, and could not make out which was the man and which the woman, because they were unclothed. How characteristic of all our views is it not, again, that commonly our eye is pained and embarrassed by the sight of an undraped human figure, and we generally find it quite disgusting: our own body first becomes intelligible to us, by our pondering on it!—RICHARD WAGNER.—The illustration in the first sentence was also contained in "*The German's Fate in Paris*" (translated in *The Meister*, No. XX.), written in Paris ten years earlier. It would seem that there were more 'British Matrons' in Dresden, than in Paris.—TR.

individuality, the modern poet has to turn, not to the *feeling*, but to the *understanding ;* since even to himself it is only a thought-out thing. For this, his method of procedure must be a hugely circumstantial one : all that the modern sentiment takes as the most comprehensible, he has, so to say, to slowly and circumspectly divest of its form and colour, *under the very eyes* of this sentiment, and, throughout this systematic stripping process, to gradually bring the Feeling round to Thinking ; since, after all, the individuality he makes-for is nothing but a thing of thought. Thus the modern poet must turn aside from the feeling, to address the understanding: to him, Feeling is the obstacle; only when he has overcome it with the utmost caution, does he come to his main purpose, the demonstration of a thought to the Understanding.—

The *understanding* is thus, from first to last, the human faculty which the modern poet wishes to address; and with it he can only parley through the *organ* of the combining, dispersing, severing and re-piecing Understanding; through abstract and conditioned Word - speech, which merely describes and filters down the impressions and acquirements of the Feeling. Were our State itself a worthy object of Feeling, the poet, to reach his purpose, would have in a certain measure to pass over, in his drama, from tone-speech to word-speech : in Greek Tragedy such was very near the case, but from opposite reasons.* This Tragedy's basis was the Lyric, from which it advanced to word-speech in the same way as Society advanced from the natural, ethico-religious ties of Feeling, to the political State. The return from Understanding to Feeling will be the march of the Drama of the Future, in so far as we shall advance from the *thought-out* individuality to the genuine one. But, from the very beginning of his work, the modern poet has to exhibit a Surrounding—the State —which is void of any purely-human sentiment, and therefore is un-communicable through the Feeling's highest utterance. So that he can only reach his purpose, at all,

* " Aber aus umgekehrten Gründen " ;—*not* in the *D. M.*—Tr.

through the organ of the 'combining' Understanding, through un-emotional modern speech; and rightly does the playwright of nowadays deem it unfitting, bewildering and disturbing, to employ Music for an object which can at best be intelligibly conveyed as Thought to the Understanding, but never to the Feeling as Emotion.

———————

But what sort of shaping of the Drama, in the sense aforesaid, would be called forth by the going-under of the State, by the rise of an organically healthy Society? *

Looked at reasonably, the Going-under of the State can mean nothing else but *the self-realisement of Society's religious conviction* (Bewusstsein) *of its purely-human essence.* By its very nature, this conviction can be no Dogma stamped upon us from without, i.e. it cannot rest on historical traditions, nor be drilled into us by the State. So long as any one of life's actions is demanded of us as an outward Duty, so long is the object of that action no object of Religious Conscience; for when we act from the dictates of religious conscience we act from out ourselves, we *so* act as we cannot act otherwise. But Religious Conscience means a *universal* conscience (allgemeinsames *Bewusstsein*); and conscience cannot be universal, until it knows the Unconscious, the Instinctive, the Purely-human, as the only true and necessary thing, and vindicates it by that knowledge. So long as the Purely-human shall loom before us in any troubledness soever, as it positively can-

———

* To this sentence there was added in the *D. M.*: "this must be the object of our next inquiry." With this, "article II." came to a close; but it was followed (in the same issue) by the third article, to which a footnote was appended: "The accompanying third fragment of a larger work—in which he is already addressing himself to the life-conditions of the Drama of the Future —the author adds because he has therein endeavoured to shew, in their development from the Needs of our modern state of affairs, those life-conditions by many not felt as necessary at all, but by others deemed to entirely exclude all need of Art; and in this he has kept to the same standpoint, already taken up by him in dealing with the nature of modern dramatic poetry." This "third article" goes on, without a break, to the end of our present Chapter V.—TR.

not but do in the present state of our society, so long must
we remain the prey to a million differences of opinion as to
how the genuine Man should be. So long as, in error about
his true essence, we form notions for ourselves as to how
this essence might haply manifest, so long must we also
strive for arbitrary Forms in which this imaginary essence
is to manifest itself. So long, moreover, shall we have
states and religions, till we have but *one* Religion and *no
longer any* State. But, if this Religion must necessarily be
a universal one, so can it be none other than the true and
conscience-vindicated nature of Mankind ;* and every man
must be capable of feeling this unconsciously, and instinctively putting it into practice. This common human
nature will be felt the strongest by the *Individual* as his
own, his individual nature, such as in him it manifests itself
as the *trend to life and love :* the contentment of this trend,
it is, that drives the unit into Society ; in which, by very
reason *that he can satisfy that trend in fellowship alone,* he
attains quite of himself the religious, i.e. the common conscience, which vindicates his nature. *In the free † self-
determining of the Individuality there therefore lies the
basis of the social Religion of the Future ;* which will not
have stepped into life, until this Individuality shall have
received through Society its utmost furthering and
vindication.—

The exhaustless variety of the relations of *living* individualities to one another, the endless fill of constantly
new forms, exactly answering in their changefulness the
idiosyncrasy of these vital relations, we are not in a position to so much as conceive ; for until now we can only
apprehend each human relationship in the shape of a

* "Wenn diese Religion aber nothwendig eine allgemeinsame sein muss, so
kann sie nichts Anderes sein, als die durch das Bewusstsein gerechtfertigte
wirkliche Natur des Menschen,"—although this sentence bears a strong resemblance to the doctrines of Comte, it is really our author's own development
of a Feuerbachian theme ; there is not the slightest evidence of either Wagner
or his passing model, Feuerbach, having ever come into any contact with the
French Positivist or his writings.—TR.

† In the *D. M.* "*hindered by nothing*" here appeared.—TR.

Right conferred by historical tradition, and in its prescription by a statutory 'norm of standing.'* But we may guess the measureless wealth of living individual relationships, if we take them as purely-human, ever fully and entirely present ; i.e. if we think every extrahuman or non-present thing that in the State, as Property and historic Right, has placed itself between them, has torn asunder their ties of Love, has dis-individualised, Class-uniformed, and State-established them,—if we think this all sent far away.

Yet again, we can picture those relations in their greatest simplicity, if we take the most distinctive chief-' moments '† of individual human life,—which must also be the regulator of the life in common,—and sum in them the characteristic distinctions of Society itself : such as *youth and age, growth and maturity, ardour and repose, activity and contemplation, instinct and conscience.*

The ' moment ' of *Wont*, which we have seen at its naïvest in the maintenance of socio-ethical concepts, but in its hardening into a State-political *morale* have found completely hostile to all development of the Individuality, and finally have recognised as a demoraliser and disowner of the Purely-human,—this Wont is nevertheless a valid ' moment ' of instinctive human nature.   If we examine a little closer, we shall find in it but one aspect of Man's manysidedness, which shews-out in the individual according

* "Vorausbestimmung durch die staatlich ständische Norm."—The edition of 1852, but not the *D. M.* nor the later editions of the book, contained the following footnote : " The individuality which the State allows us, is certified to-day by our description in an official passport,—if we are State-faithful : or in a police-warrant,—if we are State-unfaithful.   The State in this way takes upon it, through its police, the labour of the poet and character-sketcher."— In the *Wagner-Liszt Correspondence*, Letter 17 (May 29, 1849), there is an interesting autobiographic silhouette of how our author used the one " certificate " to obviate the consequences of the other.—TR.

† " Hauptmomente,"—as the term "moment" is used by Wagner in a sense differing from that which *we* generally accord it, and similar to that given it by the French (more akin to "element," or "factor "), I have placed the word between single inverted commas wherever it might otherwise lead to misapprehension.—TR.

to his time of life. The human being is not the same in
maturity as in youth: in youth we yearn for deeds, in age
for rest. The disturbance of our quiet is just as grievous
to us in old age, as is the hindrance of our activity in youth.
Age's claim is vindicated, of itself, by the gradual exhaustion of the bent toward action, whose profit is *experience.*
Experience is doubtless in itself instructive and delectable,
for the experienced man himself; for the non-experienced
instructee, however, it can only have a determinant result
when either his bent-to-action is weak and easily kept
down, or the points of Experience are forced upon him as
an inexorable standard for his dealings :—but only by such
a constraint, is the natural activity of man in general to be
weakened ; this weakening therefore, which to a superficial
glance seems absolute and grounded in sheer human nature,
and by whose cause we seek to justify in turn those laws
of ours which admonish to activity,—this weakening is but
conditional.—

Just as human society received its first ethical concepts
from the Family, so did it acquire therefrom its reverence
for age. In the Family, however, this reverence was one
called forth, conducted, conditioned and motived, by Love:
the father before all *loved* his son ; of love he counselled
him ; but, also out of love, he gave him scope. In Society
this motiving love was lost, in exact degree as the reverence
for the person transferred itself to fixed ideas and extrahuman things which—unreal in themselves—did not stand
toward us in that living reciprocity wherein Love is able
to requite our reverence, i.e. to take from it its fear. The
father, now become a *God,* could no more love us; the
counsel of our elders, now become a *Law,* could no longer
leave us our free play ; the family, become a *State,* could
no more judge us according to the instinctive forbearance
of Love, but only according to the chilling edicts of moral
compacts. The State—taken at its wisest—thrusts upon
us the experiences of History, as the plumb-line for our
dealings : yet we can only deal sincerely, when through
our instinctive dealings themselves we reach experience;

an experience taught us by communications can only be resultful for us, when by our instinctive dealings we make it over again for ourselves. Thus the true, the reasonable love of age toward youth substantiates itself in this: that it does not make its own experiences the measure for youth's dealings, but points it toward a fresh experience, and enriches its own thereby; for the characteristic and convincing thing about an experience is its individual part, the specific, the *knowable*, which it acquires by being won from the spontaneous dealings of this one specific Individual in this one specific case.

The Going-under of the State means therefore the falling-away of the barrier which the egoistic vanity of Experience, in the form of Prejudice, has erected against the spontaneity of individual dealings. This barrier at present takes the place that naturally * belongs to *love*, and by its essence it is *lovelessness :* i.e. Experience eaten up with its own conceit; and at last, the violently prosecuted will to reap no more experiences,—the self-seeking narrow-mindedness of Habit, the cruel doggedness of Quiet.— Now, by Love the father knows that he has not as yet experienced enough, but that by the experiences of his child, which in love toward it he makes his own, he may endlessly enrich his being. In the aptitude for rejoicing at the deeds of others, whose import it knows to turn through love into a delight-worthy and delight-giving object for itself, consists the beauty of reposeful age. Where this repose is naturally at hand through Love, it is by no means a hindrance on the activity of youth, but the latter's furtherance. It is the giving space to the activity of youth in an element of Love ; *by the beholding of this activity, it becomes a highest artistic participation therein,— becomes the very life-element of Art in general.*†

---

* In the *D. M.* : "der Natur, wie der höchsten Vernunft gemäss," i.e. "in keeping with Nature and the highest Reason."—Tr.

† It perhaps is scarcely necessary to point to the working out of this idea in the poem of *Die Meistersinger*, especially the scene between Sachs and Walther in the first part of Act III.—Tr.

Already-experienced age is able to take according to their *characteristic import* the deeds of youth, by which the latter unconsciously evinces its instinctive thrust, and to survey them *in their full conjunction :* it thus can vindicate these deeds more completely than their youthful agent, since it knows how to explain and consciously display them. *In the repose of age* we thus win the 'moment' of highest poetic faculty ;* and only *that* more youthful man can make this faculty his own, who *wins that repose,* i.e. that justness toward the phenomena of Life.—

The loving admonition of the experienced to the inexperienced, of the peaceful to the passionate, of the beholder to the doer, is given the most persuasively and resultfully by bringing faithfully before the instinctive agent his inmost being. He who is possessed with life's unconscious eagerness, will never be brought by general moral exhortations to a critical knowledge (*zur urtheilfähigen Erkenntniss*) of his own being, but this can only succeed entirely when in a likeness faithfully held up before him he is able to look upon himself; for right cognisance is re-cognition, just as right conscience is knowledge of our own Unconsciousness. The admonisher is the *understanding,* the experienced-one's conscious power of view : the thing to be admonished is the *feeling,* the unconscious bent-to-doing of the seeker for experience. The Understanding can know nothing other than the *vindication of the Feeling ;* for, itself, it is but the quiet which follows on the begetting stir of Feeling. It can only vindicate itself, when it knows itself conditioned by instinctive Feeling ; and Understanding justified by Feeling—no longer entangled in the feelings of this unit, but *upright towards Feeling in general—is the Vernunft.†* As *Vernunft* the Understanding is so far

---

* In the *D. M.* there appeared : "oder in der bewussten liebevollen Anschauung des Erfahrenen überhaupt,"—" or in the conscious, loving 'view' of the experienced-one in general."—TR.

† This term "Vernunft" is so seldom used by Wagner, and has been endowed with so wide a range of meaning by its more frequent users, that I have thought best to retain it in its original form,—especially as it is constantly so employed in English. Carlyle has translated the word as "Reason," in opposition to

superior to the Feeling, as it can judge all-righteously the
agency of individual feelings, in their contact with their
objects and opposites ; which latter likewise act from individual feelings. It is the highest social force, itself conditioned by Society alone ; the force which knows to class
the specialities of Feeling according to their proper genus ;
in *that* to re-discover them, and by that, again, to vindicate
them. It is thus capable withal of rousing itself to utterance through Feeling, when it proposes to address itself
merely to the man-of-feeling,—and Love lends to it the
instrument therefor. It knows through the feeling of Love,
which spurs it to impart, that to the man of passion—in
midst of his instinctive dealing—that thing alone is understandable which addresses itself to his Feeling : were it to
wish to address his Understanding, then in him it would
take for granted *that* which even itself has first to win
through its communication, and it must therefore stay un-
understood.* But Feeling only grasps the akin to itself ;
just as the naked Understanding—as such—can only parley
with the Understanding. The Feeling stays cold amid the
reflections of the Understanding : only the reality of an
object kindred to itself can warm it into interest. This
object must be the sympathetic image of the instinctive
doer's own nature ; and sympathetically it can only work,
when it displays itself in an action vindicated by the selfsame feeling which, from out this action and this vindication, he *fellow*-feels (*mitfühlt*) as his very own. Through
this fellow-feeling he just as instinctively attains an understanding of his own individual nature, as by the objects and

---

the "Understanding"; but we must not forget that it connotes a higher intellectual faculty than that of "Logic," and is more akin to our loosely-rendered
"Intuition."—TR.

* In *Oper und Drama* this runs : "was er durch seine Mittheilung sich
eben selbst erst gewinnen soll, und müsste unverständlich bleiben"; the last
three words having replaced "müsste somit unverstanden bleiben" of the
D. M., I have considered that a literal translation of the latter—which really
only differs by a shade—will convey the meaning more clearly in English. But
the crux here is, that the "er" (rendered by me as "it") *may* either refer to the
"Verstand als Vernunft" or to the "man of passion."—TR.

opposites of his feeling and dealing—by whose contact his
own feeling-and-dealing had evolved itself, in the image—
he has also learnt the nature of those opposites ; and this
because, snatched out of himself by lively sympathy for his
own likeness, he is carried on to take instinctive interest in
the feelings and dealings even of his opposites, is tuned to
acknowledgment of, and justice toward these opposites,
since they no longer stand confronting the bias of his
actual dealings.

Only in the most perfect artwork therefore, in *the Drama*,
can the insight of the experienced-one impart itself with
full success ; and for the very reason that, through employment of every artistic expressional-faculty of man, the poet's
aim (Absicht) is in Drama the most completely carried
from the Understanding to the Feeling,—to wit, is artistically imparted to the Feeling's most directly receptive
organs, *the senses.* The Drama, as the most perfect art-
work, differs from all other forms of poetry in just this,—
that in it the Aim is lifted into utmost imperceptibility, by
its *entire realisation.* In Drama, wherever the aim, i.e. the
Intellectual Will, stays still observable, there the impression is also a chilling one; for where we see the poet still
will-ing, we feel that as yet he *can* not. The poet's can-
ning, however, is the complete ascension of the Aim into
the Artwork, the *emotionalising of the intellect* (die Gefühl-
swerdung des Verstandes). His aim he can only reach by
physically presenting to our eyes the things of Life in their
fullest spontaneity ; and thus, by vindicating Life itself out
of the mouth of its own Necessity ; for the Feeling, to
which he addresses himself, can understand this Necessity
alone.

In presence of the Dramatic Artwork, nothing should
remain for the combining Intellect to search for. Everything in it must come to an issue sufficient to set our

Feeling at rest thereon ; for in the setting-at-rest of this Feeling resides the repose, itself, which brings us an instinctive understanding of Life.   In the Drama, we must become *knowers* through *the Feeling.**   The Understanding tells us : " *So is it,*"—only when the Feeling has told us : "*So must it be.*"   Only through *itself,* however, does this Feeling become intelligible to itself : it understands no other language than its own.   Things which can only be explained to us by the infinite accommodations of the Understanding, embarrass and confound the Feeling.   In Drama, therefore, an action can only be explained when it is completely vindicated by the Feeling ; and it thus is the dramatic poet's task, not to invent actions, but to make an action so intelligible through its emotional Necessity, that we may altogether dispense with the intellect's assistance in its vindication.   The poet therefore has to make his main scope the *choice of the Action,*—which he must so choose that, alike in its character as in its compass, it makes possible to him its entire vindication from out the Feeling ; for in this vindication alone, resides the reaching of his aim.

An action which can only be explained on grounds of historic relations, un-based upon the Present ; an action which can only be vindicated from the standpoint of the State, or understood alone by taking count of religious Dogmas stamped upon it from without,—not sprung from common views within,—such an action, as we have seen, is only representable to the Understanding, not to the Feeling. At its most successful, this was to be effected through narration and description, through appeal to the intellect's imaginative-force ; not through direct presentment to the Feeling and its definitely-seizing organs, the senses : for we saw that those senses were positively unable to take-in the full extent of such an action, that in it there lay a mass of relations beyond all possibility of bringing to physical view and bound to be relegated, for their comprehension,

---

* " Im Drama müssen wir *Wissende* werden durch *das Gefühl.*"   Compare "Durch Mitleid wissend,"—*Parsifal.*—TR.

to the combining organ of Thought. In a politico-
historical drama, therefore, it became the poet's business
to eventually give out his Aim * quite nakedly—as such :
the whole drama stayed unintelligible and unimpressive, if
this Aim, in the form of a human 'moral,' did not at last
quite visibly emerge from amid the desert waste of
pragmatic motives, employed for sheer description's sake.
In the course of such a piece, one asked oneself instinctively : "What is the poet trying to tell us ? "

Now, an Action which is to justify itself before and
through the Feeling, busies itself with no *moral ;* its whole
moral consists precisely in its justification by the instinctive
human Feeling.   It is a goal to itself, insofar as it has to
be vindicated only and precisely by the feeling out of which
it springs.   Wherefore this Action can only be such an one
as proceeds from relations the truest, i.e. the most seizable
by the Feeling, the nighest to human emotions, and thus
the simplest,—from relations such as can only spring from
a human Society intrinsically at one with itself, uninfluenced
by inessential notions and non-present grounds-of-right: a
Society belonging to itself alone, and not to any Past.

However, no action of Life stands solitary and apart : it
has always some sort of correlation with the actions of other
men ; through which it is conditioned alike as by the individual feelings of its transactor himself.   The weakest
correlation is that of mere petty, insignificant actions ;
which require for their explanation, less the strength of a
necessary feeling, than the waywardness of whim.   But the
greater and more decisive an action is, and the more it can
only be explained from the strength of a necessary *feeling :*
in so much the more definite and wider a connexion does
it also stand with the actions of others.   A great action,
one which the most demonstratively and exhaustively dis-

---

* As a great deal will be said about this "aim" (*Absicht*) in Part III., the
present pages should be borne in mind.   Equivalents might be found in
"intention," "object," or sometimes even "tendency" ; but, with this explanation, I think the simpler word will answer best our author's meaning.
—Tr.

plays the nature of Man along any one particular line, issues only from the shock of manifold and mighty opposites. But, for us to be able to rightly judge these opposites themselves, and to fathom their actions by the individual feelings of the transactors, a great action must be represented in a wide circle of relations ; for only in such a circle, is it to be understood. The Poet's chief and especial task will thus consist in this : that at the very outset he shall fix his eye on such a circle, shall completely gauge its compass, shall scrutinise each detail of the relations contained therein, with heed both to its own measure and to its bearing on the main-action ; this done, that he then shall make the measure of his understanding of these things the measure of their understandable-ness as a work of Art, by drawing-in this ample circle towards its central point, and thus condensing it into the periphery which gives an understanding of the central Hero. This *condensation* (Verdichtung) is the work proper to the poetising intellect (*des dichtenden Verstandes*) ; and this intellect is the centre and the summit of the whole man, who from thence divides himself into the receiver and the imparter.

As an object (*Erscheinung*) is seized in the first place by the outward-turned instinctive Feeling, and next is brought to the Imagination, as the earliest function of the brain : so the Understanding, which is nothing else but the imaginative-force as regulated by the actual Measure of the object, has to advance in turn through the Imagination to the instinctive Feeling—in order to impart what it now has recognised. In the Understanding objects mirror themselves as what they actually are ; but this mirrored actuality is, after all, a mere thing of thought : to impart this *thought-out* actuality, the Understanding must display it to the Feeling in an image akin to what the Feeling had originally brought to *it ;* and this image is the work of Phantasy. Only through the *Phantasy*, can the Understanding have commerce with the Feeling. The Understanding can only grasp the full actuality of an object, when it breaks the image, in which the object is brought it by the Phantasy,

and parcels it into its singlest parts ; when it fain would
bring these parts before itself again in combination, it has
at once to cast for itself an image, which no longer answers
strictly to the actuality of the thing, but merely in the
measure wherein Man has power to recognise it.   Thus
even the simplest action confounds and bewilders the
Understanding, which would fain regard it through the
anatomical microscope, by the immensity of its ramifica-
tions : would it comprehend that action, it can only do so
by discarding the microscope and fetching forth the image
which alone its human eye can grasp ; and this comprehension is ultimately enabled by the instinctive Feeling—
as vindicated by the Understanding.   This image of the
phenomena, in which alone the *Feeling* can comprehend
them, and which the Understanding, to make itself intelligible to the Feeling, must model on that image which
the latter originally brought it through the Phantasy,—
this image, for the Aim of the poet, who must likewise take
the phenomena of Life and compress them from their view-
less many-member-edness into a compact, easily surveyable
shape,—this image is nothing else but *the Wonder.**

* " *Das Wunder,*"—in the sense of "signs and wonders," i.e. the Marvellous.—In the *D. M.* there is no break here, but the article runs on throughout the following chapter.—Tr.

V.

HE WONDER in the Poet's work is distinguished from the * Wonder in religious Dogma by this: that it does not, like the latter, *upheave* the nature of things, but the rather makes it *comprehensible* to the Feeling. The Judæo-Christian Wonder tore the connexion of natural phenomena asunder, to allow the Divine Will to appear as standing *over* Nature. In it a broad connexus of things was by no means condensed in favour of their understanding by the instinctive Feeling, but this Wonder was employed entirely for its own sake alone; people demanded it, as the proof of a suprahuman power, from him who gave himself for divine, and in whom they refused to believe till before the bodily eyes of men he had shewn himself the lord of Nature, i.e. the arbitrary subverter of the natural order of things. This Wonder was therefore claimed from *him* one did not hold for authentic in himself and his natural dealings, but whom one proposed to first believe when he should have achieved something unbelievable, something *un-understandable*. A *fundamental denial of the Understanding* was therefore the thing hypothecated in advance, both by the wonder-claimer and the wonder-worker: whereas an *absolute Faith* was the thing demanded by the wonder-doer, and granted by the wonder-getter.

Now, for the operation of its message, the poetising intellect has absolutely no concern with *Faith*, but only with an *understanding through the Feeling*. It wants to display a great connexus of natural phenomena in an image swiftly understandable, and this image must there-

* In the *D. M.* and in the edition of 1852 there here appeared the predicate " verrufene," i.e. "notorious," or " discredited." It should be added that " Wunder " is the usual German term for " miracle."—Tr.

fore be one answering to the phenomena in such a way that
the instinctive Feeling may take it up without a struggle,
not first be challenged to expound it : whereas the characteristic of the Dogmatic Wonder consists just in this, that,
through the obvious impossibility of explaining it, it
tyrannously subjugates the Understanding despite the
latter's instinctive search for explanation ; and precisely in
this subjugation, does it seek for its effect.   The Dogmatic
Wonder is therefore just as unfitted for Art, as the Poetic
Wonder is the highest and most necessary product of the
artist's power of beholding and displaying.

If we picture to ourselves more plainly the Poet's method
in the moulding of his 'wonder,' we shall see in the first
place that, in order to present in intelligible survey a great
connexus of reciprocally conditioned actions, he must compress those actions themselves to a measure in which, for all
their perspicuity, they shall yet lose nothing of the fulness of
their Contents.   A mere abridging or lopping-off of lesser
'moments' of action would of itself but mar the moments
kept; since these stronger moments of the Action can only
be vindicated to the Feeling as the climax * of its lesser
moments.   Wherefore the moments excised for sake of
poetic clearing of space must be carried over into the
retained chief-moments themselves, i.e. they must be
included in the latter in some fashion cognisable to the
Feeling.   The reason why the Feeling cannot dispense
with them is, that for an understanding of the main-action
it needs withal a sentience of the motives from which it
sprang, and which enounced themselves in those lesser
moments-of-action.   The crest (*Spitze*) of an action is in
itself a fleeting moment, which is utterly meaningless as a
pure matter-of-fact, if it does not appear as motived by
ideas (*Gesinnungen*) that in themselves lay claim to our
fellow-feeling : a heaping of such moments must rob the
poet of all power of vindicating them to our Feeling ;
whereas it is this very vindication, this exposition of

---

* Or "intensification, enhancement," — the German original being
"*Steigerung.*"—TR.

motives, that has to fill the artwork's space,—which would be completely thrown away, were it filled with a mass of non-vindicable moments of action.

In the interest of intelligibleness, therefore, the poet has so to limit the number of his Action's moments, that he may win the needful space for the motivation of those retained. All those motives which lay hidden in the moments excised,* he must fit into the motives of his Main-action in such a way that they shall not appear detached ; because in detachment they would also demand their own specific moments of action, the very ones excised. On the contrary, they must be so included in the Chief-motive, that they do not shatter, but *strengthen* it as a whole. But the strengthening of a motive makes also necessary a strengthening of the moment-of-action itself, which is nothing but the fitting utterance (*die entsprechende Äusserung*) of that motive. A strong motive cannot utter itself through a weak moment - of - action ; both action and motive must thereby become un-understandable.—In order, then, to intelligibly enounce a Chief-motive thus strengthened by taking into it a number of motives which in ordinary life would only utter themselves through numerous moments-of-action, the action thereby conditioned must also be a strengthened, a powerful one, and in its unity more ample than any that ordinary life brings forth; seeing that in ordinary life the selfsame action would only have come to pass in company with many lesser actions, in a widespread space, and within a greater stretch of time. The poet who, in favour of the perspicuity of the thing, would draw-together not only these actions but this expanse of space and time as well, must not merely *cut off* parts, but *condense* the whole intrinsic contents. A condensement of the shape of actual life, however, can be comprehended by the latter only when—as compared with itself—it appears magnified, strengthened,

---

* In the *D. M.* there occurred : "and which alone made those moments appear worthy of regard."—TR.

unaccustomed. It is just in his busy scattering through
Time and Space, that Man cannot understand his own
life-energy : but the image of this energy, as brought within the compass of his understanding, is what the Poet's
shapings offer him for view ; an image wherein this energy
is condensed into an utmost-strengthened 'moment,' which,
taken apart, most certainly seems wondrous and unwonted,
yet shuts within itself its own unwontedness and wondrousness, and is in nowise taken by the beholder *for a Wonder*
but apprehended as the *most intelligible* representment of
reality.

In virtue of this Wonder, the poet is able to display
the most measureless conjunctures (*Zusammenhänge*) in
an all-intelligible Unity. The greater, the farther-reaching
the conjuncture he desires to make conceivable, only the
stronger has he to intensify the attributes of his shapings.
Time and Space, to let them appear in keeping with the
movement of these figures, he will alike condense from
their amplest stretch, to shapings of his Wonder ;—the
attributes of infinitely scattered moments of Time and
Space will he just as much collect into one intensified
attribute, as he had assembled the scattered motives into
one Chief-motive ; and the utterance of this attribute he
will enhance as much, as he had strengthened the action
issuing from that motive. Even the most unwonted shapes,
which the poet has to evoke in this procedure, will never
truly be *un-natural ;* because in them Nature's essence is
not distorted, but merely her utterances are gathered into
one lucid image, such as is alone intelligible to artist-man.
The poetic daring, which gathers Nature's utterances into
such an image, can *first for us* be crowned with due
success, precisely because *through Experience we have gained
a clear insight into Nature's essence.*

So long as the phenomena of Nature were merely an
'objective'* of man's Phantasy, so long also must the

---

* "*Objekt*,"—for the English "object" our author always uses " *Gegenstand*,"
in the stricter sense of our term, or " *Zweck* " in its sense of "a goal."—TR.

human imagination (*Einbildungskraft*) be subjected to
them : moreover, their semblance governed and determined
its view of the human phenomenal-world in such a way,
that men derived the inexplicable in that world—that is
to say, the unexplained—from the capricious orderings of
an extranatural and extrahuman Power, which finally in
the Miracle upheaved both Man and Nature. When the reaction against belief in miracles set in, even the Poet had to
bow before the prosaic rationalism of the claim, that poetry
should also renounce its Wonder ; and this happened in
the times when natural phenomena, theretofore regarded
only with the eye of Phantasy, began to be made the object
of scientific operations of the Understanding. The scientific Understanding, however, was so long unsettled about
the essence of these phenomena, as it believed that only in
an anatomical disclosing of all their inner minutiæ could
it set them comprehensibly before it. Positive about this
essence have we only been, from the time when we learnt
to look on Nature as a living Organism, not as an aimfully
constructed Mechanism ; from the time when we grew
clear, that she was not a thing *created*, but herself the *forever becom-ing ;* that she includes within herself the begetter
and the bearer, the Manly and the Womanly ; that Time
and Space, by which we earlier had held her circumscribed,
were but abstractions from her own reality ; that, further,
we may rest content with this knowledge in general,
because we no longer need, for its confirmation, to assure
ourselves of farthest distances by the calculations of
Mathematics,—since in closest nearness, and in the tiniest
fact of Nature, we may find proofs for the selfsame thing
as that which the remotest distance can only send us in
confirmation of our knowledge of Nature. Thenceforth,
however, we also know that we are here *to enjoy* Nature,
because we *can* enjoy her, i.e. we are qualified for such
enjoyment. But the *most reasonable* (vernunftigste) enjoyment of Nature is that which satisfies our *universal* aptitude
for delight : in the universality of man's organs of
reception, and in the highest enhancement of their aptitude

for delight, lies alone the measure according to which he
has to enjoy ; and the artist, who addresses himself to this
highest aptitude for delight, has therefore to take this
measure alone for the measure also of the phenomena he
wishes to impart as a connected whole. This measure
needs only to so far follow Nature's utterances, in her
phenomena, as they have to answer to her intrinsic essence ;
nor does the poet disfigure that essence through his
strengthening and intensifying, but—precisely in his utterance of it—he merely compresses it to a measure answering that of the most ardent human longing to understand
a vast connexus of phenomena. It is just the fullest
understanding of Nature, that first enables the poet to set
her phenomena before us in wondrous shaping ; for only in
such shaping, do they become intelligible to us as *the
conditionments of human actions intensified.*

Nature in her actual reality is only seen by the *Understanding,* which *de-composes her into her separatest of parts ;*
if it wants to display to itself these parts in their living
organic connexion, then the quiet of the Understanding's
meditation is involuntarily displaced by a more and more
highly agitated mood, which at last remains nothing but a
mood of Feeling. In this mood, Man unconsciously refers
Nature once more *to himself ;* for it is his individually
human feeling, that has given him precisely the mood
wherein he has apprehended Nature according to one
particular impression. In Feeling's highest agitation, Man
sees in Nature a sympathising being ; and in truth the
character of her phenomena governs also the character
of man's mood, past all escaping. Only in the utmost
egoistic coldness of the Understanding, can he withdraw
himself from her immediate sphere of operation,—albeit
even then he must confess to himself, that her more mediate
influence still determines him.—In his times of great
commotion man sees no longer any *hazard,* in his encounter
with natural phenomena : whereas the utterances of Nature,
though grounded on an organic concord of phenomena, yet

brush against our daily life with all the semblance of Caprice, and in our moods of indifference or egoistic pre-occupation—when we have neither lief nor leisure to ponder on their founding in a natural concord—they appear to us as Hazard; which, according to our human purpose of the moment, we seek to either turn to our advantage or turn away as to our dis-advantage. Man deeply-moved, when he suddenly turns from his inner mood to face surrounding Nature, finds in her either an intensifying aliment, or an alterative stimulus, of his mood, —according to her passing aspect. By whatever Being he feels dominated or supported in such a fashion, to that Being man ascribes a power great in exact measure as he finds himself in a great mood. His own sense of hanging-together with Nature he instinctively feels expressed, as well, in a great hanging-together of Nature's passing phenomena with himself, with his own mood; his own enhanced or altered mood he recognises again in Nature, whose mightiest utterances he thus refers to himself, equally as he feels himself determined by them. In this sense of a great reciprocal operation the phenomena of Nature crowd together, before his Feeling, into a definite shape to which he assigns an individual emotion answering to their impression upon him and his own mood; to this shape he finally attributes organs—intelligible to himself—wherewith to speak-out that emotion. Then he *speaks* with Nature, and she *answers* him.—In this his colloquy with Nature does he not understand her better, than the regarder of her through the microscope ? What does the latter under-stand of Nature, excepting what he has no need to under-stand ? But the former perceives that part of her which is necessary to him in the highest agitation of his being, in an agitation wherein he understands Nature according to an infinitely greater compass, and understands her in such a way as the widest-reaching Understanding can never picture to itself. Here Man *loves* Nature; he ennobles her, and uplifts her to a sympathising sharer in the highest

mood of Man, whose physical existence she has unconsciously conditioned from out herself.*

If, then, we wish to define the Poet's work according to
its highest power thinkable, we must call it *the—vindicated
by the clearest human Consciousness, the new-devised to answer
the beholdings of an ever-present Life, the brought in Drama
to a show the most intelligible,—the
Mythos.*

We now have only to ask ourselves, through *what expressional means* this Mythos is the most intelligibly to be
displayed in Drama. For this, we must go back to that
'moment' of the whole artwork which conditions its very
essence ; and this is the necessary *vindication of the action
through its motives,* for which the poetising Understanding
turns to face the instinctive *Feeling,* upon the latter's unforced fellow-feeling to ground an understanding of them.
We have seen that the condensation—so necessary for a
practical understanding — of the manifold moments-of-
action, immeasurably ramified in actual reality (*in der
realen Wirklichkeit*), was conditioned by the poet's longing
to display a great conjuncture of human life's phenomena,
through which alone can the Necessity of these phenomena
be grasped. This condensation he could only bring about,
in keeping with his main scope, by taking-up into the
motives of the moments chosen for actual representment
all those motives which lay at bottom of the moments-of-
action that he had discarded ; and by vindicating their
adoption, before the judgment-seat of Feeling, in that he
let them appear as a strengthening of the Chief-motives ;

---

* What are a thousand of the finest Arabian stallions, to their purchasers
who in English horse-marts prove their points and try their qualities of use,
compared with what his horse *Xanthus* was to *Achilles,* when it forewarned
him of his death ? Honestly, I would not exchange that soothsaying horse of
the godlike racer even for Alexander's highly-trained *Bucephalus,* who, as is
known, bestowed on Apelles' equine portrait the flattery of a neigh !—
R. WAGNER.—This note was not in the *D. M.*—TR.

which latter, in turn, conditioned of themselves a strengthening of their corresponding moments-of-action.   Finally we
saw that this strengthening of a moment of action could only
be achieved by lifting it above the ordinary human measure,
through the poetic figment (*durch Dichtung*) of the Wonder
—in strict correspondence with human nature, albeit exalting and enhancing its faculties to a potency unreachable in
ordinary life;—of the Wonder, which was not to stand
beyond the bounds of Life, but to loom so large from out
its very midst, that the shows of ordinary life should pale
before it.—And now we have only to come to definite
terms, as to *wherein should consist the strengthening of the
Motives* which are to condition from out themselves that
strengthening of the Moments of Action.

What is the meaning, in the sense indicated above, of a
"Strengthening of the Motives"?

It is impossible—as we have already seen—that a heaping-up of motives can be the thing we mean; because
motives thus crowded together, without any possible utterance as action, must remain unintelligible to the Feeling;
and even to the Understanding—if explicable—they would
still be reft of any vindication.*   Many motives to a scanty
action (*Viele Motive bei gedrängter Handlung*), could only
appear petty, whimsical and irrelevant, and could not
possibly be employed for a great action, excepting in a
caricature.   The strengthening of a motive cannot therefore consist in a mere addition of lesser motives, but in the
complete absorption of *many motives* into this *one*.   An
interest (*Interesse*) common to divers men at divers times
and under divers circumstances, and ever shaping itself
afresh according to these diversities : such an interest—
once that these men, these times and circumstances are
typically alike at bottom, and in themselves make plain an

---

* From " we mean," to the end of this sentence, and also the subsidiary
clause in the next, " excepting as a caricature," have been added since the
article in the *D. M.*, but appear in all the editions of the book.—TR.

essential trait of human nature—is to be made the interest
of *one* man, at one given time and under given circumstances.   In the Interest of this man all outward differences
are to be raised into *one* definite thing ; in which, however,
the Interest must reveal itself according to its greatest,
most exhaustive compass.   But this is as good as saying,
that from this Interest all which savours of the particular-
istic and accidental must be taken away, and it must be
given in its full truth as a necessary, purely human *utterance
of feeling* (Gefühlsausdruck).   Of such an emotional-utter-
ance *that* man is incapable, who is not as yet at one with
himself about his necessary Interest : the man whose feelings have not yet found the object strong enough to drive
them to a definite, a necessary enunciation ; but who, faced
with powerless, accidental, unsympathetic outward things,
still splits himself into two halves.   But should this mighty
object front him from the outer world, and either so move
him by its strange hostility that he girds up his whole individuality to thrust it from him, or attract him so irresistibly
that he longs to ascend into it with his whole individuality,
—then will his Interest also, for all its definiteness, be so
wide-embracing that it takes into it all his former split-up,
forceless interests, and entirely consumes them.

   The moment *of this consumption* is the act which the poet
has to prepare for, by strengthening a motive in such sort,
that a powerful moment-of-action may issue from it ; and
this preparation is the last work of his enhanced activity.
Up to this point his organ of the poetising intellect, *Word-
speech,* can do his bidding ; for up to here he has had to set
forth interests in whose interpreting and shaping a necessary
feeling took no share as yet,—interests variously influenced
by given circumstances from Without, without there being
any definite working on Within in such a way as to drive
the inner Feeling to a necessary, choiceless activity, in its
turn determining the outer course of things.   Here still
reigned the combining Understanding, with its parcelling
of parts and piecing-together of this or that detail in this

or that fashion ; here it had not directly to *display*, but merely to shadow forth, to draw comparisons, to make like intelligible by like,—and for *this*, not only did its organ of Word-speech quite suffice, but it was the only one through which the intellect could make itself intelligible.—But where the thing prepared-for is to become a *reality*, where the poet has no longer to separate and compare, where he wants to let the thing that gainsays all Choice and definitely gives itself without conditions, the determinant motive strengthened to a determinative force—to let this proclaim itself in the very Utterance (*Ausdruck*) of a necessary, all-dominating feeling,—there he can no longer work with the merely shadowing, expounding * Word-speech, *except he so enhance it* as he has already enhanced the motive : and this he can only do by pouring it into *Tone-speech.*

* In the *Deutsche Monatsschrift*—to which we may now bid farewell, as the last of its " three articles " ends with this chapter—there here appeared " unintelligible to the Feeling," as a predicate of " Word-Speech."—It may be as well to point out that the word " *Ausdruck*," which I have here, and in a few other passages, translated as " Utterance," is commonly rendered by " Expression." Neither equivalent is quite satisfactory, though the best we have ; and particularly the latter has given rise to much confusion in the minds of musicians. " Utterance," of course, is more strictly allotted to the word of similar derivation, " *Äusserung*," but Wagner himself has often interchanged the two words in this Part II.—TR.

ONE-SPEECH is the beginning and end of Word-speech : as the *Feeling* is beginning and end of the Understanding, as *Mythos* is beginning and end of History, the *Lyric* beginning and end of Poetry. The mediator between beginning and middle, as between the latter and the point of exit, is *the Phantasy*.

The march of this evolution is such, however, that it is no retrogression, but a progress to the winning of the highest human faculty ; and it is travelled, not merely by Mankind in general, but substantially by every social Individual.

Just as in the unconscious Feeling lie all the germs for evolution of the Understanding, while this latter holds within it a necessitation to vindicate the unconscious feeling, and the man who from out his Understanding vindicates this Feeling is first the man of *Vernunft;* just as in Mythos justified by History, which alike grew out of *it*, is first won a really intelligible image of Life : so does the Lyric also hold within itself each germ of the intrinsic art of Poetry, which necessarily can but end with speaking out the vindication of the Lyric ; and this work of vindication is precisely the highest human Artwork, the *Entire Drama* (das *vollkommene Drama*).

The primal organ-of-utterance of the inner man, however, is *Tone-speech*, as the most spontaneous expression of the inner Feeling stimulated from without. A mode of Expression similar to that still proper to the beasts was, in any case, alike the first employed by Man ; and this we can call before us at any moment,—as far as its substance goes,—by removing from our Word-speech its dumb articulations (*die stummen Mitlauter*), and leaving nothing but the open sounds (*die tönenden Laute*). In these vowels, if we think of them as stripped of their consonants, and picture to ourselves the manifold and vivid play of inner feelings, with all their range of joy and sorrow, as given-out in them alone, we shall obtain an image of man's first emotional language ; a language in which the stirred and high-strung Feeling could certainly express itself through nothing but a joinery of ringing tones, which altogether of itself must take the form of Melody. This melody, which was accompanied by appropriate bodily gestures in such a way that it appeared, itself in turn, to be nothing but the simultaneous inner expression of an outer announcement through those gestures, and therefore also took its time-measure—its Rhythm—from the changeful motion of those gestures, in such a manner that it returned it to them as the melodically-vindicated measure for their own announce-ment,—this *rhythmic melody*, which we should do wrong to set down as of poor effect and beauty, in view of the infinitely greater variety of man's emotional fund as com-pared with that of the beasts, and especially in view of its endless capacity for enhancement through interaction between the inner expression of the voice and the outer expression of the gestures,*—this melody, both by its nature and its origin, so thoroughly decreed the Measure for the word-verse, that the latter appears to have been governed by it to the extent of positive subordination,— as we still may see to-day by inspecting any genuine *Volkslied ;* in which we shall always find the word-verse plainly governed by the melody, and so much so, that it often has to accommodate itself, even for the sense, to the melody's most intimate requirements.

This matter shews us very palpably the rise of Speech.†

---

* The wood-bird, the animal which expresses its emotion the most melodi-ously, lacks all power of accompanying its song by gestures.—RICHARD WAGNER.

† I take the rise (*Entstehung*) of Speech from out of Melody, not as in a chronologic, but as in an architectonic order. —R. WAGNER.

P

In the Word, the ringing tones of pure emotional-speech
seek as much to bring themselves to a distinguishment
from one another, as the inner Feeling seeks to discriminate
between the outer objects working on the senses, to tell its
tale about them, and finally to make intelligible its inner
thrust toward such a tale itself. In pure Tone-speech, with
its tale of the received impression, the Feeling gave only
itself to be understood; and this, supported by the gestures,
it was quite competent to do, through its countless raisings
and sinkings, prolongings and abridgings, intensifyings and
abatings of the open sounds. To denote and distinguish
between outer objects themselves, however, the Feeling
must cast about it for something answering-to and
embodying the impression of the object, for a distinctive
garment wherewith to clothe the open tone ; and this it
borrowed from the Impression, and through it from the
object itself. This garment it wove from dumb articulations,
which it fitted on to the open sound as a prefix or suffix,*
or even as both together, so that it was enveloped in them
and held down to a definite, distinguishable announcement ;
in the same way as the object, thus distinguished, marked
off and announced itself to the outer world by a garment—
the animal by its skin, the tree by its bark, &c. The
vowels thus clothed, and parcelled by such clothing, form
the *roots of speech* through whose fitting and fixing together
the whole sensuous edifice of our endless-branching Word-
speech has been erected.

Let us first notice, however, with what instinctive fore-
sight this Speech but very gradually left its nursing mother,
Melody, and her breast-milk the open tone. In keeping
with an unaffected view of Nature and a longing to impart
the impressions of such a view, Speech set only the kindred
and analogous together, in order not only to make plain
the kindred by its analogy and explain the analogous by

---

* "An= oder Ablaut,"—i.e. the initial or terminal inflection, given by the
mouth to the simple vowel sound as it leaves the *larynx ;* thus in "sound,"
"s" would be the *Anlaut,* "ou" the *tönender Laut,* and "nd" a double
Ablaut.—Tr.

its kinship, but also, through an Expression based on analogy and kinship of its own 'moments,' to produce a still more definite and intelligible impression upon the Feeling. Herein was evinced the sensuously composing (*sinnlich dichtende*) force of Speech. Through taking the open sound, employed for purely subjective expression of the feelings inspired by an object—in scale with its impression,—and clothing it with a garment of mute articulations, which stood to the Feeling as an objective expression borrowed from an attribute of the object itself, it had arrived at moulding different 'moments' of expression, in its speech-roots. Now, when Speech set these roots together according to their kinship and alike-ness, it made plain to the Feeling both the impression of the object and its answering expression, in equal measure, through an increased strengthening of that Expression ; and hereby in turn, it denoted the object as itself a strengthened one,—namely, as an object strictly-speaking multiple, but *one* in essence through its kinship and alike-ness. This 'composing moment' of Speech is its *alliteration* or *Stabreim*, in which we recognise the very oldest attribute of all poetic speech.

In *Stabreim* the kindred speech-roots are fitted to one another in such a way, that, just as they sound alike to the physical ear, they also knit like objects into one collective image in which the Feeling may utter its conclusions about them. Their sensuously cognisable resemblance they win either from a kinship of the vowel sounds, especially when these stand open in front, without any initial consonant * ; or from the sameness of this initial consonant itself, which characterises the likeness as one belonging peculiarly to the object † ; or again, from the sameness of the terminal consonant that closes up the root behind (as an assonance), provided the individualising force of the word lies in that terminal.‡ The distribution and arrangement of these

---

* " Erb' und eigen."   " Immer und ewig." ⎫
† " Ross und Reiter." " Froh und frei."   ⎬ RICHARD WAGNER.
‡ " Hand und Mund."   " Recht und Pflicht." ⎭

rhyming roots takes place by similar laws to those that
lead us in every walk of Art to repeat, as necessary for an
understanding, those motives on which we lay chief weight,
and which we therefore so bestow between lesser motives,
in turn conditioned by them, that they stand out plainly as
the conditioning and essential ones.

As I must reserve till later a fuller treatment of this subject,
for the purpose of demonstrating the Stabreim's possible
operation upon our Music, I will at present content myself
with pointing out in how strict a relation the Stabreim, and
the Word-verse rounded-off thereby, once stood to that
melody which we have to consider as the earliest message of
a more complex human feeling, albeit a feeling rounding off
its complexity into a unity. By that Melody we have to
explain not only the dimensions of the Word-verse, but
also the position and, in general, the attributes of the Stabreim which governed those dimensions ; while the production of that Melody, again, was conditioned by man's
natural capacity of breath and the possibility of giving out
a number of stronger intonations in one breath. The duration of an outflow of the breath through the organ of song
governed the dimensions of a segment of the melody, in
which one pregnant portion of the sense must come to a
conclusion. But this possible duration governed also the
number of special intonations in one melodic segment: if
these special intonations were of impassioned strength, and
thus more rapidly consumed the breath, then this number
was diminished,—or if, their strength being less, they did
not require so swift a breath-consumption, then their
number was increased. These intonations, which fell
together with the gestures and thereby disposed themselves to a rhythmic measure, were in Speech condensed
into the alliterative root-words, whose number and position
they conditioned in the same way as the melodic segment,
itself conditioned by the breath, determined the length and
compass of the Verse.—How simple is an explanation and
understanding of all *Metrik*, if only we take the reasonable
pains to go back to the natural conditionments of all human

art-ability, from which alone can we also reach again to genuine art-production !—

But let us follow for the present the evolutionary career of *Word-speech*, and reserve for ourselves a later return to the Melody it left behind.—

In exact degree as poesis (*das Dichten*) ceased to be a function of the Feeling and became a transaction of the Understanding, did the creative league of Gesture-, Tone-, and Word-speech, originally united in the Lyric, disband itself ; Word-speech was the child that left its father and mother, to help itself along in the wide world alone.—As the number of objects and their relations to his Feeling increased before the adolescent's eye, so accumulated the words and combinations of Speech which were to answer to those added objects and relations.   So long as this growing man still kept his eye on Nature, and was able to grasp her by his Feeling, so long also did he invent linguistic roots in characteristic keeping with the objects and their relations. But when amid the eventual stress of life he turned his back on chis fruitful fountain of his powers of speech, then all his inventive-force was blighted, and he had to content himself with the harvest handed down to him but no longer a pos-session to be ever-newly reaped ; in such-wise that, according to his need, he took his heritage of speech-roots and pieced them doubly and trebly together for extranatural objects, pared them down for sake of this his piecing, and above all marred them past all knowledge by evaporating the ring of their sounding vowels to the hasty clang of Talk ; while, by heaping-up the dumb articulations needful for combining un-related roots, he wrinkled grievously the living flesh of Speech.   When Speech had thus lost an instinctive under-standing of her own roots—only possible through Feeling, —she naturally could no longer answer *in these* to the intonations of that fostering mother-melody.   She either contented herself—where Dance remained an inseparable portion of the Lyric, as in Greek antiquity—with snuggling as briskly as possible to the *Rhythm* of the melody : or she sought—where Dance had more and more completely swerved away from Lyric, as among the modern nations —for another bond of union with the melodic breathing-snatches ; and this she procured in the *end-rhyme*.

The End-rhyme—to which we must also come back, on account of its attitude towards our music—set itself up at the exit of a melodic segment, without being able to answer the intonations (*Betonungen*) of the melody itself. It no longer knit the natural band of Tone- and Word-speech, in which the Stabreim brought its radical affinities to the melodic intonations within the purview of both the outer and the inner sense ; but it merely fluttered at the loose end of the ribands of melody, toward which the word-verse fell into a more and more arbitrary and uncomplying attitude. —The more confusedly and circuitously this Word-speech must proceed, at last, to designate objects and relations belonging solely to social Convention, and no longer to the self-determining nature of things ; the more she must busy herself to find terms for concepts which, themselves skimmed-off from natural phenomena, were to be employed in turn for combinations of these abstractions ; the more, for this, she must screw up the original meaning of roots to accommodate a twofold and threefold meaning, ingeniously laid under them but merely to be *thought out*, no longer to be *felt ;* and the more elaborately she had to equip the mechanical apparatus which was to bolster up, and set in motion, this system of screws and levers : so much the more shrewish and estranged did she become towards that primal melody (*Urmelodie*),—till at last she lost even the remotest memory of it, when, out of breath and reft of tone, she must flounder into the grey morass of *Prose*.

The Understanding, condensed from Feeling through the Phantasy, acquired in Prosaic word-speech an organ through which it could make itself intelligible *alone*, and in direct

ratio as it became un-intelligible to Feeling. In modern
Prose we speak a language we do not understand with the
Feeling, since its connection with the objects, whose impression on our faculties first ruled the moulding of the speech-
roots, has become incognisable to us ; a language which we
speak as it was taught us in our youth,—not as, with waxing self-dependence of our Feeling, we haply seize, form,
and feed it from ourselves and the objects we behold ; a
language whose usages and claims, based on the logic of
the Understanding, we must unconditionally obey when
we want to impart our thoughts. This language, in our
Feeling's eyes, rests therefore on a *convention* which has a
definite scope,—namely, to make ourselves thus far intelligible according to a given norm, in which we are to think
and to *dominate* our feelings, that we may demonstrate to
the Understanding an aim of the Understanding. Our
Feeling—which quite of itself found unconscious expression in the primitive Speech—we can only *describe* in
this language ; and describe in a far more circuitous way
than an object of the Understanding, because we are
obliged to screw ourselves *down* from our intellectual
language to its real stock, in the same way as we screwed
ourselves *up* from that stock to *it*.—Our language accordingly rests upon a State-historico-religious convention,
which in France, under the rule of Convention personified,
under Louis XIV., was also very logically fixed into a
settled 'norm,' by an Academy under orders. Upon no
living and ever-present, no really felt *conviction* does it rest,
for it is the tutored opposite of any such conviction. In a
sense, we cannot discourse in this language according to
our innermost emotion, for it is impossible to *invent* in it
according to that emotion ; in *it*, we can only impart our
emotions to the Understanding, but not to the implicitly
understanding Feeling ; and therefore in our modern evolution it was altogether consequent, that the Feeling should
have sought a refuge from absolute intellectual-speech by
fleeing to absolute tone-speech, our Music of to-day.

In modern Speech no *poesis* is possible,*—that is to say,
a poetic Aim cannot be *realised* therein, but only spoken
out *as such.*

The poet's Aim is never realised, until it passes from the
Understanding to the Feeling. The Understanding, that
merely wants to impart an Aim which can be *entirely*
imparted in the language of the Understanding, does not
concern itself with a *uniting* aim, but its aim is a dissever-
ing, a *loosening* one. † The Understanding poetises only
when it grasps the scattered fragments as a connected
whole, and wants to bring this whole to an infallible impression. A connected whole is only to be *fully surveyed*
from a *remoter* standpoint, in keeping with the object and
the aim ; the image, which thus offers itself to the eye, is
not the actual reality of the object, but merely that reality
which the eye can take in as a *connected whole.* An actual
reality only the *loosening* Understanding is able to know
according to its details, and to impart through its organ,
modern intellectual-speech ; the ideal, the sole intelligible
reality only the *composing* (dichtende) Understanding is
able to comprehend as a connected whole, but can intelligibly impart it only through an organ which, being itself
a concentrator *(ein verdichtendes),* shall answer also to the
concentrated object, in that it imparts it the most intelligibly to the Feeling. A great conjuncture of phenomena
—through which alone they are individually explicable—
is only to be displayed, as we have seen, through a concentration of these phenomena ; this concentration
(*Verdichtung*), as applied to the phenomena of human
life, means their simplification, and for its sake a *strengthening* of the moments-of-action—which, again, could only
proceed from motives likewise strengthened. But a motive
can gain an access of strength only through the ascension

---

* " In der modernen Sprache kann nicht *gedichtet* werden."

† In the German the antithesis is between "*verbindend*" ("binding together") and "*auflösend*" ("setting loose"). The obvious allusion is to
"*gebundene Rede*"—poetry, or rather, *verse*—and "*ungebundene Rede*"—
"loosened speech," i.e. *prose.*—TR.

of the various intellectual-moments contained in it, into one decisive 'moment'-of-*feeling;* while the Word-poet can arrive at imparting this convincingly, only through the primal organ of the soul's inner feeling,—through *Tone-speech.*

But the poet must see his Aim unrealised, were he to lay it bare so undisguisedly that he waited for the instant of highest need, to lay hands upon the redeeming utterance of Tone-speech. If *first* where Melody has to enter as the most perfect utterance of a high-strung feeling, he wanted to transpose the *naked* word-speech into *full-clad* tone-speech, he would plunge both intellect and feeling into one common depth of bewilderment, from which he could only rescue them by the most unblushing revelation of his Aim: to wit, by openly revoking all pretence of Art-work and imparting his Aim, as such, to the Under-standing, while he offered to the Feeling a mere emotional expression un-governed by the Aim, an expression both diffluent and superfluous, — that of our modern Opera. The *ready-made* (fertige) melody is unintelligible to the Understanding that up to its entry has been the only principle at work, even for the expounding of nascent feelings; in that melody it can only take an interest in ratio as it has itself passed over into the Feeling, which arrives, amid its *growing* stir, at the per-fection of its most exhaustive method of *expression.* In the growth of this expression, towards its utmost pleni-tude, the Understanding can only take an interest from the instant when it steps upon the soil of Feeling. This soil the poet definitely treads, however, from the time when he urges onward from the *aim* of Drama towards its *realising;* since the longing for this realisement *is already* the necessary, the strenuous stir, within him, of the selfsame Feeling to which he wants to communicate a *thought-out* object and gain for it a sure, redeeming comprehension.—The poet can only hope to realise his Aim, from the instant when he *hushes* it and keeps it secret to himself: that is to say, when, *in the language* wherein alone it could be imparted as a naked intellectual-aim, he no longer speaks it out at all. His redeeming, namely his realising work first begins from the time when he is able to unbosom himself in the new, redeeming and realising tongue; in which at last, and alone, he can also deliver the most convincingly the deepest Content of his Aim,—to wit, from the time when the Art-work itself begins : and that is, from the earliest entry of the Drama.

A Tone-speech to be struck-into from the outset, is therefore the organ of expression proper for the poet who would make himself intelligible by turning from the Under-standing to the Feeling, and who for that purpose has to take his stand upon a soil on which alone he can have any commerce with Feeling. The strengthened moments-of-action, which the poetising Understanding has descried, can—by reason of their necessarily strengthened motives—only come to an intelligible show upon a soil which in itself is raised above the ordinary life and its habitual methods of expression ; upon a soil which thus towers (*hervorragt*) above that of the ordinary means of expres-sion, in the same way as those strengthened shapes and motives tower over those of ordinary life. Yet this Expression can as little be an unnatural one, as those actions and motives may dare to be un-human and un-natural. The poet's shapings have to fully correspond with real Life, in so far as they are merely to display the latter in its most succinct cohesion, and in the utmost force of its arousal ; and thus also, their Expression should be nothing but that of the most deep-roused human *feeling*, according to its highest power of self-enunciation. Unnatural, on the contrary, would the poet's figures seem, if, amid the highest enhancement of their motives and ' moments ' of action, they enounced them through the organ of ordinary life ; unintelligible, moreover, and positively ridiculous, if they employed this organ by turns with that unwonted, heightened one,—just as much as though, before our very eyes, they were to exchange from time to time the soil of

THE PLAY AND DRAMATIC POETRY.

work.*

If now we pry a little closer into the Poet's business, we
shall see that the realisement of his Aim consists solely in
the making possible an exhibition of the 'strengthened
actions' of his characters (*seiner gedichteten Gestalten*)
through an exposition of their motives to the Feeling ;
and that this, again, can only be effectuated through an
Expression which shall in so far claim his active aid, as *its
invention and establishment first makes possible the displaying of those motives and actions.*

This Expression is therefore the prime condition of the
realisement of his Aim, which without it could never step
from the realm of thought into that of actuality. But the
sole effectual Expression, here, is *an altogether different* one
from that of the poetic Understanding's own organ of speech.
The Understanding is therefore driven by necessity to wed
itself with an element which shall be able to take-up into it
the poet's Aim as a fertilising seed, and so to nourish and
shape this seed by its own, its necessary essence, that it
may bring it forth as a realising and redeeming utterance
of Feeling.

This element is that same mother-element, the womanly,
from whose womb—the *ur*-melodic † expressional-faculty,—
there issued Word and Word-speech, so soon as it was fecundated by the actual outward-lying objects of Nature ; just as
the Understanding throve from out the Feeling, and is thus
the condensation of this womanly into a manly, into an element fitted to impart. Now, just as the Understanding has
to fecundate in turn the Feeling,—just as amidst this fecundation it is impelled to find itself encompassed by the

---

* In fact, this has formed a preponderantly weighty 'moment' of our
modern Comic-art.—R. WAGNER.

† In Volume I., p. 169, I pointed out the impossibility of rendering into
English this prefix "*ur*" ("primeval," conf. "ere," "yore" &c.) ; I now can
only throw myself on my reader's mercy, for employing the useful little syllable without further ado.—TR.

Feeling, in *it* justified, by it mirrored back, and in this mirroring recognisable, i.e. first cognisable, by itself,—just so is the intellectual Word impelled to recognise itself in Tone, the Word-speech to find itself justified in Tone-speech.* The stimulus which rouses this impulse and whets it to the highest agitation, lies outside the one impelled, and in the object of his yearning ; whose charm is brought him first through Phantasy — the all-puissant mediatrix between Feeling and Understanding,—but this charm cannot content him until he pours himself into that object's full reality. This charm is the influence of the "eternal womanly," which draws the man-ly Understanding out of its egoism,—and this again is only possible through the Womanly attracting that thing in it which is kindred to itself : but That in which the Understanding is akin to the Feeling is *the purely-human,* that which makes-out the essence of the human *species* as such. In this Purely-human are nurtured both the Manly and the Womanly, which only *by their union through Love become first the Human Being.*

The impetus necessary to the poetic intellect, in this its poesis, is therefore *Love,*—and that the love *of man to woman.* Yet not that frivolous, carnal love, in which man only seeks to satisfy an appetite, but the deep yearning to know himself redeemed from his egoism through his sharing in the rapture of the loving woman ; and *this yearning* is *the creative moment* (das dichtende Moment) of the Understanding. The necessary bestowal, the seed that only in the most ardent transports of Love can condense itself from his noblest forces—*this procreative seed is the poetic Aim, which brings to the glorious loving woman, Music, the Stuff for bearing.*

Let us now lend ear to this act of Birth.

* Would it be thought trivial of me, if I were to remind the reader—with reference to my exposition of that myth—of Œdipus who was born of Jocasta, and who begot with Jocasta the redemptrix, Antigone ?—R. WAGNER.

THIRD PART.

THE ARTS OF POETRY AND TONE
IN THE
DRAMA OF THE FUTURE.

(*DICHTKUNST UND TONKUNST*
IM
DRAMA DER ZUKUNFT.)

In Letters to Uhlig, *No.* 19 (*December,* 1850), *Wagner* *writes :* "*Part III.—Here first, do I begin."—*

I.

ERETOFORE the Poet has in two ways endeavoured to tune the organ of the Understanding, absolute Word-speech, to an emotional expression which might help him to convey his message to the Feeling : through the verse's *measure*—on the side of *Rhythmik ;* through its *end-rhyme*—on the side of *Melodik.*—

For measuring their verse, the poets of the Middle Ages still kept definitely to *the melody,* in respect both of the number of syllables, and especially of their emphasis (*Betonung*). But after the verse's at last purely outward dependence on a stereotype melody had degenerated into slavish pedantry—as in the schools of the Meistersingers, —in more recent times there sprang from Prose a Measure altogether independent of any real melody ; and this was brought about by taking for model the rhythmic structure of Greek and Latin verse,—such as we now have under our eyes in the form of Literature. The attempts at copying and appropriating this model were at first restricted to the next of kin, and launched out so very gradually that we could not grow fully aware of their fundamental error until, on the one side, we had acquired a more intimate acquaintance with the ancient *Rhythmik,* while on the other, our very attempts at copying it had brought us to an insight into the impossibility and fruitlessness of this copying. We know *now,* that what begot the endless variety of Grecian *Metrik* was the indivorcible, the living collaboration of the Dance's gesture with the Tone-Word's speech ; and we know that all the hence-arisen verse-forms were strictly conditioned by a Speech which had so moulded itself through just this partnership, that we can scarcely grasp an iota of its rhythmic peculiarities from the standpoint of *our own* language, whose moulding principle has been quite an other one.

The special mark of Grecian culture lies in its paying so preponderant an attention to man's bodily appearance, that we have to regard the latter as the basis of all Greek art. The lyric and the dramatic artwork were the speech-enabled spiritualising of this body's motion, and the monumental plastic-art was finally its open deifying. As for the art of Tone, the Greeks only felt urged to develop it sufficiently to serve as a prop for Gesture, whose tale was already expressed melodiously by Speech itself. In its accompaniment of Dance's motion their sounding Word-speech won so sure a prosodic Measure,—i.e. so delicately balanced a physical standard for the weight or lightness of each syllable and its ordering in point of time-length,—that the instinctive speaking-accent, with its emphasis of syllables which bear no 'quantitative' weight, had absolutely to stand back as against this purely sensuous ruling. Yet this ruling was no arbitrary one, but derived, even for speech, from the natural attributes of the root-syllable's vowel sound, or this sound's position toward the strengthened consonants ; while on the other hand, by its heightening (*Hebung*) of the speaking-accent the Melody made good again the latter's ousting by the Rhythm.*

Now, the metres of Greek verse-building have come down to us without this reconciling melody (as their architecture without its quondam ornament of colour), and still less can we explain the endless *changefulness* of these metres from the changeful movements of the dance, because we no longer have before our eyes those movements, any more than we have that melody before our ears.—A verse-measure abstracted from the Greek *Metrik*, under such ·conditions, must therefore unite in itself every conceivable

---

* Here, for sake of clearness, I have been obliged *both* to transpose some of the clauses of a sentence, and to divide its original body into two. I notice this, as it is one of the very few cases, in *Oper und Drama*, where Wagner's so-called "involved style" presents any really serious difficulties to the literal translator.—TR.

element of contradiction. For its counterfeiting purposes it demanded, before all else, a ruling of our syllables into 'longs and shorts,' which was utterly against their natural disposition. In a language already dissolved into the rankest prose, liftings and lowerings (*Hebungen und Senkungen*) of the speaking-tone can only be dictated by the *accent* which we place upon certain words or syllables *for sake of intelligibleness.* This Accent, however, is by no means good for once and all, as the 'quantity' (*das Gewicht*) of Greek prosody was good for every case; but it varies in exact degree as this word or that syllable in the sentence is of stronger or weaker *import* for the meaning. In our speech we can only imitate a Greek μετρον by, on the one hand, arbitrarily coining the Accent itself into a prosodic value, or on the other, sacrificing the Accent to an *imaginary* prosodic value. Hitherto both plans have been tried in turn, so that the bewilderment, which such rhythmic-posing verses have inflicted on the Feeling, could only be smoothed away again by an arbitrary arrangement on the part of the Understanding: for a better explanation it set the Greek 'schema' above the word-verse, and thereby told itself much the sort of thing that the painter once told the viewer, when he wrote beneath his picture: "This is a cow."

How incapable is our language of any accurately rhythmic utterance in Verse, is shewn the plainest by that simplest of all metres in which she has been accustomed to clothe herself, in order—as modestly as possible—to shew herself in at least some sort of rhythmic garb. We mean the so-called *Iambic,* in which she loves to present herself to our eyes—and alas! to our ears also—as a five-footed monster. Taken on its own merits, the unloveliness of this metre irks the Feeling, so soon as it is set before us without a break, as in our spoken plays: but when—as indeed is inevitable—the most grievous violence is done to the live Accent of speech, for sake of this monotonous rhythm, then the hearing of such verses becomes a positive martyrdom; for, led astray from a correct and

Q

rapid comprehension of the subject-matter, through the
mutilation of the speaking-accent, the hearer next is
violently held down to abandon his feelings to a painfully
fatiguing ride on the hobbling Iambic, whose clattering
trot must rob him of the last shred of sense and understanding.—An intelligent actress was once so distressed by
the iambics, such as they are ambled on to the stage by
our modern poets, that she had all her rôles written out in
prose, so as not to be tempted *by their look* to exchange
the natural speaking-accent for a sense-destroying scansion
of the verse.   Through this sensible procedure this artist
most certainly discovered that the pretended iambic was
an illusion of the poet, which vanished so soon as ever the
Verse was written out in prose and this prose was declaimed
in an intelligible fashion ; most certainly she found that
each line, when spoken with natural feeling and intoned
with sole regard to an unmistakable delivery of its meaning, contained but *one*, or at the utmost *two* syllables which
called for a special lingering together with a sharper intonation ; that to these one or two accented syllables the
remainder bore a quite equable relation, unbroken by any
pause, any swelling or sinking, any rise or fall ; while
prosodic 'longs and shorts' could only figure among them
through the expedient of stamping the root-syllables with
an accent altogether foreign to our modern habit, and
thoroughly obstructive, nay destructive of the understanding of a phrase—namely an accent which, in favour of
the Verse, must shew itself as a rhythmic retardation (*als
ein rhythmisches Verweilen*).

I admit, that good verse-makers are distinguished from
bad ones by just the fact that they only place the 'longs' of
the Iambic upon the root-syllables, and the 'shorts' on the
prefix or suffix : but if the thus-determined 'longs,' as is
certainly the intention of the Iambic, are delivered with
rhythmical exactitude—say, in the proportion of the whole
notes of a bar to its half notes—, that very treatment
constitutes an offence against our linguistic usage, and an

offence which completely blocks any true and intelligible expression in consonance with our feeling.   Were any prosodically increased 'quantity' present to our Feeling, in hearing these root-syllables, then it would have been quite impossible for the musician to let those iambic verses be declaimed in any rhythm you please, and above all to rob them of their distinctive 'quantity' in such a way, that he should allot indiscriminately to long or short notes the supposititious long and short syllables.   But the musician was bound to the Accent alone; and first in music does this Accent gain importance, from its bearing on syllables which—as a chain of rhythmically uniform moments—in ordinary speech behave to the main-accent like a gradual upstroke *: for it here has to answer to the rhythmical weight of the 'good and bad' parts of the bar, and to win a marked distinction through raising or sinking the tone (*durch Steigen oder Sinken des Tones*).—As a rule, however, the Poet further saw himself compelled, in the Iambic, to give up all thought of turning the root-syllables into prosodic 'longs,' and to choose at lief or hazard either this or that, from out a row of equally accented syllables, whereto to accord the honour of a prosodic 'length'; whereas, next-door to it, he was constrained to degrade a root-syllable into a prosodic 'short,' so as to dispose his words intelligibly.—

The secret of this Iambic has become patent on our acting stages.   Intelligent actors, concerned to address the hearer's Understanding, have spoken this verse as naked prose; unintelligent ones, unable to grasp the content of the verse by reason of its beat, have declaimed it as a sense- and tone-less melody, alike un-intelligible as un-melodious.

---

* " Und erst in der Musik gewinnt dieser Accent von Sylben, die in der gewöhnlichen Sprache—als eine Kette rhythmisch ganz gleicher Momente— zum Hauptaccente sich wie ein steigender Auftakt verhalten, eine Bedeutung." I here give the German clause, since the "von"—meaning either "of" or "from"—gives rise to a little uncertainty, albeit not vitally affecting the *general* sense.—TR.

Where, as among the Romanic peoples, a *Rhythmik*
based on prosodic longs and shorts has never been attempted in spoken verse, and the verse-line therefore has
only been governed by the number of syllables, there the
end-rhyme has been set fast as an indispensable condition
of the verse's very existence.

In this End-rhyme lies the characteristic essence of the
Christian Melody, as whose verbal residue it is to be
regarded.   Its significance we may figure to ourselves at
once, by calling to mind the *chorale* of the Church.   The
melody of this chant is absolutely neutral in its rhythm; it
strides on, step by step, in completely even beats (*Takt-
längen*), merely pausing at the end of a breath to take its
breath anew.   The division into stronger and weaker bar-
parts is a substitution of later date; the original church-
melody knew nothing of such a division.   For *it*, the root
and coupling syllables were quite alike; Speech had no
authority over it, but only an aptitude for being resolved
into an emotional expression, whose substance was fear of
the Lord and desire of Death.   Only where the breath
gave out, at the close of a melodic segment, did Word-
speech take a share in the melody, through the rhyme of
its ending syllable; and this rhyme was so definitely an
affair of the melody's last-held note, that in the case of so-
called feminine endings the short after-syllable alone
needed to rhyme, and the rhyme of such a syllable was
deemed a fitting pendant for a preceding or succeeding
masculine end-rhyme : a positive proof of the absence of
any *Rhythmik* in either this melody or this verse.

Finally divorced from this melody by the secular poet,
the word-verse would have been wholly unrecognisable as
Verse, without its end-rhyme.   Seeing that the breathing-
periods did not so obviously mark off the lines, as in the
chanted melody, and that the syllables were uniformly
dwelt-on without the smallest distinction,—their *number*,
the line's sole governing factor, could not have parcelled-
off the verse-lines at all recognisably, had not the end-

rhyme so audibly denoted the moment of severance that it made good the lacking 'moment' of Melody, the taking of a fresh deep breath.   This End-rhyme therefore, since it was also dwelt on as the stanza's rounding-off (*da auf ihm zugleich als auf dem scheidenden Versabsatze verweilt wurde*), acquired so weighty a significance for spoken verse, that all the other syllables of the line had to rank as a mere preparatory onset on its closing syllable, as a lengthened upstroke for the down-beat of the rhyme.

This movement towards the closing syllable was thoroughly in keeping with the character of the Romanic peoples' speech, which, after its heterogeneous mixing of fragments from alien and outlived tongues, had modelled itself in such a fashion, that the Feeling was completely debarred from any understanding of the primal roots. This we may learn the plainest from the French language, in which the speaking accent has become the absolute antithesis of an intonation of the root-syllables, such as must be natural to the Feeling when there still remains a vestige of connection with the roots of speech.   The Frenchman never lays stress upon any but the final syllable of a word, however far ahead the root may lie, in compound or elongated words, and even if this final syllable is a mere inessential appendage.   Moreover, in his phrase he drives all the words together into one monotonously hastening onset upon the closing word, or rather— the closing syllable; and on this he lingers with a strongly lifted accent, even when this closing word—as customary —is by no means the weightiest of the phrase: for, in direct opposition to this speaking accent, the Frenchman habitually constructs his phrase so as to drive all its determinative moments into its commencement; whereas the German, for instance, relegates them to its close.   This strife between the Content of the phrase and its Expression through the speaking-accent, we may easily explain by the influence of the end-rhymed verse upon the speech of everyday.   So soon as this latter is roused by any particular excitement, it involuntarily expresses itself in accordance with the character of that verse, the remnant of the older melody ; just as on the other hand the German, in a like event, speaks out in Stabreims—e.g. "Zittern und Zagen," "Schimpf und Schande."—

Thus the chief characteristic of the End-rhyme is, that, without any integral connection with the phrase, it appears as a help-in-need for establishing the Verse, and a help to which the expression of ordinary speech feels driven whenever it wishes to give utterance to a heightened emotion. As compared with the ordinary verbal expression, the end-rhymed verse is the attempt to communicate a heightened matter in such a way as to produce a corresponding impression on the Feeling, and this by very means of an expression differing from that of everyday.—This everyday expression, however, was the organ of communication between the Understanding on the one part and the Understanding on the other ; through an expression different from this, through a *heightened* one, the communicator wanted, in a sense, to avoid the Understanding, i.e. to address himself just to that which differs from the Understanding, namely to the Feeling. This he sought to attain by rousing the physical organ of speech-reception—which took up the Understanding's message in a quite indifferent un-consciousness—to a consciousness of its functions, inasmuch as he sought to evoke in it a purely sensuous pleasure in the Expression itself. The word-verse which closes with an end-rhyme may well incite the sentient organ of hearing to give heed so far, that it feels captivated by the listening for a return of the rhyming period : but hereby it is only attuned to just giving heed, i.e. it falls into a state of strained expectancy, which must be *satisfied in the full capacity* of the hearing-organ if the latter is to be stirred into such active interest, and finally to be so completely contented, that it may transmit the delightful acquisition to man's whole receptive-faculty. Only when the *whole* power of man's Feeling is completely stirred to interest in an object conveyed to it through a recipient sense, does that object win the force to expand its concentrated essence

again, in such a way as to bring the Understanding an infinitely enriched and sapid food.   But as every communication is aimed at a *mutual-understanding*, so also the poet's
aim at last makes only for a communication to the Understanding : to reach this positive understanding, however, he
does not assume it in advance, in the quarter to which he
addresses himself, but in a sense he wishes to get it first
begotten by a comprehension of his aim ; and the bearing-
organ for this begettal is, so to say, man's Feeling-power.*
This Feeling-power, however, is not a consenting party to that
birth, until it has been set into the highest state of agitation
through the thing received, and thus acquires the force for
bearing.   But this force comes first to it through Want (*Noth*),
and Want through the overfill to which the thing received
has thriven : only that which overburdens a bearing organism,
compels it to the act of birth ; and the bringing forth an
understanding of the poetic-aim is the recipient Feeling's
impartal of this aim to the inner Understanding,—which we
must look on as the ending of the bearing Feeling's Want.

Now, the Word-poet, who cannot impart his Aim to the
nearest recipient organ, that of Hearing, so amply that this
organ shall be roused into that highest agitation wherein it
is driven, in turn, to impart the thing received to the *whole*
receptive-faculty,—the Word-poet, if he wants to enchain
this organ for long, can only degrade and blunt it, when

---

* "Da es bei jeder Mittheilung doch nur auf *Verständniss* abgesehen ist, so
geht auch die dichterische Absicht endlich nur auf eine Mittheilung an den
Verstand hinaus : um aber zu diesem ganz sicheren Verständnisse zu gelangen,
setzt sie ihn da, wohin sie sich mittheilt, nicht von vornherein voraus, sondern
sie will ihn an ihrem Verständnisse sich gewissermassen erst erzeugen lassen,
und das Gebärungsorgan dieser Zeugung ist, so zu sagen, das Gefühlsvermögen
des Menschen."—I have quoted this sentence in full, as it is the most difficult
to interpret in all the book.   Its *drift* is plain enough, from the context ; but
our author has here allowed himself the perilous pleasure of a word-play upon
Verstand and *Verständniss* (" Understanding " in the abstract and the concrete)
in the extremest manner of Feuerbach.   An additional stumbling-block is
presented to the translator, by the "sie" and the "ihn," as we have no
gender for our "it " ; I have therefore been forced to replace the "sie "—
referring to the "poet's aim "— by "he " (i.e. "the poet ") in the portion of
the sentence *after* the colon, in order to avoid a conflict between the "it "s.—
A reference to page 207, in Chapter IV. of Part II. will prove of service.—TR.

he makes it forget, in a sense, its infinite capacity for reception,—or else he renounces all appeal to its infinite
power of aid, and employs it again as a mere slavish go-
between for the transference of thought to thought, for the
parleying of the Understanding *with* the Understanding :
which is as much as to say that the poet abandons his Aim,
he ceases his *poesis*, he merely stirs in the recipient Understanding its stock of things already known, of things brought
to it earlier through the senses ; he arranges the old in new
combinations, but imparts to it nothing new.—Through a
mere enhancement of Word-speech by the rhymed verse,
the poet can reach nothing beyond the forcing of the
recipient ear to an unsympathetic, puerilely superficial
attention, which—busied with its own object, just the in-
expressive Word-rhyme—cannot at all extend its field
within.   The poet, whose Aim was not this mere arousal
of so unsympathetic an attention, must at last look quite
aside from the coöperation of the Feeling and try to dissi-
pate again its fruitless stir, in order to be able once more
to address the Understanding undisturbed.

How that highest, bearing power of the Feeling is alone
to be aroused, we shall learn a little better when we have
first inquired in what relation our modern Music stands to
this rhythmic or end-rhymed verse of our modern Poetry,
and what influence this verse has been able to exert on her.

Divorced from the Word-verse, which had cut itself adrift
from her, Melody had gone on her own particular path of
evolution. We have already followed this somewhat closely,
and recognised that Melody—as the surface of an endlessly
developed Harmony, and borne on the wings of a complex
Rhythmik borrowed from the bodily Dance and unfolded
into rankest fill—had inflated herself to the pitch of laying claim to govern Poetry and ordain the Drama, as a

self-dependent entity in Art. Word-verse, likewise thriven to independence, could not exert any shaping influence upon this Melody, wherever it came in contact with her, on account of its ricketiness and incapacity for emotional expression; on the contrary, in any brush with Melody its own entire falsity and nothingness must come to open show. The rhythmic-verse was resolved by Melody into its truly quite un-rhythmic factors, which then were newly patched together according to rhythmic Melody's absolute good-pleasure : while the End-rhyme was drowned, past any trace or hearing, in the mighty billows of her sound. When Melody held *strictly* to the Word-verse and arranged her ornament so as to bring into relief the *sensuous* purpose of its structure, she disclosed the very thing in this verse which the intelligent declaimer, concerned for an understanding of its Content, had thought needful to conceal : namely its poverty-stricken outward Setting (*Fassung*), which disfigured the right pronunciation of the words and confounded all their meaning. This Setting might do the smallest harm, when it was not markedly driven-in upon the senses; but it cut off all possibility of the Content's being understood, so soon as ever it aired its own importance before the sense of hearing and thus induced the latter to post itself as a rigid barrier between the message and the inner receptivity. Moreover, when Melody thus subordinated herself to the Word-verse, when she contented herself with giving its rhymes and rhythms just precisely the roundness of her singing tone, then she not only exposed the lie and ugliness of the verse's sensuous Setting—together with the stultification of its Content,— but she robbed her self of all power of shewing herself in sensuous beauty and raising the verse's Content to an enthralling 'moment'-of-Feeling.

Wherefore that Melody which remained conscious of her aptitude for infinite emotional-expression,—acquired on Music's own domain,—paid no heed at all to the sensuous setting of the Word-verse, since it must grievously affect her shaping from her own resources. She

chose instead the task of announcing herself, entirely
for herself as independent vocal-melody, in an expression
which rendered the emotional-content of the words according to its broadest generality ; and indeed in a specifically
musical setting, toward which the word-verse merely held
the position of the explanatory label beneath a painting.

Where the melody did not go so far as to cast away the
Content of the verse, and employ the vowels and consonants of its syllables as a mere material for the singer's
mouth to chew, there the connecting bond between the
verse and melody remained the *speaking accent.*—Gluck's
endeavour, as I have already mentioned, was only directed
to gaining from the speaking accent a vindication for the
melodic accent, which before his time had been mostly
wayward as regards the verse. If, however, in his sole
concern for a melodically-strengthened but otherwise faithful reproduction of the natural speaking-expression, the
musician held to the *rhetorical accent* as the only thing
that could afford a natural and intelligible bond between
the talk and the melody,—then he had at like time to
completely upset the verse : for he had to lift out of it the
Accent, as the only thing to be dwelt on, and must let fall
all the other intonations, whether of an imaginary prosodic
'quantity' or of the end-rhyme. He thus passed over the
Verse for the same reasons as those which decided the
intelligent actor to speak it as naturally-accented Prose.
But the musician herewith *dissolved into prose* not only the
verse, but also his own melody ; for, of that melody which
merely reinforced by Tone the rhetorical accent of a verse
already disbanded into prose, there remained nothing over
but *a musical prose.*

As a matter of fact the whole dispute, in the different
conceptions of Melody, has revolved round the question as
to whether, and how, the melody should be governed by
the word-verse. The ready - made melody, essentially
obtained from Dance—the melody as which alone our
modern ear can conceive the essence of Melody at all—
will by no manner of means accommodate itself to the

speaking-accent of the word-verse. This accent shews itself now in this, now in that member of the verse, and never returns to the same position in the verse - line; because our poets have flattered their fancy with the will-o'-the-wisp of either a prosodically rhythmic verse, or a verse become melodic through its end-rhyme, and for sake of this phantom have forgotten to take for the verse's only rhythm-setting 'moment' the actual living Accent of Speech. Nay, in non-prosodic verse these poets have not even paid heed to definitely placing their speaking-accent on the only landmark of this verse, its End-rhyme; but the more habituated they have become to the use of rhyme, the more frequently have they taken any entirely un-emphasised end-syllable and used it for an end-rhyme.

But a melody can only stamp itself at all seizably upon the ear, through its containing a repetition of definite melodic moments in a definite rhythm; if such moments either do not return at all, or make themselves unrecognisable by returning upon parts of the bar which do not rhythmically correspond, then the melody lacks the very bond of union which first makes of it a melody,—just as the word-verse first becomes a genuine verse through a precisely similar bond. A melody thus united in itself, however, will not fit a word-verse which only possesses this uniting bond in imagination, and not in reality: here the speech-accent, to be emphasised according to the verse's *sense* alone, does not answer to the necessary return of the melismic and rhythmic accents of the melody, and the Musician who does not wish to sacrifice his melody, but to give it forth before all else,—since in it alone can he intelligibly address the Feeling,—sees himself therefore compelled to regard the speech-accent only where it *accidentally* coincides with the melody. But this is tantamount to giving up all cohesion of the melody with the verse: for, once the musician leaves the speaking accent out of count, far less can he feel any compunction as to the verse's imaginary prosodic rhythm, and at last he treats this verse

—the original instigating ' moment of speech '—purely and
solely according to his melodic good pleasure ; a course in
which he feels completely justified, so long as he remembers
to render as effectively as possible, in his melody, the
general emotional-contents of the verse.

Had the Poet ever come by a genuine longing to raise
his vehicle of Speech to the persuasive plenitude of
Melody, then he must first of all have bestirred himself to
so employ the speaking Accent as the only measure-giving
'moment' for his verse, that in its symmetrical return
(*entsprechenden Wiederkehr*) it should establish a whole-
some Rhythmos, as necessary to the verse itself as to the
melody.   But we nowhere see the slightest trace of this :
or if we recognise a trace, it is where the verse-maker
gives up *à priori* all pretence of a poetic aim ; where
he proposes, not to create (*dichten*), but, as the Absolute
Musician's humble servant and word-purveyor, to merely
patch together certain counted-out and rhyming syllables,
with which the Musician, in supreme contempt for the
words, then does whatever he listeth.

How significant it is, on the other hand, that certain
beautiful verses of Goethe's—verses in which the poet
bestirred himself, so far as in him lay, to reach a certain
melodic swing—are commonly designated by musicians
as *too beautiful*, too perfect for musical setting!   The
truth of the thing is, that a musical setting completely
answering the sense of these verses, too, would resolve
them into prose, and from out this prose must first *re*-bear
them as an independent melody ; for our musical Feeling
is instinctively aware that that *verse*-melody withal is a
mere *imaginary* one, its semblance a pretty fiction of the
Phantasy, and thus that it is a melody quite other than
the Musical one, which has to manifest itself in altogether
definite and sens-ible reality.   If, then, we hold those verses
too beautiful to set to music, we are only saying that it
pains us to think of destroying them as Verse,—a thing we

allow ourselves to do with fewer qualms of conscience,
whenever a less respect-able effort of the poet is placed
before us.   But at the same time we thus admit, that we
can form no idea of a correct relation between Verse and
Melody.

The most recent melodist, after he had passed in review
all the fruitless attempts at devising a mutually redeeming,
a creatively furthering union of the Word-verse with the
Tone-melody, and above all had observed the evil influence
which a faithful reproduction of the Speaking-accent
exerted on the Melody, even to its distortion into a kind
of musical prose,—this melodist, so soon as on the other
hand he declined to disfigure or completely give the lie to
the verse through a frivolous melody, saw himself induced
to compose melodies wherein he might altogether avoid any
vexatious contact with Verse ; which he respected in itself
but found a drag on Melody.   He named his product " *Songs
without Words* "; and very properly must songs-*without*-
words be the outcome of disputes in which one could only
come to an issue by leaving them unsettled.—This now so
favourite " Song without words " is the faithful translation
of our whole music into the language of the pianoforte,
for the use of our art-commercial-travellers.   In it, the
Musician tells the Poet : " Do as you please, and I will do
as *I* please ! We shall get on best together, when we
have nothing to do with each other."—

Let us now see how we are so to get at this " Musician
without Words," through the driving force of the highest
Poetic-aim, that we may lift him off his quilted piano-stool,
and place him in a world of highest artistic faculty ; which
shall open out to him at last the begetting power of the
Word,—of the Word, whereof he disembarrassed himself
with such feminine ease,—of the Word which *Beethoven*
got born for him from out the giant labour-pains of
Music !

F we want to keep on reasonable terms with Life, we have to win *from the Prose of our ordinary speech* the heightened Expression in which the poetic Aim shall manifest itself in all its potence to the Feeling. A verbal expression which tears asunder the bond of connection with ordinary speech, by basing its physical manifestment on imported 'moments' foreign to the nature of our ordinary speech—such as that prosodic rhythm above-denoted, — can only bewilder the Feeling.

In modern speech no other intonations are employed than those of the prosaic *speaking-accent*, which has no fixed dwelling in the natural stress of the Root-syllables, but in each fresh phrase is lodged *wherever* needful for the *purpose* of an understanding of one particular aim, in keeping with that phrase's sense. The speech of modern daily life differs from the older, poetic speech in this : that, for sake of an understanding, it needs a far more copious use of words and clauses, than did the other. In our language of daily life we discuss matters having no more touch with the meaning of our own roots of speech, than they have with Nature at large ; it therefore has to take the most complicated turns and twists, in order to paraphrase the meanings of primitive or imported speech-roots—which have become altered or newly accommodated to our social relations and views, and in any case estranged from our Feeling,—and thus to bring them to a conventional understanding. As our sentences are diffuse and endlessly expanded, to admit this apparatus of accommodation, they would be made completely unintelligible if the speaking-accent gave prominence to the root-syllables by a frequent emphasis. A comprehension of these phrases must have

its path smoothed for it, by the accent being employed but
very sparingly, and only for their weightiest moments;
whereas all the remaining moments, however weighty the
significance of their roots, must naturally be left entirely
un-emphasised, for very reason of their frequency.

If, now, we give a little thought to what we have to
understand by the compression and concentration of the
moments-of-action and their motives, as necessary to a
realisement of the poetic Aim; and if we recognise that
these operations, again, can only be effected through a
similarly compressed and concentrated Expression: then
we shall be driven at once to see *how* we have to deal with
our language.   Just as we cut away from these ' moments '
of action, and for their sakes from their conditioning
motives, all that was accidental, petty, and indefinite;
just as we had to remove from their Content all that
disfigured it from outside, all that savoured of the State,
of pragmatically Historical and dogmatically Religious,—
in order to display that Content as a purely Human one
and dictated by the Feeling: so also have we to cut away
from the verbal expression all that springs from, and
answers to, these disfigurements of the Purely-human and
Feeling-bidden (*des Gefühlsnothwendigen*); and to remove
it in such a way that this purely-human core shall alone
remain.—But the very thing which marred the purely-
human content of a verbal utterance, is the same which
so stretched out the Phrase that its speaking-accent had to
be most sparingly distributed, while a disproportionate
number of the words must necessarily be left un-emphasised.   So that the poet, who wanted to assign a prosodic
weight to these un-emphasisable words, gave himself up to
a complete illusion; as to which a conscientious scanning of
his verse, out loud, must have in so far enlightened him, as
he saw the phrase's sense disfigured and made unintelligible by such a method of delivery.   Certainly, the beauty
of a verse has hitherto consisted in the poet's having cut
away from his phrase, as much as possible, whatever
auxiliary words too cumbrously hedged-in its Main-accent:

he has sought for the simplest expressions, needing the fewest go-betweens, in order to bring his Accents closer together; and for this purpose he has also freed his subject-matter, as much as he could, from a burdensome Surrounding of historico-social and state-religious relations and conditionings. But the poet has never heretofore been able to bring this to such a point, that he could impart his subject unconditionally to the Feeling and nothing else,—any more than he has brought his vehicle of expression to a like enhancement; for this enhancement to the highest pitch of emotional utterance could only have been reached precisely in an ascension of the verse into the melody,—an ascension which, as we have seen because we *must* see, has not as yet been rendered feasible. Where the poet, however, has believed that he had condensed the speaking-verse itself into a pure moment-of-Feeling, without this ascension of his verse into actual Melody, *there* neither he, nor the object of his portrayal, has been comprehended either any longer by the Understanding, or by the Feeling. We all know verses of this sort, the attempts of our greatest poets to tune Words, without music, into Tones.

Only *that* poetic Aim whose nature we have already explained above, and in its necessary thrust toward realisement, can succeed in so freeing the prose-phrase of modern speech from all its mechanical apparatus of qualifying words, that the genuine Accents may be drawn together into a swiftly-seizable message. A faithful observance of the mode of expression we employ when our Feeling is highly wrought, even in ordinary life, will supply the poet with an unfailing measure for the number of accents in a natural Phrase. In frank emotion, when we let go all conventional consideration for the spun-out modern phrase, we try to express ourselves briefly and to the point, and if possible, *in one breath.* But in this succinct expression we emphasise far more strongly than usual— through the force of feeling—and also shift our accents closer together; while, to make these accents *im*press the

hearer's Feeling as forcibly as we want to *ex*press in them
our own feelings, we dwell on them with sharply lifted
voice. These Accents round themselves instinctively into
a phrase, or a main section of a phrase, during the outflow
of the breath, and their number will always stand in direct
ratio to the excitement ; so that, for instance, an ireful, an
active emotion will allow a greater number of Accents to
be emitted in one breath, whereas a deep, a *suffering* one
will consume the whole breath-force in fewer, more long-
drawn tones.—

The Accents being governed by the breath, and shaping
themselves to either a whole phrase or a substantial section
of a phrase according to the subject of expression, the poet
will therefore regulate their number by the particular
emotion to which he gives his immediate sympathy; and
he will see to it that his coil of words is rid of that excess
of auxiliary and explanatory lesser-words peculiar to the
complicated phrase of Literature : at least so far, that
their numerical bulk—despite the slurring of their intonation—shall not consume the breath in vain.—The harm of
our complex modern phrase, as regards the expression
of Feeling, has consisted in its being overstocked with
unemphatic side-words, which have taken up the speaker's
breath to such an extent that, already exhausted, or for
sake of 'saving' himself (*aus sparender Vorsicht*), he could
only briefly dwell on the main-accent ; and thus an understanding of the hastily accented main-word could only be
imparted to the Understanding, but not to the Feeling :
since it needs the *fulness* of a sensuous expression, to
rouse the Feeling's interest.—In a compact construction
the side-words, merely retained by the poet in their smallest
necessary number, will behave to the words emphasised by
the Speaking-accent like the mute consonants to the sounding vowels, which they enclose in order to individualise
and condense them from a vague ejaculation (*aus einem
allgemeinen Empfindungsausdrucke*) to an expression illus-
trative of a particular object. A massing of consonants
around a vowel, without any justification before the Feel-

R

ing, robs that vowel of all emotional ring ; just as a massing
of side-words around a main-word, when merely dictated
by the meddlesome Understanding, shuts-off that main-
word from the Feeling. In the eyes of Feeling, a doubling
or trebling of the consonant is only of necessity when the
vowel thereby gains a drastic colouring, in harmony with
a drastic property of the object which the root expresses ;
and in the same way, an extra number of subsidiary words
is only justified before the Feeling when the accented
main-word is specifically enhanced thereby in its expression, but not when it is lamed—as in the modern
phrase.

We thus arrive at the natural basis of Rhythm, in the
spoken verse, as displayed in the *liftings and lowerings*
(Hebungen und Senkungen) of the accent ; while this
accent's utmost definiteness and endless variety can only
come to light through its intensifying into Musical
Rhythm.

Whatever number of liftings of the voice we may decide-
on for one breath, and thus for one phrase or segment of a
phrase, in keeping with the mood to be expressed, yet they
will never be of equal strength among themselves.   In the
first place a *completely equal strength* of accents is not permitted by the sense of a clause, which always contains
both *conditioning* and *conditioned* ' moments,' and, according
to its character, either lifts the condition*or* above the condition*ee*, or the other way about.   But neither does the
Feeling permit an equal strength of accents ; since the
Feeling, of all others, can only be roused to interest
(*Theilnahme*) by an easily grasped and physically marked
distinction between the moments of expression.   Though
we shall have to learn that this interest is finally to be
determined the most surely through a Modulation of the
musical tone, for the present we will neglect that means of
enhancement, and merely bring home to ourselves the

influence which an unequal strength of accents must necessarily exert upon the Rhythm of the phrase.

Now that we have drawn the Accents together and freed them from their surrounding load of side-words, and mean to shew their differentiation into weaker and stronger ones, we can only do it in a way that shall completely answer to the *good and bad halves of the musical bar*, or—which is the same thing at bottom—to the 'good and bad' bars of a musical period. But these good and bad bars, or half-bars, only make themselves known to the Feeling, as such, through their standing in a mutual relation whose path, again, is paved and lighted by the smaller, intermediate fractions of the bar. Were the good and bad half-bars to stand entirely naked side by side—as in the *chorales* of the Church—they could only make themselves known to Feeling as the merest ridge and hollow of the accent,* whereby the 'bad' bar-halves of a period must entirely lose their own accent, and in fact would cease to count at all as such : only by the intervening fractions of the bar acquiring rhythmic life, and being brought to a share in the accent of the bar-halves, can the weaker accent of the 'bad' half-bars be also made to tell.—Now, the accented Word-phrase governs of itself the characteristic relation of those bar-fractions to the bar-halves, and that through the *hollows* of the accent and the ratio of these 'hollows' to the 'ridges.' In ordinary pronunciation the unemphatic words and syllables, which we place on the slope of the wave, mount upwards to the main-accent through a swelling of the emphasis, and fall away again through a slacking of the emphasis. The point to which they fall, and from which they mount to a fresh main-accent, is the weaker, minor accent, which—in keeping with both the *sense* and the *expression* of the phrase—is governed by the main-

---

* " Hebung und Senkung,"—the technical equivalent is " arsis and thesis " ; seeing that *Oper und Drama* was not written for a mere professional public, however, and that our author has avoided all academic labels wherever possible, I have preferred the common terms as applied to a wave, or undulation, since the equivalent which I have employed earlier, " liftings and lowerings," would be too cumbersome for protracted use.—TR.

accent as much as is the planet by the fixed star. The number of preparatory or after (*nachfallende*) syllables depends solely on the sense of the poetic diction ; of which, however, we presuppose that it shall express itself in utmost succinctness. But the more necessary it may seem to the poet, to increase the number of his preparatory or after syllables, so much the more characteristically is he thus enabled to liven the rhythm and give the Accent itself a special importance,—just as, on the other hand, he may specialise the character of an Accent by placing it close beside the following one, *without* any preparation or after-thought.

His power here is boundless in variety : but he cannot become fully conscious of it, until he intensifies the rhythm of the Speaking-accent into the rhythm of Music, in its endless livening by Dance's varied motion. The purely musical beat affords the poet possibilities of speech-expression which he was forced to forego, from the outset, for his merely spoken word-verse. In merely spoken verse the poet had to restrict the number of syllables in a 'hollow' to two at the utmost, since with *three* he could not have avoided an emphasis being placed on one of them, which naturally would have thrown his verse awry at once. This false accentuation he would never have had to fear, if genuine prosodic longs and shorts had stood at his behest; but since he could only allot his emphasis to the speaking-accent, and since its incidence must be assumed as possible on every root-syllable, for sake of the verse,—it passed his wit to find a means of indicating the proper accent so unmistakably, that it should not be given to root-syllables on which he wished *no* emphasis to be placed. We are here speaking, of course, of verses communicated by means of writing, and read as written: the living Verse, un-belonging to literature, we have in nowise to understand as without its rhythmic-musical Melody; and if we take a good look at the monuments of Grecian Lyric which have come down to us, we shall find that a merely recited Greek verse presents us with the embarrassment—whenever we deliver it in accordance with the instinctive accentuation of Speech—of placing the accent on syllables which were left unemphasised in the original rhythmic melody, *as being included in the upstroke.* In merely spoken verse we can never employ more than two syllables in the 'hollow,' because more than two syllables would at once displace the correct accent, and the resulting dissolution of the Verse would force us into the necessity of speaking it out as nothing but a washy Prose.

The truth is, that in spoken, or to-be-spoken verse we lack the 'moment' that might fix the duration of the crest of the wave (*Hebung*) in such a way, that by it we could accurately measure out the hollows. According to our sheer pronouncing powers, we cannot stretch the duration of an accented syllable beyond the length of two un-accented syllables, without falling into the fault of drawling, or—as in fact we call it—"sing-song." In ordinary speech this "sing-song," where it does not really become an actual singing and thus completely do away with ordinary speech, is rightly held for a fault; for, as a mere toneless drawling of the vowel, or even of a consonant, it is rightdown ugly. Yet at the bottom of this tend to drawling—where it is not a sheer habit of dialect, but shews itself involuntarily, in an access of emotion—there lies a something which our Prosodists and Metricists would have done well to regard, when they set themselves the task of explaining Grecian metres. They had nothing in ear but our hurried speak-ing-accent, cut loose from the melody of Feeling, when they invented the measure by which two 'shorts' must always go to one 'long'; the explanation of Greek metres, in which six or more 'shorts' are matched at times by two or even a single 'long,' must have readily occurred to them if they had had in ear for that so-called 'long' the *long-held note of a musical bar,* such as those Lyrists still had at least in *their* ear when they varied the setting of words to known Folk-melodies. This sustained and rhythmically measured Tone, however, is a thing the poet of our speaking-verse had no longer in his ear, whereas he now knew only the

brief-lived accent of Speech. But if we hold fast by this
Tone, whose duration we not only can accurately determine in the musical bar but also divide into its rhythmic
fractions in the most varied manner, then we shall obtain
in those fractions the rhythmically vindicated, the mean-
ingly distributed, melodic moments-of-expression for the
syllables of the 'hollow'; while their number will have
solely to be regulated by the sense of the phrase and the
intended effect of the expression, since we have found in
the musical beat the certain Measure in accordance with
which they cannot fail of coming to an understanding.)

This beat, however, the poet has to regulate solely by
the Expression he intends ; he himself must make it into
a knowable Measure, and not have it haply thrust on him
as such.   This he does by distributing the Accents,
whether stronger or weaker, in such sort that they shall
form a phrase- or breathing-segment to which a following
one may correspond, and that this following one may
appear necessarily conditioned by the first ; for only in
a necessary, an enforcing or assuaging repetition, can a
weighty moment-of-expression display itself intelligibly to
Feeling.   The arrangement of the stronger and weaker
accents is therefore what sets the Measure for the particular kind of beat, and for the rhythmic structure of the
'period.'—Let us now gain an idea of such a measure-
setting arrangement, as issuing from the poet's Aim.

We will take the case of an expression which is of such
a character as to allow the emphasising of three accents in
one breath, whereof the first is the strongest, the second
the weakest (as is almost always to be assumed in such a
case), and the third again a lifted one : here the poet would
instinctively arrange a phrase of two even bars, whereof
the first would have the strongest accent on its 'good'
half, and on its 'bad' half the weaker one, while the second
bar would have the third, the other lifted accent on its
down-beat.   The 'bad' half of the second bar would serve
for taking breath, and for the upstroke toward the first
bar of the second rhythmic phrase, which must suitably

reiterate its predecessor.   In this phrase the 'hollows' would
mount as an upstroke for the down-beat of the first bar, and
fall away as a downstroke to its 'bad half'; from which,
again, they would mount to the 'good half' of the second
bar.   Any strengthening of the *second* accent, as called-
for by the sense of the phrase, would be easily effected
rhythmically (apart from a melodic rise of pitch) by allowing either the depression between it and the first accent, or
the upstroke toward the third, to completely drop out,—
which must necessarily draw increased attention to just
this intermediate accent.—

I trust that this illustration—to which a host of others
might readily be added—will suffice to indicate the endless
variety of *common-sense* (sinnvollen) rhythmic devices at the
service of the Word-verse, when its speaking-expression, in
entire keeping with its Content, makes up its mind to the
necessary ascension into musical Melody, and in such a way
that it predetermines the melody as the realisement of its
own intrinsic aim.   Through the number, position, and
importance of the Accents, and through the greater or lesser
volubility (*Beweglichkeit*) of the 'hollows' between the
'ridges,' and their exhaustless relations to the latter, the
sheer faculty of Speech itself affords so ample a variety of
rhythmic forms, that their wealth, and the thence-sprung
fecundation of man's purely Musical powers, must only
shew itself still more immeasurable through each fresh
art-creation that issues from the Poet's inner stress.

The rhythmically-accented verse of Speech has already
brought us so close to the held tone of Song, that we now
must necessarily draw nearer to the matter lying at its
bottom.

If we continue to keep this one thing in eye, that the
Poetic Aim can only be realised through its complete
transmission from the Understanding to the Feeling : then

here, where we are busied with figuring the *act* of realisement through that transmission, we must examine closely
into the capacity of each factor of Expression for a direct
communication to the senses; since the Feeling can only
apprehend directly through the senses. With this end in
view, we had to cut away from the Word-phrase all that
made it unimpressive to the Feeling, all that made it a sheer
organ of the Understanding; we thereby compressed its
Content to a purely human one and seizable by the Feeling,
and we gave this Content a just as compact verbal
Expression : inasmuch as, by drawing them closer to one
another (and especially through a repetition of their
sequence), we lifted the necessary Accents of emotional
discourse to a Rhythm instinctively enthralling to the ear.

Now, the Accents, of a phrase thus ordered, cannot fall
anywhere but on parts of speech in which the purely human
Content, the thing seizable by Feeling, expresses itself the
most decisively ; therefore they will always fall on those
significant root-syllables wherein was originally expressed
by us, not only a definite object seizable by the Feeling,
but also the sensation (*Empfindung*) which answers to that
object's impression * upon us.

Until we are able, so to say, to 'feel back' our sensations
—made utterly unintelligible to ourselves by State-politics
or religious dogmas—and thus to reach their original truth,
we shall never be in a position to grasp the sensuous substance of our *roots of speech*. What scientific research has
disclosed to us, can only instruct the Understanding, but
never bring the Feeling to an understanding of them ; and
no scientific instruction, were it made so popular as to reach
down to even our Folk-schools, would be able to wake this
understanding of our speech. Only from an unruffled, a
loving intercourse with Nature, from a necessary Need for
purely human understanding of her : in short, it can only
come from a *Want*, such as the Poet feels when he is

---

* " Eindruck,"—it should be pointed out that our author here uses " impression " from the point of view of the object that impresses, and thus sets it half
way between " expression " and " sensation."—TR.

driven to impart himself with convincing sureness to the Feeling.—Science has laid bare to us the organism of speech ; but what she shewed us was a *defunct* organism, which only the Poet's utmost Want can bring to life again : and that by healing up the wounds with which the anatomic scalpel has gashed the body of Speech, and by breathing into it the breath that may ensoul it into living motion. *But this breath is—Music.*— —

Pining for redemption, the Poet stands at present in the winter frost of Speech, and looks yearningly across the snow-flats of pragmatic prose, with which are cloaked the erst so richly dizened fields, the sweet countenance of loving Mother Earth. But here and there, under the warm gushes of his sorrowing breath, the stubborn snow begins to melt ; and lo !—from out Earth's bosom sprout before him fresh green buds, shooting forth all new and lush from the ancient roots he took for dead,—until at last the sun of a new and never-aging human springtide mounts aloft, dissolves away the snow, and lets the buds all burgeon into fragrant blossoms welcoming the sun with smiling eye.—

In those old primal roots, as in the roots of plants and trees—so long as they still can keep an anchorage in the solid soil of Earth,—there must be dwelling an ever new-creative force, if so be they are not yet torn completely from the soil of the Folk itself. Beneath the frosty mantle of its civilisation the Folk preserves, in the instinctiveness of its natural mode of speech, the roots through which it holds to the soil of Nature ; and everyone may come by an instinctive understanding of them, if he turns from the hubbub of our State-society conversation to seek a loving intercourse with Nature, and thus unbars these roots to his Feeling, through an ' unconscious ' use of their *kindred* properties. The Poet, however, is the *knower of the unconscious*, the aimful demonstrator of the instinctive ; the Feeling, which he fain would manifest to fellow-feeling, teaches him the expression he must use ; but his Understanding shews him the Necessity of that expression. If the poet, who thus speaks from consciousness to un-

consciousness, would fain take count of the natural sway
(*Zwang*) which bids him use *this* expression and none
other, then he learns to know the nature of this expression ;
and, in his impulse to impart, he wins from that nature the
power of mastering this expression itself in all its necessity.—
Now, if the poet pries into the nature of the word which is
forced upon him by his Feeling, as the only word to fit an
object or an emotion woken by that object, he discovers
this constraining force in the *root* of this word, which has
been invented or found (*erfunden oder gefunden*) through
the Necessity of man's earliest emotional stress. If he
plunges deeper into the organism of this Root, in order to
track the emotion-swaying force he knows must dwell
within it, since that force has made so determinant an
impression on his Feeling,—then he perceives at last the
fountain of that force in the purely *sensuous* body of this
root, whose primal substance is the *open sound*.

This Open-sound is the embodied inner feeling, which
wins the stuff for its embodiment in the moment of its outward manifestal, and wins, indeed, precisely *that* stuff
which manifests itself—according to the particularity of the
stimulus—through the vowel of this root. In this uttering
of the *inner feeling* there also lies the strenuous reason why
the root arouses the corresponding inner feeling of the
fellow-man to whom that utterance reaches ; and this
emotional-sway—if the poet would bring it to bear on
others in the way he has experienced it himself—can only
be effected through the greatest fulness in the enunciation
of the open-sound wherein alone the specific inner feeling
can impart itself the most exhaustively and convincingly.

But this Open-sound, whose full enunciation becomes
quite of itself a Musical Tone, is regulated in the speech-
root by the *closed sounds* (Mitlauter), which convert it from
a moment of *general* expression into the particular expression of this one object, or of this one emotion. The
Consonant thus has two chief functions, which, on account
of their decisive weightiness, we have accurately to note.

The first function of the *consonant* consists in this : that it raises the open-sound of the root to a definite characteristic, by firmly hedging-in its infinitely fluid element, and through the lines of this delimitation it brings to the vowel's colour, in a sense, the drawing which makes of it an exactly distinguishable shape. This function of the consonant is consequently the one turned *outward* from the vowel. Its object is to definitely sever from the vowel whatever is to be differentiated therefrom, and to place itself as a sort of boundary-fence between the two. This important position the consonant takes up *before* the vowel, as its initial sound (*Anlaut*). As a terminal sound (*Ablaut*), *after* the vowel, the consonant is of less importance for hedging it from without, inasmuch as the vowel must already have shewn itself in its characteristic quality before the sounding of the terminal, and the latter will therefore be more conditioned by the vowel itself, as its necessary set-off (*Absatz*). On the other hand, the consonantal closing sound is of determinative weight whenever it is so strengthened as to affect the sound of the vowel, and thus is raised, itself, into the characteristic moment of the root.

We shall return to the influence exerted by the consonant upon the vowel itself. For the present we have to deal with its outward function, and this it exercises the most determinatively in its position *before* the vowel, as an initial sound. In this situation the consonant shews us, in a sense, the countenance (*Angesicht*) of the root, whose body is filled by the vowel's warmly streaming blood, and whose hinder side is turned from the eye, in the terminal. If we may understand by the root's " countenance " the whole physiognomic exterior of man, which he turns to face us as we meet him, we shall gain an accurate designation for the decisory importance of the initial consonant. In it the Individuality of the oncoming root is first shewn us ; just as man first shews himself as an individual through his physiognomic exterior, and by this exterior we hold until the inner being has been able to display itself to us through a broader unfolding. This physiognomic surface of the

speech-root imparts itself—so to say—to the eye of our
speech-intelligence ; and to this eye the poet has to commend
it in the most effective way, if he is seeking to bring his
shapings before eye and ear alike, so as to gain full comprehension by the Feeling. But, just as one phenomenon,
among many, can rivet the ear's intelligent attention only
through presenting itself in a repetition which does not fall
to the others' lot, and in virtue of this repetition it is singled
out by the ear as a salient feature of especial interest : so
also to the " eye " of Hearing it is necessary that there
should be a *repeated* presentment of any phenomenon which
is to display itself as a distinct and definitely knowable
thing. Only through the enunciation of at least two corresponding Accents, in a connexion embracing both the
subject and the predicate, could the rhythmic word-phrase
—knit according to the breath's necessity—intelligibly
impart the meaning of its Content. In his thrust to open
up to *Feeling* an understanding of the phrase as an utterance
of *feeling,* and in his consciousness that this thrust can be
satisfied only through the keenest interest of the directly
recipient sense-organ, the poet has now to commend these
Accents to the Hearing in the most effective manner
possible ; and to do this, he must present them in a garb
which not only shall distinguish them completely from the
unemphasised root-words of the phrase, but shall also make
this distinction obvious to the " eye " of Hearing by displaying itself as a *like*, a kindred garb of *both the accents.* The
physiognomic likeness of the root-words, accented according
to the sense of language,* makes them swiftly recognisable
by that " eye," and shews them in a kinship which is not

---

* " Die Gleichheit der Physiognomie der durch den Sprachsinn accentu-
irten Wurzelwörter " &c.—This is one of a good many instances, in this
region of the book, where Wagner has allowed his own acute " sense of language " to lead him into that "stubbornness of style " to which he alludes on
page 6 (i.e. in the Dedication of the Second Edition, 1868), and which I take
to be a desire, manifested from time to time, to work one particular word and
its derivatives through every shade of meaning, in illustration of the matter
in hand.   This method naturally places unusual difficulties in the translator's
path, seeing that hardly a word in this book can be dropped without detracting
from the main argument.—TR.

only swiftly seizable by the sensory organ, but is in truth indwelling also in the *sense* of the root.

The *sense* of a root is the ' objective ' sensation embodied therein *; but first by its *embodiment* does a sensation become *understandable*, and this body itself is alike a *sensuous* one, and one that can be determinately apprehended by nothing but the answering sense of Hearing. The poet's utterance will therefore be a swiftly understandable one, if he concentrates the to-be-expressed sensation to its inmost essence (*Gehalt*) ; and this inmost essence will necessarily be a *unitarian* (einheitliche) one, in the kinship of its conditioning and its conditioned moments. But a unitarian sensation instinctively utters itself in a uniform (*einheitlichen*) mode of *expression ;* and this uniform expression wins its fullest enablement from that *oneness* of the speech-root which reveals itself in a kinship of the conditioning and conditioned chief-moments of the phrase. A sensation [or " emotion "] such as can vindicate its own expression through the *Stabreim* of rootwords which call instinctively for emphasis,† is comprehensible to us beyond all doubt,—provided the kinship of the roots is not deliberately disfigured and made unknowable through the sense of the phrase, as in our modern speech ; and only when this sensation, so expressed, has brought our Feeling to instinctively grasp it as *one thing*, does that Feeling warrant any mixing of it with another. In the *Stabreim*, again, poetic speech has an infinitely potent means of making a *mixed* sensation swiftly understandable by the already biased (*bereits bestimmten*) Feeling ; and this means we may likewise call a *sensuous* one,—in the significance that it, too, is grounded on a comprehensive, and withal a definite *sense* in the speech-root. In the first place, the purely sensuous aspect of the Stabreim is able to unite the physical expression of one sensation with that of another, in such a way that the

---

* "Der *Sinn* einer Wurzel ist die in ihr verkörperte Empfindung von einem Gegenstande."

† "Eine Empfindung, die sich in ihrem Ausdrucke durch den *Stabreim* der unwillkürlich zu betonenden Wurzelwörter rechtfertigen kann," &c.

union shall be keenly perceptible to the ear, and caress it
by its naturalness. But further—through this innate power of
the similar ' clang '—the *sense* of the Stabreim-ed rootword
which introduces the fresh sensation already dawns upon
the ear as one *essentially akin,* i.e. as an antithesis included
in the genus of the main-sensation ; and now, in all its
general affinity with the first-expressed sensation, it is
transmitted through the captivated Hearing to the Feeling,
and onward through this, at last, to the Understanding
itself.*

In this respect the capacity of the immediate receiver,
Hearing, is so unbounded that it can knit the farthest-
removed sensations, so soon as ever they are brought it in
a physiognomic resemblance, and can transfer them to the
Feeling as kindred, purely human ones.   Against this all-
embracing, all-uniting power of the sentient organ, what
boots the naked Understanding? which foregoes this
wonder-help, and degrades the sense of hearing to a servile
porter for its bales of industrial goods ! This sentient
organ is so self-surrendering to him who lovingly addresses
it, so lavish with its fund of love, that it can take the
subversive Understanding's myriad tatters, remake them
as a Purely-human, a first and last and ever One, and offer
them to the Feeling for its highest, most enravishing delight.—Draw nigh this glorious sense, ye Poets ! But draw
nigh it as entire men, in full trust !   Give it the amplest ye
can ever compass, and what your Understanding nevermore can bind ; this sense will bind it up for you, and give
it back as an unending whole.   So come to it with all your
hearts, and eye to eye ; offer it your countenance, the visage
of the Word,—but not the hinder draggled side, which ye
trail dully after you in the End-rhyme of your prosaic talk,
and try to palm upon the ear,—just as though the payment
of this childish tinkle, which one offers as a sop to savages
and fools, would earn your words unhindered entrance
through its gateway to the brain's unresting threshing-

* " Die Liebe bringt Lust und—Leid, " [" Love brings delight and—Load "].
—R. WAGNER.

ground. The Ear is no child; it is a staunch and loving woman, who in her love will make that man the blessedest who brings *in himself* the fullest matter for her bliss.

And how little as yet we have offered this Ear, with our mere bringing it the consonantal Stabreim; albeit, through *that* alone, it has already opened-up to us the understanding of all Speech! Let us search farther, and see how this understanding of Speech may raise itself to the highest understanding of Man, through the utmost arousal of the Ear.—

We have to return once more to the Consonant, to set it before us in its second function.—

The force that enables it to present to the Ear the seemingly most diverse objects and feelings, as allied through their initial rhyme,—this outward efficacy the Consonant acquired from nothing but its situation towards the sounding Vowel of the root, in which, again, it exercises its *inward* function through determining that vowel's character.—Just as the consonant hedges the vowel from without, so does it also bound the vowel within : i.e. it determines the specific nature of the latter's manifestment, through the roughness or smoothness of its inward contact therewith.* This weighty inward working of the consonant, however, brings us into so direct a contact with the vowel, that our comprehension of it must largely depend on a consideration of

---

* The Singer, who has to get the full tone out of the vowel, is acutely sensitive to the difference between the effects of energetic consonants—such as K, R, P, T—, or indeed, strengthened ones—such as Schr, Sp, St, Pr—, and softer, weak ones—such as G, L, B, D, W,—upon the open sound. A strengthened terminal—nd, rt, st, ft—where it is radical—as in "Hand," "hart," "Hast," "Kraft"—, so definitely lays down the nature and duration of the vowel's utterance, that it downright insists on the latter's sounding brief and brisk ; and, being thus a characteristic token of the root, it fits itself for rhyme—as Assonance (as in "Hand und Mund").—R. WAGNER.

the vowel itself, to which we are irresistibly pointed as the intrinsic content of the root.

We have called the enclosing consonants the garment of the vowel, or more precisely, its physiognomic exterior. In view of their inward agency, let us call them still more accurately the fleshy covering of the human body, organically ingrown with the interior ; we thus shall gain a faithful image of the essence both of Consonant and Vowel, as well as of their organic relations to one another.—If we take the vowel for the whole *inner organism* of man's living body, which prescribes from out itself the shaping of its outward show, as offered to the eye of the beholder : then we have to ascribe to the consonants—beyond the outward function of displaying themselves to the eye, as that aforesaid show — the additional weighty office of bringing to the inner organism, through the branching conduits of the sense-organs, those outward impressions which in turn determine this inner organism to a particular employment of its faculty of utterance. Just as the fleshy covering of the human body has a skin which hedges it outwards from the eye, so has it also a skin turned inwards to the inner vital organs * : yet through this inner skin it is nowise completely sundered from these organs, but clings together with them in such a fashion as to win from them its nourishment and power of outward shaping.—The blood, that bodily sap which in unbroken flow alone can mete out life, this blood drives onward from the heart, in virtue of that connection of the fleshy covering with the inner organs, and thrusts to the outermost skin of this flesh ; from thence, leaving behind it the needful nourishment, it flows back to the heart again ; and the heart, as though in an overfill of inner riches, now pours forth through the lungs—which had brought the outer air-stream

---

* I may be allowed, perhaps, to add the explanation, that this " inner skin " is what is anatomically known as the *peritoneum, pleura,* &c. ; while the outer portion of the eyeball, the lining of the mouth &c., and the chief *internal* apparatus of the ear, are all formed from embryonic doublings inward of the outer integument.—TR.

for the blood's enlivenment and freshening—this air-stream pregnant with its own impassioned content, this directest outward manifestal of its inmost living warmth.—This heart is the *open sound*, in its richest, least dependent energy. Its livening blood, which it outwardly condensed into the consonant, it turns back from this consonant to its primal seat, since its overfill could never be consumed in that condensement; and now, with its blood directly livened by the air-stream, the heart in utmost fulness breathes *itself* without.

Toward Without the inner man, as a *tone*-emitter, addresses himself to Hearing; just as his outer shape had turned toward Sight. We have recognised the consonant as this *outer* shape of the root-vowel ; and, since vowel and consonant alike addressed the *Hearing*, we were obliged to figure this Hearing as endowed with both a hearing and a seeing faculty, so as to claim the latter's service for the consonant—as it were, the outer speaking man. In the Stabreim we have pictured this consonant in its outermost and weightiest function, as regards both sense and sound, and it there displayed itself to the Hearing's "eye": on the other hand the vowel, whose innate vitalising property we have lately learnt, imparts itself to the very " ear " of Hearing. But only when it is able to display its utmost quality, in the same fulness and self-dependence as we have allowed the consonant to unfold in the Stabreim ; only when it can shew itself as not merely a sounding *vowel* (tönender *Laut*) but a sounding *tone* (lautender *Ton*), is it in a position to engross the infinite capacity of the " ear " of that Hearing whose "seeing power" we demanded at its highest for the consonant: only then, can this " ear " be filled to such a pitch, that it falls into that excess of ecstasy where it needs must impart its boon to man's All-feeling, and rouse it into highest stir.—Just as that man alone can display himself in full persuasiveness, who announces himself to our ear and eye at once: so the message-bearer of the inner man cannot completely convince our Hearing, until it addresses itself with equal

persuasiveness to both " eye and ear " of this Hearing.
But this happens only through *Word-Tone-speech*, and poet
and musician have hitherto addressed but half the man
apiece : the poet turned towards this Hearing's eye alone,
the musician only to its ear. Yet nothing but the whole seeing and hearing,—that is to say, the completely *understanding* Ear, can apprehend the inner man past all mistake.—

That strenuous force which dwelt in the Speech-root,
and necessarily determined the poet, in his search for the
surest expression of a feeling, to employ this one particular
word as alone complying with his Aim,—that force the
poet recognises with full conviction as inherent in the
sounding vowel, so soon as ever he sets it before him at its
fullest, as the genuine, breath-souled (*athembeseelten*) *tone*.
In this Tone speaks out the most unmistakably the vowel's
emotional content, which an innermost Necessity bade clothe
itself in this vowel and none other ; just as this vowel,
confronted with the outer object, condensed for its outer
covering this consonant and none other.   To resolve this
vowel into its highest emotional expression, to let its utmost fulness broaden out and consume itself in the heart's-
tone of Song : for the poet this means, to make the erewhile wilful, and therefore disquieting factor of his poetic
Expression into an un-wilful, into a thing which as determinately renders back the feeling as it determinatively
seizes it.   He therefore gains full quieting in nothing but
the fullest stir of his Expression ; only by employing his
expressional-faculty according to its highest innate power,
can he make it to the organ of Feeling, which in its turn
imparts itself directly to the Feeling ; and from his own
faculty of Speech, does this organ thrive, so soon as ever
he measures and employs it in its *whole* capacity. —

To impart a feeling with utmost plainness, the poet has
already ranged his row of words into a musical bar, according to their spoken Accents, and has sought by the Consonantal Stabreim to bring them to the Feeling's understanding in an easier and more sensuous form ; he will still more
completely facilitate this understanding, if he takes the

vowels of the accented root-words, as earlier their consonants, and knits them also into such a rhyme as will most definitely open up their understanding to the Feeling. An understanding of the vowel, however, is not based upon its superficial analogy with a rhyming vowel of another root; but, since *all the vowels are primally akin to one another*, it is based on the *disclosing of this* Ur-*kinship* through giving full value to the vowel's *emotional content, by means of musical Tone*. The vowel itself is nothing but *a tone condensed :* its specific manifestation is determined through its turning toward the outer surface of the Feeling's 'body'; which latter—as we have said—displays to the 'eye' of Hearing the mirrored image of the outward object that has acted on it. The object's effect on the body-of-Feeling, itself, is manifested by the vowel through a direct utterance of feeling along the nearest path, thus expanding the individuality it has acquired from without into the universality of pure emotion*; and this takes place in the Musical Tone. To That which bore the vowel, and bade it outwardly condense itself into the consonant,—to That the vowel returns as a specific entity, enriched by the world outside, in order to dissolve itself in *it*, now equally enriched.† This enriched, this individually established, this Tone expanded to the universality of Feeling, is the redeeming 'moment' of the poet's Thought ; and Thought, in this redemption, becomes an immediate *outpour of the Feeling*.

By the poet's resolving the Vowel of his accentuated and

* " Die Wirkung des Gegenstandes auf den Gefühlskörper selbst giebt der Vokal durch unmittelbare Äusserung des Gefühles auf dem ihm nächsten Wege kund, indem er seine, von Aussen empfangene Individualität zu der Universalität des reinen Gefühlsvermögens ausdehnt " &c.—

† Reference should here be made to the "heart, breath, &c." simile on page 272, and to its resumption as a metaphor, on page 274. With regard to its immediate terms, this sentence is a singular proof of how *little* Wagner needed to borrow from Schopenhauer, when he wrote his *Tristan und Isolde* poem, and how close his own reflections had brought him to that Pantheism which forms the substantial basis of " *Die Welt als Wille und Vorstellung.*" —TR.

stabreimed root-word into its mother-element, the Musical
Tone, he now enters definitely upon the realm of Tone-speech.
From this instant he has to attempt no further regulation
of his Accents according to a measure of kinship which
shall be cognisable by that "eye" of Hearing; but now
that the vowels have become musical tones, their kinship,
as needful for their swift adoption by the Feeling, is regulated by a measure which is cognisable solely to the "ear"
of Hearing, and surely and imperiously grounded on that
"ear's" receptive idiosyncrasy.—Already in Word-speech
the prime affinity of all vowels is shewn so definitely, that
when root-syllables lack an initial consonant we recognise
their aptitude for Stabreim by the very fact of the vowel's
standing open in front, and we are by no means governed
by a strict outward likeness of the vowel; we rhyme, for
instance, "eye and ear" ("Aug' und Ohr").* This *Ur*-
kinship, which has preserved itself in Word-speech as an
unconscious moment of feeling, the full-fledged Tone-speech
brings quite unmistakably to Feeling's consciousness. Inasmuch as it widens the specific vowel into a musical
tone, it tells our Feeling that this vowel's particularity is
included in an *ur*-akin relationship, and born from out
this kinship; and it bids us acknowledge as the mother of
the ample vowel-family the purely human Feeling, in its
immediate facing outwards,—the Feeling, which only faces
outwards so as to address itself, in turn, to our own purely
human Feeling.

Wherefore the Word-poet can no farther demonstrate to
our Feeling the kinship of the vowel sounds, already turned
to tones; this the *Tone-poet* alone can compass.

----

* How admirably our language characterises in this rhyme the two most
open-lying organs of reception, through the vowels likewise lying open toward
without; it is as though these organs herein proclaimed themselves as turned,
with the whole fill of their universal receptive-force, directly and nakedly from
within outwards.—R. WAGNER.

III.

HE characteristic distinction between the *Word-poet* and the *Tone-poet* consists in this : the Word-poet has concentrated an infinitude of scattered moments of action, sensation, and expression,—only cognisable by the Understanding,—to a point the most accessible to the Feeling ; now comes the Tone-poet, and has to expand this concentrated, compact point to the utmost fulness of its emotional-content. In its thrust towards an impartal to the Feeling, the procedure of the poetising (*dichtenden*) Understanding was directed to assembling itself from farthest distances into the closest (*dichtester*) cognisability by the sensory faculty; from here, from the point of immediate contact with the sensory faculty, the poem has now to broaden itself out, exactly as the recipient sensory-organ—likewise concentrated upon an outward-facing point, for sake of taking-in the poem— now broadens itself to wider and yet wider circles, under the immediate influence of the acquisition, until it rouses at last the whole inner emotional faculty.

The perversity of the makeshift procedure of the lonely Poet and the lonely Musician has hitherto lain in precisely this : to address the Feeling at all seizably, the Poet wandered into that vague diffuseness in which he became the delineator of a thousand details, intended to set a definite shape before the Phantasy as knowably as possible ; the Phantasy, bombarded by a host of motley details, at last could only master the proffered object by trying to grasp these perplexing details one by one, and thereby losing itself in the function of pure Understanding ; to which latter alone could the poet return, when, dazed by the massy reaches of his own delineations, he finally looked round him for a familiar foothold. On the other hand, the

Absolute Musician saw himself driven, in his shapings, to condense an endless element of Feeling into a definite point such as the Understanding best might apprehend ; for this purpose he had more and more to renounce the fulness of his element, to labour to concentrate the feeling to a thought—albeit a task impossible in itself,—and finally to commend to arbitrary Phantasy this imaginary concentrate, only produced through completely discarding all emotional expression and counterfeiting some chosen outward object.—Music thus resembled the good God of our legends, who came down from heaven to earth, but, to make himself visible there, must assume the shape and vesture of a common man of every-day : in the ofttimes ragged beggar not a creature recognised the God. But the true Poet has one day to come, who with the clairvoyant eye of poet's-Want, in its utmost craving for redemption, shall recognise in the dust-stained beggar the redeeming God ; shall take from him his rags and crutches ; and, wafted upwards by his longing, shall soar with him to endless spaces, whereon the enfranchised God knows well to breathe undreamt delights of blissful Feeling. So the chary speech of daily life, in which we are not yet what we *can* be, nor therefore give forth what we *can* give forth,—this language we will cast behind us : in the Artwork to speak a tongue in which alone we are able to give forth what we *must*, if we *are* entirely what we can be.

Now, the Tone-poet has so to regulate the verse's tones by their kinship of Expression, that they not only shall make known the emotional-content of this or that vowel, as a vowel *apart*, but shall at the same time shew this content as one akin to *all* the tones of the verse, and display to the Feeling this kindred content as *one specific member of the* Ur-*Kinship of all tones.*

To the Word-poet the disclosure of a kinship of his lifted Accents,—such as should be obvious to the Feeling, and through this at last to the Understanding itself,—was only possible through the consonantal Stabreim of the root-words. What determined this kinship, however, was merely the particularity of their common consonant ; no other consonant could rhyme with it, and therefore the kinship was restricted to one specific family, which was cognisable to the Feeling precisely and only through its making itself known as a completely shut-off family. The Tone-poet, on the contrary, has at his disposal a clan whose kindred reaches to infinity ; and whereas the Word-poet had to content himself with presenting to the Feeling merely the specially accented root-words of his phrase, as allied in sense and sound through the complete alikeness of their initial consonants, the Musician, on the other hand, has before all to display the kinship of his tones in such an extension that, starting with the Accents, he pours it over *all*—even the least emphasised—vowels of the phrase ; so that not alone the vowels of the Accents, but all the vowels in general display themselves to the Feeling as akin to one another.

Just as the Accents in the phrase did not first of all acquire their special light through its sense alone, but through their being thrown into physical relief by the un-emphasised words and syllables that lay in the 'hollow,' so have the chief-tones to win their special light from the lesser tones, which must bear precisely the same relation to them as the up- and down-strokes bear to the 'ridges.' The choice and significance of those minor words and syllables, as well as their bearing on the accentuated words, were governed in the first place by the intellectual-content of the phrase ; only in degree as this intellectual-content, through a condensation of its bulk, was intensified into a compact utterance conspicuous to the sense of Hearing, did it transform itself into an emotional-content. Now, the choice and significance of the lesser tones, as also their bearing on the Chief-tones,

are in so far independent of the intellectual-content of' the
phrase as the latter has already condensed itself to an
emotional-content, in the rhythmic verse and by the
Stabreim; while the full realisement of this emotional-
content, through its most direct communication to the
senses, is further to be accomplished solely in that quarter
where the pure language of Feeling has already been
recognised as the only efficacious one, in that the Vowel
has been resolved into the Singing-tone. From the
instant of the musical intonation of the vowel in word-
speech, the Feeling has become the appointed orderer of
all further announcements to the senses, and henceforward
Musical Feeling alone prescribes the choice and significance both of lesser tones and chief tones; and that,
according to the nature of the Tone-clan (*Tonverwand-
schaft*) whose particular member has been chosen to give
the necessary emotional expression to the phrase.

This kinship of the Tones, however, is musical *harmony;*
and we here have first to take it according to its superficial extension,* in which the unit families of the broad-
branched clan of *tone-varieties* display themselves [in open
rank]. If we keep in eye at present its aforesaid *horizontal*
extension, we expressly reserve the all-determining attribute of Harmony, in its *vertical* extension towards its
primal base, for the decisive moment of our exposition.
But that horizontal extension, being the surface of Harmony, is its physiognomy as still discernible by the poet's
eye: it is the water-mirror which still reflects upon the
poet his own image, while at the same time it presents
this image to the view of him whom the poet wanted to
address. This image, however, is in truth the poet's
realised Aim,—a realisement which can only fall to the
lot of the musician, in his turn, when he mounts from the
depths, to the surface of the sea of Harmony; and' on that
surface will be celebrated the glorious marriage of Poetry's
begetting Thought with Music's endless power of Birth.

That wave-borne mirror-image is *Melody.* In it the

* " Ausdehnung in der Fläche," or " flat dimensions."—TR.

poet's Thought becomes an instinctively enthralling moment of Feeling; just as Music's emotional-power therein acquires the faculty of definite and convincing utterance, of manifesting itself as a sharp-cut human shape, a plastic Individuality. Melody is the redemption of the poet's endlessly conditioned thought into a deep-felt consciousness of emotion's highest freedom (*höchster Gefühlsfreiheit*): it is the willed and achieved Unwilful, the conscious and proclaimed Unconscious, the vindicated Necessity of an endless-reaching Content, condensed from its farthest branchings into an utmost definite utterance of Feeling.

If now we take this melody that appeared on the horizontal plane of Harmony, as the mirrored image of the poet's thought, and is ranged in the primordial Tone-clan by adoption into one particular family of that clan— the special Key,—if we take this melody and hold it up against that *mother-melody* whence Word-speech once was born : then there is evinced the following most weighty difference, which we must here take definitely into view.

Starting with an infinitely confluent fund of Feeling, man's sensations gradually concentrated themselves * to a more and more definite Content; in such sort that their expression in that *Ur*-melody advanced at last, by Nature's necessary steps, to the formation of Absolute Word-speech. The most characteristic mark of the oldest Lyric is this, that in it the words and verse proceeded from the tones and melody; just as bodily Gesture, starting with the vague suggestions of the dance-movement, only understandable in frequent repetitions, abridged itself to the more measured, more definite Mimetic-gesture. In the evolution of the human race, the more the instinctive faculty of Feeling

* "Aus einem unendlich verfliessenden Gefühlsvermögen drängten sich zuerst menschliche Empfindungen zu einem allmählich immer bestimmteren Inhalte zusammen," &c.—

(*Gefühlsvermögen*) condensed itself to the arbitrary faculty
of Understanding ; and the more, in consequence, the content of the Lyric departed from an Emotional-content
(*Gefühlsinhalt*) to become an Intellectual-content,—so
much the more palpably did the Word-poem depart
from its original 'hang-together' with that *Ur*-melody,
and merely use it, in a manner, to make its own delivery
of a cold Didactic Content as palatable as possible to the
rooted habits of the Feeling. Melody itself, such as it
once had blossomed from man's primitive emotional
faculty as a necessary expression of feeling, and in its
fitting union with word and gesture had developed to that
fulness which we still may observe to-day in the genuine
Folksmelody,—this melody those reflective poets-of-the-
Understanding (*Verstandesdichter*) were unable to mould
or vary to meet the contents of their diction (*dem Inhalte
ihrer Ausdrucksweise*). Still less was it possible for them
to find in that mode of diction, itself, a spur to fashioning
fresh melodies : since just the progress of general evolution,
in this great Cultural period, was a stepping forth from
Feeling into Understanding ; and the growing intellect
would only have felt hindered in its experimentings, had
it been in any way driven to invent fresh expressions for
emotions which lay so far behind it.

Wherefore, so long as the Lyric form was welcomed
and demanded by the public, these poets—whom the Content of their poems had made incapable of inventing
melodies—addressed themselves to varying the poem, but
not the melody ; the latter they left all unassailed, and
merely lent to the expression of their poetic thoughts an
outward Form, which they laid below the unaltered melody
as a variation of its text. The so exuberant Form of
Greek speaking-Lyric, such as it has come down to *us*,
and specially the choruses of the Tragicists, we can never
explain as necessarily conditioned by the *content* of these
poems. The mostly didactic and philosophic content
of these chants stands generally in so vivid a contrast
with its sensuous expression, in the profusely changing

Rhythmik of the verses, that we can only conceive this manifold investiture, not as having emanated from the Content of the poetic-aim, but as conditioned by the melody and obediently conforming to its immutable demands.—Even to-day we know the most sterling Folk-melodies only with later texts, which on this or that outward occasion have been engrafted on *them*, the favourite melodies that stood so handy; and—though on a far lower level—when our modern Vaudeville-poets, particularly the French, write verses to well-known melodies and curtly refer the performer to their names, they behave not unlike the Greek Lyricists and Tragic-poets: who in any case composed to melodies belonging to the oldest Lyric art, and surviving—notably in the sacred rites—in the mouth of the Folk, those verses whose wondrous wealth of Rhythm still fills us with amazement at the present day, now that we no longer know their melodies.

But a positive proof of the Greek Tragic-poets' aim, both as to content and form, is afforded by the whole progress of their dramas; which unquestionably move from the lap of the Lyric to an intellectual Reflection, just as the Song of the chorus embouches into the merely spoken iambic Talk of the characters. What sets the working of these dramas in so enthralling a light for us, however, is precisely the Lyric element preserved in them, and recurring more strongly in their crises; that Lyric element which the poet employed with full and deliberate consciousness, exactly as the Didacticist who delivered his educational poems to youth in school, in the stirring strains of lyric song. Yet a deeper look will shew us that the Tragic poet was less open and honest of aim when he clothed it in the lyric garb, than where he undisguisedly expressed it in the merely spoken dialogue: and in this didactic probity, but artistic disingenuousness, there lies the downfall of Greek Tragedy; for the Folk soon noticed that it did not want instinctively to move their Feeling, but arbitrarily to rule their Understanding. Euripides had to shed blood beneath

the lash of Aristophaneian ridicule, for this open blurting
of the lie. That the more and more deliberately didactic
poetry must next become the practised rhetoric of the
forum (*zur staatspraktischen Rhetorik*), and at last the
downright prose of literature, was the extreme, but
altogether natural consequence of the evolution of Understanding out of Feeling, and—for artistic Expression—of
Word-speech out of Melody.—

But *that* Melody to whose birth we now are listening,
forms a complete contrast to the primal Mother-melody ;
and after the above more detailed observations, we may
briefly denote its course as an advance from Understanding
to Feeling, from Word-speech to Melody: as against the
advance from Feeling to Understanding, from the Mother-
melody to Word-speech.   Upon the path of progress from
Word-speech to Tone-speech we reached the horizontal
surface of Harmony, on which the word-phrase of the poet
mirrored back itself as a musical melody.   How, starting
from this surface, we are to master the whole immeasurable
depths of Harmony, that aboriginal womb of all the kin of
Tones, and bring it into ever more extended realisement
of the poet's Aim ; how we are to plunge the poetic Aim,
as a begetting 'moment,' into the full profundity of this
*Ur*mother-element, in suchwise that we may prompt each
atom of its vast emotional chaos to conscious, individual
manifestment, yet in a compass never narrowing but ever
stretching wider : in a word, the artistic advance that shall
consist in broadening a conscious, definite Aim into an
infinite and, for all its boundlessness, an exact and definitely
manifested emotional-Power,—this must be the subject of
our concluding argument.

———————

Let us first settle one thing further, however, so as to
come to an understanding about the results of to-day's
inquiry.

Whereas we have taken Melody—such alone as we have hitherto denoted *—as the acme of emotional-expression in Word-speech, to which the Poet must necessarily climb ; and on this height we have already seen the Word-verse mirrored back from the surface of musical Harmony : yet, upon closer examination, we are astonished by the discovery that this melody is precisely the same, to all appearance, as that which rose from the immeasurable depths of *Beethoven's* music, in the "Ninth Symphony" to greet the shining light of day. The appearance of this melody on the surface of the Harmonic sea was made possible, as we have seen, solely by the urgence of the Musician to look upon the Poet eye to eye ; the Poet's word-verse alone was able to keep it afloat upon that surface, on which it else had merely been a fleeting vision and, without this holdfast, would have swiftly sunk back to the bottom of the sea. This melody was the love-greeting of the woman to the man, and the open-armed "Eternal Womanly" here shewed itself more loveable than the egoistic Man-ly ; for it is Love itself, and only as the highest love-entreaty (*Liebesverlangen*) is the Womanly to be taken,—be it revealed in woman or in man. For all the wonders of that meeting, the man yet left the loving woman : what to this woman was the highest sacrificial incense of a life-time, to the man was a mere passing fume of love. Only the poet whose Aim we have here expounded, will feel driven so irresistibly to a heart-alliance with the "eternal womanly" of Tone-art, that in these nuptials he shall celebrate alike his own redemption.

Through the redeeming love-kiss of that Melody the poet is now inducted into the deep, unending mysteries of Woman's nature : he sees with other eyes, and feels with other senses. To him the bottomless sea of Harmony, from which that beatific vision rose to meet him, is no longer an

---

* "Die Melodie, wie wir sie bis jetzt nur bezeichneten" &c.—From the ambiguity of "nur," this clause *may* mean, "such as we have merely indicated hitherto" ; but I incline to the belief that it is intended to distinguish the "verse-melody" from the "orchestral melody" to be dealt with in Chapter V.—TR.

object of dread, of fear, of terror, such as earlier it seemed
in his imaginings of the strange and unknown element* ;
now, not only can he float upon the surface of this ocean,
but—gifted with new senses—he dives into its lowest depth.
From out the lonely, fearsome reaches of her mother-home
the woman had been self-driven, to wait the nearing of the
beloved ; now, with his bride, he sinks him down, and
learns the hidden wonders of the deep.   His insight pierces,
clear and tranquil, sheer to the ocean's primal fount ;
whence he sends the wave-shafts mounting to the surface,
to run in ripples at the sun-rays, to softly plash beneath
the soughing west-wind, or manlike rear their crests against
the north-wind's storm.†   For the very winds of heaven,
does the poet now command,—since those winds are nothing but the breath of never-ending Love ; of the Love
in whose delight the poet is redeemed, and through its
might becomes the lord of Nature.

Let us examine now, with sober eye, this reign of the
Tone-wed Poet.—

The bond-of-kinship of those tones whose rhythmic-
moving chain, with its links of 'ridge and hollow,' makes
out the Verse-melody, is first of all made plain to Feeling
in the Key (Tonart) ; for it is this which prescribes the particular tone-ladder [or *scale*] in which the tones of that
melodic chain are contained as separate rungs.—Hitherto,
in the necessary endeavour to impart his poem to the
Feeling, we have seen the poet engaged in drawing-together

---

* *Siegfried*, last scene : "Wie end' ich die Furcht? wie fass' ich Muth?"
et seq.—TR.

† I append the German of this clause, as its most musical *Stabreim* is so
obviously intentional : "Von dem aus er die Wogensäulen ordnet, die zum
Sonnenlichte emporsteigen sollen, um an seinem Scheine in wonnigen Wellen
dahinzuwallen, nach dem Säuseln des Westes sanft zu plätschern, oder nach
den Stürmen des Nordes sich männlich zu bäumen."—TR.

the organic units of his diction—assembled from circles wide apart,—and removing from them all that was heterogeneous, so as to lead them before the Feeling, especially through the [Stab-]rhyme, in the utmost displayable kinship. At bottom of this thrust of his there lay an instinctive knowledge of Feeling's nature, which takes-in alone the homogeneous (*das Einheitliche*), alone the thing that in its oneness includes alike the conditioned and the conditioner; of Feeling, which seizes the imparted feeling according to its generic essence, so that it refuses to heed the opposites contained therein, *quâ* opposites, but is guided by the nature of the *genus* in which those opposites are reconciled. The Understanding loosens, the Feeling binds; i.e. the Understanding loosens the genus into the antitheses which lie within it, whereas the Feeling binds them up again into one harmonious whole. This unitarian Expression the poet most completely won, at last, in the ascension of his Word-verse into the melody of Song; and the latter wins its unitarian Expression, its unfailing operation on the Feeling, through instinctively displaying to the senses the inner kinship of its tones.*

The *Key* (Tonart) is the most united, most closely kindred *family* of the whole *tone-genus;* it shews itself as truly of one kin with the *whole* tone-genus, however, where it advances to an alliance with other Keys, through the instinctive inclination of its individual members. We here may suitably compare the tone-key with the ancient patriarchal families of the various human stems: by an instinctive error the kinsmen of these families considered them-

* "Diesen einheitlichen Ausdruck gewann der Dichter am vollständigsten endlich im Aufgehen des, nach Einheit nur ringenden Wortverses in die Gesangsmelodie, die ihren einheitlichen, das Gefühl unfehlbar bestimmenden Ausdruck aus der, den Sinnen unwillkürlich sich darstellenden Verwandtschaft der Töne gewinnt."—I here must confess myself beaten in the attempt to *readably* work-in the "nach Einheit nur ringenden" into the body of the text; and therefore note that this omitted subsidiary clause lays stress upon the fact that the "Word-verse" merely *strove* for unity of expression, whereas the "Song-melody" was naturally fitted to *attain* it.—TR.

selves as a peculiar people, and not as members of the entire human race; yet the Individual's sexual love was not enkindled by a wonted, but solely by an un-wonted object, and thus it climbed the barriers of the patriarchal family, to knit alliances with other families. In a prophetic transport Christianity proclaimed the oneness of the human race: the art which owes its most characteristic development to Christianity, the art of Music, has taken up that evangel into itself, and has transformed it, as our modern Tone-speech, into a sybaritic message to the sensuous Feeling.* If we take those *ur*-patriarchal national melodies, the genuine heirlooms of particular stems, and compare them with the Melody which the advance of Music through the Christian evolution has made possible to us to-day, we shall find as their characteristic token, that they almost never move away from one definite key, appearing positively engrown therewith : whereas the Melody possible to *us*, has acquired the most unheard variety of power of placing its initial chief-key in alliance with the remotest tone-families, by means of harmonic Modulation ; so that in a larger composition the *ur*-kinship of all keys is presented to us, as it were, in the light of one particular chief-key.

This boundless power of extension and alliance so intoxicated the modern musician, that, upon recovery from his bout, he has deliberately looked round him for that earlier straitened family-melody, so as to make himself intelligible by copying its simplicity. The looking-round for that patriarchal straitenedness reveals to us the real weak side of our whole art of Music, in which we heretofore had made our reckoning—so to say—without our host. From the Fundamental note of Harmony, Music had spread itself into a huge expanse of waters, in which the Absolute-musician swam aimlessly and restless to and fro, until at last he lost his nerve : before him he saw nothing but an endless surge of possibilities, albeit he was conscious in

---

* " Zu schwelgerisch entzückender Kundgebung an das sinnliche Gefühl," —the "entzückend" (enravishing) is here employed as a half-contrast to Christianity's "Verzückung " (transport, or ecstasy).—Tr.

himself of no definite purpose to which to put those possibilities,—just as the Christian all-humanitarianism (*Allmen-
schlichkeit*) was merely a floating sentiment, without any
holdfast to vindicate it as a definite feeling; and this holdfast is the *actual* Man. Thus the musician was bound to
wellnigh bewail his immoderate power of swimming; he
yearned back to his primal homeland's quiet creeks, where
the water flowed restfully between its narrow shores, and
always in one definite tide. What moved him to this
return, was nothing but the experienced aimlessness of his
rovings on the high seas; to put it strictly, the admission
that he possessed a faculty which he was unable to use,—
the Yearning for the Poet.

Beethoven, the daringest of swimmers, spoke plainly out
this yearning; not only, however, did he strike again that
patriarchal melody, but he spoke aloud the poet's verse
thereto. Already in another place I have drawn attention
to an uncommonly weighty 'moment' in this regard, to
which I must here come back, since it now has to serve us
for a new anchorage in the dominion of experience. That
patriarchal melody—as I shall continue to call it, in token of
its historic bearings,—that melody which Beethoven strikes
in the "Ninth Symphony," as found at last for *fixing* the
Feeling (*zur* Bestimmung *des Gefühles*), and of which I earlier
asserted that it did not arise *from out* the poem of Schiller,
but rather was invented outside the word-verse and merely
spread above it: that melody shews itself wholly confined
to the tone-family ties which rule the movements of the old
national *Volkslied*. It contains as good as *no* modulation,
and appears in so marked a simplicity of key, that in it the
aim of the musician, to go back upon the historic fount of
Music, is spoken out without disguise. This aim was a
necessary one for Absolute Music, which does not stand on
a basis of Poetry: the musician who wishes to intelligibly
address the Feeling in Tones alone, can do this only through
tuning-down his endless powers to an extremely straitened measure. When Beethoven wrote down that melody,
he said:—So only, can we absolute musicians give out an

T

understandable message. But the march of evolution of
all things human is no returning to the old, but a constant
stepping forward : each turning back, whatever, shews itself
no natural, but an artificial movement. Even Beethoven's
return to the patriarchal melody, like this melody itself,
was an artificial one. Neither was the bare construction of
this melody the artistic goal of Beethoven ; much rather do
we see how deliberately, though only for an instant, he so
far lowered the pitch of his melodic inventiveness : it was
merely to strike the natural foundation of all Music, where
he not only might reach his hand to greet the Poet, but also
grasp the poet's own. Once that with this simple, straitened melody he feels the Poet's hand within his own, he
strides towards the poem itself ; and from out this poem
—shaping after its spirit and its form—he passes forward
to an ever bolder and more manifold building of his tones :
at last to set before us wonders such as we had never
dreamt of, wonders such as the " *Seid umschlungen, Millionen !* ", the " *Ahnest du den Schöpfer, Welt ?* " and finally
the un-misunderstandable combination of the " *Seid umschlungen* " with the " *Freude, schöner Götterfunken !* "—all
arisen from the puissance of *poetic* (*dichtenden*) tone-speech.
If, now, we compare the broad melodic structure of the
whole musical setting of the verse " *Seid umschlungen* " with
the melody which the master, in his absolute-musical capacity, so to say merely spread above the verse " *Freude,
schöner Götterfunken*," we shall gain an exact understanding
of the distinction between that patriarchal melody—as I
have called it—and the melody which grows forth upon the
word-verse through the working of the Poetic Aim. As
the former made itself intelligible only in the most straitened of tone-family ties, so the latter—not only *without*
becoming un-understandable, but to first become *right* understandable by the Feeling—can stretch the narrower
kinship of the Key to the broad *ur*-kinship of all Tones,
through alliance with other keys akin ; and thus it widens
the surely-guided feeling, into the endless Purely-human
Feeling.—

The Key of a melody is that which presents to Feeling its various included tones in their earliest bond of kinship. The incitement to widen this narrower bond to a richer, more extended one, is derived from the Poetic Aim, insofar as that has already condensed itself in the speaking-verse to a moment-of-feeling; while this extension is governed by the particular expressional character of single chief-tones, which have themselves, in turn, been prompted by the verse. These Chief-tones are, in a sense, the adolescent members of the family, who yearn to leave its wonted surrounding for an unhindered independence: this independence, however, they do not gain as egoists, but through encounter with another being, a being that lies outside the family. The maiden attains her independence, her stepping beyond the family, only through love of the youth who, himself the scion of another family, attracts her over to him. Thus the tone which quits the circle of the Key is a tone already prompted and attracted by that other key, and into the latter must it therefore pour itself according to the necessary law of Love. The leading-tone (*Leitton*) that urges from one key into another, and by this very urgence discloses its kinship with that other key, can only be taken as prompted by the motive of Love. The motive of Love is that which drives the 'subject' (*Subjekt*) out beyond itself, and compels it to an alliance with another. For the unit tone, this motive can spring from nothing but a [general] connection which determines *it* in particular; but the connection that determines the Melody, resides in the 'sensuous' expression of the Word-phrase, which again has been first of all determined by the sense of that phrase. If we look closer, we shall see that the selfsame principle is here at work, as that which had bound remoter-lying sensations together in the Stabreim.

For the sentient ear, as we have seen, the Stabreim already coupled speech-roots of opposite emotional expression (as "*Lust und Leid*," "*Wohl und Weh*"), and thus presented them to the Feeling as generically akin. Now, in a far higher measure can musical Modulation make such a union perceptible to the Feeling.   If we take, for instance, a stabreimed verse of completely like emotional-content, such as : " *Liebe giebt Lust zum Leben,*" * then, as a like emotion is physically disclosed in the Accents' stabreimed roots, the musician would here receive no natural incitement to step outside the once selected key, but would completely satisfy the Feeling by keeping the various inflections of the musical tone to that one key alone.   On the contrary, if we take a verse of mixed emotion, such as : " *die Liebe bringt Lust und Leid,*" then here, where the Stabreim combines two opposite emotions, the musician would feel incited to pass across from the key first struck in keeping with the first emotion, to another key in keeping with the second emotion, and determined by the latter's relation to the emotion rendered in the earlier key.   The word " *Lust*" (" delight ")—which, as the climax of the first emotion, appears to thrust onward to the second—would have in this phrase to obtain an emphasis quite other than in that : " *die Liebe giebt Lust zum Leben*" ; the note sung to it would instinctively become the determinant leading-tone, and necessarily thrust onward to the other key, in which the word " *Leid*" (" sorrow ") should be delivered. In this attitude toward one another, " *Lust und Leid*" would become the manifestment of a specific emotion, whose idiosyncrasy would lie precisely in the point where two opposite emotions displayed themselves as conditioning one the other, and thus as necessarily belonging together, as actually akin ; and this manifestment is possible alone to Music, in her faculty of harmonic Modulation, because in virtue thereof she exerts a binding sway upon the 'sensuous' Feeling such as no other art has force for.

Let us next see how musical Modulation, hand in hand with the verse's Content, is able to lead back again to the first emotion.—Let us follow up the verse " *die Liebe bringt Lust und Leid*" with a second : " *doch in ihr Weh auch webt sie Wonnen,*" †—then " *webt,*" again, would become a

---

* " Love gives delight to living."—
" But with her woe she weaves things winsome."—TR.

tone leading into the first key, as from *here* the second emotion returns to the first, but now enriched, emotion. To the Feeling's sensory organ the Poet, in virtue of his Stabreim, could only display this return as an advance from the feeling of "*Weh*" to that of "*Wonnen,*" but not as a rounding-off of the generic feeling "Liebe"; whereas the Musician becomes completely understandable by the very fact that he quite markedly goes back to the first tone-variety, and therefore definitely denotes the genus of the two emotions as one and the same,—a thing impossible to the poet, who was obliged to change the root-initial for the Stabreim.—Only, by the *sense* of both verses the Poet indicated the generic bond uniting the emotions; he thus desired its realisement to the Feeling, and determined the realising process of the Musician.   For his procedure, which, if unconditioned, would seem arbitrary and unintelligible, the Musician thus obtains his vindication from the Poet's aim,—from an aim which the latter could only suggest, or at utmost, merely approximately realise for fractions of his message (precisely in the Stabreim), but whose full realisement is possible precisely to the Musician; and that, through his power of employing the Ur-kinship of the tones to harmoniously display to Feeling the primal unity of the emotions.

We may easiest gain a notion of how immeasurably great this power is, if we imagine the sense of the above-cited pair of verses as still more definitely laid down: in such sort that, between the advance from the one emotion and the return thereto in the second verse, a longer sequence of verses shall express the most manifold gradation and blend of intermediate emotions,—in part corroborating, in part reconciling,—until the final return of the chief-emotion. Here, to realise the poetic aim, the musical Modulation would have to be led across to, and back from, the most diverse keys; but all the adventitious keys would appear in an exact affinitative relation to the primary key, which itself will govern the particular light they throw upon the expression, and, in a manner, will lend them first their very capability of giving that light.* The chief-key, as the ground-tone of the emotion first struck, would reveal its own ur-kinship with all the other keys, and thus, in virtue of the intensified Expression, would display the dominant Emotion (*die bestimmte Empfindung*) in such a height and breadth, that only emotions *kindred to it* could dominate our Feeling, so long as its utterance lasted ; that this one Emotion, in virtue of its intensity and its extension, would usurp our whole emotional faculty ; and thus this unique emotion would be raised to an all-embracing one, an omni-human, an unfailingly intelligible.

If the poetico-musical '*period*' has thus been denoted, in accordance with its domination by one Chief-key,† then we may provisionally denote *that* artwork as the most perfect of Expression, in which many such periods present themselves in utmost fulness, for the realisement of a loftiest poetic Aim ; and *so* present themselves that they condition each the other, and unfold themselves to a total breadth of utterance wherein the nature of Man, along one decisory Chief-line,—i.e. along a line competent to sum in itself Man's total essence (just as a Chief-key is able to sum in itself all other keys)—wherein this nature is displayed to Feeling in the surest and most seizable of fashions. This artwork is the Perfected Drama, wherein that comprehensive line of human nature will manifest itself to the Feeling in a continuous, a mutually conditioning (*sich wohl bedingenden*) chain of moments of feeling : a chain of such strength and force of conviction, that *the Action*,—as the necessary, the most definite utterance of the emotional-content of 'moments' intensified into a comprehensive joint-motive,—that that *Action* may issue from this wealth of conditions as their last instinctively demanded, and thus completely intelligible moment.

* By way of illustration, I may point to the "Tristan's Ehre..." passage in the first Act of *Tristan und Isolde.*—TR.

† "Ist hiermit die dichterisch-musikalische *Periode* bezeichnet worden, wie sie sich nach einer Haupttonart bestimmt" &c.—i.e. "if we have thus established the groundwork of that unit of poetry and music, combined, which we are to call by the name of a 'Period.'"—TR.

Before we proceed to argue from the character of the poetico-musical 'period' to the Drama which has to grow from amid the reciprocally-conditioning evolution of many such needful periods, we must first, however, exactly define *that other* 'moment' which conditions the emotional expression even of the unit melodic-period : that power which lies within the realm of Music proper,* and which is to place at our disposal the incomparably 'binding' organ through whose peculiar aid we first can bring about the Perfected Drama. In the *vertical* dimension of Harmony —as I have already called it, where it moves upwards from its base,—will this organ arise for us, if we allot to Harmony itself the possibility of taking a fully sympathetic share in the total Artwork.

---

* As I have had to slightly expand this portion of an extremely concentrated sentence, I append its German original :—" *das* Moment . . . welches auch die einzelne melodische Periode nach ihrem Gefühlsausdrucke aus dem Vermögen der reinen Musik heraus bedingt," &c.—TR.

IV.

P to the present, we have shewn the condition for a melodic advance from one tone-variety to another as lying in the Poetic Aim, in so far as the latter itself had already revealed its emotional-content ; and by this shewing we have *proved* * that the instigating *ground* for melodic motion, to be justi-fied even in the eyes of Feeling, can be supplied by nothing but that Aim. Yet what *enables* this advance, so necessary to the Poet, naturally does not lie in the domain of Word-speech, but quite definitely in that of Music alone. This own-est element of music, *Harmony* to wit, is merely in *so* far still governed by the poetic-aim, as it is the other, the womanly element into which this aim pours itself for its own realisement, for its redemption. For this is the *bear-ing* element, which takes up the poetic-aim solely as a begetting seed, to shape it into finished semblance by the prescripts of its own, its womanly organism. This organism is a specific, an individual one, and *no* begetter, but a bearer : it has received from the poet the fertilising seed, but the fruit it forms and ripens by its own in-dividual powers.

That Melody which we have seen appearing on the *surface* of Harmony, is conditioned as to its distinctive, its purely-musical expression by Harmony's upward-working depths alone : as it manifests itself as a horizontal chain, so is it connected by a plumbline with those depths. This plumbline is the harmonic Chord, a vertical chain of tones in closest kinship, mounting from the ground-tone † to the

---

* " Und bei diesem Nachweis *be*wiesen [haben], dass der veranlassende *Grund* zur melodischen Bewegung, als ein auch vor dem Gefühle gerechtfer-tigter, nur aus dieser Absicht entstehen könne."—

† " Grundton," i.e. the " fundamental note," or " bass."—Tr.

surface. The chiming (*Mitklingen*) of this chord first gives
to the melodic note the peculiar significance wherein it, and
it alone, has been employed to mark a distinctive moment
of the Expression. Now, just as the ground-tone, with the
chord determined by it, first gives to the melody's unit note
a particular expression—seeing that the selfsame tone upon
another of its kindred ground-tones acquires a quite other
significance,—so each melodic progress from one Key to
another is likewise governed by the changing ground-tone,
which of itself prescribes the harmony's leading-tone, as
such. The presence of that ground-tone, and of the harmonic chord thereby determined, is indispensable in the
eyes of Feeling, if this latter is to seize the melody in all its
characteristic expression. But the presence of the ground-
harmony means—its *concurrent sounding out* (Miterklingen).
The sounding-out of the harmony to a melody, is the first
thing that fully persuades the Feeling as to the emotional-
content of that melody, which otherwise would leave to it
something undetermined.   But only amid the fullest determination of every 'moment' of expression, is the Feeling
itself determined to a swift, direct and instinctive interest;
and a full determination of the Expression, again, can only
mean *the completest impartal to the Senses, of all its necessary
moments.*

So, the ear imperiously demands the concurrent sounding of the harmony to a melody, because thereby it first
obtains an entire fulfilling—and thus a satisfying—of its
sensory faculty, and thereafter it can devote itself with the
necessary composure to [an appreciation of] the melody's
apt emotional expression. The concurrent sounding of the
harmony to a melody is therefore no impediment, but the
sole facilitation, to the Hearing's understanding. Only if
the harmony were unable to utter itself as Melody,—i.e. if
its melody had neither a dance-rhythm nor a word-verse to
vindicate it and assure its recognition by the Feeling, but
were to shew itself as a mere chance apparition on the
surface of chords capriciously built-up on a shifting bass,—
only such a naked show of Harmony, as this, would disquiet

the unassisted Feeling; for it would bring it merely incitations, but no satisfaction of the mood incited.

Our Modern Music, in a sense, has evolved from naked Harmony. She has wilfully committed herself to the endless fill of possibilities which offered themselves in the shifting of the ground-tones, and of the chords derived therefrom. Insofar as she has remained faithful to this her origin, she has only worked bewilderingly and benumbingly upon the Feeling, and her motleyest manifestments, in this sense, have merely offered a relish to a kind of intellectual gluttony on the part of our artists themselves, but no pleasure to the non-music-understanding laity. Wherefore the layman, provided he did not *affect* an understanding of music, held only by the shallowest surface of the melody, such as was presented him in the purely sensuous * charm of the singing-organ; while to the absolute musician he cried: " I don't *understand* your music; it's too learned for me."—In opposition to all this, *that* Harmony which is to sound out as the purely-musical basis of the poet's melody, has nothing at all to do with an understanding, in the sense in which it is understood at present by the learned class-musician, and *not* understood by the layman: in the delivery of that melody it has rightdown *not* to draw the attention of the Feeling to its agency, *as* Harmony; but, as even though *silent* it would condition the melody's characteristic expression, albeit its silence would infinitely hinder any understanding of this expression,—nay, could only consign it to the music-pedant to think out for himself,—so the concurrent sounding of the harmony has to render needless all abstract excursions of the musical Art-understanding, and to conduct before the Feeling the musical emotional-content of the melody, as a thing instinctively knowable, a thing to be seized without any distracting toil, and easily and swiftly comprehensible.

Whereas, then, the Musician has hitherto constructed his

* I may call to mind the " castrato-knifelet."—R. WAGNER.

music out of its harmony, so to say, the Tone-poet now will add to a melody conditioned by its speaking-verse the other necessary, purely-musical condition, already implicit in that melody : he will add the concurrent Harmony, as though merely for its making obvious. Within the poet's melody the harmony is already contained as well, though as it were unspoken-out : quite without his heeding, it has conditioned the expressional significance of the tones which the poet appointed for the melody. This expressional significance (*ausdrucksvolle Bedeutung*), which the poet had unconsciously in ear, was already the fulfilled condition, the plainest utterance of the harmony ; but for him it was merely a thing of thought, and not yet physically discernible. Yet it is to the Senses, the directly recipient organs of the Feeling, that he imparts himself for his redemption, and to them must he therefore bring the melodic utterance of the harmony *together with* the stipulations for that utterance ; for an *organic* artwork is only such as includes within itself, and imparts the most discernibly to others, alike the conditioned and the conditioner. Up to now, our Absolute Music has given us Harmonic conditionments ; in his Melody the poet would merely impart the thing conditioned, and would therefore remain as unintelligible as she,—unless he fully made known to the ear the Harmonic stipulations of a Melody already warranted by the word-verse.

The *harmony*, however, only the *musician* can invent, and not the poet. Wherefore the melody which we have seen the poet inventing from out the word-verse, was more a *discovered* one—as being conditioned by Harmony—than one *invented* by him. The conditions for this Musical melody must first have been to hand, before the poet could find it as already validly conditioned. Before the poet could find this melody, to his redemption, the musician had already conditioned it by his own-est powers : he now brings it to the poet as a melody warranted by its harmony ; *and only Melody such as has been made possible by the very essence of our Modern Music,** is the melody that can redeem the poet,—that can alike arouse and satisfy his stress.*

Poet and Musician herein are like two travellers who have started from *one* departure-point, from thence to journey straight ahead in opposite directions. Arrived at the opposite point of the Earth, they meet again ; each has wandered round one half the planet. They fall a-questioning one another, and each tells each what he has seen and found. The Poet describes the plains, the mountains, valleys, fields, the men and beasts, which he has met upon his distant journey through the mainland. The Musician has voyaged across the seas, and recounts the wonders of the ocean : on its breast he has often been nigh to sinking, and its deeps and strange-shaped monsters have filled him half with terror, half with joy. Roused by each other's stories, and irresistibly impelled to learn for themselves the Other which each has not yet seen,—so as to make into an actual experience impressions merely taken up in fancy,— they part again, each to complete his journey round the Earth. At their first starting-point they meet at last once more; the Poet now has battled through the seas, the Musician has stridden through the continents. Now they part no more, for both now *know* the Earth: what they earlier had imagined in their boding dreams, as fashioned thus and thus, has now been witnessed by them in its actuality. They are One; for each knows and feels what the other feels and knows. The Poet has become musician, the Musician poet: now they are *both* an entire Artistic Man.

At the point where their roads first met, after wandering round the first half of the Earth, the mutual discourse of the Poet and Musician was *that melody* which we now have in eye,—the melody whose utterance the Poet had shaped from out his inmost longing, but whose manifestment the

---

* That is to say, by modern Harmony, as appears from the two preceding paragraphs.—TR.

Musician conditioned from amid his own experiences. When they pressed their hands in fresh farewell, each had in mind what he himself had not as yet experienced, and to gain this crowning experience they quitted each other anew.—Let us take the Poet first, in his mastering the experiences of the Musician. These he now reaps for himself, albeit guided by the counsel of the Musician, who had already sailed the open seas upon his sturdy ship, had found the course to firm-set land, and now has accurately mapped out for him the chart. On this new voyage we shall see the Poet become the selfsame man as the Musician upon his own new journey across the other Earth-half, as traced-out for him by the Poet; so that we now may look on both these journeyings as one and the same thing.

When the Poet now commits himself to the vast expanse of Harmony, as it were to prove the truth of that [other] melody the Musician had " told of," he no longer finds the wayless tone-wastes which the Musician had first encountered on his earlier voyage ; to his delight he meets with the wondrous bold, the passing new, the infinitely delicate, yet giant-bolted framework of the ship that first sea-wanderer had built; the Poet mounts on board it, to safely make the passage of the waves. The Musician had taught him the handling of the helm, the trimming of the sails, and all the cunningly devised expedients for breasting storms and tempests. Sailing the wide seas at the helm of this glorious ship, the Poet, who before had toiled to measure hill and valley step by step, now rejoices at his consciousness of Man's all-conquering might ; let the billows rear them never so proudly, from *its* high deck they seem to him the willing, faithful bearers of his lofty fortune, that fortune of the Poetic Aim. This ship is the strong, enabling implement of his widest and his mightiest will ; with fervent love his thanks go forth to the Musician, who invented it in direst stress of weather, and now has made it over to his hands : for this trusty ship is the conqueror of the endless floods of Harmony, — *the Orchestra*.

Harmony is in itself a mere thing *of thought :* to the
Senses it becomes first actually discernible as *polyphony,* or,
to define it still more closely, as *polyphonic symphony.*

The first, the natural symphony is afforded by the
harmonious sounding-together of a polyphonic tone-mass
of like constituents. The most natural tone-mass is the
Human Voice, which shows itself in wide diversity of range
and timbre (*Klangfarbe,*—lit. clang-tint) according to the
sex, age, and idiosyncrasy of the vocally-gifted individual;
through the harmonious coöperation of these individualities,
it becomes the most natural revealer of Polyphonic symphony. The *Christian religious* Lyric invented this
symphony : in it Man's plurality (*die Vielmenschlichkeit*)
seemed united into an emotional-expression whose subject
was not the individual longing, as the utterance of a severed
personality, but the individual longing as infinitely
strengthened through the utterance of precisely the same
longing by an altogether like-needing community ; and
this longing was the yearning for dissolution into God, into
the conceptual personification of the highest ' power ' * of
the longing individual personality itself. To this ' raising
the power ' of a personality which he felt to be null and
void in itself, the Individual as it were encouraged himself
by the similar longing of a Community, and through his
intimate harmonic blending with that Community,—as
though to draw from a like-attuned faculty in common the
force which he felt was lacking to the unit personality.
But in the course of Christian manhood's evolution, the
secret of this longing was destined to be laid bare ; and
indeed, as its purely-individual Personal Content. As a
purely-individual personality, however, man no longer
fastens his longing on God, on a merely conceptual being,
but he materialises (*verwirklicht*) the object of his longing
into a real (*Realen*), a physically present thing, whose
attainment and enjoyment are practically achievable by
him. With the extinction of the purely religious spirit of

---

* "Potenz," i.e. " power " in the mathematical sense.—TR.

Christianity there also vanished all necessary significance of the polyphonic church-song, and together with it, its idiomatic form of manifestment. Counterpoint, as the first stirring of a sheer Individualism intent on ever clearer utterance of self, began with sharp and acrid tooth to eat into the simple symphonic vocal-tissue, and turned it more and more visibly into an artificial consonance of inwardly-discordant individual utterances—often only toilsomely to be upheld.—In Opera at last the Individual loosed himself completely from the vocal union, to display himself as an unchecked Personality, alone and self-dependent. Where dramatic personages unbent themselves to part-song, this happened—in the specific Operatic style—for mere sake of physically reinforcing the individual expression ; or—in the true Dramatic style—as a simultaneous display, effected through the utmost art, of individualities continuing to assert their several characteristics.

If we now picture to ourselves the Drama of the Future, in its realisement of the Poetic Aim defined by us above, we shall find therein no room at all for the exhibition of individualities so subsidiary in their reference to the drama that they may be employed for the purpose of giving a polyphonic rendering to the harmony, through their merely symphonising share in the melody of the main personages. With its compression and strengthening both of motives and actions, we can conceive no sharers in the plot but such as at all times exert a decisive influence on it through their necessary individual doings (*Kundgebungen*),—therefore none but personages who themselves require a symphonic support for the musical enouncement of their individuality, that is to say, a many-voiced *elucidation* (Verdeutlichung) of their melody ; but never such as may serve for the mere harmonic vindication of the melody of another person,—excepting in the rarest of events, and those entirely warranted and necessary to a higher understanding of the thing.—Even the *Chorus*, as hitherto employed in Opera, and according to the significance there assigned it in even the most favourable cases, will have to

vanish from *our* drama*; *it,* too, can have a vital and convincing effect, in Drama, only when its sheer pronounce-
ments *en masse* are completely taken from it. A Mass
can never interest, but only dumbfound us: none but
accurately distinguishable individualities can lead our
interest captive. It is the necessary care of the poet
who strives throughout for plainest understandableness,
to give to a more numerous Surrounding—wherever
such be needful—the character of individually sharing in
the motives and actions of his drama: nothing does he
wish to cover up, but to disclose All. To the Feeling,
which he addresses, he wants to open the whole living
organism of a human action; and this he attains only
when he presents each several portion of that organism in
the warmest, most spontaneous play. The human Surrounding of a dramatic action must appear to us as though
that particular action, and the persons involved therein,
loomed large above this Surrounding merely by reason
that they and it were shewn from precisely the one side
turned towards the spectator, and in the illumination of
precisely this one now-falling light. But our Feeling must
be so decided in respect of this Surrounding, that we cannot be assailed by the supposition that an action, and the
persons involved therein, would rouse our interest just as
strongly if they were shewn beneath a different light, and

---

* I add the German of this clause, and of the last clause of the preceding
sentence, since a *misreading* thereof has often been cast in the teeth of *Die
Meistersinger* and *Parsifal:* "keinesweges aber—ausser in nur selten erschein-
enden, vollkommen gerechtfertigten und zum höchsten Verständnisse noth-
wendigen Fällen—zur bloss harmonischen Rechtfertigung der Melodie einer
anderen Person dienen können.—Selbst der bisher in der Oper verwendete
Chor wird nach der Bedeutung, die ihm in den noch günstigsten Fällen dort
beigelegt ward, in *unserem* Drama zu verschwinden haben ;"—I would draw
particular attention to the "*nach der Bedeutung dort.*" Further, in *Letters to
Uhlig,* No. 16, dated Sep. 20, 1850 (i.e. only four months, at the outside,
before writing the above), Wagner speaks of composing his *Siegfried*—the
Siegfried's Tod—as "the accomplishment of the conscious mission of my life,"
and, among his projects for the contemplated production of that work in
Zurich, he says: "I would try to form a *chorus* here, consisting, for the most
part, of amateurs."—TR.

if we were watching the show-place from another side.* In other words, the Surrounding must so display itself to our Feeling, that we can attribute to each of its members the capability of motives and actions which, under other circumstances than the precise ones set before us, would captivate our interest to an equal degree. What the poet places in the background, is thus withdrawn solely out of regard for the necessary sight-point of the spectator, who would not be able to cast his eye across a too profusely distributed action, and to whom the poet therefore only turns the one easily-grasped physiognomy of the object he wishes to display.

To make the Surrounding exclusively into a lyric 'moment,' must unconditionally degrade it in the drama, and would at the same time assign to the Lyric itself an altogether false position in Drama. In the Drama of the Future—the work of the poet who imparts himself from out the Understanding to the Feeling—the lyric outpour must be a necessary outcome of motives pressed together before our very eyes, not stream forth all unmotived from the start. The poet of this Drama will not proceed from the feeling to its [later] vindication, but will give us the feeling itself [as already] vindicated by the Understanding. This vindication goes on in the presence of our own Feeling, and takes place through the conversion of the 'will' of the transactors into an instinctively necessary 'must,' i.e. 'can'; the moment of realisation of this will, through instinctive must to can, is the Lyric Outpour in its utmost strength, as the overflowing into Deed. The 'lyric moment' has therefore to grow out of the drama itself, to appear as necessarily conditioned by its course. So that the dramatic

---

* There is some ambiguity in the opening of this sentence: "Unser Gefühl muss in dieser Umgebung aber so bestimmt sein, dass wir durch die Annahme nicht verletzt werden können." This might possibly be rendered : "that we might not be *hurt* by the idea that," &c., i.e. "we should not resent the supposition, were it to occur to us"; I fancy, however, that in that case our author would have used the subjunctive "könnten," instead of "können." Precisely the same difficulty crops up, at times, with every writer who deals with hypothetical contingencies.—TR.

U

Surrounding cannot un-conditionally appear in the garb of
Lyric, as has been the case in our Opera, but it, too, has
first to *mount* to Lyric, and that through sharing in the
Action ; wherefore it has not to convince us as a lyric
mass, but as a well-distinguished memberhood of self-set
individualities.

Not the so-called *Chorus*, then, nor the main characters
themselves, are to be used by the poet as a symphonic body
of musical tones for bringing to light the Harmonic stipulations of the melody.   Only in the full tide of lyric outpour,
when all the Characters and their Surrounding have been
strictly led-up to a joint expression of feeling, is there offered
to the tone-poet a polyphonic mass of voices to which he may
make over the declaration of the Harmony.   Yet even here
it will remain the tone-poet's necessary task, not to give out
the dramatic unit's share in the emotional-outpour as a
sheer harmonic bolstering of the melody, but—precisely
amid this harmonic concord—to allow the individuality of
the personage concerned (*des Betheiligten*) to make itself
known in a definite, and withal a melodic utterance ; and
just in *this*, will have to be avouched his highest faculty, as
lent him by the standpoint of our Musical art.   But the
standpoint of our independently developed art of Music
supplies him also with the immeasurably puissant organ for
making plain the Harmony ; an organ which, besides the
satisfaction of this positive Need, possesses the further
power of characterising the Melody in a way completely
barred to the symphonic Vocal-mass : and this organ is the
Orchestra.

We have now to consider the *Orchestra* not merely, as I
termed it above, as the conqueror of the waves of Harmony,
but as itself those conquered waves.   In it the Harmonic
element, that conditions the melody, is turned from a
'moment' of sheer declaration of those conditions, into an

at all times characteristic accessory-organ for realising the Poetic Aim.   From being merely a thing imagined by the poet, and never to be realised in Drama by the same tone-mass in which the vocal melody appears,—the naked harmony becomes in the Orchestra an altogether real and special agent ; a factor through whose help the Perfected Drama is first truly placeable within the power of the poet.

The Orchestra is Harmony's realised Thought, in its highest, living-est mobility.   It is the condensement of the members of the vertical Chord to a self-dependent display of their affinitative inclinations, in a *horizontal* direction along which they may expand themselves with freest power of motion,—with a motive power that has been lent the Orchestra by its first creator, Dance-rhythm.—

We have to notice first of all the important point, that the instrumental orchestra is something quite different from the vocal tone-mass, not only in its power of expression, but also, and quite definitely, in its *colour* (klangfarbe).   In a manner, the musical instrument is an echo of the human voice, but so constituted that we can only detect in it the Vowel resolved into the musical Tone, and no longer the word-determining Consonant.   In this loosening from the Word, the instrumental tone is like that *Ur*-tone of all human speech, which only with the advent of the consonant condensed itself into the genuine vowel ; and in its bindings— parallel with those of modern word-speech—it becomes a specific tongue, which retains alone an emotional, and not an intellectual kinship with actual human Speech.   Now, this pure Tone-speech completely loosened from the Word, or remaining a stranger to the consonantal evolution of *our* speech, in turn has won a specific individual property from the individuality of the instruments, through which alone it was utterable ; and this property is determined by the *consonant-like* character of the instruments, in much the same way as Word-speech is determined through its consonantal

articulations. In its determinant influence on the quality
of the tone entrusted to it, one might term a musical instrument the consonantal *onset of the Root*,* displaying itself as
a *Stabreim binding together* all the tones executable upon
it. The kinship of the instruments to one another might
thus be easily decided by the likeness of this initial sound,
according as it shewed itself as a softer or harsher delivery,
so to say, of the consonant they originally shared in common. As a matter of fact, we possess families of instruments
that own an originally like initial, which merely shades off
according to the respective character of the offspring, in a
similar way to e.g. the consonants *P,B* and *W* in word-speech;
and just as with *W* we stumble across a resemblance to *F*,
so the pedigree of the instrumental families might easily be
discovered to embrace a very complex ramification, whose
exact tracing, and a characteristic employment of its members in groups arranged according to their likeness or
diversity, could not but present us with an Orchestra endowed with far more *individual powers of speech* than have
even yet appeared,—seeing that the Orchestra is at present
a long way from being known enough in its interpreting
capacity.† But this knowledge can only come to us, in any
event, when we shall assign to the Orchestra a more intimate
share in Drama than has hitherto been the case, where it
is mostly employed as a mere luxurious piece of finery.

The *particularity* of the Orchestra's faculty of speech—
which must necessarily result from its idiosyncrasy of
sound — we reserve for a concluding inquiry into its

---

* "Den konsonirenden *wurzelhaften Anlaut*" &c.—
† "Nach seiner sinnvollen Eigenthümlichkeit."—For "sinnvoll" I can
neither find nor concoct a suitable equivalent. The nearest approach would
be "meaning," as used adjectivally, or rather, "full of meaning"; but the
full idea would be : "that appears to be thinking for itself," and therefore a
term somewhat akin to "significative" or "suggestive."—In the succeeding
paragraph, I must explain that "sinnlich" presents one with the usual difficulties attendant upon the utter confusion of almost all our English adjectives
derived from "sense"; for the most part I have preferred to translate this
word as "physical," but *here* it was obviously necessary to employ "sensuous,"
albeit with a caution against its being taken in a derogatory significance.—TR.

functions. In order to be properly equipped for that
inquiry, we must in the first place settle one thing : *the
complete difference in the purely sensuous utterance of the
Orchestra, from the likewise purely sensuous utterance of the
Vocal tone-mass.* The Orchestra is as different from that
Vocal-tone-mass as the above-named Instrumental consonant from the consonant of Speech, and consequently, as
are the 'open sounds' which are respectively conditioned
or determined by the one and the other. The instrumental-
consonant governs once and for all *each* tone producible
upon that instrument : whereas the vocal tone of Speech,
by the very play of its initial sounds, is always coming-by
an other, an infinitely varied tint. It is this that makes the
tone-organ of the human voice the richest and completest,
to wit the most organically-conditioned, of them all.
Compared with *it*, the most complex blend of orchestral
tone-colours conceivable must needs seem poverty-stricken,
—an experience which certainly cannot be made by those
people who hear the human voice employed by our modern
singers in imitation of the orchestral instrument, with a
total omission of the consonants and retention of one
solitary favoured vowel ; and who straightway go themes-
selves and handle that human voice as an instrument, by
writing, for instance, duets between a soprano and a
clarinet, a tenor and a French horn.

Were we entirely to neglect the fact that the Singer,
whom *we* mean, is a human being artistically representing
human beings, and that the artistic outpours of his Feeling
are ordered by the highest necessity of transforming a
thought into a Man : yet even the purely sensuous aspect
of his articulate voice (*Sprachgesangston*), in the infinite
variety that comes from its characteristic play of vowels
and consonants, would prove it not only a far *richer* tone-
organ than the orchestral instrument, but also one entirely
distinct therefrom ; and this distinction of the physical
organ of tone determines also, once for all, the whole
attitude which the Orchestra has to take towards the
Acting Singer.

The orchestra, in the first place, has to assure us that the tone, the melody, and the characteristic phrasing (*Vortrag*) of the singer, are validly conditioned and vindicated by the inner sphere of Musical Harmony. This faculty the orchestra wins as a tone-body set loose from the song-tone and the singer's melody: a body voluntarily, and—for sake of justifying its own independence—sympathetically subordinating itself to the singer; but it never wins it by attempting to actually mingle in the song-tone. If we allow a melody sung by the human voice to be accompanied by instruments in such a fashion, that that integral factor of the whole harmony which lies in the notes (*Intervallen*) of the melody shall be left out of the harmonic body of the accompaniment, and kept, as it were, for the singing voice to make good : then we shall become aware at once that the harmony is absolutely incomplete, and the melody has *not* been harmonically vindicated ; precisely because our ear, detecting the great distinction between the sensuous tone-colour of the instruments and that of the human voice, instinctively *severs* the one from the other, and thus receives the mere impression of two diverse ' moments '—a melody not adequately vindicated by its harmony, and a defective harmonic accompaniment. This uncommonly weighty experience, which has never yet been properly followed up, may explain a large share of the ineffectiveness of our opera-*melodik* of hitherto, and teach us about the countless errors into which we have fallen in our handling of vocal melody, when coupled with the orchestra. And this is the very spot, to provide ourselves with that instruction.

Absolute Melody, such as we have employed in Opera hitherto, and such as our purely musical good-pleasure has reconstructed by ringing the changes on our old acquaint-ances, Volkslied and Dance-melody—in the absence of a Word-verse that should necessarily shape *itself* into a melody,—this Absolute Melody, looked at closely, was ever a thing translated from the instruments into the human voice. By an involuntary error we have always thought of the human voice as a, merely to be specially courted, orchestral instrument ; and as such we have woven it also into the orchestral accompaniment. This inter-weaving sometimes happened in the manner I have already instanced, namely the human voice was employed as an integral factor of the instrumental harmony,—but some-times it was effected by the accompaniment reduplicating the melody, in addition to its own harmonic duties ; where-by the orchestra at any rate was rounded into an intelli-gible whole, but by that very finish it exposed the melody's character as belonging exclusively to instrumental music. Through the complete adoption of the melody into the orchestra, as thus found needful, the musician confessed that this melody was one which, completely vindicated in its harmony by nothing but the *whole like mass* of tone, could also be intelligibly delivered by that mass alone. The human voice's delivery of the melody, on top of this har-monically and melodically completed body of tone, seemed utterly superfluous and like a second, disfiguring head un-naturally planted on its shoulders. The hearer quite in-stinctively perceived this incongruity : he never understood the singer's melody, until it came to him rid of the play of vowels and consonants—obstructive to *this* melody—which disturbed his comprehension of its Absolute self; until he heard it delivered by the instruments alone. That not until they have been played to the public by the Orchestra, in concerts or at the change of guard,—or on some har-monic instrument,—that not till then, have our most favourite operatic melodies been really understood by the public; and that they have first gained currency with it, when it could hum them without words,—this notorious fact might have long since enlightened us as to Opera's entirely false conception of vocal melody. This melody was Vocal only inasmuch as it was assigned to the human voice, to deliver in its purely instrumental capacity,— a capacity in whose unfoldment the voice felt terribly

hampered by the vowels and consonants of the words, and
for whose sake Vocal-art has also quite logically taken a
development such as we may see to-day arrived at its most
ingéné pitch of wordlessness, amongst our modern opera-
singers.

But this disparity between the tone-colour of the
Orchestra and that of the Human Voice has come the most
startlingly to light, where serious tone-masters * have striven
for a characteristic garment for dramatic melody.   Since
they involuntarily had in ear that aforesaid "instrumental-
melody," as their motives' only bond of purely-musical
comprehensibility, they sought to give it a suggestive and
exact expression by means of an uncommonly ingenious
instrumental accompaniment, harmonically and rhythmically accenting note by note, and word for word ; and thus
they arrived at turning out musical periods in which, the
more carefully that instrumental accompaniment was inter-
woven with the motives of the human voice, yet the ear
instinctively took up two separate things—an unseizable
voice-part whose conditionments and explanation had been
transferred to the accompaniment, and an accompaniment
which in itself remained an inexplicable chaos, through its
instinctive severance from the voice.   The fault at bottom
of this practice was thus a twofold one.   Firstly : an ignoring
of the determinative nature of Poetic Song-melody, for
which there was substituted an Absolute Melody, drawn
from instrumental music; and secondly : an ignoring of the
thorough difference in tone-colour † between the Human

* "Ernste Tonmeister,"—from the expression "characteristic," it is evident that the reference is to Meyerbeer.—TR.

† The abstract musician did not even detect the complete immiscibility of the
timbres, for instance, of the pianoforte and the violin. A major portion of
his artistic life's-joy consisted in playing pianoforte sonatas with violin, &c.,
without becoming aware that he was only bringing an imaginary music to
light, not bringing to the ear a real one. Thus his hearing was swamped by
his sight ; for what he heard, was nothing but a group of harmonic abstractions, to which alone his sense of hearing still was sensitive, whereas the living
flesh of musical expression was bound to stay entirely unheeded by him.—
R. WAGNER.

Voice and the Orchestral Instruments, with which one had intermingled the voice for purely musical ends.

If we turn aside a moment, to denote the peculiar character of Song-melody, it is with the object of once more calling plainly to mind the fact that, not only in sense but also in sound, it has sprung from, and is conditioned by, the Word-verse. As touching its sense, its source lies in the nature of the Poetic Aim, in its struggle for an understanding through the Feeling,—as touching its physical semblance, in the organ of the Understanding, namely Word-speech. Starting from this conditioning source, it develops into an enouncement of the purely emotional Content of the verse, through a dissolution of the vowel into the musical tone ; and here it turns its purely musical side towards the element of Music proper, from which alone this side obtains the enablement for its appearance, whereas it keeps the other side of its total aspect (*gesammterscheinung*) turned unswervingly towards the significative (*sinnvollen*) element of word-speech, from whence it took its first conditions. In this attitude the Verse-melody becomes the uniting bond and messenger between Word-speech and Tone-speech, as the offspring of the marriage of Poetry with Music, the embodied love-moment of both arts. But it thus is more withal, and stands on a higher level, than Poetry's verse or Music's absolute melody ; and its appearance—alike conditioned by, and redeeming either side—becomes only possible in the event of their *each* supporting its plastic, independent message. This must be *upheld* by both conditioning elements, but well *distinguished* from them ; and, for the welfare of both arts, they must continuously vindicate it, but never swamp it by admixture of their individualities with its own.*

If we want to figure to ourselves this melody's correct

---

* I have been obliged here to sort out the constituents of one sentence, and arrange them into two.—TR.

relation to the orchestra, we may do it in the following image.

A little while back we compared the Orchestra, as the *conqueror* * of the waves of Harmony, to an ocean-ship : this was in the sense wherein we take "sea-voyage" ("*Seefahrt*") as synonymous with "a voyage aboard" ("*Schiffahrt*"). For sake of a fresh and independent simile,† we must now consider the Orchestra, in its capacity of "conquered Harmony"—as we were bound to call it later, —no longer as the ocean, but as a limpid mountain-lake, lit by the sun-rays to its very bottom ; a lake whose whole surrounding shores are plainly visible from every point upon it.—From tree-stems reared upon the rocky soil of hills rolled down from everlasting, a *boat* has now been built ; bound fast with iron clamps, well-found with oars and rudder, it has been shaped and fitted closely to the Aim of its carrying by the waters, of ploughing its way athwart them. This boat, now launched upon the lake, urged forward by the pulsing oars, and guided by its helm, is the *verse-melody* of the Dramatic Singer, when borne upon the sounding surges of the Orchestra. The boat is a thing quite other than the mirror of the lake, and yet it has been carpentered and fitted with sole regard to the water and exact adjustment to its qualities ; on land the boat is. of no use at all, or at most for breaking into common fire-wood, to feed the burgher's kitchen hearth. Only on the lake, does it become a joyous thing of life ; carried and yet self-moving, moved and yet ever at rest ; drawing ever back to it our gaze, when it sweeps across the lake ; like the human-shewing Aim of the whole existence of that throbbing sheet of waters, which before had seemed to us without a purpose.—Yet, the pinnace does not float upon the surface of the water-mirror : the lake can carry it in one

* "Bewältiger,"—"ruler," or "tamer" ; we all know the allegorical lady who "rules the waves."—TR.

† Never can an object be completely like the thing with which it is compared, but only assert its likeness in one direction, not in all ; completely alike, are never the objects of organic, but only those of mechanical formation.—R. WAGNER.

steady track, only on condition that it plunges in the water the one full portion of its fronting body.   A flimsy plank, that merely grazed the surface of the lake, would be tossed hither and thither by the waves, whichever way their waters streamed ; whereas a lumpish stone, again, must be drowned at once beneath them.   But not only with one full side of its body does the boat embed itself within the lake, but the helm which governs its direction, and the oar which gives its motion, both gain alike that governing and moving force from nothing but their contact with the water, which first empowers the effective pressure of the guiding hand. With every forward thrust, the oar cuts deep into the ringing reach of waters ; raised out, it lets the clinging drip flow back again in drops of Melody.

There is no need to underline this likeness, to make clear my meaning as to the relation involved in the contact of the word-tone-melody of the human voice with the orchestra; for this relation is completely set forth therein,— as will be still more obvious to us if we call our old friend, the Opera-melody proper, the fruitless attempt of the Musician to condense into a seaworthy boat the waters of the lake themselves.

It only remains for us to consider the Orchestra in its capacity of an independent (*selbständiges*) element, in itself distinct from that Verse-melody ; and to assure ourselves of its aptitude for carrying that melody, not only through making manifest the harmony conditioning it [*sie*, i.e. the melody] from a purely musical standpoint, but also through its own peculiar, its endlessly expressive faculty of speech : for carrying it, as the lake the pinnace.

V.

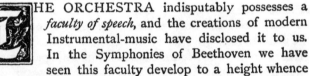

HE ORCHESTRA indisputably possesses a *faculty of speech*, and the creations of modern Instrumental-music have disclosed it to us. In the Symphonies of Beethoven we have seen this faculty develop to a height whence it felt thrust on to speak out That which, by its very nature, it can not speak out. Now that in the Wordverse melody we have brought it That which *it* could not speak out, and have assigned to it, as carrier of this kindred melody, the office in which—completely eased in mind—it is to speak out nothing but what its nature fits *it* alone to speak: now, we have plainly to denote this Speaking-faculty of the Orchestra as the faculty of uttering the *unspeakable*.

This definition, however, is not to convey the idea of a merely imaginary thing, but of a thing quite real and palpable.

We have seen that the Orchestra is no mere compost of washy tone-ingredients, but consists of a rich association of instruments—with unbounded power of adding to its numbers; whilst each of these is a definite individuality, and invests the tone produced by it with an equally individual garment. A tone-mass without some such individual distinction between its members is nowhere to be found, and can at best be thought, but never realised. But what determines the Individuality, in the present case, is—as we have seen—the particular idiosyncrasy of the unit instrument, whose consonant-like timbre converts into a thing apart, as it were, the vowel of the tone produced. Whereas, however, this consonantal timbre can never lift itself to the suggestiveness of the Wordspeech-consonant's appeal to Feeling's understanding, nor is it capable of that consonant's change and consequent play of influence upon the vowel, so neither can the Tone-speech of an instrument ever condense itself to an expression such as that attainable solely by the organ of the Understanding, namely Word-speech; yet, as pure organ of the Feeling, it speaks out the very thing which Word-speech in itself can *not* speak out,— without further ado, then : That which, looked at from the standpoint of our human intellect, is *the Unspeakable*. That this Unspeakable is not a thing unutterable *per se*, but merely unutterable through the organ of our Understanding; thus, not a mere fancy, but a reality,—this is shewn plainly enough by the Instruments of the orchestra themselves, whereof each for itself, and infinitely more richly in its changeful union with other instruments, speaks out quite clearly and intelligibly.*

Let us first take into view that Unspeakable which the Orchestra can express with greatest definition, and indeed, in union with another thing unspeakable,—*with Gesture*.

The bodily Gesture, as determined by an inner emotion which proclaims itself in the significant movements of certain members most capable of expression, and finally in the features of the face,—this bodily Gesture is insofar a thing unutterable, as Speech can only hint-at or describe it, whereas those members or those features were the only channels for its actual utterance. Something that Word-speech can fully impart, i.e. an object communicable *by* the Understanding *to* the Understanding, has no need at all of accompaniment or reinforcement by Gesture ; nay, unneedful gestures could only mar the message. With such a message, however, as we have seen above, neither is the sensory organ of the recipient Hearing roused, but merely serves as an uninterested go-between. But a message

---

* This easy explanation of the " Unspeakable " one might extend, perhaps not altogether wrongly, to the whole matter of Religious Philosophy ; for although that matter is given out as *absolutely* unutterable, from the standpoin of the *speaker*, yet mayhap it is utterable enough if only the fitting organ be employed.—R. WAGNER.

This note should be remembered by those who aver that Wagner's "metaphysical " view of Music, in the *Beethoven* essay, was *merely* derived from Schopenhauer.—TR.

which Word-speech cannot fully and convincingly convey to *Feeling*—which here has also to be roused,—thus an expression which borders on Passion (*Affekt*), imperatively needs strengthening through a concomitant gesture. We thus see that where the Hearing is to be roused to greater 'sensuous' interest, the messenger involuntarily has to address the eye as well : Eye and Ear must mutually assure each other of a higher-pitched message, before they can transmit it convincingly to the Feeling.

Now, the gesture, in its needful message to the eye, delivered precisely That which word-speech was incompetent to express,—had the latter been able to do so, the gesture would have been superfluous and disturbing. The eye was thus aroused by the gesture in a way which still lacked its fitting counterpart, of a message to the ear : but this counterpart is needful, for rounding the expression into one completely understandable by Feeling. True that the word-verse, roused into melody, at last dissolves the intellectual-content of the original verbal message into an emotional-content : but in this melody there is not as yet contained that 'moment' of the message to the ear which shall completely answer to the gesture; for precisely in this [verse-]melody, as the *most highly roused* expression of the words, lay the first *incitement* to intensify the gesture, —namely, to supply the corroborative 'moment' which the melody still needed, and needed just because it could not as yet bring anything of its own to exactly correspond thereto. The verse-melody, then, has contained only the antecedent condition for the gesture. That, however, which is to vindicate the gesture before the judgment-seat of Feeling, in the same way as the speaking-verse was to be vindicated through the melody, or the melody to be vindicated—or better : *elucidated*—through the harmony,— That lies beyond the power of *this* melody which arose from out the *speaking*-verse, and which with one essential aspect of its body remains strictly conditioned by Word-speech ; for it was Word-speech, that could not deliver the particular tale of Gesture, and therefore called the latter to

her aid ; and now, she positively cannot find a completely
fitting vehicle for conveying it to the longing Ear.—But
now there comes the language of the Orchestra, completely
sundered from this Word-speech ; and that tale of Gesture's,
which was unutterable in Word-Tone speech, the Orchestra
is just as able to impart to the Ear as the gesture itself
imparts it to the Eye.

This faculty the Orchestra has won from its accompaniment of the most physical of all gestures, the *Dance-gesture*,
to which such an accompaniment was a necessity dictated
by its very essence, to make its message understandable ;
since the gestures of Dance, like Gesture in general, bear
much the same relation to the orchestral melody as the
word-verse bears to the vocal melody thereby conditioned.
So that Gesture *and* Orchestral-melody, together, first form
such a whole, a thing so intelligible in itself, as Word-Tone-
melody forms for *its* part.—Their most physical point of
contact, i.e. the point where both—the one in Space, the
other in Time : the one to the eye, the other to the ear—
displayed themselves as altogether like and mutually conditioned,—Dance-gesture and Orchestra had this common
point in *Rhythm ;* and after each departure from it, to this
point they must perforce return in order to stay or to
become intelligible, for it is *it* that lays bare their prime
affinity.   But from this point both Gesture and Orchestra
expand, in equal measure, to their respective idiosyncrasies
of speaking-power.   Just as Gesture reveals to the eye a
thing which *she alone* can utter, so the Orchestra conveys
to the ear a something exactly answering to that revelation,
precisely in the same way as Musical Rhythm, at the
starting-point of their kinship, explained to the *ear* the
thing revealed to the *eye* in the most palpable moments of
the dance.   The setting down of the uplifted foot was the
same thing to the eye, as to the ear was the accentuated
downbeat of the bar ; and thus also the mobile instrumental
tone-figure, melodically uniting the down-beats of the bar,
is altogether the same thing to the ear, as to the eye is the
movement of the feet, or other expressive members of the
body, in the intervals between their exchange.

Now, the farther Gesture departs from her definite, but at like time her most straitened basis,—that of the dance ; the more sparingly she distributes her sharpest accents, in the most manifold and delicate expressional nuances to attain an endless aptitude for speech : so much the more manifold and delicate become the tone-figures of Instrumental speech, which, to convincingly impart the Unspeakable of Gesture, now wins a melodic Expression immeasurable in its wealth of idiom.   Nor can either its content or its form be characterised in Word-speech, for very reason that they are already *completely* made known to the ear through the Orchestral-melody, and only further wait adoption by the eye ; and that, as the content and form of the gesture answering to this melody.

That this idiomatic language of the Orchestra is a long way from having evolved in Opera to the fulness of which it is capable, is to be explained by the fact—already mentioned in its proper place—that, with its utter lack of a genuine dramatic basis, the Opera has always drawn its by-play directly from the pantomimic dance.   These Ballet-mimetics had the very narrowest range of movement and gesture, and at last were stereotyped into settled make-believes, because they altogether lacked the necessary conditions that might have prescribed, and alike explained, a greater multiplicity.   Such conditions are contained in Word-speech ; and indeed, no word-speech *dragged-on* to help, but one that *summons* Gesture to lend *her* help. As though instinctively aware of its potentiality, the Orchestra sought in absolute Instrumental-music, set loose from pantomime, for that heightened power of speech which it thus could not gain in Pantomime or Opera ; and we have seen that this effort, when put forth in its highest force and sincerity, must lead to the longing for a justification through the Word, and through Gesture prompted by the Word.   We now have only to learn, from the other side, how the complete realisement of the Poetic Aim is in turn to be effected by nothing but the highest, the most lucid vindication of the Word-verse-melody through the perfected language of the Orchestra, in its alliance with Gesture.

In its will to realise itself in Drama, the Poetic Aim stipulates for the highest and most manifold expression that Gesture owns: yes, it demands from her a force, diversity, a finesse and mobility, such as nowhere but in Drama can come to 'necessary' show, and which are therefore to be *invented* of a quite specific character; for the Dramatic Action, with all its motives, is an action lifted high above life, and intensified to the point of Wonder. The compact moments and motives of action were only to be made intelligible to Feeling by means of an equally concise expression, which was to rise from the word-verse to a melody immediately determining the Feeling. Now, just as this utterance intensifies itself to Melody, so it necessarily requires an intensifying of the gestures which it prompts, a lifting of them above the measure of those of ordinary Talk (*Redegebärde*). Moreover this Gesture, in keeping with the character of Drama, is no mere monologue of a solitary individual, but intensifies itself to utmost manifoldness,—so to say, to a "many-voiced" gesture, — through the characteristic reaction of the mutual encounter of *many* individuals. The dramatic-aim not only draws within its sphere the inner emotion *per se*, but, for sake of its own realising, it specifically demands that this emotion shall be proclaimed in the outer, bodily appearance of the performers. Pantomime contented itself with typical masks, for the stature, bearing, and dress of the performers: the all-enabled Drama tears away these typical masks—since it possesses the warranty therefor, in its faculty of Speech,—and shews the performers as specific Individualities, proclaiming themselves precisely *thus* and not otherwise. Wherefore the dramatic-aim prescribes the stature, mien, bearing, motion and dress of the performer, down to their tiniest detail, so that at every instant he may appear as this one, this swiftly and definitely knowable Individuality, in full distinction from its fellows. This drastic distinction of the

X

one individuality is only to be achieved, however, when all
its fellows, when all the individualities in touch with it,
display themselves with an equally sure and drastic
definition.

Let us now picture to ourselves such sharp-cut individualities as these, appearing in the endless change of
correlations from whence evolve the divers moments and
motives of the Action ; and let us figure the infinitely
enkindling impression which their aspect must produce on
our captive eye : then we shall comprehend alike the Hearing's need of an impression intelligible to *it*, in turn, and
completely answering to this impression on the Sight,—an
impression through which the latter shall appear supple-
mented, vindicated, or elucidated ; for "At the mouth of
two witnesses shall the (whole) matter be (first) established."

What the ear is longing to distinguish, however, is precisely the Unspeakable of the impression received by the
eye,—That whose self and motion the poetic-aim merely
summoned through its nearest organ, Word-speech, yet
cannot now convincingly impart to Hearing. Were this
show not present to the eye, then poetic Speech might feel
warranted in imparting to Phantasy a description of the
thing imagined ; but now that at bidding of the highest
Poetic-aim it offers itself directly to the eye, a verbal
description not only is entirely superfluous, but would stay
quite unimpressive to the ear. That which Poetry could
not speak out, however, is imparted to the ear by precisely
the language of the Orchestra ; and just from the longing
of the Ear, incited by her sister Eye, does this language
win a new immeasurable power : a power forever slumber-
ing, *without* this incitation, or—if woken by its own initiative
—proclaiming itself un-understandably.

Even for this enhancement of its task, the Orchestra's
power-of-speech relies in the first place on a kinship with

the language of Gesture, such as we have seen it displaying in the dance. In tone-figures peculiar to the individual character of specially appropriate instruments, and shaping themselves into the specific Orchestral-melody * through an equally appropriate blending of these characteristics, it speaks out That which is now revealing itself to the eye in physical Show and by means of Gesture; and speaks it out *so far* as there has been no need for any third party—to wit, for intermeddling Word-speech—to explain the Show and Gesture, for their understanding by the eye, or to interpret their meaning to the directly-seizing ear.

Let us come to closer terms about this matter.—We commonly say: "I read it in thine eye"; which means: "In a way intelligible to *it* alone, my eye perceives in the look of thine an instinctive feeling indwelling in thee, which I instinctively, in turn, now feel with thee."—Now, if we extend the eye's receptivity to a faculty for taking in the whole outward stature of the man it looks on, his appearance, bearing and gestures, then we have to admit that the eye can grasp and understand the utterance † of this man, past all mistake: provided only, he manifests himself in *full instinctiveness*, is entirely at one with himself within, and utters his inner promptings with undisguised sincerity. But the moments in which man declares himself thus plainly, are solely those of most perfect repose or highest agitation: what lie between these extremes, are transitions which only partake of the character of genuine passion in direct ratio as they either approach their state of highest agitation, or return therefrom, appeased, to a harmonious repose. These transitions consist of a mixture of arbitrary,

---

* "Zur eigenthümlichen Orchestermelodie,"—i.e. as distinguished from the "remembrances and forebodings" which the Orchestra borrows from the "verse-melody," in its capacity immediately to be discussed.—This paragraph presented some difficulty until I realised that the "so far" (*so weit*), *italicised* in the German, naturally implies "but no farther," and thus constitutes a link between the present and the preceding section.—TR.

† "Äusserung,"—I may remind the reader that "utterance" does not necessarily imply "speech," but merely "a giving, or shewing, out."—TR.

reflective Will (*reflektirter Willensthätigkeit*) with non-conscious, necessary Emotion (*Empfindung*) : their guidance along the necessary channel of instinctive feeling,—with an unflagging flow towards, and final disembouchment into true Emotion, no longer hemmed and conditioned by the reflective Understanding,—*this* is the substance of the Dramatic poet's Aim,* and for this he finds the sole empowering expression in just the Wordverse-Melody, the blossom of that organic speech of Word-and-Tone which turns its one side to the reflective Understanding, but its other to the instinctive Feeling. Gesture (meaning thereby the whole message of man's outward semblance to the eye) takes but a conditional share in this transition, since she has only *one* aspect, and that, the emotional side wherewith she fronts the eye : whereas the side which she conceals from the eye is the very same as that which Word-Tone-speech turns toward the Understanding, and would therefore stay entirely hidden from the Feeling, were it not that *both* sides of Word-Tone-speech address the ear,—albeit one of them less forcibly—and that the ear may thus acquire an added faculty of intelligibly conveying to the Feeling even this side averted from the eye.

This faculty the ear acquires through the language of the Orchestra, which is able to attach itself just as intimately to the verse-melody as earlier to the gesture, and thus to develop into a messenger of the very *Thought* itself, transmitting it to Feeling : and, indeed, of that Thought which the present † verse-melody—as the utterance of a mixed emotion, not yet fully at one with itself—neither can nor will speak out ; but which can still less be imparted by the gesture to the eye, since Gesture is the most present thing

---

* Literally " the Content of the poetic Aim in Drama" (*der Inhalt der dichterischen Absicht im Drama*).   Although I have been obliged to employ "substance" instead of "content," in this particular sentence, I wish to lay stress upon the latter term, as a connecting bond with earlier chapters ; whilst the "Aim" itself should be taken in the light of pages 102 and 208-10.—Tr.

† "Gegenwärtige,"—it is rather amusing to find that our English diction- aries are compelled to clear up their definitions of "present" by negatives such as "not past or future."—Tr.

of all, being conditioned by the emotion given out in the verse-melody, and therefore in this instance is as indefinite as itself, or expresses alone this indefiniteness without being able to clearly illustrate the genuine emotion. In the Verse-melody not only is Word-speech combined with Tone-speech, but also the thing which both these organs express : to wit, the absent with the present, the thought with the emotion. The *present* part of it is the instinctive feeling, in its necessary pour into the musical expression of the melody; the non-present part is the abstract thought, in its bondage to the word-phrase, as an arbitrary moment of reflection.—Let us define more closely what we have to understand by this " thought."

Here, also, we shall soon arrive at a clear idea, if we take the thing from an artistic standpoint, and go back to its ' sensuous ' derivation.

A thing we cannot utter through any single medium, nor through them all combined, even if we *would,*—such a thing is naught and nothing. On the other hand, everything for which we find an expression is also something real, and we may recognise its reality if we take the trouble to decipher the expression which we *instinctively* employ for the thing. The expression : Thought, is very easily explainable, if only we go back to its sensuous speech-root. A " thought " * is the " thin " image in our mind, of a non-present, but yet a real " thing." † By its [of the word " thought "] origin, this Non-present is a real, a physically

---

* " Ein Gedanke ist das im ' Gedenken ' uns ' dünkende ' Bild eines Wirklichen, aber Ungegenwärtigen."—Of course it is impossible to fit this derivation with current English words, but it is probable that " thing " is derived from the same root as " think," while Ogilvie tells us that in Icelandic " thanki " is the term for " mind." To these derivations one might add " than " and " then," each of which implies either absence or distance.—TR.

† In a similar way we may prettily explain " Geist " (ghost, or spirit) by its kindred root " giessen " (to pour out) : its natural meaning is " that which *pours itself out* " from us, just as the perfume is that which spreads itself, which pours itself, from the flower.—R. WAGNER.—This note was continued in the

apprehended object, which has made a definite impression on us in another place, or at another time : this *im*pression has lain hold upon our feeling,* and, to impart the latter to our fellows, we have been forced to invent an *ex*pression which shall convey the object's generic impression in terms of the sentience of mankind at large. We thus could only take the object up into us according to the impression which it made upon our senses ; and this impression, regulated in its turn by our sensory *faculty*, is the image that appears to be (*dünkt*) the object itself, when we *think of* it (*im* Gedenken). 'Thinking-of' and 'remembering,' then, are really one and the same thing ; and a 'thought' is the image impressed upon our sensory faculty by an object, yet moulded by that faculty itself and now brought

first edition, by : " The ' Spirit ' of Theology, on the other hand, is based upon a reversal of this natural process ; for there—in keeping with the Christian mythos—it has become the thing poured out *upon* us from above."—TR.

* " Empfindung " is one of those words which we never can render exactly, in English, as will be seen from the interpretations given in *Flügel's Dictionary*, viz : " sensation ; sense ; perception ; feeling ; sentiment " ; to which I may add " emotion." Strictly speaking, it is " something which we have *found* outside us, and taken *into* us." From the translator's point of view, it is much to be regretted that our author should have so religiously adhered to the *one* term here, seeing that his own " memory " was one of the most remarkable of his mental features, and therefore a more varied exposition of the nature of that faculty—even at the cost of a digression—would have been of the greatest value. As I have been compelled to make an arbitrary selection of the equivalents for " Empfindung," I append the original : "Dieses Ungegenwärtige ist seinem Ursprunge nach ein wirklicher, sinnlich wahrgenommener Gegenstand, der auf uns an einem anderen Orte oder zu einer anderen Zeit einen bestimmten Eindruck gemacht hat : dieser Eindruck hat sich unserer Empfindung bemächtigt, für die wir, um sie mitzutheilen, einen Ausdruck erfinden mussten, der dem Eindrucke des Gegenstandes nach dem allgemein menschlichen Gattungsempfindungsvermögen entsprach. Den Gegenstand konnten wir somit nur nach dem Eindrucke in uns aufnehmen, den er auf unsere Empfindung machte, und dieser von unserem Empfindungsvermögen wiederum bestimmte Eindruck ist das Bild, das uns im *Gedenken* der Gegenstand selbst dünkt. Gedenken und Erinnerung ist somit dasselbe, und in Wahrheit ist der Gedanke das in der Erinnerung wiederkehrende Bild, welches —als Eindruck von einem Gegenstande auf unsere Empfindung—von dieser Empfindung selbst gestaltet, und von der gedenkenden Erinnerung, diesem Zeugnisse von dem dauernden Vermögen der Empfindung und der Kraft des auf sie gemachten Eindruckes, der Empfindung selbst zu lebhafter Erregung, zum Nachempfinden des Eindruckes, wieder vorgeführt wird."—TR.

back by musing Memory—that witness to both the force of the impression and the lasting power of its receiver,—brought back to re-arouse the Feeling, itself, into an after-sense of the impression.   We here have nothing to do with Thought's development to the power of combination, i.e. of binding together all self-won or transmitted images of objects passed away from 'presence,' but whose impressions are treasured-up in memory,—with Thinking, such as we meet it in philosophic Science,—for the Poet's path leads out of Philosophy and into Art-work, into a *realisement of the thought* in physical presence.

Only one point more, have we to determine.   A thing which has not made an impression on our feelings (*Empfindung*) at the first, neither can we *think* it; and the antecedent emotional-phase (*Empfindungserscheinung*) is the conditionor of the shape in which the thought shall be enounced.   So that even Thought is roused by the emotion, and must necessarily flow back again into Emotion; for *a thought is the bond between an absent and a present emotion, each struggling for enouncement.*

Now, as it were before our eyes, the poet's Verse-Melody materialises * the thought,—i.e. the non-present emotion recalled by memory,—converting it into a present, an actually observable emotion.   In its sheer words this Verse-Melody contains the non-present but *conditioning* emotion, as described from memory and thought; in its purely musical melody it contains the *conditioned*, the new, the 'present' emotion into which that instigating thought resolves itself, as into its kindred new embodiment. Evolved and vindicated, before our eyes, by the recollection of an earlier emotion; directly moving, and surely influencing the sympathetic Feeling, by its sound : the emotion

---

* "Verwirklicht,"—lit. " realises " ; but the meaning is so obviously that of : " makes palpable to the senses," that perhaps "materialises "—in the sense given it by the Spiritualists—will best convey the idea.   This whole paragraph is one of the hardest to *translate* in all the book, owing to the play with " Gedenken " (recollection) and " Gedanke " (thought), and also to an exceptionally complex construction, apparently the fruit of over-haste.   I must therefore beg for a little extra indulgence here.—TR.

manifested in this melody is a thing which now belongs as much to us, to whom it has been imparted, as to him who has imparted it; and just as it comes back to him hereafter as a thought,—i.e. a remembrance,—so can *we*, also, preserve it as a thought.—Pondering on this last emotional-phase, and driven by its memory, in turn, to the enouncement of yet a new, of yet another 'present' emotion, our informant now takes up this reminiscence as a mere non-present 'moment,' briefly shadowing or hinting it to the Understanding's recollection; exactly as in the previous verse—wherein it came to a definite melodic show, now handed over to the memory—he employed the reminiscence of an earlier emotion, no longer actively within our mind, for the *thought* engendering a fresh emotion. But *we*, we who receive the new message, are able, through our Hearing, to hold fast that now merely-thought-of emotion *in all its pure-melodic record*: it has become the property of pure Music, and, when brought again to physical show by the Orchestra's appropriate expression, to us it appears as *the presentment, the realisement*, of what the actor has just told us as a mere *thing of thought*. Such a melody, once imparted to us by the actor as the outpour of an emotion, and now expressively delivered by the orchestra at an instant when the person represented merely nurses that emotion in his memory,—such a melody materialises for us this personage's Thought. Nay, even where the present speaker appears no longer conscious of that emotion, its characteristic sounding by the orchestra is able to stir within us an emotion which—in its filling-out of a conjuncture, its clearing-up of a situation, through suggesting motives that are well enough contained therein but cannot come to vivid light within its representable moments—for us becomes a *thought*, yet in itself is *more* than Thought, for it is the thought's *Emotional-content brought to presence*.

Here, when employed for the highest realisement of the poetic-aim, the musician's power is rendered boundless, through the Orchestra.—Without the stipulations of such an aim, the absolute musician has heretofore imagined that he had really to do with thoughts and combinations of thoughts. Yet, when musical themes were point-blank christened "thoughts," this was either a thoughtless misnomer, or the token of an illusion on the part of the musician ; he gave the name of "thought" to a theme in whose conception he had certainly thought something himself, but which no one understood, except at utmost those he told in sober words what he had thought, thereby inviting them to think this something into the theme for themselves as well. Music cannot think : but she can materialise thoughts, i.e. she can give forth their emotional-contents as no longer merely recollected, but made present. This she can only do, however, when her own manifestment is conditioned by a Poetic Aim, and when this latter, again, reveals itself as no mere thing of thought, but a thing expounded in the first place by the organ of the Understanding, namely Word-speech. A musical motive (*Motiv*) can produce a definite impression on the Feeling, inciting it to a function akin to Thought, only when the emotion uttered in that motive has been definitely conditioned by a definite object, and proclaimed by a definite individual before our very eyes. The omission of these condition-ments sets a musical motive before the Feeling in a most indefinite light ; and an indefinite thing may return in the same garment as often as one pleases, yet it will remain a mere recurrence of the Indefinite, and we shall neither be in a position to justify it by any felt necessity of its appear-ance, nor, therefore, to associate it with anything else.—But a musical motive into which the thought-filled Wordverse of a dramatic performer has poured itself—so to say, before our eyes—is a thing conditioned by Necessity : with its return a *definite* emotion is discernibly conveyed to us, and conveyed to *us* through the physical agency of the Orchestra, albeit now unspoken by the performer ; for the latter *now* feels driven to give voice to a fresh emotion, derived in turn from that earlier one. Wherefore the con-current sounding of such a motive unites for us the conditioning, the non-present emotion with the emotion

conditioned thereby and coming at this instant into voice;
and inasmuch as we thus make our Feeling a living witness
to the organic growth of one definite emotion from out
another, we give to it the faculty of thinking : nay, we here
give it a faculty of higher rank than Thinking, to wit, the
instinctive *knowledge* of a thought made real in Emotion.

Before we proceed to a discussion of the results which
follow from the Orchestra's above-suggested faculty of
speech, for the shaping of the Drama, we must determine
another of its salient capabilities, so as to take that faculty's
full compass. — The capability to which we here refer,
comes to the Orchestra from a union of those aptitudes
which have accrued to it from its alliance with Gesture, on
the one hand, and its remembrance of the Verse-melody on
the other. Just as Gesture, originating in the most physical
of Dance's postures, has evolved to the most intellectual
Mimik ; just as Verse-melody, from a mere thinking of an
emotion, has advanced to the most ' present ' enouncement
of an emotion : so the speaking-faculty of the Orchestra—
which has won from both its shaping force, and fed and
flourished on their utmost ripening—so does it grow from
out this double source to a highest special capability,
wherein we see the two divided arms of the orchestral
river, now richly tinged by tributary brooks and streams,
as though unite again into one common flow. To wit :
where gesture lapses into rest, and the melodic discourse
of the actor hushes,—thus where the drama prepares its
future course in inner moods as yet unuttered,—there may
these still unspoken moods be spoken by the Orchestra in
such a way, that their utterance shall bear the character of
a *foreboding* necessitated by the poet's Aim.

A Foreboding is the herald of an emotion as yet unspoken-out,—because as yet unspeakable, in the sense of
our customary word-speech. Unspeakable, is any emotion
which is not as yet defined ; and it is undefined, so long as

it has not been yet determined through a fitting *object.* The first thrill of this emotion, the Foreboding, is thus its instinctive longing for definement through an object; through an object which it predetermines, in its turn, by the force of its own need; moreover, an object which must answer to it, and for which it therefore waits. In its manifestment as a foreboding, I might compare the emotional-fund to a well-tuned harp, whose strings are sounding to the touch of passing winds, and wait the player who shall grasp them into shapely chords.

Such a presentiment as this, has the poet to wake within us, *in order, through its longing, to make us necessary sharers in the creation of his artwork.* By calling forth this longing, he provides himself with the conditioning force, in our aroused receptiveness, which alone can make it possible for him to shape the creatures of his fancy in accordance with his settled Aim. In the evocation of moods such as the poet needs must wake in us, if he is to procure our indispensable assistance, absolute Instrumental-speech has already proved itself all-powerful; since precisely the arousing of indefinite, of presaging emotions, has been its most characteristic effect; but this aptitude could only become a weakness, wherever it wanted to give a definite shape, withal, to the emotions it had roused. Now, if we apply to the 'moments' of the Drama this extraordinary, this unique enabling aptitude of Instrumental-speech; if we entrust it to the poet, to be set in motion for the furtherance of a definite aim: then we must come to terms as to *whence* this language has to take the sensuous moments-of-expression in which it is to clothe itself, to accord with the Poetic Aim.

We have already seen that our Absolute Instrumental-music was obliged to borrow the sensuous 'moments' for its expression, either from a Dance-rhythm familiar to our ear of yore, and from the thence-sprung Tune—or from the melos of the Folk-song, to which our ear had been equally brought up. The absolute Instrumental-composer endeavoured to raise the everlasting indefiniteness of these 'moments' into a definite Expression, by fitting them together according to their kinship or contrast; by increasing or diminishing the strength, and hastening or slackening the speed, of their delivery; and finally by an idiomatic characterisation, which he sought among the manifold individualities of the tone-instruments themselves. In virtue of all this, he presented an image to the Phantasy; and eventually he could but feel compelled to explain the object of his description, by giving it an exact, an extra-musical label. So-called " Tone-painting " has been the manifest last stage (*Ausgang*) of our absolute Instrumental-music's evolution; in it this art has sensibly chilled down its own expression, no longer addressing itself to the Feeling, but to the Phantasy: an experience which anyone may make for himself, by hearing a Mendelssohnian, or still more (*gar*) a Berliozian orchestral composition, on top of a tone-piece by Beethoven. Nevertheless it is not to be denied, that this evolutionary course was a ' necessary' one, and the definite veering-off into tone-painting was prompted by more upright motives than, for instance, the return to the fugal style of Bach. Above all must it not be forgotten, that the sensuous power (*das sinnliche Vermögen*) of Instrumental-speech has been uncommonly enriched and heightened through this same Tone-painting.

We have now to recognise that not only can this power be heightened beyond all measure, but its expression be at the same time rid of its chillingness, if the tone-painter may but address himself again to Feeling, in place of Phantasy. This opportunity is offered him, when the subject of his mere describings to Thought is revealed in actual presence, to the Senses; and indeed, as no mere help towards an understanding of his tone-picture, but as conditioned by a highest Poetic Aim, for whose realisement the tone-picture is itself to be the helper. The subject of the tone-picture could be nothing but a moment from the life of Nature, or of Man himself. But it is precisely such moments from natural or human life, to whose delineation the Musician has hitherto felt drawn, that the Poet now needs in preparation for weighty dramatic crises (*Entwickelungen*), and it has been to the utmost detriment of his intended artwork, that the whilom Absolute Playwright must abjure these moments in advance—because, the more completely were they to impress the eye, yet without the supplementary aid of an emotion-guiding music their stage-effect was bound to be held unjustified, disturbing and detractive, not furthersome and helping.

Those indefinite presentiments, which the poet must necessarily arouse in us, will always have to be allied with some sort of Show (*Erscheinung*) that presents itself to the eye. This will be a 'moment' of the Natural Surrounding, or, in fact, of the Human centrepiece of that Surrounding: in any case, a 'moment' whose motion is not as yet determined by any *definitely* revealed emotion ; for the latter can only be expressed by Word-speech, in its aforesaid alliance with gesture and music,—by that very Word-speech whose definite announcement we have here to pave the way for, through its evocation by our longing. No language is capable of so *movingly* (bewegungsvoll) expressing a preparatory Repose, as that of the Orchestra : to develop this repose into an impatient longing, is its most peculiar office. What is offered our eye by a scene of Nature or a still and silent human figure, and through that eye attunes our feelings into placid contemplation, this same thing Music can present to our emotions in such a way that, starting from the 'moment' of Repose, she moves them to a state of strained Expectancy,* and thus awakes the longing which the poet needs on our part to assist him in the revelation of his aim. Nay, for this stirring of our Feeling towards a definite object, the poet needs to prepare our eye for the determinant (*bestimmende*) Show itself,—to wit, he must not even present us with the scene from Nature, nor with his human characters, until our roused expectancy

---

* Wagner's dramas present so many examples of this, that I need only instance Tannhäuser's posture in the change from the first to the second 'set' of *Tannhäuser*, Act I.—TR.

demands their presence and sanctions their behaviour, as fulfilling the necessities prefigured by it.—

In the exercise of this uttermost faculty, musical Expression will remain quite vague and non-determinant, till it takes into it the poetic Aim above-denoted. For the physical 'moments' of the preparatory tone-piece, however, this Aim is able so to draw upon the definite phenomenon about to be realised, that they shall answer just as closely to that phenomenon as its eventual appearance answers to the expectations woken in us by the premonitory music. Thus heralded, the actual phenomenon steps before us as a fulfilled longing, a justified foreboding; and, bearing in mind that the poet must lead his drama's shows before the Feeling as towering over those of wonted life—in fact, as Wondrous,—we now have to admit that these shows would not display themselves as such, or would appear outrageous and unintelligible, if their eventual naked revelation could not be so conditioned by our preparatory feeling of their necessity, as to make us downright demand them in fulfilment of an expectation. But only to an Orchestral-language thus inspired by the Poet, is it possible to rouse in us this necessary expectancy; wherefore without the Orchestra's artistic aid the Drama of Wonders (*das wundervolle Drama*) can neither be planned nor carried out.

VI.

E now have gathered all the connecting ties for our drama's single * Expression, and have only still to come to terms as to *how* they are to be knit with one another, in order to answer as a single *Form* to the single Substance; for only through the possibility of this oneness of Form, can the Substance also shape itself as *one*.—

The life-giving focus of dramatic Expression is the *verse-melody* of the performer: toward it leads-on the absolute orchestral-melody, as a *foreboding;* from it is led the instrumental-motive's "thought," as a *remembrance.* The Foreboding is the ray of light which, falling on an object, brings out to vivid truth of show the tint peculiar to that object, and conditioned by its substance; the Remembrance is the garnered tint itself, which the painter borrows from the object, to bestow it on others akin thereto. What greets the eye, is the ever 'present' show and motion of the imparter of the verse-melody, the dramatic gesture of the performer; to the ear this is elucidated by the orchestra, which plays its original, its most necessary part as the harmonic carrier of the verse-melody.—In the total expression of the performer's every message, to the ear alike as to the eye, the *orchestra* thus takes an unbroken share, supporting and elucidating on every hand: it is the moving matrix of the music, from whence there thrives the uniting bond of all Expression.—*The Chorus of Greek*

* " Einig,"—this derivative of " ein " (one) was rendered by the *Musical World* translator (1855-6) as "oneful," and I have felt half tempted to improve upon that eccentric coinage by inventing another word, "onefold"—analogous to our "twofold" or the German "einfältig"; but perhaps "single" will be sufficiently explicit, if the reader will only bear in mind the text : " If therefore thine eye be single, thy whole body shall be full of light."—TR.

Tragedy has bequeathed to us its emotional (*gefühlsnothwen-dige*) significance for the drama *in the modern Orchestra alone*, and therein, free from any hampering, has evolved to an immeasurable wealth of utterance ; its physical (*reale*), its individual human semblance, however, has been lifted from the ὀρχήστρα and placed upon the stage,—there to unfold the germ of human Individuality, indwelling in the Greek Chorus, to the topmost flower of self-dependence as the immediate doer or sufferer in the drama itself.

Let us now consider how the poet, from amid that Orchestra in which he has become entirely a musician, turns back to face the Aim which led him thither ; and, indeed, to completely realise it through the boundless amplitude of means of Expression, which now he has acquired.

The Poetic Aim was to be realised, in the first place, in the Verse-melody ; in the Harmonic Orchestra we have learnt to recognise the carrier and elucidator of *pure* Melody. It now remains for us to ascertain how that Verse-melody comports itself towards the drama, and what furtherance the Orchestra can bring to this relation.

We have already gained from the Orchestra the capability of awaking forebodings and remembrances. The Foreboding we have taken as the herald of the matter that finally proclaims itself in the gesture and verse-melody,— the Remembrance, on the other hand, as a derivative from that matter. We now must settle What it is, that has to fill the general body of the drama, and fill it in such a way as to make these forebodings and remembrances a real dramatic necessity, an accessory to its thorough under-standing.

The moments in which the orchestra might speak out thus independently, must in any case be such as do not yet permit the full ascension of the spoken thought into the musical emotion, on the part of the dramatis personæ.

Just as we have watched the growth of the musical melody from out the speaking-verse, and have recognised that growth as conditioned by the very nature of this verse ; just as we have had to conceive the vindication of the melody—i.e. the understanding given it by the conditioning word-verse—not merely as a something to be thought or worked out by the artist (*künstlerisch Auszuführendes*), but as something necessarily to be brought organically to pass before our very Feeling, an act of birth to be carried on (*Vorzuführendes*) in its presence : so have we to picture the dramatic Situation as growing from conditionments which mount, before our eyes, to a height whereon the Verse-Melody appears the only fit, the necessary expression of a definitely proclaimed emotion.

A ready-made melody—so we have seen—remained unintelligible to us, because open to arbitrary interpretings ; a ready-made Situation must remain just as unintelligible, even as Nature herself remained unintelligible to us so long as we looked on her as something *made*—whereas she is intelligible enough, now that we know her as the Be-ing, i.e. the forever Becom-ing : a Being (*ein Seiendes*) whose Becoming is ever present to us, alike in farthest as in nighest spheres.   By leading forth his Artwork in continuous organic growth, and making our selves organic helpers in that growth, the poet frees his creation from all traces of his handiwork ; whereas, should he leave those traces unexpunged, he would set us in that chill of feelingless amazement which takes us when we look upon a master-piece of mechanism.—Plastic art can display alone the Finished, i.e. the Motionless ; wherefore it can never make of the beholder a confident witness to the becoming of a thing.   In his farthest strayings, the Absolute Musician fell into the error of copying plastic art in this, and giving the Finished in place of the Becoming.   The Drama, alone, is the artwork that so addresses itself in Space and Time to our eye and ear, that we take an active share in its becoming, and therefore can grasp the *Become* as a necessity, as a thing which our Feeling clearly understands.

Y

Now, the poet who wishes to make of us the active witnesses and sole enablers of his artwork's Becoming (*Werdens*), has to guard himself from taking even the smallest step that might break the bond of this organic growth (*Werdens*) and thus affront our captivated Feeling by an arbitrary demand : his most important ally would be made disloyal to him at once. Organic growth, however, means a growing from below upwards, an advance from lower to higher forms of organism, a binding of needy moments into one satisfying moment.* Wherefore, just as the Poetic Aim was to gather up the moments of the Action and their motives, collecting them from such as were actually to hand in daily life, albeit infinitely scattered there, and ramified past any survey ; just as it was to compress these moments and motives, for sake of their intelligible display, and to strengthen them in such cohesion : so for their *realisement* the poet has to go to work in exactly the same way as with their composition *in his thought ;* for his Aim can only be realised through its making our Feeling a partner in its thinking work of composition (*an ihrer gedachten Dichtung*).

The thing the Feeling grasps the surest, is our ordinary view of daily life, in which we deal from need or inclination precisely as we have been accustomed to. If, then, the poet has gathered his motives from this life and its wonted viewings, he must also bring us the shapings of his fancy, in the first place, with an exterior (*Äusserung*) which shall not be *so* foreign to this life as to be completely unintelligible to men involved therein. He has therefore to shew his characters at first in predicaments (*Lebenslagen*) having a recognisable likeness with such as we have found, or at least might have found, ourselves in ; only from such a foundation, can he mount step by step to situations whose force and wondrousness remove us from the life of every-

---

* "Die Verbindung bedürftiger Momente zu einem befriedigenden Momente." For this sentence we must recall the Feuerbachian formula of Vol. I, page 80 (*Art-work of the Future*), where "need and satisfaction" are dealt with.—Tr.

day, and shew us Man in the highest fulness of his power. Just as, through the removal of everything which might savour of the Accidental,* in the encounter of strongly pronounced individualities, these situations grow to a height on which they appear lifted above the wonted human measure,—so has the *Expression* of the doers and the done-by to necessarily lift itself by well-found stages, from one that is still in touch with customary life, to one raised high above it : in fact, to such an one as we have already indicated in the Musical Verse-melody.

But we now must fix our lowest point for both the Situation and the Expression, the point from which we are to start on that upward journey. If we look a little closer, we shall see that this point is precisely the same as that on which we must place ourselves in order to impart, and thus to realise, the Poetic Aim at all ; and that lies where this Aim parts company with the daily life from which it sprang, to hold up to it its poetical image. Upon this point the poet sets himself aface to those involved in daily life, with an announcement of his aim,† and calls aloud for their attention. He cannot be rightly heard until this attention is *willingly* yielded him, — until our feelings, distracted by the affairs of daily life, just as much collect themselves to a feeling of intent expectancy as the poet, in his Aim, has already collected from that same life the moments and motives of his Dramatic Action. The willing expectation, or expectant Will of the hearer, is thus the first enabler for the artwork ; and it determines the manner of Expression which the poet must bring to meet it,—not merely so as to be understood, but to be understood in the measure demanded by the hearer's strained expectance of something out of the common.

---

* " Zufällig,"—reference should here be made to pp. 219-22 *antea*, and their " Hazard " (Zufall) &c. To myself it seems probable that this portion of the text was drafted contemporaneously with that earlier chapter.—Tr.

† " Mit dem lauten Bekenntnisse seiner Absicht,"—it is evident, from the context, that our author means us to understand : " with the announcement that he has a living story to tell us." This volume contains many similar instances —some of which I have already noted—of a quasi-poetical ' ellipsis.'—Tr.

From the very first, the poet has to make use of this expectancy for the enunciation of his Aim, and that, by guiding this indeterminate feeling in the direction of that Aim. No language is more competent for this, as we have seen, than the indefinitely determining language (*die unbestimmt bestimmende*) of pure Music, of the Orchestra. The Orchestra gives voice to the very expectancy that possesses us before the appearing of the artwork; according to the particular bent demanded by the poetic-aim it guides our general feeling of suspense, and works it into a Foreboding, which necessarily calls for a definite phenomenon to finally fulfil it.* When the poet leads the object of this expectancy upon the scene, as a dramatic personage, it is obvious that he would only affront and disillusion the awakened Feeling, were he to allow that person to express himself in a tongue recalling suddenly the most habitual utterance of the life from whence we have just been transported.† This personage, too, must pronounce himself in that tongue which has already aroused our emotion, if he is to correspond at all with what this emotion has been led to expect. In this Tone-speech must the dramatic person speak, if we are to understand him with our kindled Feeling : but, he must also speak in such a way as to *determine* the emotions roused in us; and our vaguely roused emotions can only be determined by their being given a fixed point round which they may gather as human Fellow-feeling,

---

* In this place I need but cursorily mention, that I do not allude to the modern Operatic Overture. Every man of common sense must know that these tone-pieces—provided there was aught to understand in them at all—should have been performed *after* the drama, instead of *before* it, if they were meant to be understood. Vanity has betrayed the musician—even in the most favourable cases—into wanting to fulfil the Foreboding in the very Overture itself, and that, with an absolute-musical certainty about the whole plot of the drama.—R. WAGNER.—That our author was perfectly aware that he was condemning his own *Tannhäuser*-overture (in its earlier form) *as* an Overture, is proved by a letter to Uhlig dated March 20, 1852. On the other hand, his *Rheingold* Introduction (then unwritten) is the completest fulfilment of the above suggestions.—TR.

† The everlasting tradition of entr'acte-music in our plays is an eloquent witness to the lack of any art-ideas on the part of our playwrights and stagemanagers.—R. WAGNER.

and whereat they may condense themselves to a specific sympathy for this one man, involved in this particular plight, influenced by this surrounding, ensouled by this will, and engaged in this project. These necessary conditions for displaying an individuality to the Feeling, can be convincingly set forth in nothing but Word-speech,—in that language which is instinctively intelligible to ordinary life, and wherein we mutually impart a plight or Will such as must be resembled by those laid bare by the dramatic person, if these latter are to be *understood* by us at all. As our kindled mood, however, has already claimed that this word-speech shall not be one at total variance with that tone-speech which has so lately moved us, but one already* welded with it—as it were the interpreter, but alike the partner, of the roused emotion—, so by this very fact, the Content (*Inhalt*) to be set forth by the dramatis personæ is prescribed as one as much uplifted above the matters of our daily life, as the Expression itself is raised above the language of that life.   And the poet has only to hold by the characteristics of this Expression,—he has only to take care to fill it with a Content such as shall justify it,—to become fully conscious of the heightened standpoint which the sheer Means of Expression has provided for the reaching of his Aim.

This standpoint is already so lofty a one, that the poet *can*—because he positively *must*—allow the Unwonted and Wondrous, as needed for the realisement of his aim, to take their development immediately from here.   The Wondrous of his dramatic individualities and situations he will develop in exact degree as its fit Expression stands at his behest,—namely, as the language of the impersonator, after accurately laying down the basis of the Situation as one borrowed from Man's Life and intelligible thereto, can lift itself from the already tonal Word-speech into actual Tone-speech ; from which there blooms at last the Melody, in answer to the sure and settled Feeling, in utterance of the

* " Bereits," here used as " schon,"—i.e. "from the first articulate word and onward."—Tr.

purely human kernel of the sure and settled Individuality
and Situation.*—

A Situation arising from this basis, and waxing to such
a climax, forms in itself a plainly differentiated member of
the drama. While this Drama, both in content and in
form, consists of a chain of such organic members, conditioning, supplementing and supporting one another:
exactly as the organic members of the human body,—
which then alone is a complete and living body, when it
consists of all the members whose mutual conditionings and
supplementings make up its whole; when none are lacking to it; but, also, when none are too many.

But the Drama is an ever new, an ever newly-shaping
body; and it has only *this* in common with its human
prototype,—that it is living, and draws its life from inner
life-needs. This Life-need of the drama, however, is a
diverse one; for it does not shape itself from an always
like-remaining Stuff, but takes this Stuff from the endless
varieties of a measurelessly complex life, of divers men in
divers circumstances; while the latter, again, have only
one thing in common,—namely, that they just are Men
and *human* circumstances. The never equal individuality
of men and circumstances obtains through mutual re-
agence an ever novel physiognomy, which brings to the
poetic-aim a constantly fresh series of Necessities, for it to
realise. From out these Necessities the drama has ever to
shape itself afresh and other-wise, in answer to those changing individualities; and nothing, therefore, has borne
stronger witness to the incapacity of past and present art-
periods, for shaping the genuine Drama, than when Poet
and Musician have sought in advance for Forms, and set

---

* "Als deren Blüthe die Melodie erscheint, wie sie von dem bestimmten,
versicherten Gefühle als Kundgebung des rein menschlichen Empfindungs-
inhaltes der bestimmten und versicherten Individualität und Situation gefordert
wird."

up Forms, which were to make the Drama possible to them so soon as they should pour into these Forms any Stuff they chose to dramatise. No Form was more balking and unfit for achievement of the genuine Drama, however, than the Opera-form with its once-for-all division into vocal numbers, quite heedless of the dramatic matter : however much our opera-composers might toil and moil to stretch them out and multiply them, the unyielding, disconnected botchwork could only fall to rags and tatters in the long run,— as we have seen in its own place.

Against this, let us take a hasty glance at the Form of our supposed drama, so as to assure ourselves that—for all its necessary and fundamental, its ever newly-shaping change—it is a Form essentially, nay, uniquely *one*. But let us also consider *what* it is, that makes this unity possible.

Unity of artistic Form is only thinkable as the emanation (*Kundgebung*) of a united Content : a united Content, however, we can only recognise by its being couched in an artistic *Expression* * through which it can announce itself *entirely* to the Feeling. A Content which should prescribe a twofold Expression, i.e. an expression which obliged the messenger to address himself alternately to the Understanding and the Feeling,—such a content could only be itself a dual, a discordant (*uneiniger*) one.—Every artistic aim makes primarily for a united Shape, for only in degree as an announcement approaches such a shape, does it become at all an artistic one : but it necessarily begins to cleave in two, from the instant when it can no longer be entirely imparted through the Expression placed at its disposal. Since it is the instinctive Will of every artistic Aim, to impart itself to Feeling, it follows that the cloven Expression is incompetent to entirely rouse the Feeling : but an Expression must entirely rouse the Feeling, if it would entirely impart thereto its Content. This entire arousing of the Feeling was impossible to the sheer Word-poet, through *his* expressional organ ; therefore what he

* " Ausdruck,"—" means of expression " would be a clearer rendering, but too long-winded for such frequent use.—Tr.

could not impart through that to Feeling, he was obliged to announce to Understanding, so as to compass the full utterance of the content of his Aim : he must hand over to Understanding, to be thought out, what he could not give to be perceived by Feeling; and, when it came to the decisive point, he could only speak out his 'tendence' as a mere 'sentence,' * i.e. as a naked, unrealised aim ; whereby he was compelled to degrade the Content of his aim, itself, to a non-artistic one. ·

Now, if the work of the sheer Word-poet appears as a non-realised poetic Aim, on the other hand the work of the Absolute Musician is only to be described as altogether bare of such an Aim ; for the Feeling may well have been entirely roused by the purely-musical expression, but it could not be *directed*. By reason of his inadequate means of Expression, the poet was obliged to split the Content into an emotional and an intellectual one, and thus to leave the kindled Feeling in a state of restless discontent, —fitly matched by the unallayable brooding on this restlessness of the Feeling, into which he plunged the Understanding. The musician no less constrained the Understanding to seek for some lurking Content, in this Expression of his which so completely stirred the Feeling, yet brought it no appeasement of its utmost stir. The poet gave this Content as a 'sentence': the musician— in order to make some show of an Aim, in truth not extant,—as a title to his composition. Both, in the long run, had to turn away from Feeling, to the Understanding; the poet—so as to fix a feeling, incompletely roused : the musician—to exculpate himself in the eyes of a feeling roused in vain.

If, then, we wish to accurately denote that Means of Expression which, in virtue of its own unity, shall make possible a Unity of Content, let us define it as one which can the most fittingly convey to Feeling a widest-reaching Aim of the poetic Understanding. Such an Expression

---

* " Seine Tendenz nur als Sentenz."—TR.

must *contain the poet's Aim in each of its separate ' moments,' albeit in each of them concealing that aim from the Feeling, —to wit, by realising it.**—Even to Word-Tone-speech this entire cloaking of the poetic Aim would be impossible, were it not that a second, a concurrent organ of Tone-speech could be allied therewith ; so that wherever Word-Tone-speech—as the directest harbourer of the poet's Aim, and for sake of keeping it in touch with the moods of ordinary life—is obliged to so thin down its own Expression, that it can only clothe that Aim with an almost diaphanous veil of Tone, there this second organ is able to maintain an even balance of the one Emotional-expression.

The Orchestra, as we have seen, is this compensatory organ for preserving the Unity of Expression. Wherever, for a plainer definement of the dramatic Situation, the Word-Tone language of the dramatis personæ abates itself in such a way as to expose its closest kinship with the language of daily life,—with the organ of the Understanding, —there the Orchestra makes good this sunk expression, through its power of musically conveying a Foreboding or Remembrance ; so that the awakened Feeling remains in its uplifted mood, and never has to follow on that downward path by transforming itself into a purely intellectual function. This constant height of Feeling—never to be diminished, but only still further augmented—is governed by the constant height of the Expression, and the latter by the constancy, i.e. the unity, of the Content.

Let us not forget, however, that the Orchestra's equalising moments-of-expression are never to be determined *by the caprice of the musician,* as a random tricking-out of sound, but *only by the poet's Aim.* Should these ' moments ' utter anything not connected with the Situation of the dramatis personæ, anything superfluous thereto, then the Unity of Expression is itself disturbed by this departure from the

---

* " This apparently paradoxical sentence (in fact, this whole short paragraph) is by no means easy to render into English ; yet the editor of the *Musical World*, of March 1, 1856, might have spared his gibes, had he chosen to remember the old Latin maxim : " ars est *celare* artem."—TR.

Content. A mere absolute-musical embellishment of droop-
ing or inchoate situations—a favourite Operatic device for
the self-glorification of Music, in so-called "ritornelles" and
interludes, and even in the song-accompaniments,—such
a trick upheaves at once the Unity of Expression, and
casts the interest of the ear on Music no longer as an
expression, but, in a manner, as herself the thing expressed.
No : those 'moments,' too, must be governed by nothing
but the poetic-aim, and in such a way that, as either a Foreboding or a Remembrance, they shall always direct our
Feeling solely to the dramatic personage and whatever hangs-
together therewith, or outgoes therefrom.   We ought
never to hear these prophetic or reminiscent melodic-
moments, except when we can feel that they are comple-
mentary to the utterance of the character upon the stage,
who either will not or cannot just now expose to us his full
emotion.

These Melodic Moments, in themselves adapted to maintain our Feeling at an even height, will be made by the orchestra into a kind of guides-to-Feeling (*Gefühlswegweisern*)
through the whole labyrinthine (*vielgewundenen*) building
of the drama. At their hand we become the constant fellow-
knowers of the profoundest secret of the poet's Aim, the
immediate partners in its realisement. Between them, as
Foreboding and Remembrance, there stands the Verse-
melody as the borne and bearing individuality, conditioned
by an emotional-surrounding consisting of moments of
utterance drawn alike from its own promptings and from
those of others, already experienced or yet to be experienced. These referential moments, for rounding-off the
emotional-expression, withdraw into the background so
soon as ever the individual comes to oneness with himself,
and thus advances to the fullest expression of the Verse-
melody : *then* the orchestra will merely support this melody
in its elucidatory function * ; but when the full colours of

* " Nach seinem verdeutlichenden Vermögen,"—i.e. as what our author
has called the " *harmonic* vindicator of the melody " ; see pages 303, 306, 310,
313, 315 and 318.—Tr.

exhaustive definition, and denote the most perfect Unity of artistic Form as that in which a widest conjuncture of the phenomena of Human Life—as Content—can impart itself to the Feeling in so completely intelligible an Expression, that in all its 'moments' this Content shall completely stir, and alike completely satisfy, the Feeling. *The Content, then, has to be one that is ever present in the Expression, and therefore the Expression one that ever presents the Content in its fullest compass ; for only Thought can grasp the absent, but only the present can be grasped by Feeling.*

In this unity of the *Expression*, ever making present, and ever embracing the full compass of the Content, there is at like time solved, and solved in the only decisive way, the whilom problem of the *unity* of *Time and Space.**

Time and Space, as abstractions from the real living attributes of the Action, could only chain the attention of our drama-*constructing* poets because a single, a completely realising Expression did not stand at their service for the poetic Content planned by them. Time and Space are thought-out attributes of actual physical phenomena ; and so soon as the latter are thought about, they have in truth already lost their force of manifestment : the body of these abstractions is the Real, the Sense-appealing, of an action which displays itself in a definite spacial surrounding, and in a period of motion conditioned thereby. To set the unity of the Drama in the unity of Space and Time, means to set it at *naught* (in *Nichts* setzen) ; for Time and Space are nothing in themselves, and only become some-thing through their being *annulled* by something *real*, by a Human Action and its Natural Surrounding. This Human Action must be the thing united in itself, i.e. the thing that hangs-together ; by the possibility of making its connexion a

---

* " Einheit des Raumes und der Zeit,"—it is interesting to compare this passage with : " zum Raum wird hier die Zeit," *Parsifal*, Act I.—T<small>R</small>

surveyable one, is conditioned the assumption of its time-length, and by the possibility of a completely adequate representment of the Scene is conditioned its extension in Space; for it wills but one thing,—to make itself intelligible to Feeling.

In the singlest Space and the most compact Time one may spread out an Action as completely discordant and disconnected as you please,—as we may see to our heart's content in our Unity-pieces. On the contrary, the Unity of an Action consists in its intelligible connexion; and only through *one* thing can this reveal itself intelligibly,—which thing is neither Time nor Space, but *the Expression*. If in the preceding pages we have ascertained *what* is this unitarian, i.e. this continuous Expression, which at all times keeps the Continuity in presence; and if we have shewn it as a thing by all means possible : then in this Expression we have also won back the severed by the necessity of Space and Time * as a thing once more united, and a thing made ever present where needful for an understanding; for its 'necessary' Presence lies not in Time or Space, but in the *impression* which is made on us within them. The limitations of Space and Time, which arose from lack of this Expression, are upheaved at once by its acquirement; both Time and Space are annihilated, through the actuality of the Drama.

The genuine Drama, then, is influenced no longer by aught that lies outside it; but it is an *organic Be-ing and Becom-ing*, evolving and shaping itself by those inner conditions which itself lays down for its only contact with outside—in turn conditioning *it*,—namely by the Necessity of making its message understandable, and understandable *as the thing it is and becomes ;* whilst it wins its intelligible Shape by bearing from its own, its inmost Need, the all-empowering Expression for its Content.

------

* " Das in Zeit und Raum nothwendig Getrennte."—TR.

VII.

N the argument just ended I have indicated possibilities of Expression such as a poetic Aim *can* press into its service, and such as the highest Poetic Aim *must needs* employ for its realisement. The verification of those possibilities of Expression depends solely on the highest poetic Aim: but this latter cannot be taken in hand, till the Poet becomes conscious of those possibilities.—

Whoever, on the other hand, may have understood me to be occupied with setting up an arbitrarily concocted System, according to which all poets and musicians should construct their work in future,—he has wilfully mis-understood me. Moreover, he who chooses to believe that the New, which I haply have said, reposes on an absolute assumption and is not identical with Experience and the nature of the object dealt with,—he will not be *able* to understand me, even though he wished it.—The New that I may have said, is nothing other than the Unconscious in the nature of the thing, and has become conscious to me, as a thinking artist, merely because I have grasped in its continuity a thing which artists heretofore have taken only in its severance. I thus have *invented* nothing new, but merely *found* that continuity.—

It only remains for me to denote *the relation between poet and musician* which follows from the argument above. To do this briefly, let us first ask ourselves the question: "Has the poet to *restrict* himself in presence of the musician, and the musician in presence of the poet?"

Freedom of the Individual has hitherto seemed possible through nothing but a—wise—restriction from without:

moderation of his impulses, and thus of the force of his
abilities, was the first thing required of the unit by the
State-community.   The full effectuation of an Individuality
had to be looked on as synonymous with an infringement
of the individuality of others, whereas the individual's self-
restraint was reckoned as his highest wisdom and virtue.—
Taken strictly, this virtue, preached by sages, besung by
didactists, and finally claimed by the State as the duty of
subservience, by Religion as the duty of humility,—this
virtue was a virtue never coming forth ; willed, but not
practised ; imagined, but not realised : and so long as a
virtue is demanded, it will never in truth be exercised.
Either the exercise of this virtue was an act despotically
imposed—and thus without that merit of virtue imagined
for it ; or it was a necessary, an unreflective act of free-will,
and then its enabling force was not the self-restricting
Will,—but *Love*.

   Those same sages and lawgivers who claimed the practice
of self-restraint through reflection, never reflected for an
instant that they had thralls and slaves beneath them,
from whom they cut off every possibility of practising that
virtue ; and yet these latter were in fact the only ones
who really restrained themselves for another's sake,—
because they were compelled to.   Among that ruling and
'reflecting' aristocracy the self-restraint of its members,
toward one another, consisted in nothing but the prudence
of Egoism, which counselled them to segregate themselves,
to take no thought for others; and this policy of *laisser
aller* (Gehenlassen)—clever enough at giving itself a quite
agreeable outward show, in forms it borrowed from those
of reverence and friendship—yet was only possible to these
gentry on condition that other men, mere slaves and
chattels, should stand ready to maintain the hedged-off
self-dependence of their masters.   In the terrible demoralisation of our present social system, revolting to
the heart of every veritable Man, we may see the necessary consequence of asking for an impossible virtue, and
a virtue which eventually is held in currency by a barbarous

Police. Only the total vanishing of this demand, and of the grounds on which it has been based,—only the up-heaval of the most un-human inequality of men, in their stationings toward Life, can bring about the *fancied* issue of that claim of self-restriction: and that, by making possible *free Love*. But Love will bring about that fancied issue in a measurelessly heightened measure, for it is not at all a *self-restraint*, but something infinitely greater,—to wit, *the highest evolution of our individual powers—together with the most necessitated thrust towards our own self-offering for sake of a beloved object.*—

Now, if we apply this criterion to the case above, we shall see that self-*restriction* of either the Poet or the Musician, in its ultimate consequences, would only bring about the drama's death, or rather, would withstand its ever being brought to life. So soon as poet and musician restricted one another, they could have no other end in view, than each to let his own particular talent shine out for itself; and seeing that the object, on which they were bringing these lights of theirs to shine, was just the Drama, the latter would naturally fare like the sick man betwixt two doctors, each endeavouring to display his special scientific skill in an opposite direction: with the strongest constitution in the world, the invalid would go to the ground.—If Poet and Musician, however, do not restrict each other, but rouse each other's powers into highest might, by Love; if in this Love they are all that ever they can be; if they *mutually go under* * in the offering that each brings each,—the offering of his very highest potence,—then the Drama in its highest plenitude is born.—

If the *poet's Aim*—as such—is still at hand and visible, then it has not as yet gone under into the Musical Ex-pression; but if the *musician's Expression*—as such—is still apparent, then it, in turn, has not yet been inspired by the Poetic Aim. Only when the Expression, as a marked and

---

* "*Gehen sie . . . gegenseitig in sich unter*,"—this somewhat quaint expression is evidently an allusion to that "Going-under of the State," dealt with on page 201 et seq.—TR.

z

special thing, goes under in the realisement of this Aim,
only *then* is neither Aim nor Expression any longer at
hand, but the reality which each had *willed* is can-ned.
And this reality is the Drama; in whose presentment we
must be reminded no more of Aim or Expression, but its
Content must instinctively engross us, as a Human Action
vindicated 'necessarily' before our Feeling.*

Let us tell the *Musician* then that every, even the tiniest
moment of his Expression *in which the poetic-aim is not
contained*, and which is not conditioned 'necessarily' by
that Aim and its realisement,—that every such moment is
superfluous, disturbing, bad ; that each utterance of his is
unimpressive if it stays unintelligible, and that it becomes
intelligible only by taking into it the Poet's aim ; that
he himself, however, as realiser of the poetic-aim, stands
infinitely higher than in his arbitrary dealings without that
aim,—for, as a conditioned, a 'satisfying' message, his own
is an even higher one than that of the conditioning, the
'needy' Aim in itself, albeit the latter is the highest aim
man has ; that, finally, in the conditionment of his message
by this Aim, he will be incited to a far richer exhibition of
his powers than ever he was while at his lonely post, where
—for sake of utmost understandableness—he was obliged
to *restrain himself*, i.e. to hold himself to a function not
belonging to him as Musician : whereas he now is necessarily challenged to the most unrestrained unfoldment of
his powers, precisely because he needs and must be *nothing
but musician*.

To the *poet* let us say, that if his Aim—in so far as it is
to be displayed to the ear—*cannot be entirely realised in the
Expression of his musician ally*, then neither is it a highest
Poetic Aim at all ; that wherever his Aim is still discernible, he has not completely poetised it ; and therefore, that
he can only measure *the height of poetry* to which his Aim
has reached, by *the completeness* wherewith it is realisable
in the *musical Expression*.

* For the pendants to this paradox the reader should refer to pages 233 and
345 ; all three passages will gain vastly in comprehensibility, by the comparison.—TR.

So, let us finally denote the measure of poetic worth as follows :—as Voltaire said of the Opera : " What is too silly to be said, one gets it sung," so let us reverse that maxim for the Drama which we have in view, and say : *What is not worth the being sung, neither is it worth the poet's pains of telling.*

After what has been said above, it might seem almost superfluous to ask the further question : Whether we ought to think of the Poet and Musician as *two persons*, or as *one ?*

The Poet and Musician, whom we mean, are very well thinkable as two persons. In fact the Musician, in his practical intermediation between the poetic aim and its final bodily realisement through an actual scenic representation, might necessarily be conditioned by the Poet as a separate person, and indeed, a *younger* than himself—if not necessarily in point of years, yet at least in point of character. This younger person, through standing closer to Life's instinctive utterance—especially (*auch*) in its lyric moments,—might well appear to the more experienced, more reflecting Poet, as more fitted to *realise* his aim than he himself is ; and from this his natural inclination towards the younger, the more buoyant man—so soon as the latter took up with willing enthusiasm the poetic-aim imparted to him by the older—there would bloom that fairest, noblest Love, which we have learnt to recognise as the enabling force of Art-work. By the very fact that the Poet saw his —here necessarily merely hinted—aim completely comprehended by the younger man, and that this younger man was competent to understand it, there would be knit that bond of Love in which the Musician becomes the 'necessary' bearer ; for the latter's share in the conception is the bent to spread abroad, with warm and flowing heart, the boon received. Through this bent, incited in another, the Poet himself would win an ever waxing warmth toward his begettal, which must needs determine him to the helpfulest

interest in the birth itself.   Just the twofold energy of this
Love must needs exert an infinite artistic force, inciting,
enkindling, and empowering on every hand.

Yet if we consider the present attitude assumed by Poet
and Musician toward one another, and if we find it ordered
by the same maxims of self-restriction and egoistic severance, as those which govern all the factors of our modern
social State: then we cannot but feel that, in an unworthy
public system where every man is bent on shining for
himself alone, *there* none but the individual Unit can take
into himself the spirit of Community, and cherish and
develop it according to his powers—how inadequate soe'er
they be.   Not to *two*, at the hour that is, can come the
thought of jointly making possible the Perfected Drama;
for, in parleying on this thought, the two must necessarily
and candidly avow the impossibility of its realisement in
face of Public Life, and that avowal would nip their
undertaking in the bud.   Only the lonely one, in the thick
of his endeavour, can transmute the bitterness of such a
self-avowal into an intoxicating joy which drives him on,
with all the courage of a drunkard, to undertake the making
possible the Impossible ; for he, *alone*, is thrust forward by
two artistic forces which he cannot withstand,—by forces
which he willingly lets drive him to self-offering.*—

* I here am obliged to make express mention of myself, and, indeed, with
a single eye to removing from the reader's mind any suspicion that with the
above account of the Perfected Drama I had attempted an explanation of my
own artistic works, in any sense as though I had fulfilled my present demands
in my own operas, and had thus already brought to pass this hypothetic
Drama.   No one can be better aware than myself, that the realisation of this
Drama depends on conditions which do not lie within the will, nay, not even
within the capability (*Fähigkeit*) of the Unit,—were this capability an infinitely
greater than my own,—but only in Community, and in a mutual co-operation
made possible thereby : of both which factors, nothing but the direct antithesis
is now to hand.   Nevertheless I will admit that my artistic works have been
of the greatest weight to me ; for alas ! so far as I can see around me, they
must be my only witnesses to the existence of an endeavour from whose results
alone, small as they are, that thing was to be learnt which—striving from
unconsciousness to consciousness—I now have learnt ; and which—let us hope,
for the welfare of Art—I now can speak aloud with full conviction.   Not of
my achievements, but of That which they have brought within my consciousness, of That which I now can utter with conviction, am I proud.—R. WAGNER.

Let us further take a glance at the present *public* aspect of our musico-dramatic art, so as to make plain to ourselves why the Drama, such as we have dealt with, cannot possibly come to an appearance just now; and, were it *ventured* notwithstanding, how it could not evoke an understanding, but only the utmost bewilderment.

———————

We have had to recognise *Speech* itself as the indispensable basis of a perfect Artistic Expression. That we have lost all emotional comprehension of our spoken language, we have had to regard as an irreplaceable loss for any artistic message to the Feeling. Therefore, if we have pointed out the possibility of a re-livening of Speech, for the purpose of artistic expression, and have deduced the perfected Musical Expression from a language thus brought again within the Feeling's understanding,—then we most certainly have taken our foothold upon a supposition which can only be realised through Life itself, not through the unaided Artistic Will. If we may assume, however, that the artist, upon whom there had dawned the *necessity* of Life's evolution, would also have to advance with fashioning Consciousness to meet that evolution,—then we must surely deem him justified in the endeavour to lift his prophetic Boding to the level of an artistic Deed ; and in any case it would be to his credit, to have henceforth moved along a more reasonable (*vernünftigsten*) artistic path.

Now, if we cast our eye across the languages of those European nations which hitherto have borne an active and original share in the evolution of the Musical Drama, of Opera,—and these are but the Italians, French, and Germans—, we shall find that, of those three nations, the *German* alone possesses a language whose daily usage still hangs directly and conspicuously together with its Roots.

Italians and Frenchmen speak a tongue whose radical meaning can only be brought home to them by a study of older, so-called dead languages : one might say that their language—as the precipitate from a historic period of Folk-mingling, whose conditioning influence upon these races has altogether lapsed—that their language speaks for them, not *they* speak in their language. If, then, we grant that from a Life set free of all Historic pressure, and stepping into intimate communion with associate Nature, there may arise for these tongues, as well, quite new and hitherto undreamt conditions for their emotional transformation,—and if we certainly may rest assured that Art, to be *all* that in this new life it *should* be, will exert an uncommonly weighty influence upon that transformation,—yet we can but recognise that such an influence would spring the most resultfully from that art which should ground its Expression upon a language whose hang-together with Nature is even now more obvious to the Feeling, than is the case with either the French, or the Italian tongue. That evolution of the Artistic Expression, with its prophetic influence upon that of daily Life, cannot take its start from artworks whose verbal basis lies within the French, or the Italian tongue ; but, of all the modern operatic dialects, the German alone is fitted to re-liven Art's Expression in the manner we have recognised as needful : for very reason that it is the only one which in daily life has retained the accent on the root-syllable, whilst in those others an arbitrary convention abrogates the rule of Nature, and sets the accent on syllables of ' inflection '—altogether meaningless *per se*.

It is the chief and fundamental factor, then, the ' moment ' of Speech, that points us to the German nation in the Drama's struggle for a completely warrantable, a highest artistic Expression ; and were it possible for the unaided Artistic Will to call the perfect Dramatic Artwork to light of day, at present this could only happen in the German tongue. But what conditions the executability of this Artistic Will, lies firstly in the fellowship of *imperson-*

ating artists. Let us therefore observe the doings of the latter upon our German stage.—

Italian and French singers are accustomed to render none but musical compositions expressly written for their mother-tongue : little as this speech may stand in a completely natural connection with the musical melody, yet one thing at least is undeniable in the performances of French and Italian singers—to wit, the attention paid to a right rendering of the *talk*, as such. Although this is more noticeable among the French than the Italians, yet everyone must be struck by the distinctness and energy wherewith the latter, too, speak out their words, more especially in the drastic phrases of the Recitative. But above all must this one thing be credited to both,—that a natural instinct prevents them from ever disfiguring the sense of the talk through a false delivery.

German singers on the contrary are accustomed, for by far the greater part, to sing in operas which have been merely translated into German from the French or Italian. Neither a poetic, nor a musical intelligence has ever been set in motion for these translations, but they have been put together by people who knew nothing of either music or poetry, and went to work in much the same commercial spirit as one transposes newspaper articles or business advertisements. Taken in the mass, these translators were before all else not musical ; they rendered an Italian or French text-book, for itself as word-poem, into a so-called Iambic metre which they ignorantly took to represent the really quite unrhythmic measure of the original ; and these verses they got written under the music by some poor hack of a music-copyist, with instructions to dribble out a syllable to every note. The poetical labours of the translator had consisted in furnishing the vulgarest prose with the absurdest end-rhymes ; and since he had often had the most painful difficulty in finding these rhymes themselves,—all heedless that they would be almost inaudible in

the music,—his love toward them had made him distort the
natural order of the words, past any hope of understanding.
This hateful Verse, contemptible and muddled in itself, was
now laid under a music whose distinctive Accents it nowhere
fitted: on lengthy notes there came short syllables, on
longer syllables the shorter notes ; on the musical 'ridge'
there came the verse's 'hollow,' and so the other way
around.* From these grossest offences against the sound,
the translation passed on to a complete distortion of the
sense; and it really took such considerable pains to stamp
the latter on the ear, by countless textual repetitions, that
the ear instinctively turned away from the text and devoted
its sole attention to the purely melodic utterance.—In such
translations as these, were the operas of Gluck presented to
German Art-criticism : operas whose very essence consists
in a faithful declamation of the words. Whoever has seen
a Berlin score of a Gluckian opera, and has convinced his
own eyes of the nature of the German textual lining wherewith these works have been set before the public, may get
an inkling of the character of that Berlin school of art-
æsthetics which has derived its standard for dramatic
declamation from the operas of Gluck. From Paris one
had heard so much about this dramatic declamation,
through literary channels, and now one has been so astound-
ingly clever as to recognise it for oneself in performances
given in those translations—which cast all proper declamation to the winds.—

But, far more important than their effect upon Prussian
Æsthetics, has been the influence of these translations on
our German *opera-singers*. They soon found themselves
compelled to abandon the vain attempt to bring this
textual lining into accordance with the notes of the
melody ; they accustomed themselves to paying less and
less heed to the text, as conveying any *sense ;* and through

---

* I lay stress upon these grossest offences, not that they have *invariably*
occurred in our translations, but since it has been possible for them to happen
over and over again—without disturbing either singers or audience. I make
use of the superlative, merely so as to betoken the most obvious physiognomy
of the thing.—R. WAGNER.

this disregard of theirs they emboldened the translators to an ever more thorough slovenliness in the prosecution of their labours, which, in the form of printed textbooks, gradually came to be put into the hands of the public for exactly the same purpose as the explanatory programme of a pantomime. Under such conditions the dramatic singer at last relinquished even the useless trouble of pronouncing the vowels and consonants, seeing that they were only a hindrance and difficulty to the singing voice, which he now employed as a musical instrument pure and simple. Thus, both for himself and the public, there was nothing left of the drama beyond its Absolute Melody—whose methods, in such a state of affairs, he even transferred to the *Recitative*. Since in the mouth of the translated German singer its groundwork was no longer the *diction*, this Recitative—wherewith at first he hadn't at all known what to do—soon gained for him a quite peculiar worth : it was such a respite from the time-beat of the Melody, and, free from the annoyance of the conductor's bâton, the singer here found a pleasing opportunity for production of his voice. To him the speechless Recitative was a chaos of disconnected notes, from which he might pick out the one or two that specially suited his register ; upon such a tone, occurring about once in every four or five notes, his delighted vocal vanity now pounced, and held it till the breath gave out. Wherefore the singer had a great partiality for making his first appearance with a recitative ; for it gave him the best opportunity of shewing himself—by no means as a dramatic elocutionist—but as the possessor of a good sound larynx and an excellent pair of lungs. This notwithstanding, the public held by its opinion that so-and-so was an eminently *dramatic* singer : one understood by the epithet precisely the same thing as what one praised in a violin-virtuoso, when he was clever enough to make his purely-musical execution both interesting and entertaining, by means of harmonics and double-stops.*

---

* "Abstufungen und Übergänge,"—I will not pledge myself that this is the correct translation ; ior the ordinary use of these words would mean

One can easily imagine the artistic results, if one were suddenly to set before these singers the Wordverse-Melody as to which we lately came to terms.   They would the less be able to deliver it, as they have already habituated themselves to getting through operas composed to German texts with exactly the same practices as in the translated operas ; and in this matter they have been backed by our modern German opera-composers themselves.—Time out of mind, the German language has been handled by German composers according to an arbitrary norm, which they borrowed from the treatment they had found applied to Speech in the operas of that foreign nation whence the Opera was first exported to us. The absolute Opera-melody—with those marked peculiarities of rhythm and melismus which it had evolved in Italy, in passable concordance with an arbitrarily accentuable tongue—had been the standard for our German opera-composers from the very first; this melody had been copied by them and varied on, and to *its* demands had the idiosyncrasies of our language and its accent to conform.   From everlasting, the German tongue has been treated by our composers as a mere translated lining for this melody ; and whoever wishes to convince himself of the truth of what I say, he need only examine, for instance, Winter's "Unterbrochenes Opferfest." Beyond the purely arbitrary accent given to the sense of the phrase, even the ' sensuous ' accent of the root-syllables is often completely subverted, in favour of the melismus ; moreover certain compound words, of double root-accent, are decried as downright un-composable, or—if they positively must be used—are set to an accent altogether foreign to the spirit of our speech.   Even the else so conscientious Weber is often quite reckless of the words, to please the melody.—Nay, in the very latest days, German opera-composers have actually *copied* the speech-affronting tone-accent of those translations, maintaining it as an enlargement of the domain of operatic language,—so that singers

"gradations and transitions," which, however, would not have much point here.—Tr.

to whom one were suddenly to present a Word-verse-Melody, such as we mean, would be absolutely incapable of delivering it in *our* sense.

The characteristic of *this* melody consists in its musical-expression being definitely conditioned by the speaking-verse, in its qualities both of sense and sound: only from amid these conditions has it taken this one particular musical shape, and our ever present fellow-feeling of these conditions, again, is the necessary postulate for its under-standing. Now, were this melody cut loose from its conditions,—as our singers most certainly would loose it from the speaking-verse,—it would stay quite unintelligible and unimpressive ; if nevertheless it could work an impres-sion through its purely musical factors, at least it would not work in the sense demanded by the Poetic Aim ; for, even if that melody *per se* should please the ear, there still would be a complete annihilation of the dramatic aim which assigns to that particular melody the significance of a warning voice from memory, whenever it is referred-to later in the orchestra,—a significance which can belong to it only when it has been seized and treasured-up by us, not as Absolute Melody, but as answering to a definitely uttered sense. Wherefore a drama couched in the Word-Tone speech aforesaid, but executed by our speechless singers, could make nothing but a purely musical impres-sion upon its hearers ; and, the right conditions for its comprehension having fallen out of count, this impression would be pretty much as follows :—

The speech-less Song perforce must prove indifferent and wearisome to us, wherever we did not find it chain our interest and captivate our ear through its promotion to the rank of Absolute Melody, cut loose from the word-verse both by giver and receivers. When recalled to mind by the orchestra, as a significant dramatic motive, this Melody would only wake our recollection of its naked self, and not of the motive erewhile proclaimed in it ; therefore its recur-rence at another stage of the drama would draw away our attention from the present moment, but not explain it for

us. Our ear not having roused our *inner* feeling, but
merely been woken to a thirst for outward, i.e. un-motived
change of pleasures,—this melody, now deprived of all
significance, could wellnigh only weary it by its return ;
so that ‖the very thing which really answered in the most
sensitive fashion to a suggestive wealth of Thought, would
take-on all the semblance of an importunate poverty of
utterance. Again the ear, when merely *musically* excited,
demands a satisfaction in the sense of the close-trimmed
musical structure to which it has been accustomed, and
would be utterly bewildered by the broadening of this
structure so as to cover *the whole drama ;* for that broad
extension of the musical Form, withal, can only be taken-in
and understood, in all its unity, by a Feeling attuned to
the actual Drama. To a Feeling *not* thus attuned, but
pinned down to purely sensuous Hearing, that broad and
unitarian Form to which the petty, narrow, disconnected
forms had been enlarged, would remain out-and-out
unknowable ; ergo, the whole musical edifice needs must
make the impression of a ragged, piecemeal, unsurveyable chaos, whose being and existence we could account-
for by nothing so much as the caprices of a fantastic,
incompetent and puzzle-brained musician.

But what would still more strengthen this impression of
ours, would be the haphazard freaks of a bridleless and
rampant Orchestra ; for the orchestra can never satisfy the
Absolute Hearing, unless it consistently emits its tale in
firm-knit, melodiously accented dance-rhythms.

We have seen that the first thing to which the Orchestra
has to devote its own peculiar faculty of expression, is the
Action's *dramatic gesture.* Let us observe, then, what
influence would be exerted upon the necessary gestures,
by the circumstance that the singer is singing without
any speech. The singer, who does not know that he is
the representative of a definite dramatic Personality,
primarily expressed by Speech ; the singer, who consequently does not perceive the connection of his dramatic
message with that of the personalities who come in

contact with him ; the singer, who thus does not even know *what* he is expressing,—is certainly in no position to convey to the eye the gestures requisite for an under-standing of the Action. Once that his delivery has become that of a wordless musical instrument, he will either not express himself at all by Gesture, or he will employ it in much the same way as the instrumental virtuoso who in certain places of his register, and certain moments of his execution, finds himself compelled to resort thereto as a physical help in need. These physic-ally necessary moments of Gesture, however, have been instinctively present to the rational (*vernünftigen*) poet and musician: he knows well enough when they will occur; but he has at like time brought them into harmony with the sense of the dramatic-expression, and thus has robbed them of the quality of a mere physical expedient. For he has taken a gesture conditioned by the physical organism, for the production of this particular note and this particular musical-expression, and has set it in unison with *that* gesture which is to answer withal to the sense of the message delivered by the dramatic personality ; and this he has done in such a way, that the Dramatic Gesture—which at any rate must have its ground in a physically conditioned one—shall vindicate this physical gesture from a higher standpoint, shall give it an import needful to the dramatic understanding of the thing, and thus shall cloak and cancel its purely physical aspect.

Now our theatrical singer, schooled by the rules of Absolute Vocalisation, has been taught a convention in accordance wherewith he is to accompany his delivery by certain stage-gestures. This convention has been borrowed from Dance-pantomime, and consists in nothing more or less than a genteel moderation of the gestures physically conditioned by the delivery of the notes,—gestures which degenerate with less tutored singers into grotesque ex-aggeration and vulgarity. This Conventional Gesture, in itself, results in nothing but an extirpation of the last vestige of verbal sense in the melody ; moreover it only applies to those places, in the Drama, where the performer really sings : so soon as he ceases to do this, he deems himself also absolved from any further concernment with Gesture. Our opera-composers, indeed, have used these pauses in the singing for their orchestral interludes, where either the individual instrumentists have had to display their special skill, or the composer himself has elected to draw the public's attention to his own art of instrumental weavery. These intervals, again, are filled by the singers according to certain rules of stage-decorum, provided they are not too busy with bowing their thanks for reaped applause : one goes to the other side of the proscenium, or passes to the back—as though to see whether anyone is coming,—then comes to the front again, and casts one's eyes toward heaven. It is considered less seemly in such pauses, albeit allowable and warranted in cases of dilemma, to lean over to one's partners, engage them in polite conversation, arrange the folds of one's dress, or finally, to do just nothing at all and patiently wait till the orchestral clouds of Fate roll by.*

Let one take this byplay of our opera-singers, which has been positively dictated to them by the spirit and form of those translated operas in which, almost exclusively, they have been wonted heretofore to sing ; and let one hold up to it the necessary demands of the Drama such as *we* mean : then, from the utter non-compliance with these demands, we may argue to the bewildering impression which the Orchestra must make upon the hearer. It will be remembered that, in its faculty of expressing the unspeakable, we have assigned to the orchestra the special task of supporting the dramatic gestures, of interpreting them, nay, in a sense, of making them first possible, through its language bringing to our thorough understanding the Unspeakable of Gesture. Wherefore it takes the most unresting interest in the Action, Motives and Expression,

---

* Is there any need for me to notice the exceptions, whose very lack of influence has proved the power of the general rule ?—R. WAGNER.

at every instant; on principle, its enouncements *in them-selves* must have no predetermined form, but gain their singleness of Form from nothing but its sharing in the drama's progress, from its becoming *one* with Drama. Conceive, then, an energetic gesture of passion, suddenly manifested by the performer, and as swiftly vanishing ; conceive it accompanied and expressed by the orchestra, precisely as that gesture needed :—in the complete har-mony between the two factors, such a collaboration cannot fail of an enthralling, a determinant effect. But behold! the conditioning gesture is absent from the stage, and we see the performer in some indifferent attitude or other : will not the sudden outburst, and as rapid vanishing of the orchestral tempest, appear to us an outbreak of insanity on the part of the composer ?—We could name, if we chose, a thousand of such cases : let the following couple serve by way of instance.

A loving maid has just dismissed her lover. She moves to a point whence she can gaze after him, into the dis-tance ; her gesture involuntarily betrays that he is once more turning to face her, as he goes away ; she waves him a last, a mute love-greeting. The orchestra accompanies and explains this graceful movement, bringing before us the full emotional-content of that dumb farewell, by musing on the melody which the representatrix had earlier made known to us in the actual words of greeting wherewith she welcomed her lover. But, if this melody has been sung on that first occasion by a *speechless* singeress, its mere return *per se* does not produce that speaking, memory-waking impression on us which it ought to do; to us it merely seems the repetition of a perhaps agreeable theme, which the composer brings on again because it had pleased himself and he feels warranted in coquetting with it. If the singeress goes still farther, however, and merely takes this postlude as an " orchestral ritornelle "; if she does not carry out that byplay at all, and remains standing indifferently in the foreground—just to wait till a ritornelle is over: then nothing can be more tiresome to the hearer than just that interlude; for, reft of any sense or meaning, it is simply a retardation, and had better be cut out.*

Our second case is one where the gesture explained by the orchestra is of downright decisory importance.—A situation has just been rounded off; obstacles have been set aside; and the mood is one of satisfaction. The poet wishes, however, to deduce from this situation its 'necessary' successor, and this aim of his can only be realised by letting us feel that that mood is *not* completely satisfied, in truth, those obstacles are *not* entirely set aside. He is concerned to make us recognise that the seeming quietude of his dramatis personæ is merely a self-illusion, on their part; and thus to so attune our Feeling, that we ourselves may frame the necessity of a further, an altered development of the situation, through our co-creative sympathy: to this end he brings before us the gesture of a mysterious personage whose motives, as hitherto divulged, have inspired us with anxiety as to a final satisfactory solution; and he makes this gesture *threaten* the chief character. This threat is meant to fill us with *foreboding*, while the orchestra is to elucidate the character of that foreboding,—and this it can only do by knitting it with a *remembrance;* wherefore he prescribes for this weighty moment the emphatic repetition of a melodic phrase which we have already heard as the musical expression of words referring to the threat, and which has the characteristic property of recalling to us the image of an earlier situation; and now, in union with the threatening gesture, this phrase becomes for us a prophecy, engrossing and instinctively determining our Feeling. — But, *this threatening gesture is omitted;* the situation leaves on us the impression of complete appeasement; merely the orchestra, contrary to all expectation, suddenly strikes in with a musical phrase whose sense we have not been able

---

* The allusion, of course, is to Act II. of *Tannhäuser*, while the following illustration refers to the close of Act II. of *Lohengrin.*—TR.

to catch from the earlier utterances of a speechless singer, and whose appearance at this juncture we therefore hold for a fantastic caprice on the part of the composer, to be severely frowned down.

Let this suffice to indicate the further humiliating consequences, for an understanding of our drama!—

To be sure, I here have dwelt upon the most preposterous offences; but that they *can* arise in every Operatic performance, even at theatres conducted in the very best spirit, no one will deny who has examined into the nature of such performances from the Dramatic standpoint; while their existence will give us a notion of the artistic demoralisation which has eaten into our stage-singers, and *chiefly* through the aforesaid circumstance, that they mostly sing nothing but translated works.   For, as said above, one does not find these particular faults among the Italians and French, or at least in nothing like the same degree,— and, with the Italians for the simple reason, that their operas never make any claims upon them but such as they are perfectly able to fulfil in their own fashion.

Precisely on the German stage—that is to say in the very language in which, for the present, it could be the most completely brought to pass—the Drama we propose would call up nothing but the wildest confusion and most complete misunderstanding.   Performers who cannot feel the Aim of Drama as a something present in their nighest fundamental organ—that of Speech,—can neither conceive what this Aim really is ; were they to attempt to do so from a purely musical standpoint—as customary,—they could not but misunderstand it, and in their embarrassment they would realise everything except that Aim.

To the *public*,* then, there would be left nothing but the

* By this term, " the public," I can never think of those units who employ their abstract Art-intelligence to make themselves familiar with things which

music, cut off from all dramatic aim ; and this music would
only make an impression on its hearers exactly *where* it
seemed to depart from that aim in such a way as to offer,
entirely for itself, a pleasant tingling to the ear. From the
apparently unmelodic song of the Singer—that is to say,
" unmelodic " in the sense of our wonted instrumental-
melody transplanted to the voice—the public would have
to look about for enjoyment in the playing of the Orchestra ;
and here it might perhaps be fascinated by one thing,
namely the instinctive stimulus of an extremely changeable
and variegated *instrumentation.*

To raise the strangely potent language of the Orchestra
to such a height, that at every instant it may plainly manifest to Feeling the Unspeakable of the Dramatic Situation,
—to do this, as we have already said, the musician inspired
by the poet's Aim has not to haply practise self-restraint ;
no, he has to sharpen his inventiveness to the point of
discovering the most varied orchestral idioms, to meet the
necessity he feels of a pertinent, a most determinate Expression. So long as this language is incapable of a
declaration as individual as is needed by the infinite variety
of the Dramatic Motives themselves ; so long as the
message of the Orchestra is too monochrome to answer
these motives' individuality,—so long may it prove a disturbing factor, because not yet completely satisfying : and

are never realised upon the stage. By " the public " I mean that assemblage
of spectators without any specifically cultivated Art-understanding, to whom
the represented drama should come for their complete, their *entirely toilless
Emotional-understanding ;* spectators, therefore, whose interest should never
be led to the mere art-media employed, but solely to the artistic object realised
thereby, to the drama *as a represented Action, intelligible to everyone.* Since
the public, then, is to *enjoy* without the slighest effort of an Art-intelligence, its
claims are grievously slighted when the performance—for the reasons given
above—does not realise the dramatic-aim ; and it is completely within its rights,
if it turns its back on such a representment.   On the other hand the connoisseur who, in defiance of the performance, takes pains to think out the unrealised
dramatic-aim for himself, by aid of the text-book and a critical interpretation
of the music—which generally receives good treatment at the hands of our
orchestras,—from this connoisseur such a mental strain is exacted, as must rob
him of all *enjoyment* of the artwork, and convert into a toilsome labour the very
thing which was meant to instinctively delight and enthrall him.—R. WAGNER.

therefore in the Complete Drama, like everything that is not *entirely* adequate, it would divert attention toward itself. To be true to our aim, however, such an attention is absolutely *not* to be devoted to it; but, through its everywhere adapting itself *with the utmost closeness* to the finest shade of individuality in the Dramatic Motive, the Orchestra is irresistibly to guide our whole attention *away from itself*, as a *means of expression*, and direct it to the *subject expressed*. So that the very richest dialect of the Orchestra is to manifest itself with the artistic object of not being noticed, in a manner of speaking, of *not being heard at all:* to wit, not heard in its *mechanical*, but only in its *organic* capacity, wherein it is One with the Drama.

How must it discourage the poet musician, then, were he to see his drama received by the public with sole and marked attention to the mechanism of his Orchestra, and to find himself rewarded with just the praise of being a "very clever Instrumentalist"? How must he feel at heart —he whose every shaping was prompted by the Dramatic Aim,—if art-literarians should report on his drama, that they had read a textbook and had heard, to boot, a wondrous music-ing by flutes and fiddles and trumpets, all working in and out?—

But, could this Drama possibly produce any other effect, under the circumstances detailed above?—

And yet! are we to give up being Artists? Or are we to abandon all necessary insight into the nature of things, because we can draw no profit thence?—Were it no profit, then, to be not only an Artist, but a *Man* withal; and is an artificial know-nothingness, a womanish dismissal of knowledge, to bring us more profit than a sturdy consciousness, which, if only we put all seeking-of-self behind us, will give us cheerfulness, and hope, and courage above all else, for deeds which needs must rejoice ourselves, how little soever they be crowned with an outward success?

For sure! Even now, it is only knowledge that can prosper us; whilst ignorance but holds us to a joyless, divided, hypochondriacal, scarcely will-ing and never can-ning make-believe of Art, whereby we stay unsatisfied within, unsatisfying without.

Look round you, and see where ye live, and for whom ye make your art!—That our artistic comrades for the representment of a dramatic artwork are not forthcoming, we must recognise at once, if we have eyes the least whit sharpened by Artistic Will. Yet how greatly we should err, if we pretended to explain this by a demoralisation of our opera-singers due entirely to their own fault; how we should deceive ourselves, if we thought necessary to regard this phenomenon as accidental, and not as conditioned by a broad, a general conjuncture!—Let us suppose for an instant, that in some way or other we acquired the power of so working upon performers and performance, from the standpoint of artistic intelligence, that a highest Dramatic-aim should be fully carried out,—then for the first time we should grow actively aware that we lacked the real enabler of the artwork, a Public to feel the need of it, and to make its Need the all-puissant fellow-shaper. The Public of our theatres has no *need* for Artwork ; it wants to *distract* itself, when it takes its seat before the stage, but not to *collect* itself ; and the Need of the seeker after distraction is merely for artificial *details*, but not for an artistic *unity*. If we gave it a whole, the public would be blindly driven to tear that whole to disconnected fragments, or, in the most fortunate event, it would be called upon to understand a thing which it altogether *refuses* to understand; wherefore, in full consciousness, it turns its back on any such artistic aim. From this result we should only gain a proof *why* such a performance is absolutely out of the question at present, and why our opera-singers are bound to be exactly what they are and what they cannot else be.

To account to ourselves for this attitude of the Public towards the performance, we must necessarily pass to a judgment on this Public itself. If we cast a look at earlier ages of our theatric history, we can only regard this Public as involved in an advancing degradation. The excellent work, the pre-eminently *fine* that has been done already in our art, we surely cannot consider it as dropped upon us from the skies ; no, we must conclude that it was prompted withal by the *taste* of those before whom it was produced. We meet this Public of fine taste and feeling, at its most marked degree of active interest in art-production, in the period of the Renaissance. Here we see princes and nobles not only sheltering Art, but so engrossed with its finest and its boldest shapings, that the latter must be taken as downright summoned into being by their enthusiastic Need.   This noble rank—nowhere attacked in its position ; knowing nothing of the misery of the thralls whose life made that position possible ; holding itself completely aloof from the industrial and commercial spirit of the burgher life ; living away its life of pleasure in its palaces, of courage on the field of battle,—this nobility had trained its eyes and ears to discern the beautiful, the graceful, nay, even the characteristic and energetic ; and at *its* commands arose those works of art which signal that epoch as the most favoured artistic period since the downfall of Greek Art.   The infinite grace and delicacy in Mozart's tone-modellings—which seem so dull and tedious to a public bred to-day on the grotesque—were delighted-in by the descendants of that old nobility ; and it was to Kaiser Joseph that Mozart appealed, from the mountebankish shamelessness of the singers of his "*Figaro.*"   Nor will we look askance at those young French cavaliers, whose enthusiastic applause at the Achilles-aria in Gluck's "*Iphigenia in Tauris*" turned the wavering balance in favour of that work ;—and least of all will we forget that, whilst the greater courts of Europe had become the political camps of intriguing diplomats, in Weimar a German

royal family was listening with rapt attention to the loftiest
and most graceful poets of the German nation.

But the rulership of public taste in Art has passed over
to the person who now pays the artists' wages, in place of
the nobility which erstwhile recompensed them ; to the
person who orders the artwork for his money, and insists
on ever novel variations of his one beloved theme, but at
no price a new theme itself : and this ruler and this order-
giver is—*the Philistine.* As this Philistine is the most
heartless and the basest offspring of our Civilisation, so is
he the most domineering, the cruelest and foulest of Art's
bread-givers.   True, that everything comes aright to him :
only, he will have nothing to do with aught that might
remind him that he is to be a *man,*—either on the side of
beauty, or on that of nerve.   He *wills* to be base and
common, and to this will of his has Art to fit herself : for
the rest,—why ! nothing comes to him amiss.—Let us turn
our look from him as quickly as may be !—

Are we to make bargains with such a world?—No, no !
For even the most humiliating terms would leave us sheer
outside the pale.—

Hope, faith and courage can we only gain, when we
recognise even the modern State-philistine not merely as a
conditioning, but likewise as a conditioned factor of our
Civilisation ; when we search for the conditionments of
this phenomenon, too, in a conjuncture such as that we
have just examined in the case of Art.   We shall not win
hope and nerve until we bend our ear to the heart-beat of
history, and catch the sound of that sempiternal vein of
living waters which, however buried under the waste-heap
of historic civilisation, yet pulses on in all its pristine
freshness.   Who has not felt the leaden murk that hangs
above us in the air, foretelling the near advent of an earth-
upheaval ?   And we who hear the trickling of that well-
spring, shall we take affright at the earthquake's sound?

Believe me, no ! For we know that it will only tear aside the heap of refuse, and prepare for the stream that bed in which we soon shall even *see* its living waters flow.

Where now the statesman loses hope, the politician sinks his hands, the socialist beplagues his brain with fruitless systems, yea, even the philosopher can only hint, but not foretell,—since all that looms before us can only form a series of un-wilful happenings, whose physical show no mortal man may preconceive,—there it is the *artist*, whose clear eye can spy out shapes that reveal themselves to a yearning which longs for the only truth—*the human being*. The artist has the power of seeing beforehand a yet unshapen world, of tasting beforehand the joys of a world as yet unborn, through the stress of his desire for Growth. But his joy is in imparting, and—if only he turns his back on the senseless herds who browse upon the grassless waste-heap, and clasps the closer to his breast the cherished few who listen with him to the well-spring,—so finds he, too, the hearts, ay, finds the senses, to whom he can impart his message. We are *older* men and *younger :* let the elder not think of himself, but love the younger for sake of the bequest he sinks into his heart for new increasing,—the day will come when that heirloom shall be opened for the weal of brother Men throughout the world !

We have seen the Poet driven onward by his yearning for a perfect Emotional-expression, and seen him reach the point where he found his Verse reflected on the mirror of the sea of Harmony, as musical Melody : unto this sea was he compelled to thrust ; only the mirror of this sea could shew him the image of his yearning ; and this sea he could not create from his own Will, but it was the Other * of his being, That wherewith he needs must wed himself, but which he could not prescribe from out himself,

* " Das Andre, das ich ersehne," *Walküre*, act ii ; " Ein andrer ist's,—ein andrer, ach ! " *Parsifal*, act ii.—TR.

nor summon into being.—So neither can the artist prescribe from his own Will, nor summon into being, that
Life of the Future which once shall redeem him : for it
is the Other, the antithesis of himself, for which he yearns,
toward which he is thrust ; That which, when brought him
frʋm an opposite pole, is for the first time present for him,
first takes his semblance up into it, and knowably reflects
it back.   Yet again, this living ocean of the Future cannot
beget that mirror-image by its unaided self : it is a mother-
element, which can bear alone what it has first received.
This fecundating seed, which in *it* alone can thrive, is
brought it by the Poet, i.e. the Artist of the Present ;
and this seed is the quintessence of all rarest life-sap,
which the Past has gathered up therein, to bring it to
the Future as its necessary, its fertilising germ : *for this
Future is not thinkable, except as stipulated by the Past.*

Now, the *melody* which appears at last upon the water-
mirror of the harmonic ocean of the Future, is the clear-
seeing eye wherewith this Life gazes upwards from the
depth of its sea-abyss to the radiant light of day.   But the
verse, whose mere mirror-image it is, is the own-est poem
of the Artist of the Present, begotten by his most peculiar
faculty, engendered by the fulness of his yearning.   *And
just as this verse. will the prophetic Artwork of the yearning
Artist of the Present once wed itself with the ocean of the
Life of the Future.*—In that Life of the Future, will this
Artwork be what to-day it yearns for but cannot actually
be as yet : for that Life of the Future will be entirely what
it *can* be, only through its taking up into its womb this
Artwork.

*The begetter of the Artwork of the Future is none other
than the Artist of the Present, who presages that Life of
the Future, and yearns to be contained therein.   He who
cherishes this longing within the inmost chamber of his
powers, he lives already in a better life ;—but only One can
do this thing :—*

the Artist.

SUMMARY.

DEDICATION OF SECOND EDITION

(to Constantin Frantz).

Reception accorded to first edition ; had obviously fallen into hands of mere *professional musicians.* Recent demand, for purposes of ferreting out subversive tenets. Worries of a new edition (4). Politician, artist, and *German Spirit.* Eccentricity of his old [political] opinions. Theatre-public and " the wounds of which my successes are bleeding still." *Oper und Drama:* difficulties of exposition, and stubbornness of style. Theorising æstheticians ; the artist and the earnest thinker ; the only true success (7).

PREFACE TO FIRST EDITION.

Anger roused by his endeavours to forecast, in *Art-work of Future.* Sloth and sense of honour. Another grudge will now be roused, by exposition of worthlessness of modern operatic affairs. Not a smothered growl, but categorical defiance, is needed. "This one personage" [Meyerbeer] and "the Error." Prudence and prejudice v. exile and artistic courage. Of all things the most dangerous is half-heartedness. The *ulterior* object of the book (11).

INTRODUCTION.

An error is never done with, till all its possibilities have been exhausted. Modern Opera an asylum for the madness of the world. Fumbling Criticism and "gradual" progress ; lives by "Though, But, and Ne'ertheless." To crush the Error and root up Criticism, artists themselves must practise criticism (14). Replies to an article on "Modern Opera": musical *characteristique* and Meyerbeer ; Mendelssohn's early death ; was Mozart a lesser musician? The Drama's *whole;* but its architect? Error's crown of errors ; the *open·death of Opera.* The riddle's solution : "a means of Expression has been made the end" (17). The briefest survey of Opera's evolution teaches this ; it arose in Italy, where "the Drama never developed to any significance," *not* from the medieval Folk-play ; vocal dexterities. Metastasio and opera-librettists : the obliging servants of the Musician. The genuine Drama on a basis of Absolute Music !

FIRST PART.—OPERA AND MUSIC.

Chapter I.

Music thrust into a false position toward Poetry ; desiring to outline definitely the thing to-be-expressed. *Earnest,* and *frivolous* lines of Opera.

Earnest line.—The Aria was the basis of Opera : the Folk-song with its word-poem left out. Into the Dramatic Cantata was dovetailed next the

378 SUMMARY.

Ballet. Art-dexterities; the aim of Drama merely lodged, not housed (25). Recitative borrowed from plain-song; a theatric scaffolding of Greek mythology.—Gluck simply revolted *consciously* against the singing Virtuoso; sceptre of Opera passes definitely to the Composer, who henceforth rules the Poet still more strictly (28). Gluck's successors; their enlargement of Form of aria, duet &c., increasing warmth of Expression. The Ensemble. Cherubini, Méhul and Spontini attain all that Gluck could have desired. Spontini's belief that he had reached the acme of operatic Form; the honest, confident voice of the Absolute Musician (30).

The opera-circus; the poet the musician's groom. Dramatic sketches of one settled pattern, and trite rhetorical phrases (32). A make-believe of Drama, without a real dramatic *aim*: music not merely its expression, but its *content*; "modern Dramatic opera" the actual advent of the madness (34).

Chapter II.

Gluck's *reflective* Opera compared with naïve line of Italy, the home of modern music; but a German, Mozart, mirrored back the brightest flower of Italian music. Mozart's procedure contrasted with Mendelssohn's cautious steps. In none of Mozart's instrumental works is Music so richly furthered, as in his operas; but never could he write *beautiful* music, unless inspired by the text (37). He would have helped to pen the truest *drama*, if only he had met the *poet*; but he left the formal skeleton of Opera unaltered. His imitators. Essence of the *Aria* absolute-musical. The Folk had brooked no tune without its words: the man of luxury heard the Folk-song and distilled its scent (40). Rossini—the uncommonly handy modeller of artificial flowers: Mozart, in his death, bore away his Life; Spontini embalmed himself alive, and Rossini tore away the cerecloths. He meant to *live*, and struck the ear-delighting *absolute-melodic* Melody; Alexander's sword and the naked Deed; "delicious melodies." Rossini and his singers, band, and poet (43). His complaisance to opera-public; a Rossinian *"Don Giovanni"* was possible. A reactionary, like Prince Metternich: "Do you ask for Opera and State? Here you have them." Visit of Europe's idol to the moody Beethoven—unreturned.—With Rossini died the Opera; yet a wonderful fresh lease of life was to be drawn—the Bankers presently would make it for themselves. In expiation for his sins, Rossini became a fish-purveyor and church-composer (47).

Chapter III.

Since Rossini, Opera's history that of operatic *melody*. Gluck and his serious followers had deceived themselves with their dramatic "declamation"; the public only listened to the Tune. But Rossini had not *exhausted* Melody's essence; deeper-feeling musicians and the utterance of human Feeling; Weber reaches back to Folk-song. Stir of waking Freedom; national *masses*, not *men*; National line of Opera parallel with political evolution (50). Weber and the "Folk's-bloom": goes down to seek it in the meadows; unhappy man! he *plucked it*; set in a costly vase, it sheds its petals; the flower bloomed no more (52). Characteristics of German Folk-melody—mainly harmonic; broad and general emotional expression; sincerity; purely-human; the *German* spirit. Weber made this the actual factor of his Opera. *Freischütz* and *Tancredi*:

sinnig v. *sinnlich.* Weber's stammering proves Music incapable of becoming, in herself, the genuine Drama (54).

French composers follow in the wake ; but the inner contents of their native Couplet (whose *musical* essence was the Contredanse) had been sucked dry by Vaudeville and Comic Opera ; so the hunt in foreign lands began (56). Auber gallops through the Naples markets, makes Rossini a handsome bow, and gives to Paris *Masaniello.* Rossini returns the compliment with *Guillaume Tell.* A new recipe for galvanising half-paralysed Opera ; German art-critics classify, —the "national." Society rooting up the orchard of the Folk, and German critics calling it " higher *Charakteristik* " and " *Emanzipation* of the Masses " (59).

Chapter IV.

The Folk and the Hero : his deeds it celebrates in Epos and re-enacts in Drama. Greek Tragedy and chorus ; Shakespeare resolves chorus into definite individuals ; Opera takes the hollow masks : " Prince and Princess." The Surrounding, i.e. Opera-chorus. Mozart and his Osmin and Figaro : Modern Opera and colourless characters (62). Not the Folk was wanted, but the *Mass ;* thundrous Unison and nimble noise ; " Huguenots " and Prussian Guard.

A mask the more. Not *men* from the Poet, but *puppets* from the Mechanician. Historic costume and " historic " music ; hymns,—Religion shall take a turn upon the stage (65). " Emancipation of the Church," since the only serviceable historic music lay there ; but only as a side-dish. Creation out of nothing, and Something from two negatives—" emancipated Metaphysics." The *outlandish* becomes another Mode ; " no," where one means " yes " ; feign craziness, to be deemed " historico-characteristic,"—Neoromantic (68).

Chapter V.

All that has really *shaped* Opera has issued from Absolute Music, never from Poetry. Vocal melody and mechanism of the Instrument ; *instrumental-*melody the main factor in this fictive drama. Instrumental music had won itself an idiomatic speech; Beethoven's error in wishing to express definite emotions therein (71). A Pythian oracle misunderstood by his followers, as to the works of second half of his artistic life. His efforts to voice his longing ; sketches and finished pictures. People found a quarry of quaint melodic, harmonic, or rhythmic features in his musical sketches, for their Music-for-all-the-world ; his *secret* un-spoken, they made a Programme appeal to Phantasy (74). While German composers jogged along with respectability and compromise, a Frenchman took up the extreme ; master and pupil. Berlioz stared at Beethoven's enigmatic penstrokes, till he grew giddy ; opium-eater's fancy, a witch-like chaos ; enormous musical intelligence and technical power. The supernatural, i.e. un-natural. Berlioz and his orchestra ; lies buried beneath his machines (77). Formerly the Orchestra had employed nothing but dance-rhythms for its accompaniment of the dramatic action ; now that the Symphonists had broken up that rhythmic Form, Meyerbeer borrows from Berlioz the fragments, and lifts them into the voice itself. A " frivolous and flimsy *melodique* " now constitutes dramatic-musical *Characteristique* (80).

Chapter VI.

Gluck strove consciously to correctly express the emotion indicated in the text ; Mozart, by nature, could never speak incorrectly ; grey was grey, with him, and red red, but infinitely shaded ; characters of *Don Giovanni* and Hoffmann. Mozart, Rossini and Weber, and their librettists. Weber in *Freischütz* forced the poet to erect the stake on which he was to be burnt alive ; in *Euryanthe* he demanded that the very ashes of his poetess should not remain ; wished to crown his noble Melody as the Muse of Drama (83). If *Euryanthe's* text had been the work of a veritable poet, Weber would have known how to treat it, but he broke his broader melody to pieces, fitted them as a mosaic, and added a fine coat of melodic varnish, to preserve a show of Absolute Melody. This half-melody left the public undecided, *wherefore* the critics could not take proper stock of the work ; yet never have the contradictions of the operatic genre been manifested so plainly : attempt to combine absolute, self-sufficient melody with unflinchingly true dramatic expression. Weber breathes away his life through *Oberon's* wonder-horn (87).

Meyerbeer, no mother-tongue ; compared with Gluck ; rhetoric and musical expression. M. the starling in the furrow ; taking the word from "the man in front " ; the weather-cock of European music ; in Paris at one bound ; the Frenchified Weber and be-Berliozed Beethoven fall into clutches of *Robert the* grim *Devil*. Only the dead masters have deserved a martyr's crown ; illusion v. madness ; odious exploitation of opera-affairs, but on the side of "madness" M. an object of regret and warning, not of scorn (90). Retrospect. The result could not have come about, without the Poet's confederacy ; the Poet held the title-deeds ; French comic opera ; translated by Scribe and Auber into pompous phraseology of "Grand Opera." The Poet still held the reins of the opera-coach, but ousted by M ; opera-confabulations with Scribe, whose brain he must have unhinged (93). Historical hanky-panky and a "Prophet" of the sharpers ; a dramatic hotch-potch with many adjectives ; springing the whole thing into the air. An inscenation of the Berliozian orchestra, but degraded to Rossini's vocal trills and *fermate ;* something for every man in his own line. A delicate compliment to M. The *musician* crowned as the only *authentic poet* (95).

"Effect," i.e. a "Working, without a cause " ; the object-of-expression reduced to stage-machinery. Example : a hero of the Folk and the entrenched oppressors ; a thundrous hymn and "involuntary " sunrise ; the real "hero " *not to hand,*—M.'s *Prophète :* characteristically-costumed "communistic" tenor, and master-stroke of mechanism ; Absolute Effect (99).

Compared with most of his musical contemporaries, we are tempted to set down M.'s musical capacity at zero ; yet in places he lifts himself to the very greatest artistic power, when the Poet supplies a strong dramatic situation : fourth Act of *Huguenots*. But these are exceptions ; the musician's "madness" ; Music sunk to utmost spiritual penury ; loss of all power of natural Expression. The *means* of Expression wished to prescribe the *aim* of Drama (102).

Chapter VII.

Participation of the Poet in the sane relationship that is to come. Survey of Music's essence. Harmony and Rhythm the shaping organs, but Melody the first real *shape*, of Music. Melody the eye of man. Greek Art, Christianity, and Folk's-melody. Church-song and Harmony ; Dance and Rhythm. Bookish music and men to be made from chemical decoctions : this Man is Melody ; opera-composers stripping its skin to clothe a puppet. Instrumental music and Beethoven's yearning (106). Beethoven lets melody *be born* before our very eyes ; for compassing the act of *begetting*, however, he required the Poet ; his Ninth Symphony and its " *Freude* "-melody. He breaks the narrow Form, and repieces the component parts, thus *practising* the inner organism of Music in Bearing ; but at last his music's Expression (in this Choral Symphony) is worked up to a dramatic directness, answering the highest sense of Schiller's words. Artistic Deed (110).

Music a woman ; Woman's nature *love ;* receiving, conceiving, and bearing. Woman's honourable pride, will, and individuality ; the constraint of Love. Three types of loveless women : Italian Opera the wanton ; French Opera the coquette ; "German" Opera the prude. True Music, and Woman surrendering her *whole* being. Woman's Deed, to be *entirely what she is ;* beautiful instinctiveness and Love's necessity. Mozart the typical Musician.

Who must be the Man (the poet) this Woman is to love so unreservedly ?

SECOND PART.—THE PLAY AND POETRY.

Introductory.

In his Laocöon, Lessing dealt only with descriptive, i.e. epic poetry, drawing a line between it and plastic art ; at any rate he did not mean the *acted* drama : misunderstood by modern æsthetes. Purity necessary to the art-*variety :* reading a romance of Goethe's in a picture-gallery, amidst statues, while a symphony of Beethoven's is being played. True Drama is no art-*variety.* Literary-drama evolving in the same way as the pianoforte ; hammers —but no men : yet both had their origin in the living tone of human Speech (123).

Chapter I.

Twofold origin of Modern Drama : the Romance, and the misunderstood Greek Drama. Shakespeare and Racine, the two extremes.

Man's inner conflict, at the Renaissance. Middle Ages had brought forth the narrative poem, with its extravagant combinations ; the newer era brings forth Drama, i.e. the condensement into a definite utterance to the senses (127). Shakespearian Drama sprang from Life ; the mummers of the Folk become actors : "Give me your stage, I give you my speech." Narrowing the Folk-stage to the Theatre. Mystery-plays and whole adventures of a lifetime ; a fitting pendant to the monstrously discursive medieval Histories ; mask-like dearth of character. Shakespeare curtailed also the time-length of perform-ance ; but left the *scene* to Phantasy, thus leaving open a door for utter con-fusion in dramatic art for over two centuries (130).

The Romanic nations, at period of Renaissance, endeavouring to distract the inner conflict by outward show. Painting and Architecture had made their eye exacting; it demanded the Scene; stability and unity of scene. Aristotle's rules and Racine's tragédie; Talk upon the stage, and behind the scene the Action (133).

Modern Drama a hybrid of Shakespearian and Racinian; Germany its soil; a Luther, but no Shakespeare. While all Europe took up Art, Germany remained a meditant barbarian; only what was done with, outside, took flight to Germany; Shakespeare's drama imported by the Folk, Italian opera by the Princes. Operatic ostentation of scene; had Shakespeare felt this *scenic* necessity, he would have still further condensed his dramatic Stuff (136). German actors of last century adapting his plays, by omitting lesser scenes; literary readers found how much these plays thus suffered; Tieck's proposal to restore the sceneless stage. English—and later, Germans—employing elaborate stage-mountings and rapid change of scene; the modern poet, bewildered by this mass of realisms and actualisms, writes literary-dramas for dumb reading, or turns to the pseudo-antique (139).

Goethe began his dramatic career with a full-blooded Feudal-Romance, *Götz;* written from literary standpoint, but cut and revised for stage. He next chose his stuff from Burgher-romance—in *Egmont*—which presented less difficulties for 'mounting'; submitting to cramping maxims, but not the cramped spirit of the burgher public. In *Faust* he merely retained the advantages of a dramatic mode of statement; the *thrust of Thought toward Actuality*, but still half "abstract." *Faust* the water-shed beween Burgher-romance and Drama of Future. Seeking for pure artistic Form, he turns back—in *Iphigenia*—to method of the French; finally returns to undramatised Romance, to present the choicest flower of his modern world-view (142).

Schiller also began with dramatising the Romance, domestic and political, till he reached naked History itself, and endeavoured to make a drama of that. Faced with the modern Scene, he found it impossible to preserve the chronicler's fidelity of Shakespeare, and attempted a poetic adaptation; but, if we alter the facts and actions, we alter their motives, and therefore the historic characters themselves: neither History, nor yet a Drama. His *Wallenstein* trilogy; Shakespeare in three plays would have given us the whole Thirty-years War (145). Schiller drops History more and more, and follows Goethe into artistic speculation: his *Bride of Messina* goes even farther in its imitation of Greek Form, adopting the Greek "Fate"; but neither the sophisticated medieval Stuff comes to an effect, nor the antique Form to clear view; he turns back to dramatised Romance in *William Tell,* to save his poetic freshness. His poetic Ideal excluded actual Life: the highest Art to be a thing of dreams. Thus he hovered between heaven and earth, and our whole dramatic poetry hovers after him: compelled to strip its plumes, and address the dumb reader as a naked novel (148).—(Epitome of the chapter)—Revivals of old Greek tragedy; literary Lyrics; French realistic Romance; revolutionary force of the Folk. *We have no Drama;* our literary drama a product of mechanism; true Music can have nothing to do with *it* (151).

Chapter II.

Man's poetic *beholding*, and *imparting :* i.e. natural, and artistic. Phantasy, measure, and a view in common ; only from the Greek world-view has the genuine Drama blossomed as yet ; its stuff was *Mythos.* The Folk's joint poetic-force ; Man, disquieted by multiplicity of Nature's phenomena, seeks a Cause ; anthropomorphism, the most succinct of shapes. Art is the fulfilment of a longing to know oneself in the likeness of an object of one's love or adoration ; Mythos—God, Hero, Man (155). Greek Tragedy the artistic embodiment of spirit and content of Greek mythos ; the shapes of Thought presented by actual *men ;* a complete and plastic whole. A great idea requires a great, decisive action. Myth, the poem of a life-view in common.

Even the newer world has won its shaping-force from Myth ; mingling of two great mythic rounds in the medieval Romance. a) Christian mythos— man become a stranger to himself, through Law and State, seeks redemption into an extramundane Being (158). Jesus, *transfiguration through Death ;* a smile on the wan cheeks and blanching lips ; unsuffering, reposeful bliss. Yearning for Death became the content of all Christian art, unlike the Greek ; unfitted for Drama, which needs an *increasing* movement. Passion-plays were only pictures ; the Legend, the Christian Romance ; Music alone could fitly *represent* the Christian Content (160).

b) Second cycle of myths—Germanic Saga ; here, also, beholdings of Nature grow into picturings of Gods and Heroes. Sun-myths and ancestor-worship ; one definite type, with variations shaped by Folk's poetic intuitions. Christianity laid hands on the *root,* but could not touch the branches ; splintering the Germanic Epos into its individual fractions ; a monstrous mass of actions, no longer understood. Christian religious view lighting up the *corpse* of Mythos (163). The "spiritual" poem of Chivalry and the leavings of Paganism ; Crusades and medley of fables from East and West ; gulping down the *outlandish.* Stress to flee from an un-understood reality to a world of fancy ; close-packed images ; yearning to realise ; voyages of discovery and scientific research,—the world at last uncloaked as it really is. Medieval romance destroyed, and delineation of reality. Knowledge of Nature to be followed by knowledge, and shaping, of Human Life (165).

Intrinsic contradictoriness of Christian life-view ; the *maintenance* of man's inner discord became the Church's life-task ; imposing her authority on worldly rulers, she drove them to consolidate the State against the Individual. Man's outward thrust turns against both oppressors ; but he has first to explore the *actuality* of human life ; to be portrayed, artistically, in Romance alone (168).

Man can only be comprehended in conjunction with his Surrounding, with human Society, and this latter by tracing back Historic relations to their source. From amid this wilderness of facts to unearth the real Man, the Investigator must become a poet ; but his method opposed to the dramatist's ; the historic personage's "idea" based on a view current at the time, therefore only to be explained through the Surrounding, and this by a mass of details. Drama goes organically from within outwards—a simple Surrounding enriched by development of the Individuality : Historical Romance goes mechanically from without inwards—a complex Surrounding feeding an empty individuality

(172). This Romance reached its highest pitch as art-form by moulding
types, compressing whole historic periods into the caprices of one individual,
and thus fitting them for our modern forged Historical Drama; the latter
again exposed true History's unsuitableness for Drama. Romance stepped
down again, and sought for Actuality in faithful portraiture of social life of
Burgher class (175). But the externals of Burgher-society were a characterless
mask; lifted, the whole unloveliness of human society was revealed. Schiller
and Goethe turned away rom the sight—the latter, in *Wilhelm Meister*, to
hang on man's true shape a *cloak* of artistic beauty. But an artistic bond is no
longer possible, where everything is struggling to disband; the Romance
becomes Journalism, political articles, and a summons to the people.

Whoever at this instant steals away from Politics, belies his own being;
the Poet cannot come again to light till we have no more politics. Napoleon
I, and politics now filling rôle of "Fate"; we must lay to heart this saying,
before we can discover *what* is the true subject-matter for our Drama (178).

Chapter III.

Greek "Fate" was the inner Nature-necessity, *ours* is the arbitrary
political State. Nature-necessity is shewn the strongest in the instinctive life-
bent of the Individual; misinterpreted by the Greek, from Society's standpoint
of use-and-wont.

The Œdipus-myth.—Instinctive feelings that prompt all Family love (181).
Wont the instinctive basis of human Society, growing into an ethical conception, but unable to stamp out individual instinct; the war of these two
instincts typified by the Sphinx; its riddle still unsolved, and *we* must solve it,
by reconciling the Individual and Society (183). As the Individual—
Œdipus—had sinned against Society unconsciously, so the Individual—
Antigone—consciously defends the holiest social sentiments against the State
—Creon. Eteocles and broken oaths; in him the Theban burghers recognised
the principle of Property as a guarantor of order and quiet; Polynices represented the Purely-human, Society in its widest, most natural sense (185).
The burghers shift their responsibility upon their Gods and Rulers. Creon
had remarked that public opinion only wished to avoid open scandals, but was
most indulgent to sins against the Purely-human; he strikes Humanity across
the face and cries Long live the State! (188). One sorrowing heart in all this
State: Antigone knew nothing of politics,—she *loved*. What kind of love
was this? The topmost flower of all: pure Human Love. Self-annihilation
in the cause of sympathy. The love-curse of Antigone annulled the State; it
fell crashing to the ground, to become in death a *human being*.

Wondrous! that this should have been the Greek Tragedy chosen for
Potsdam! The work whose art-Form was found the purest, had also the
purest-human Content (190).

The Mythos true for all time; the poet's only task to expound it. In
Œdipus-myth a picture of man's history, from beginnings of Society to downfall
of State. Rulership and ownership. The *abstract* State; thinkers and "sinfulness" of human nature. The political State lives solely on the *vices of
society*, whose *virtues* come solely from the individual. From the free self-

determining Individuality to *organise* Society, is the conscious task of the Future (194).

Chapter IV.

It was the poet's necessary task to display the Individual's struggle to throw off the bonds of political State or religious Dogma ; but this Individuality was *no* purely-human one, merely the reflex of the State. No one can depict an Individuality without the Surrounding that conditions it ; wherefore the poet who dealt with our modern Society, or any like it, had to deal with a mass of circumstantial detail, from it to reconstruct the Individuality, and finally to present it to abstract Thought ; with *him* Feeling is the obstacle, and his organ of utterance can only be unemotional Word-speech : from the very first, the modern poet has to exhibit a Surrounding—the State—which is void of any purely-human sentiment, and therefore un-communicable through Feeling's highest organ, Music. The return from Understanding to Feeling, will be the march of the Drama of the Future (200).

The matter of this Drama.—Conscience v. Duty. So long shall we have states and religions, till we have but *one* Religion, and no longer *any* State. In the free self-determining of the Individuality there lies the basis of the social Religion of the Future. The infinite variety of relationships [for the poet to dramatise] when the State &c shall have passed away. Life's " chief-moments " : youth and age, ardour and repose, &c. (203). The 'moment' of Wont. Experience rejoicing at the deeds of others—and thereby enriching itself—the very life-element of Art. With the man of instinct no moral exhortations can have the efficacy of a likeness lovingly held up to him. Feeling, Understanding, and *Vernunft*. Through fellow-feeling man gains knowledge of, and uprightness towards his opposites, when snatched out of himself by the hand of Art (207).

The Drama differs from all other forms of poetry, in that its Aim is lifted into utmost imperceptibility, through its *entire realisation ;* Life, as vindicated by its own Necessity ; we must become *knowers* through the Feeling ; " so *must* it be." The dramatic poet's task is not to *invent* actions, but to make an action intelligible through its *emotional* motivation (209). The simplest relationships and condensation of Action, drawing it round its central point ; no naked ' moral,' nor " what is the poet trying to tell us ? " Only through the Phantasy can Understanding parley with Feeling ; the *Wonder* (212).

Chapter V.

Religious miracles demand an absolute Faith, a fundamental denial of the Understanding ; the Poet has nothing to do with Faith, but must be understood by Feeling. The Dogmatic Wonder unfitted for Art, the Poetic Wonder the highest product of the artist's beholdings. Its moulding : the stronger moments-of-action (climaxes) to be led up to by the lesser ones ; an exposition of motives has to fill the artwork's main space ; not merely to lop off parts, but to condense the whole Content, which thus seems magnified, unwonted, *wondrous*—but is yet the most intelligible presentment of reality. Nature's essence not distorted thereby, but her utterances gathered into one lucid image : possible to *us*, through our Experience having gained a clear insight into Nature (216). With the reaction against miracles, even the Poet had to bow

before the prosaic claim that he should renounce his Wonder. But we now
know Nature as a living Organism, forever *becoming*, and that we are here to
enjoy her to the full ; Man once more refers Nature to himself, he speaks with
her and *loves* her, and makes her a sympathising sharer in his highest mood
(219). Thus the highest subject for Drama is Mythos, ever *new*-devised.—
What are the requisite means of Expression ? Just as the Action and motives
have been strengthened and enhanced into a wide-embracing Interest—common
to many, but summed in one,—so must the Expression become a purely-human
emotional-utterance, Word-speech strengthened and enhanced into *Tone-
speech* (223).

Chapter VI.

Tone-speech the beginning and end of Word-speech ; the Lyric holds within
;itself each germ of the intrinsic art of Poetry ; its final vindication by the Entire
(or Perfected) Drama. Tone-speech the most spontaneous expression of the
inner Feeling stimulated from without. Animals, and Man's greater variety of
emotion and expression ; the Folkslied bending the words to fit the melody.
Rise of Speech from ringing tones and mother-melody ; the open sounds take
on a garment, like the tree its bark, (vowels and consonants) and thus form
speech-roots out of subjective and objective impressions. Stabreim the ' composing element ' of speech (227). This and its word-verse once stood in strict
relation to that *ur*-melody which we have to consider as the earliest message
of a more complex human feeling ; that melody and the number of intonations
(or accents) was governed by man's breathing-power,—the origin of Metre.

When *poesis* ceased to be a function of Feeling, and became a business of
the Understanding, the creative league (Lyric) of Gesture, Tone and Word,
disbanded ; the ring of sounding vowels became the hasty clang of Talk ; the
End-rhyme fluttering at the loose ends ; screwing up the meaning of roots to
accommodate abstractions ; floundering into the grey morass of Prose. Convention personified in Louis XIV and French Academy (231).

Poesis impossible in naked modern speech : the "ideal reality," with its
strengthened actions and motives, to be imparted solely through the language
of the inner soul—Tone-speech. This expression is not to be a "ready-made"
melody, suddenly imported, but to *grow* with the rise of the emotions.—Con-
cealment of the poet's Aim, by *realising* it.—A tone-speech to be struck-into
from the outset, not exchanged by turns with speech of daily life (234).

A fitting Expression is therefore the *a priori* condition for realising the
Poetic Aim, which otherwise could never step from thought to actuality. For
its birth, Understanding must wed Feeling, word-speech wed tone-speech, the
manly the womanly,—only by their union through Love do they become the
human being (236).

THIRD PART.—DRAMA OF THE FUTURE.
Chapter I.

The poet has tried two ways of giving Word-speech an emotional expression :
through metre—on side of Rhythm ; through end-rhyme—on side of Melody.
(a) Metre.—Modern imitations of Greek and Latin verse ; fictitious ' longs
and shorts ' ; ' schema,' the painter and his " cow " ; a fatiguing ride on the

hobbling Iambic ; the intelligent actress getting her verse written out in prose; root-syllables, our linguistic usage, and a chain of rhythmic uniformities (243).

(b) End-rhyme.—The verbal residue of Christian Melody ; the *chorale* and its neutral rhythm ; only where the breath gave out, came the rhyme,—perchance a feminine ending ; the whole verse-line a preparation for its closing syllable ; quite in keeping with speech of Romanic races, particularly French, —contrasted with German. Through an expression differing from that of everyday the poet wanted to avoid the Understanding and address the Feeling, but the ear stood sentinel to bar the way ; the word-poet at last renounces Feeling, for Understanding.— How does our modern Music stand to this modern Verse ? (248)

Melody could do nothing with this rickety word-verse, but break it into its quite unrhythmic factors, and repiece them at her own good pleasure,—or else, follow their 'setting,' and become a *musical prose*. Gluck's endeavour to emphasise the speaking-accent completely upset the verse. The ready-made melody will never fit the fluctuating accents of our verse ; to be seized by the ear, it must contain a repetition of definite melodic moments in a definite rhythm ; the poet became a mere word-purveyor to the absolute musician. Goethe's verses deemed "too beautiful" for musical setting : Mendelssohn's "songs *without* words." How are we to lift this musician off his piano-stool, by power of Beethoven's *Word?* (253)

Chapter II.

To keep touch with Life, we must win our poetic Expression from the speech of everyday. But the prosaic speaking-accent has no fixed dwelling in the *root*-syllables, because our sentences are too diffuse ; we must condense them, casting away superfluous qualifying words, and come to the brief diction of frank emotion—the phrase *in one breath ;* its number of words and accents to be governed by the character of the emotion ; a massing of words shuts off the main-word from the Feeling (257).

The natural basis of Rhythm, in spoken verse, furnished by rise and fall of word-accent ; a completely equal strength of accents is permitted neither by the *sense* of the phrase, nor by the ear of Feeling ; their differentiation corresponding to 'good and bad' bars, or bar-halves, of Music. Enlivenment of rhythm by regulation of number of preparatory or after syllables ; in spoken verse the poet could only give two 'shorts' to one 'long,' but Greek Lyric shews us often six or more—explanation, the long-held musical note. The Accents to form a speaking-phrase, to which a second shall correspond ; this sets the musical *beat ;* example—three word-accents distributed in two bars ; an endless variety of rhythmic devices possible to Word-verse wed to Melody (263).

Consideration of the separate factors of Expression.—These Accents must fall on *significant* root-syllables ; an understanding of speech-roots will never come from Scientific instruction, but from loving intercourse with Nature. The poet and the snow-flats of pragmatic Prose ; these buried roots still harbour life, among the Folk ; the poet, "the knower of the unconscious," must master their meaning, to utter it to others. The *inner* Feeling dwelling in the *vowel*-sound (266).

The Consonant.—Its *outward* function : to hedge one vowel from the other, give drawing to its colour, and thus define the predicates of a subject. The poet takes his close-drawn Accents and clothes them with like initial consonants—on principle of Repetition—to express their kinship : i.e. Stabreim. But un-like, as well as like, sensations may be thus expressed, through their *generic* oneness. The visage of the word, and not its draggled tail (270).

Inward function of Consonant : to determine the vowel's own character, by its roughness or smoothness of contact ; bringing to the inner organism those outward impressions which determine that organism to a specific utterance. Heart, blood, flesh, and breath. The "eye and ear" of Hearing. In Tone resides the Vowel's emotional-content ; all vowels are primarily akin, and therefore rhyme with one another (unlike the consonants) ; in musical tone the vowel's individuality is expanded to universality of pure Emotion; Thought, thus redeemed, becomes an outpour of Feeling ; the mother of the ample vowel-family is purely-human Feeling, in its longing for *utterance* (276).

Chapter III.

Distinction between Word-poet and Tone-poet : Word-poet has concentrated the scattered 'moments of action' &c. to one point, the most accessible to Feeling ; Tone-poet broadens out this point, till it fills the whole emotional-faculty. Perverse attempts of poets and musicians to reverse this process. The good God, as beggar, and the true Poet.

The Tone-poet has at his service a clan of sounds whose kindred reaches to infinity ; musical Harmony, on its horizontal plane ; the water-mirror whereon the poet's Thought is wed to music's Emotion ; this image is Melody (280).

This Melody takes an opposite path to the mother-melody whence Word-speech once was born. Starting with vague and general emotions, man's sensations gradually differentiated in such a way as to need a 'reflective' speech ; this shewn in the Greek Lyric's passing into Iambic *talk* of their dramas ; when the didactic content got the upper hand, Greek Tragedy fell,—Euripides beneath the lash of Aristophanes. But ours must be an advance from Understanding to Feeling, from Word-speech to Melody (284).

[A parenthesis]. This Melody's resemblance to that which rose from the depths of Beethoven's music, in Ninth Symphony, as the love-greeting of the 'eternal womanly' to the Poet. But the Poet must *stay* by it, must plunge with it to the bottom of the sea of Harmony, and rule its waves from thence (286).

Word-verse merely *strove* for unity of expression, but wed to Melody it *attains* it, through displaying the inner kinship of all tones. The "patriarchal" Folkslied had almost *no* modulation ; modern music has, but without a definite Aim ; Beethoven saw this, and returned to the "patriarchal melody" in his Ninth Symphony,—"So only, can we absolute musicians give out an understandable message." Only for an instant did Beethoven so lower the pitch of his melodic inventiveness ; in the "*Seid Umschlungen*" of that symphony lies the type of a melody which springs *from out* the word-verse (290). Widening the straitened ties of Key to the Ur-kinship of all Tones, through power of the Word ; the maiden and the stranger youth—typifying musical Modulation. The Stabreim of like, and of unlike emotional-content, and its expression in musical tones ; the musical 'period,' in which one chief-key dominates the adventitious keys, as the *generic* emotion includes the specific emotions ; the perfect Dramatic Artwork will consist of a continuous chain of such 'periods,' each springing from its predecessor (295).

Chapter IV.

The *ground* for melodic advance from key to key lies in the Poetic Aim, but the *enablement* lies in Harmony—the most purely-musical element, yet no begetter but a bearer. Chord, ground-tone and leading-tone ; the ear imperiously demands the *sounding-out* of the harmony to a melody, but no mere naked show of chords capriciously built-up on a shifting bass—such as learned Modern Music loves to set before the connoisseurs (299).

This "Melody vindicated by Harmony" redeems the poet.—Simile of the two travellers, Poet and Musician ; their opposite journeys round the Earth ; the Poet finds at last the Musician's ship, the empowerer of his artistic Will—*the orchestra* (301).

Harmony in itself is a mere thing of thought : to the senses it becomes discernible as Polyphony. The human voice the most natural 'tone-mass' ; its harmonic blending in the Christian hymn ; Counterpoint the first stir of Individualism ; in Opera the personal unit, with subsidiaries to display his melody's harmony ; in Drama of Future no room for personages unconcerned in the plot, and Chorus—as used in Opera—must vanish ; the harmony to be displayed and characterised by the Orchestra (306).

The Orchestra becoming an accessory for "realising the poet's Aim."—The members of the vertical Chord moving along a horizontal line of their own ; the instruments' individuality resembles that of the speaking-consonant, and thus creates a kind of instrumental Stabreim. Their tone-colour quite different from that of the human voice, thus immiscible therewith ; this determines once for all the Orchestra's attitude towards the Singing Actor. Errors of our Opera-*melodik* of heretofore (310).

Absolute Melody has always been a thing transplanted from the instrument to the human voice ; thus has often been *doubled* in the accompaniment—a second, disfiguring head unnaturally planted on its shoulders ; only gained currency when stripped of its words and played by military bands &c. Other musicians ingeniously wove it into the accompaniment, ignoring the total difference of tone-colour (312).

"Verse-melody" is the uniting bond between word-speech and tone-speech ; it must be upheld by both elements, but never confused therewith. Simile of the lake and boat, i.e. the Orchestra and the singer's Word-verse (315).

Chapter V.

The Orchestra indisputably possesses a faculty of *speech*, i.e. of uttering that which Speech cannot—the Unspeakable. FIRSTLY, in its alliance with Gesture ; this faculty was won from its early association with the gestures of Dance ; the rhythmic beat corresponds to the setting down of the foot ; in mimetic art this advances to the most delicate adjustment of nuances of bodily expression to the "tone-figures" which fill up the musical bar ; eye and ear corroborate each other's testimony (322).

"I read it in thine eye".; but the moments of such obvious emotion are solely those of perfect repose or highest agitation, and the transitional periods are filled by 'mixed sensations,' partly reflective Will and partly non-conscious Emotion, where Gesture cannot fully *define* and the Orchestra takes the place of *thought* (324).

A "thought" is nothing but the remembrance of a former feeling, but in turn it wakes a fresh emotion, and thus is the bond between a present and a non-present mood. The Verse-melody materialises this 'thought' by dressing its words in an emotional garment; this we now can treasure up in our Hearing's memory, and *thus*—though Music cannot think—a musical motive can produce a definite impression on the Feeling, inciting it to a function akin to Thought; hence the Orchestra, in its SECOND function, can bring before us the "Remembrance" of a past emotion, albeit now unspoken by the actor (329).

THIRD function of the Orchestra. Where Gesture lapses into rest and the melodic discourse of the actor hushes—where the drama prepares its future course in inner moods as yet unuttered—there the Orchestra can speak out a "Foreboding." The emotional faculty like a harp awaiting the player; through this 'longing' we become sharers in the creation of the artwork. So-called "Tone-painting" and an "extramusical label"; its chillingness only to be removed by an appeal to Feeling, through a definite scene or situation. Developing a 'preparatory repose' into an impatient longing, a strained expectancy; thus justifying, by a presentiment, the eventual appearance of the Wonder (334).

Chapter VI.

How the various factors of Expression are to be knit into one single Form, making possible a single Substance.—

What it is, that is to fill the body of the drama, and justify the Forebodings and Remembrances by calling forth the full Verse-melody: the DRAMATIC SITUATION. This must grow organically, starting from situations having a recognisable likeness with those of ordinary life, and gradually mounting above it; just as the vehicle of utterance of the dramatis personæ must start with a tone-speech not *too* remote from our daily word-speech—in order to lay down the basis of the Situation and guide our kindled Feeling to a *specific* sympathy —and rise gradually to full emotional Melody (341).

The drama to consist of a chain of such Situations, growing out of one another. The Stuff of each fresh drama will prescribe its own dramatic Form, whose *unity* will consist in Unity of its own Expression—the Verse-melody of the performers being always balanced or made good, and the hearer's Emotion maintained at a constant height, by the appropriate 'melodic moments' of the Orchestra (346).

These 'melodic moments' will answer to the *weightiest motives* of the drama, the pillars of all the edifice; they will thus be few in actual number, and ordered in accordance with the Poetic Aim; their recurrence will provide the highest Unity of Form, stretching not over mere fragments of the drama, but over its *whole*.

The problem of Unity solved: not of mere Time and Space, but of Action and Expression: an *organic* be-ing and becom-ing (350).

Chapter VII.

The preceding is no arbitrary "system," but the lesson of experience; " I have *invented* nothing new, but merely *found* the continuity of things erewhile severed."—(351).

The *living* factors of the Drama.—Firstly, poet and musician : are they to restrict each other ? Love versus "duty"; laisser-aller, social slavery, and barbarous police ; Love is the highest evolution of our individual powers, in self-offering for the beloved object. Each 'moment' of the musician's Expression must contain and answer to the poet's Aim ; what is not worth the singing, is not worth the telling (354).

Are poet and musician to be two persons or one ? May well be two, and the musician the younger, if not in years, in character. But at the hour that is, *two* heads must need lose heart when faced with present Public Life (356).

The dramatic artwork cannot be realised by the unaided Artistic Will, but needs the aid of Life ; the language it speaks must have living elements in it ; these possessed by the German tongue alone, of all three main operatic dialects (358).

But Germans mostly sing in *translated* operas, where the words are dribbled out at random to the notes.—Prussian æsthetes, and laws for dramatic declamation founded on such translations of Gluck's operas !—German singers abandoning all true delivery of the words ; licence of the Recitative, and favoured vocal notes ; German opera-composers follow in the wake, and *copy* this sense-confounding treatment. Wherefore a drama couched in the Word-Tone speech aforesaid could solely make a *musical* impression on its hearers : as follows (363). The singers would not pronounce their words ; the 'verse-melody,' thus treated as *absolute* melody, would leave no definite impression on us ; repeated by the orchestra, it would seem the mere freak of a puzzle-brained musician ; the necessary gestures would be omitted, since the singer does not realise that he should be an *actor ;* in their place "polite conversation," indifference, and arrangement of folds of dress ; the orchestral language would lose its last significance. Examples from *Tannhäuser* and *Lohengrin* (368).

To the Public there would remain nothing but the music *per se*, in fact the orchestration ; yet the orchestra, in a sense, should not be heard at all. Art-critics reporting that they had *read* a textbook, to much accompaniment of flutes and fiddles and trumpets (371).

Supposing even the artistic comrades were at hand, to *perform* the dramatic Artwork, we lack the real enabler—the Public ; its advancing degradation since the Renaissance, since Joseph II of Austria—with Mozart,—since the French nobles—with Gluck,—since the Weimar court—with Goethe and Schiller. The rulership of public taste has passed to the Philistine (374).

Near advent of an earth-upheaval ; the stream of living waters and the waste-heap. Where statesman and politician lose hope and the philosopher can only hint, the artist *sees* already a world as yet unborn ; we are older men and younger ; the heirloom (375).

The Life of the Future and the Artist of the Present (376).

INDEX

For the same reasons as in Vol. I, I have adopted the following plan of numeration for the references in this Index—viz., the figures denoting tens and hundreds are not repeated for one and the same *subdivision*, excepting where the numbers run into a fresh line of type ; thus 25, 29, 105, 112, 117 would appear 25, 9, 105, 12, 7. Where the reference is to notes &c. of my own, it is placed in brackets.—W. A. E.

A.

Above and Below, 174-6, 92, 3, 338.

Absolute : Artistic, 142 ; Effect, 99 ; Hearing, 364 ; Invention, 67 ; Melody, 42, 5, 82-6, 8, 99, 110, 42, 310, 2, 3, 61, 3 ; Monarchy, 45, 150 ; Music, 20, 37, 9, 69, 72, 6, 9, 84, 7, 8, 110, 231, 89, 90, 9, 320, 332, 40, 8 ; Musician, 30, 7, 121, 278, 88, 329, 31, 7, 44 ; Playwright, 333 ; Vocalisation, 365 ; Word-speech, 239, 77, 81 ; 'Working,' 96.

Abstract : Art, 141, 98 ; and Concrete, 123, 92 ; Learning, 13 ; Music, 74 ; State, 192.

Abstractions, 217, 30, 2, 349 ; Harmonic, 312.

Accents, 292 ; Main-, 243, 55, 7, 9 ; Melodic, 230, 43, 50, 360 ; Number of, 228, 42, 4, 55-62, 8 ; Speaking-, 240, 1, 5, 50-62, 74, 9, 358, 62 ; unequal Strength of, 258-63. See Ridge and hollow.

Accidental, the, 11, 222, 51, 5, 97, 339, 72. See Chance.

Achilles and Xanthus, 220.

Achilles-aria, Gluck's, 373.

Acting-drama, an, 140.

Action, the, 60, 91, 125 ; Behind the Scene, 133 ; Choice v. Invention of, 209 ; a Great, (xix), 156, 210-1, 21 ; Odds and ends of, 128, 56, 63, 215 ; without a Plot, 93 ; Root-, 163. See Dramatic, Main-, Motives.

Activity and Contemplation, 203-5.

Actors, see Performers, Singers &c.

Actress, an intelligent, 242, 3.

302

Actuality, 12, 36, 71, 120, 7, 38, 59, 161, 7, 8, 72, 350 ; and Thought, 140, 52, 7, 76, 97-8, 211-2, 35, 52, 300, 2, 7.

Adam and Eve, 199.

Admiration, 112.

Admonition, loving, 206.

Adolescent, the, 181, 229, 91.

Advance and Progress, 282, 4, 90, 338. See Evolution.

Adventurer, Musical, 38.

Adventures, Age of, 125, 30, 64-5.

Æstheticians, vi, 6, 14, 36, 48, 80, 121, 3, 57, 360.

Affinity, organic, 109, 230, 76, 307. See Akin.

Age, old, 181. See Youth.

Agitation of feeling, 54, 218-9, 33, 6, 247, 56, 61, 323.

Agitators, tricky, 98.

Aim, Conscious, 198 ; Intellectual, 210, 31, 4, 338. See Poetic.

Ajax and Philoctetes, 191.

Akin and kindred, the, 41, 207, 26-7, 236, 39, 68-70, 6, 9, 87, 91, 4, 308, 327, 32, 5.

Alcibiades, 186.

Alexander's Horse, 220 ; Sword, 42.

Alike, the, 221, 3, 7, 68, 79, 92.

All-day performances, 128.

All-empowering, 98, 350, 6, 72

All-faculty, 111.

All-feeling, 273, 5.

All-humanitarianism, 289, 302.

Alliteration, (xv), 227. See Stabreim.

Alps, 52, 7.

Alternation of Expression, 234, 343.

America, Discovery of, 71.

Analogy, 226-7 ; Superficial, 275.

S.

Sacrifice, 5, 90, cf. Gods, Self.
Sagas, 133, 61-4.
Sages, 352.
(S. George and dragon, 164).
S. Helena and Napoleon, 178.
S. Sophia, shrine of, 47.
Satisfaction, mood of, 368.
Savages and fools, 270.
"Saviour," Composer as, 66, 76.
Scale, 152, see Measure.
Scale, Musical, 286.
Scandal, a public, 187.
Scapegoat, 186.
Scattered, 216, 77, 305, cf. Severance.
Scene, the, 129-30, 6-40, 3, 5, 350, 5;
    and *Locale*, 61, 139; Naturalistic,
    129, 32, 6.
Scene, Change and stability of, 132,
    135, 7, 8.
Scene-painter and stage-tailor, 65, 7,
    91.
Scenery and machinery, 62, 3, 94, 6,
    98, 135.
*Schau*spiel, 127, 35.
Schema, 64; Greek, 241.
SCHILLER, 110, 39, 43-8, 76, 99.
(Schlegel, Schelling, &c., 150).
(Schönherr, J. H., 114).
(SCHOPENHAUER, xi, 275, 317).
Science, 157, 8, 264-5, 327.
Screws and levers, 230, 1.
Scribe, A. E., 92-5.
Sculpture, Greek, 104, 19.
Sea of yearning, 36, cf. 289.
Seizable, and seizing, 155, 97, 9, 209,
    210, 3, 42, 51, 6, 64, 9, 76, 7, 94,
    297, 8, 305, 23. Cf. Intelligible.
Self, unworthily concerned for, 9.
Self-Annulling, 183, 6, 9, 91; De-
    fence, 180; Dependence, 196, 231,
    249, 73, 91, 303, 6, 7, 10, 5, 36, 52;
    Determining, 188, 202, 30.
Self - Glorification (Music's), 346;
    Knowledge, 155, 206, 7; Love, 113;
    Oblivion, 37, 208; Offering, 112,
    353, 6.
Self-Restraint, 231, 351-4, 6, 70;
    Righteous, 114, 84, 6-8; Sacrifice,
    114, 88; Seeking, 185, 6, 371;
    Surrender, 111, 270.
Sensations, or emotions, 264, 9, 81,
    326; Mixed, or transitional, 269,
    291-4, 323-4, 47.
Sense of Language, 193, 268.
Sense and Sound, 259-63, 6, 73, 9, 91,
    293, 308, 13, 27, 60, 2, 3.

Senses, and sense-organs, 119, 26, 9,
    138, 52, 3, 98, 208, 26, 72, 80, 97,
    299, 302, 49, 75; transmitting to
    Feeling, 264, 8, 70, 3, 7, 93, 318,
    326, 32, 64.
'Sensuous' (*sinnlich*), 226, 40, 6, 9,
    257, 74, 91, 2, 8, 308, 10, 25, 31, 2,
    362; substance, 264, 6, 9.
Sentimental songs, 43.
Setting (*Fassung*) of verse, 249.
Severance, 157, 200, 32, 310, 2, 50, 6.
SHAKESPEARE, vii, 60, 124, 7, 30,
    134, 7, 68; and History, 143-5;
    narrowing the Stage, 128-30, 6, 9,
    but leaving it bare, 132, 5, 6, 8, 43.
Shallowness, 6, 100, 41.
Shams, 42, 53, 76, 242, 9.
Shape, 104, 6, 54, 281, 343, 50, 63.
    See Form.
Shaping, artistic, 60, 70, 108, 42, 55,
    162, 77, 212, 4, 6, 8, 22, 49, 77-8,
    338; -Impulse, 143, 7, 330, 1, 42,
    371, 3; Life, 165, 357, 75, 6.
Sharers, Sympathetic, 219, 95, 308,
    331, 7, 8, 46, 68, 72. Cf. Sym.
Shifting bass, a, 297, 8.
Shining for oneself alone, 353, 6.
Ship, the, 301, 14.
Show, outward, 152, 217, 72, 321, 3,
    324, 33, 5, 6.
Shrivelled man, a, 151, 76.
Sick man and two doctors, 353.
Side-Words, 257-9, see W.
Siegfried-saga, 161, (163, 7).
(*Siegfried, Der junge*, xii, 286; *Sieg-
    fried's Tod*, v, xiii, 304).
Sight and Smell, 40.
Simplicity, 37, 76, 105, 31, 96, 8, 203,
    210, 32, 56, 88, 9.
Sincerity, 50, 320, 3.
Sinfulness, 180, 92.
Sing-song, 26, 261.
Singer (operatic), the, 43, 99, 312, 59-
    366, 9, 72, 3; 's Throat, 18, 24, 69,
    298, 361; Wilfulness of, 26, 77.
Singer's mouth to chew, for the,
    250.
Singing-actor, 78, 309, 14, 72.
Single (*einig*), 335, 49, see Unity.
Sinnlichkeit, 53, 120, 1, 288, 332.
Sinnvoll, 308, 13.
Sketches for musical picture, 72-3, 5.
Skimmings from nat. phen., 230.
Skin, outward, 104, 6, 272.
Slaves, 90, 352, 73.
Sloths and cowards, 8.
Slovenly work, 361.
Snow-flats of Prose, 265.